119

EMBERIZA TOWNSENDII, TOWNSEND'S BUNTING.

(Now Spiza townsendii.)

FROM AN UNFINISHED DRAWING BY J. J. AUDUBON OF THE ONLY SPECIMEN EVER KNOWN, SHOT MAY 11, 1833, IN CHESTER CO., PA., BY J. K. TOWNSEND.

AUDUBON AND HIS JOURNALS

BY

MARIA R. AUDUBON

WITH ZOÖLOGICAL AND OTHER NOTES

BY

ELLIOTT COUES

ILLUSTRATED

VOLUME II.

Dover Publications, Inc.
New York

Published in Canada by General Publishing Company, Ltd., 30 Lesmill Road, Don Mills, Toronto, Ontario.

Published in the United Kingdom by Constable and Company, Ltd., 10 Orange Street, London WC2H 7EG.

This Dover edition, first published in 1986, is an unabridged republication of the 1960 Dover edition, which was a republication of the first edition originally published by Charles Scribner's Sons, New York, in 1897.

Manufactured in the United States of America
Dover Publications, Inc., 31 East 2nd Street, Mineola, N.Y. 11501

Library of Congress Cataloging in Publication Data

Audubon, John James, 1785-1851.
  Audubon and his journals.

  Reprint. Originally published: New York : Scribner,
1897.
  Includes index.
  1. Audubon, John James, 1785-1851. 2. Birds—North America. 3.
Naturalists—United States—Biography. I. Audubon, Maria Rebecca,
1843-1925. II. Title.
QL31.A9A2 1986   598.092′4 [B]   85-29258
ISBN 0-486-25143-8 (v. 1)
ISBN 0-486-25144-6 (v. 2)

CONTENTS

Volume II

LIST OF ILLUSTRATIONS.

Vol. II.

THE MISSOURI RIVER JOURNALS

1843

(*Continued*)

THE MISSOURI RIVER JOURNALS

1843

(*Continued*)

June 4, Sunday. We have run pretty well, though the wind has been tolerably high; the country we have passed this day is somewhat better than what we saw yesterday, which, as I said, was the poorest we have seen. No occurrence of interest has taken place. We passed this morning the old Riccaree[1] Village, where General Ashley[2] was so completely beaten as to lose eighteen of his

[1] " We halted for dinner at a village which we suppose to have belonged to the Ricaras. It is situated in a low plain on the river, and consists of about eighty lodges of an octagon form, neatly covered with earth, placed as close to each other as possible, and picketed round." ("Lewis and Clark," ed. 1893.)

"The village of the Rikaras, Arickaras, or Rikarees, for the name is variously written, is between the 46th and 47th parallels of north latitude, and 1,430 miles above the mouth of the Missouri. . . . It was divided into two portions, about eighty yards apart, being inhabited by two distinct bands. The whole extended about three quarters of a mile along the river bank, and was composed of conical lodges, that looked like so many small hillocks, being wooden frames intertwined with osier, and covered with earth." ("Astoria," W. Irving.)

" From the hills we had a fine prospect over the bend of the river, on which the villages of the Arikkaras are situated. The two villages of this tribe are on the west bank, very near each other, but separated by a small stream. They consist of a great number of clay huts, round at top, with a square entrance in front, and the whole surrounded with a fence of stakes, which were much decayed and in many places thrown down." ("Travels in North America," p. 166, Maximilian, Prince of Wied.)

[2] " General Ashley of Missouri, a man whose courage and achievements in the prosecution of his enterprises had rendered him famous in the Far

men, with the very weapons and ammunition that he had trafficked with the Indians of that village, against all the remonstrances of his friends and interpreters; yet he said that it proved fortunate for him, as he turned his steps towards some other spot, where he procured one hundred packs of Beaver skins for a mere song. We stopped to cut wood at an old house put up for winter quarters, and the wood being ash, and quite dry, was excellent. We are now fast for the night at an abandoned post, or fort, of the Company, where, luckily for us, a good deal of wood was found cut. We saw only one Wolf, and a few small gangs of Buffaloes. Bell shot a Bunting which resembles Henslow's, but we have no means of comparing it at present. We have collected a few plants during our landing. The steam is blowing off, and therefore our day's run is ended. When I went to bed last night it was raining smartly, and Alexis did not go off, as he did wish. By the way, I forgot to say that along with the three Prairie Marmots, he brought also four Spoon-billed Ducks, which we ate at dinner to-day, and found delicious. Bell saw many Lazuli Finches this morning. Notwithstanding the tremendous shaking of our boat, Sprague managed to draw four figures of the legs and feet of the Wolf shot by Bell yesterday, and my own pencil was not idle.

June 5, Monday. Alexis went off in the night sometime, and came on board about three o'clock this morning; he had seen nothing whatever, except the traces of Beavers and of Otters, on Beaver Creek, which, by the way, he had to cross on a raft. Speaking of rafts, I am told that one of these, made of two bundles of rushes, about the size of a man's body, and fastened together by a few sticks, is quite sufficient to take two men and two packs of Buffalo robes across this muddy river. In the course of the morning

West in conjunction with Mr. [Andrew?] Henry, of the Missouri Trading Co., established a post on the banks of the Yellowstone River in 1822." (" Capt. Bonneville," W. Irving.)

we passed Cannon Ball River,[1] and the very remarkable
bluffs about it, of which we cannot well speak until we
have stopped there and examined their nature. We saw
two Swans alighting on the prairie at a considerable distance. We stopped to take wood at Bowie's settlement,
at which place his wife was killed by some of the Riccaree
Indians, after some Gros Ventres had assured him that
such would be the case if he suffered his wife to go out of
the house. She went out, however, on the second day,
and was shot with three rifle-balls. The Indians took parts
of her hair and went off. She was duly buried; but the
Gros Ventres returned some time afterwards, took up the
body, and carried off the balance of her hair. They, however, reburied her; and it was not until several months
had elapsed that the story came to the ears of Mr. Bowie.
We have also passed Apple Creek,[2] but the chief part is
yet to be added. At one place where the bluffs were
high, we saw five Buffaloes landing a few hundred yards
above us on the western side; one of them cantered off

[1] "We reached the mouth of Le Boulet, or Cannon Ball River. This
stream rises in the Black Mts. and falls into the Missouri; its channel is
about 140 feet wide, though the water is now confined within 40; its name
is derived from the numbers of perfectly round stones on the shore and
in the bluffs just above." ("Lewis and Clark," ed. 1893.)

"We came to an aperture in the chain of hills, from which this river,
which was very high, issues. On the north side of the mouth there was a
steep, yellow clay wall; and on the southern, a flat, covered with poplars and
willows. This river has its name from the singular regular sandstone balls
which are found in its banks, and in those of the Missouri in its vicinity.
They are of various sizes, from that of a musket ball to that of a large
bomb, and lie irregularly on the bank, or in the strata, from which they often
project to half their thickness; when the river has washed away the earth
they then fall down, and are found in great numbers on the bank. Many of
them are rather elliptical, others are more flattened, others flat on one side
and convex on the other. Of the *perfectly spherical* balls, I observed some
two feet in diameter. A mile above the mouth of Cannon Ball River I saw
no more of them." ("Travels in North America," p. 167, Maximilian,
Prince of Wied.)

[2] Present name of the stream which falls into the Missouri from the east,
about five miles below Fort Rice; Chewah or Fish River of Lewis and
Clark; Shewash River of Maximilian. Audubon is now approaching
Bismarck, the capital of North Dakota. — E. C.

immediately, and by some means did reach the top of the hills, and went out of our sight; the four others ran, waded, and swam at different places, always above us, trying to make their escape. At one spot they attempted to climb the bluff, having unconsciously passed the place where their leader had made good his way, and in their attempts to scramble up, tumbled down, and at last became so much affrighted that they took to the river for good, with the intention to swim to the shore they had left. Unfortunately for them, we had been gaining upon them; we had all been anxiously watching them, and the moment they began to swim we were all about the boat with guns and rifles, awaiting the instant when they would be close under our bows. The moment came; I was on the lower deck among several of the people with guns, and the firing was soon heavy; but not one of the Buffaloes was stopped, although every one must have been severely hit and wounded. Bell shot a load of buckshot at the head of one, which disappeared entirely under the water for perhaps a minute. I sent a ball through the neck of the last of the four, but all ineffectually, and off they went, swimming to the opposite shore; one lagged behind the rest, but, having found footing on a sand-bar, it rested awhile, and again swam off to rejoin its companions. They all reached the shore, but were quite as badly off on that side as they had been on the other, and their difficulties must have been great indeed; however, in a short time we had passed them. Mr. Charles Primeau,[1] who is a good shot, and who killed the young Buffalo bull the other day, assured me that it was his opinion the whole of these would die before

[1] Charles Primeau was born at St. Louis, Mo., entered the American Fur Company as clerk, and continued in that service many years. Later he helped to form an opposition company under the name of Harvey, Primeau, & Co., which did business for a few years, until, like most of the smaller concerns, it was absorbed by the American Fur Co. He then went back to his former employers, and afterward was engaged by the U. S. Government as Indian interpreter, long holding this position. In 1896 he was living in the vicinity of Fort Yates. — E. C.

sundown, but that Buffaloes swimming were a hundred times more difficult to kill than those on shore. I have been told also, that a Buffalo shot by an Indian, in the presence of several whites, exhibited some marks on the inside of the skin that looked like old wounds, and that on close examination they found no less than six balls in its paunch. Sometimes they will run a mile after having been struck through the heart; whilst at other times they will fall dead without such desperate shot. Alexis told me that once he shot one through the thigh, and that it fell dead on the spot. We passed this afternoon a very curious conical mound of earth, about which Harris and I had some curiosity, by which I lost two pounds of snuff, as he was right, and I was wrong. We have seen Geese and Goslings, Ravens, Blue Herons, Bluebirds, Thrushes, Red-headed Woodpeckers and Red-shafted ditto, Martins, an immense number of Rough-winged Swallows about their holes, and Barn Swallows. We heard Killdeers last evening. Small Crested Flycatchers, Summer Yellow-birds, Maryland Yellow-throats, House Wrens are seen as we pass along our route; while the Spotted Sandpiper accompanies us all along the river. Sparrow Hawks, Turkey Buzzards, Arctic Towhee Buntings, Cat-birds, Mallards, Coots, Gadwalls, King-birds, Yellow-breasted Chats, Red Thrushes, all are noted as we pass. We have had a good day's run; it is now half-past ten. The wind has been cold, and this evening we have had a dash of rain. We have seen only one Wolf. We have heard some wonderful stories about Indians and white men, none of which I can well depend upon. We have stopped for the night a few miles above where the "Assiniboin" [1] steamer was burnt with all her cargo uninsured, in the year 1835. I heard that after she had run ashore, the men started to build a scow to unload the cargo; but that through some accident the

[1] The "Assiniboin" was the steamer on which Maximilian, Prince of Wied, travelled down the Missouri in 1833.

vessel was set on fire, and that a man and a woman who alone had been left on board, walked off to the island, where they remained some days unable to reach shore.

June 6, Tuesday. This morning was quite cold, and we had a thick white frost on our upper deck. It was also extremely cloudy, the wind from the east, and all about us looked dismal enough. The hands on board seemed to have been busy the whole of the night, for I scarcely slept for the noise they made. We soon came to a very difficult part of the river, and had to stop full three hours. Meanwhile the yawl went off to seek and sound for a channel, whilst the wood-cutters and the carriers — who, by the way, are called "charrettes"[1] — followed their work, and we gathered a good quantity of drift-wood, which burns like straw. Our hopes of reaching the Mandan Village were abandoned, but we at last proceeded on our way and passed the bar; it was nearly dinner-time. Harris and Bell had their guns, and brought two Arctic Towhee Buntings and a Black-billed Cuckoo. They saw two large flocks of Geese making their way westward. The place where we landed showed many signs of Deer, Elk, and Buffaloes. I saw trees where the latter had rubbed their heavy bodies against the bark, till they had completely robbed the tree of its garment. We saw several Red-shafted Woodpeckers, and other birds named before. The Buffalo, when hunted on horseback, does *not* carry its tail erect, as has been represented in books, but close between the legs; but when you see a Buffalo bull work its tail sideways in a twisted rolling fashion, *then* take care of him, as it is a sure sign of his intention to rush against his pursuer's horse, which is very dangerous, both to hunter and steed. As we proceeded I saw two fine White-headed Eagles alighting on their nest,

[1] This is an interesting note of the early French name on the Missouri of the persons about a boat whom we should call "stevedores," or "roustabouts." The French word *charette*, or *charrette*, occurs also as a personal name, and it will be remembered that there was a town of La Charette on the Lower Missouri. — E. C.

where perhaps they had young — and how remarkably late in the season this species does breed here! We also saw a young Sandhill Crane, and on an open prairie four Antelopes a few hundred yards off. Alexis tells me that at this season this is a rare occurrence, as the females are generally in the brushwood now; but in this instance the male and three females were on open prairie. We have passed what is called the Heart[1] River, and the Square Hills, which, of course, are by no means square, but simply more level than the generality of those we have passed for upwards of three weeks. We now saw four barges belonging to our company, and came to, above them, as usual. A Mr. Kipp, one of the partners, came on board; and Harris, Squires, and myself had time to write each a short letter to our friends at home. Mr. Kipp had a peculiar looking crew who appeared not much better than a set of bandits among the Pyrenees or the Alps; yet they seem to be the very best sort of men for trappers and boatmen. We exchanged four of our men for four of his, as the latter are wanted at the Yellowstone. The country appears to Harris and to myself as if we had outrun the progress of vegetation, as from the boat we observed oaks scarcely in leaflets, whilst two hundred miles below, and indeed at a much less distance, we saw the same timber in nearly full leaf; flowers are also scarce. A single Wolf was seen by some one on deck. Nothing can be possibly keener than the senses of hearing and sight, as well as of smell, in the Antelope. Not one was ever known to jump up close to a hunter; and the very motion of the grasses, as these are wafted by the wind, will keep them awake and on the alert. Immediately upon the breaking up of the ice about the Mandan Village, three Buffaloes were seen floating down on a large cake; they were seen by Mr.

---

[1] Heart River, the stream which falls into the Missouri near the town of Mandan, about opposite Bismarck, N. Dak. Here the river is now bridged by the Northern Pacific Railroad, which crosses the Missouri from Bismarck, and follows up Heart River for some distance. — E. C

Primeau from his post, and again from Fort Pierre. How much further the poor beasts travelled, no one can tell. It happens not infrequently, when the river is entirely closed in with ice, that some hundreds of Buffaloes attempt to cross ; their aggregate enormous weight forces the ice to break, and the whole of the gang are drowned, as it is impossible for these animals to climb over the surrounding sharp edges of the ice. We have seen not less than three nests of White-headed Eagles this day. We are fast ashore about sixteen miles below the Mandan Villages, and will, in all probability, reach there to-morrow morning at an early hour. It is raining yet, and the day has been a most unpleasant one.

June 7, Wednesday. We had a vile night of rain, and wind from the northeast, which is still going on, and likely to continue the whole of this blessed day. Yesterday, when we had a white frost, ice was found in the kettles of Mr. Kipp's barges. We reached Fort Clark[1] and the Mandan Villages at half-past seven this morning. Great guns were fired from the fort and from the " Omega," as our captain took the guns from the " Trapper " at Fort Pierre. The site of this fort appears a good one, though it is placed considerably below the Mandan Village. We saw some small spots cultivated, where corn, pumpkins, and beans are grown. The fort and village are situated on the high bank, rising somewhat to the elevation of a hill. The Mandan mud huts are very far from looking poetical, although Mr. Catlin has tried to render them so by placing them in regular rows, and all of the same size and form, which is by no means the case. But different travellers have different eyes ! We saw more Indians than at any

1 " Fort Clark came in sight, with a background of the blue prairie hills, and with the gay American banner waving from the flag-staff. . . . The fort is built on a smaller scale, on a plan similar to that of all the other trading posts or forts of the company. Immediately behind the fort there were, in the prairie, seventy leather tents of the Crows." (Prince of Wied, p. 171.)

Fort Clark stood on the right bank of the Missouri, and thus across the river from the original Fort Mandan built by Lewis and Clark in the fall of 1804. Maximilian has much to say of it and of Mr. Kipp.

previous time since leaving St. Louis; and it is possible that there are a hundred huts, made of mud, all looking like so many potato winter-houses in the Eastern States. As soon as we were near the shore, every article that could conveniently be carried off was placed under lock and key, and our division door was made fast, as well as those of our own rooms. Even the axes and poles were put by. Our captain told us that last year they stole his cap and his shot-pouch and horn, and that it was through the interference of the first chief that he recovered his cap and horn; but that a squaw had his leather belt, and would not give it up. The appearance of these poor, miserable devils, as we approached the shore, was wretched enough. There they stood in the pelting rain and keen wind, covered with Buffalo robes, red blankets, and the like, some partially and most curiously besmeared with mud; and as they came on board, and we shook hands with each of them, I felt a clamminess that rendered the ceremony most repulsive. Their legs and naked feet were covered with mud. They looked at me with apparent curiosity, perhaps on account of my beard, which produced the same effect at Fort Pierre. They all looked very poor; and our captain says they are the *ne plus ultra* of thieves. It is said there are nearly three thousand men, women, and children that, during winter, cram themselves into these miserable hovels. Harris and I walked to the fort about nine o'clock. The walking was rascally, passing through mud and water the whole way. The yard of the fort itself was as bad. We entered Mr. Chardon's own room, crawled up a crazy ladder, and in a low garret I had the great pleasure of seeing alive the Swift or Kit Fox which he has given to me. It ran swiftly from one corner to another, and, when approached, growled somewhat in the manner of a common Fox. Mr. Chardon told me that good care would be taken of it until our return, that it would be chained to render it more gentle, and that I would find it an easy matter to take

it along.   I sincerely hope so.   Seeing a remarkably fine
skin of a large Cross Fox[1] which I wished to buy, it was
handed over to me.   After this, Mr. Chardon asked one of
the Indians to take us into the village, and particularly to
show us the " Medicine Lodge."   We followed our guide
through mud and mire, even into the Lodge.   We found
this to be, in general terms, like all the other lodges, only
larger, measuring twenty-three yards in diameter, with a
large squarish aperture in the centre of the roof, some six
or seven feet long by about four wide.   We had entered
this curiosity shop by pushing aside a wet Elk skin stretched
on four sticks.   Looking around, I saw a number of cala-
bashes, eight or ten Otter skulls, two very large Buffalo
skulls with the horns on, evidently of great age, and some
sticks and other magical implements with which none but
a " Great Medicine Man " is acquainted.   During my survey there sat, crouched down on his haunches, an Indian
wrapped in a dirty blanket, with only his filthy head peeping
out.   Our guide spoke to him; but he stirred not.   Again,
at the foot of one of the posts that support the central portion of this great room, lay a parcel that I took for a bundle of Buffalo robes; but it moved presently, and from
beneath it half arose the emaciated. body of a poor blind
Indian, whose skin was quite shrivelled; and our guide
made us signs that he was about to die.   We all shook
both hands with him; and he pressed our hands closely and
with evident satisfaction.   He had his pipe and tobacco
pouch by him, and soon lay down again.   We left this
abode of mysteries, as I was anxious to see the interior of
one of the common huts around; and again our guide led
us through mud and mire to his own lodge, which we
entered in the same way as we had done the other.   All

[1] This Fox was probably the cross variety of the Long-tailed Prairie
Fox, *Vulpes macrourus* of Baird, Stansbury's Exped. Great Salt Lake, June,
1852, p. 309; *Vulpes utah* of Aud. and Bach. Quad. N. Am. iii., 1853, p. 255,
pl. 151 (originally published by them in Proc. Acad. Philad., July, 1852,
p. 114). — E. C.

these lodges have a sort of portico that leads to the door, and on the tops of most of them I observed Buffalo skulls. This lodge contained the whole family of our guide — several women and children, and another man, perhaps a son-in-law or a brother. All these, except the man, were on the outer edge of the lodge, crouching on the ground, some suckling children; and at nearly equal distances apart were placed berths, raised about two feet above the ground, made of leather, and with square apertures for the sleepers or occupants to enter. The man of whom I have spoken was lying down in one of these, which was all open in front. I walked up to him, and, after disturbing his happy slumbers, shook hands with him; he made signs for me to sit down; and after Harris and I had done so, he rose, squatted himself near us, and, getting out a large spoon made of boiled Buffalo horn, handed it to a young girl, who brought a great rounded wooden bowl filled with pemmican, mixed with corn and some other stuff. I ate a mouthful or so of it, and found it quite palatable; and Harris and the rest then ate of it also. Bell was absent; we had seen nothing of him since we left the boat. This lodge, as well as the other, was dirty with water and mud; but I am told that in dry weather they are kept cleaner, and much cleaning do they need, most truly. A round, shallow hole was dug in the centre for the fire; and from the roof descended over this a chain, by the aid of which they do their cooking, the utensil being attached to the chain when wanted. As we returned towards the fort, I gave our guide a piece of tobacco, and he appeared well pleased. He followed us on board, and as he peeped in my room, and saw the dried and stuffed specimens we have, he evinced a slight degree of curiosity. Our captain, Mr. Chardon, and our men have been busily engaged in putting ashore that portion of the cargo designed for this fort, which in general appearance might be called a poor miniature representa-

tion of Fort Pierre. The whole country around was overgrown with " Lamb's quarters " (*Chenopòdium album*),
which I have no doubt, if boiled, would take the place of
spinach in this wild and, to my eyes, miserable country,
the poetry of which lies in the imagination of those writers
who have described the " velvety prairies " and " enchanted
castles " (of mud), so common where we now are. We
observed a considerable difference in the color of these
Indians, who, by the way, are almost all Riccarees; many
appeared, and in fact are, redder than others; they are
lank, rather tall, and very alert, but, as I have said before,
all look poor and dirty. After dinner we went up the
muddy bank again to look at the corn-fields, as the small
patches that are meanly cultivated are called. We found
poor, sickly looking corn about two inches high, that had
been represented to us this morning as full six inches high.
We followed the prairie, a very extensive one, to the hills,
and there found a deep ravine, sufficiently impregnated with
saline matter to answer the purpose of salt water for the
Indians to boil their corn and pemmican, clear and clean;
but they, as well as the whites at the fort, resort to the
muddy Missouri for their drinking water, the only fresh
water at hand. Not a drop of spirituous liquor has been
brought to this place for the last two years; and there can
be no doubt that on this account the Indians have become
more peaceable than heretofore, though now and then a
white man is murdered, and many horses are stolen. As
we walked over the plain, we saw heaps of earth thrown up
to cover the poor Mandans who died of the small-pox.
These mounds in many instances appear to contain the
remains of several bodies and, perched on the top, lies,
pretty generally, the rotting skull of a Buffalo. Indeed,
the skulls of the Buffaloes seem as if a kind of relation to
these most absurdly superstitious and ignorant beings. I
could not hear a word of the young Grizzly Bear of which
Mr. Chardon had spoken to me. He gave me his Buffalo

head-dress and other trifles — as he was pleased to call them; all of which will prove more or less interesting and curious to you when they reach Minniesland. He presented Squires with a good hunting shirt and a few other things, and to all of us, presented moccasins. We collected a few round cacti; [1] and I saw several birds that looked much the worse for the cold and wet weather we have had these last few days. Our boat has been thronged with Indians ever since we have tied to the shore; and it is with considerable difficulty and care that we can stop them from intruding into our rooms when we are there. We found many portions of skulls lying on the ground, which, perhaps, did at one period form the circles of them spoken of by Catlin. All around the village is filthy beyond description. Our captain tells us that no matter what weather we may have to-morrow, he will start at daylight, even if he can only go across the river, to get rid of these wolfish-looking vagabonds of Indians. I sincerely hope that we may have a fair day and a long run, so that the air around us may once more be pure and fresh from the hand of Nature. After the Riccarees had taken possession of this Mandan Village, the remains of that once powerful tribe removed about three miles up the river, and there have now fifteen or twenty huts, containing, of course, only that number of families. During the worst periods of the epidemic which swept over this village with such fury, many became maniacs, rushed to the Missouri, leaped into its turbid waters, and were seen no more. Mr. Primeau, wife, and children, as well as another half-breed, have gone to the fort, and are to remain there till further orders. The fort is in a poor condition, roofs leaking, etc. Whilst at the fort this afternoon, I was greatly surprised to see a tall, athletic Indian thrashing

[1] No doubt the *Mammillaria vivipara*, a small globose species, quite different from the common *Opuntia* or prickly pear of the Missouri region. — E. C.

the dirty rascals about Mr. Chardon's door most severely; but I found on inquiry that he was called "the soldier," [1] and that he had authority to do so whenever the Indians intruded or congregated in the manner this *canaille* had done.   After a while the same tall fellow came on board with his long stick, and immediately began belaboring the fellows on the lower guards; the latter ran off over the planks, and scrambled up the muddy banks as if so many affrighted Buffaloes.   Since then we have been comparatively quiet; but I hope they will all go off, as the captain is going to put the boat from the shore, to the full length of our spars.   The wind has shifted to the northward, and the atmosphere has been so chilled that a House Swallow was caught, benumbed with cold, and brought to me by our captain.   Harris, Bell, and I saw a Cliff Swallow take refuge on board; but this was not caught.   We have seen Say's Flycatcher, the Ground Finch, Cow Buntings, and a few other birds.   One of the agents arrived this afternoon from the Gros Ventre, or Minnetaree Village, about twelve miles above us.   He is represented as a remarkably brave man, and he relates some strange adventures of his prowess.   Several *great warriors* have condescended to shake me by the hand; their very touch is disgusting — it will indeed be a deliverance to get rid of all this " Indian poetry." We are, nevertheless, to take a few to the Yellowstone.   Alexis has his wife, who is, in fact, a good-looking young woman; an old patroon, Provost, takes one of his daughters along; and we have, besides, several red-skinned single gentlemen.   We were assured that the northern parts of the hills, that form a complete curtain to the vast prairie on which we have walked this afternoon, are still adorned with patches of snow that fell there during last winter.   It is now nine o'clock, but before I go to rest

[1] The individual so designated was an important functionary in these villages, whose authority corresponded with that of our " chief of police," and was seldom if ever disputed. — E. C.

I cannot resist giving you a description of the curious exhibition that we have had on board, from a numerous lot of Indians of the first class, say some forty or fifty. They ranged themselves along the sides of the large cabin, squatting on the floor. Coffee had been prepared for the whole party, and hard sea-biscuit likewise. The coffee was first given to each of them, and afterwards the biscuits, and I had the honor of handing the latter to the row on one side of the boat; a box of tobacco was opened and laid on the table. The man who came from the Gros Ventres this afternoon proved to be an excellent interpreter; and after the captain had delivered his speech to him, he spoke loudly to the group, and explained the purport of the captain's speech. They grunted their approbation frequently, and were, no doubt, pleased. Two individuals (Indians) made their appearance highly decorated, with epaulets on the shoulders, red clay on blue uniforms, three cocks' plumes in their head-dress, rich moccasins, leggings, etc. These are men who, though in the employ of the Opposition company, act truly as friends; but who, meantime, being called "Braves," never grunted, bowed, or shook hands with any of us. Supper over and the tobacco distributed, the whole body arose simultaneously, and each and every one of these dirty wretches we had all to shake by the hand. The two braves sat still until all the rest had gone ashore, and then retired as majestically as they had entered, not even shaking hands with our good-humored captain. I am told that this performance takes place once every year, on the passing of the Company's boats. I need not say that the coffee and the two·biscuits apiece were gobbled down in less than no time. The tobacco, which averaged about two pounds to each man, was hid in their robes or blankets for future use. Two of the Indians, who must have been of the highest order, and who distributed the "rank weed," were nearly naked; one had on only a breech-clout and one legging, the other

was in no better case. They are now all ashore except
one or more who are going with us to the Yellowstone;
and I will now go to my rest. Though I have said "Good-
night," I have arisen almost immediately, and I must write
on, for we have other scenes going on both among the
trappers below and some of the people above. Many
Indians, squaws as well as men, are bartering and trading,
and keep up such a babble that Harris and I find sleep
impossible; needless to say, the squaws who are on board
are of the lowest grade of morality.

June 8, Thursday. This morning was fair and cold, as
you see by the range of the thermometer, 37° to 56°. We
started at a very early hour, and breakfasted before five,
on account of the village of Gros Ventres, where our captain had to stop. We passed a few lodges belonging to
the tribe of the poor Mandans, about all that remained.
I only counted eight, but am told there are twelve. The
village of the Gros Ventres (Minnetarees) has been cut off
from the bank of the river by an enormous sand-bar, now
overgrown with willows and brush, and we could only see
the American flag flying in the cool breeze. Two miles
above this, however, we saw an increasing body of Indians,
for the prairie was sprinkled with small parties, on horse
and on foot. The first who arrived fired a salute of small
guns, and we responded with our big gun. They had an
abundance of dogs harnessed to take wood back to the village, and their yells and fighting were severe upon our
ears. Some forty or more of the distinguished black-
guards came on board; and we had to close our doors as
we did yesterday. After a short period they were feasted
as last evening; and speeches, coffee, and tobacco, as well
as some gunpowder, were given them, which they took
away in packs, to be divided afterward. We took one
more passenger, and lost our interpreter, who is a trader
with the Minnetarees. The latter are by no means as
fine-looking a set of men as those we have seen before,

and I observed none of that whiteness of skin among them. There were numbers of men, women, and children. We saw a crippled and evidently tame Wolf, and two Indians, following us on the top of the hills. We saw two Swans on a bar, and a female Elk, with her young fawn, for a few minutes. I wished that we had been ashore, as I know full well that the mother would not leave her young; and the mother killed, the young one would have been easily caught alive. We are now stopping for the night, and our men are cutting wood. We have done this, I believe, four times to-day, and have run upward of sixty miles. At the last wood-cutting place, a young leveret was started by the men, and after a short race, the poor thing squatted, and was killed by the stroke of a stick. It proved to be the young of *Lepus townsendii* [*L. campestris*], large enough to have left the mother, and weighing rather more than a pound. It is a very beautiful specimen. The eyes are very large, and the iris pure amber color. Its hair is tightly, but beautifully curled. Its measurements are as follows [*omitted*]. Bell will make a fine skin of it to-morrow morning. We have had all sorts of stories related to us; but Mr. Kipp, who has been in the country for twenty-two years, is evidently a person of truth, and I expect a good deal of information from him. Our captain told us that on a previous voyage some Indians asked him if, "when the great Medicine" (meaning the steamer) "was tired, he gave it whiskey." Mr. Sire laughed, and told them he did. "How much?" was the query. "A barrelful, to be sure!" The poor wretches at first actually believed him, and went off contented, but were naturally angry at being undeceived on a later occasion. I have now some hope of finding a young of the Antelope alive at Fort Union, as Mr. Kipp left one there about ten days ago. I am now going to bed, though our axemen and "charettes" are still going; and I hope I may not be called up to-morrow morning, to be ready for breakfast at half-past four. Harris and Bell went off with Alexis. Bell fired at a bird, and a large Wolf immediately made its appearance. This is always the case in this country; when you shoot an animal and hide yourself, you may see, in less than half an hour, from ten to thirty of these hungry rascals around the carcass, and have fine fun shooting at them. We have had a windy day, but a good run on the whole. I hope to-morrow may prove propitious, and that we shall reach Fort Union in five more days.

June 9, Friday. Thermometer 42°, 75°, 66°. We had a heavy white frost last night, but we have had a fine, pleasant day on the whole, and to me a most interesting one. We passed the Little Missouri[1] (the real one) about ten this morning. It is a handsome stream, that runs all the way from the Black Hills, one of the main spurs of the mighty Rocky Mountains. We saw three Elks swimming across it, and the number of this fine species of Deer that are about us now is almost inconceivable. We have heard of burning springs, which we intend to examine on our way down. We started a Goose from the shore that had evidently young ones; she swam off, beating the water with wings half extended, until nearly one hundred yards off. A shot from a rifle was fired at her,

[1] "It rises to the west of the Black Mts., across the northern extremity of which it finds a narrow, rapid passage along high perpendicular banks, then seeks the Missouri in a northeasterly direction, through a broken country with highlands bare of timber, and the low grounds particularly supplied with cottonwood, elm, small ash, box, alder, and an undergrowth of willow, red-wood, red-berry, and choke-cherry. . . . It enters the Missouri with a bold current, and is 134 yards wide, but its greatest depth is two feet and a half, which, joined to its rapidity and its sand-bars, makes the navigation difficult except for canoes." ("Lewis and Clark," ed. 1893, pp. 267, 268.

"We came to a green spot at the mouth of the Little Missouri, which is reckoned to be 1670 miles from the mouth of the great Missouri. The chain of blue hills, with the same singular forms as we had seen before, appeared on the other side of this river." ("Travels in North America," Prince of Wied, p. 182.")

and happily missed the poor thing; she afterwards lowered her neck, sank her body, and with the tip of the bill only above water, kept swimming away from us till out of sight. Afterwards one of the trappers shot at two Geese with two young ones. We landed at four o'clock, and Harris and Bell shot some Bay-winged Buntings and *Emberiza pallida*, whilst Sprague and I went up to the top of the hills, bounding the beautiful prairie, by which we had stopped to repair something about the engine. We gathered some handsome lupines, of two different species, and many other curious plants. From this elevated spot we could see the wilderness to an immense distance; the Missouri looked as if only a brook, and our steamer a very small one indeed. At this juncture we saw two men running along the shore upwards, and I supposed they had seen an Elk or something else, of which they were in pursuit. Meantime, gazing around, we saw a large lake, where we are told that Ducks, Geese, and Swans breed in great numbers; this we intend also to visit when we come down. At this moment I heard the report of a gun from the point where the men had been seen, and when we reached the steamboat, we were told that a Buffalo had been killed. From the deck I saw a man swimming round the animal; he got on its side, and floated down the stream with it. The captain sent a parcel of men with a rope; the swimmer fastened this round the neck of the Buffalo, and with his assistance, for he now swam all the way, the poor beast was brought alongside; and as the tackle had been previously fixed, it was hauled up on the fore deck. Sprague took its measurements with me, which are as follows: length from nose to root of tail, 8 feet; height of fore shoulder to hoof, 4 ft. 9½ in.; height at the rump to hoof, 4 ft. 2 in. The head was cut off, as well as one fore and one hind foot. The head is so full of symmetry, and so beautiful, that I shall have a drawing of it to-morrow,

as well as careful ones of the feet.   Whilst the butchers
were at work, I was highly interested to see one of our
Indians cutting out the milk-bag of the cow and eating
it, quite fresh and raw, in pieces somewhat larger than
a hen's egg.   One of the stomachs was partially washed
in a bucket of water, and an Indian swallowed a large
portion of this.   Mr. Chardon brought the remainder on
the upper deck and ate it uncleaned.   I had a piece well
cleaned and tasted it; to my utter astonishment, it was
very good, but the idea was repulsive to me; besides
which, I am not a meat-eater, as you know, except when
other provisions fail.   The animal was in good condition;
and the whole carcass was cut up and dispersed among
the men below, reserving the nicer portions for the cabin.
This was accomplished with great rapidity; the blood was
washed away in a trice, and half an hour afterwards no
one would have known that a Buffalo had been dressed on
deck.   We now met with a somewhat disagreeable accident; in starting and backing off the boat, our yawl was
run beneath the boat; this strained it, and sprung one of
the planks so much that, when we landed on the opposite side of the river, we had to haul it on shore, and turn
it over for examination; it was afterwards taken to the
forecastle to undergo repairs to-morrow, as it is often
needed.   Whilst cutting wood was going on, we went
ashore.   Bell shot at two Buffaloes out of eight, and
killed both; he would also have shot a Wolf, had he had
more bullets.   Harris saw, and shot at, an Elk; but he
knows little about still hunting, and thereby lost a good
chance.   A negro fire-tender went off with his rifle and
shot two of Townsend's Hares.   One was cut in two by
his ball, and he left it on the ground; the other was shot
near the rump, and I have it now hanging before me;
and, let me tell you, that I never before saw so beautiful
an animal of the same family.   My drawing will be a
good one; it is a fine specimen, an old male.   I have been

hearing much of the prevalence of scurvy, from living so constantly on dried flesh, also about the small-pox, which destroyed such numbers of the Indians. Among the Mandans, Riccarées, and Gros Ventres, hundreds died in 1837, only a few surviving; and the Assiniboins were nearly exterminated. Indeed it is said that in the various attacks of this scourge 52,000 Indians have perished. This last visitation of the dread disease has never before been related by a traveller,[1] and I will write more of it when at Fort Union. It is now twenty minutes to midnight; and, with walking and excitement of one kind or another, I am ready for bed. Alexis and another hunter will be off in an hour on a hunt.

June 10, Saturday. I rose at half-past three this morning. It was clear and balmy; our men were cutting wood, and we went off shooting. We saw a female Elk that was loath to leave the neighborhood; and Bell shot a Sharp-tailed Grouse, which we ate at our supper and found pretty good, though sadly out of season. As we were returning to the boat, Alexis and his companion went off after Buffaloes that we saw grazing peaceably on the bank near the river. Whilst they were shooting at the Buffaloes, and almost simultaneously, the fawn of the female Elk was seen lying asleep under the bank. It rose as we approached, and Bell shot at it, but missed; and with its dam it went briskly off. It was quite small, looking almost red, and was beautifully spotted with light marks of the color of the Virginia Deer's fawn. I would have given five dollars for it, as I saw it skipping over the prairie. At this moment Alexis came running, and told the captain they had killed two Buffaloes; and almost all the men went off at once with ropes, to bring the poor animals on board, according to custom. One,

---

[1] At this time the account of the Prince of Wied had not been published in English; that translation appeared December, 1843, two years after the German edition.

however, had been already dressed. The other had its head cut off, and the men were tugging at the rope, hauling the beast along over the grass. Mr. Chardon was seated on it; until, when near the boat, the rope gave way, and the bull rolled over into a shallow ravine. It was soon on board, however, and quickly skinned and cut up. The two hunters had been absent three-quarters of an hour. At the report of the guns, two Wolves made their appearance, and no doubt fed at leisure on the offal left from the first Buffalo. Harris saw a gang of Elks, consisting of between thirty and forty. We have passed a good number of Wild Geese with goslings; the Geese were shot at, notwithstanding my remonstrances on account of the young, but fortunately all escaped. We passed some beautiful scenery when about the middle of the "Bend," and almost opposite had the pleasure of seeing five Mountain Rams, or Bighorns, on the summit of a hill. I looked at them through the telescope; they stood perfectly still for some minutes, then went out of sight, and then again were in view. One of them had very large horns; the rest appeared somewhat smaller. Our captain told us that he had seen them at, or very near by, the same place last season, on his way up. We saw many very curious cliffs, but not one answering the drawings engraved for Catlin's work. We passed Knife River,[1] *Rivière aux Couteaux*, and stopped for a short time to take in wood. Harris killed a Sparrow Hawk, and saw several Red-shafted Woodpeckers. Bell was then engaged in saving the head of the Buffalo cow, of which I made a drawing, and Sprague an outline, notwithstanding the horrible motion of our boat. We passed safely

---

[1] This is the Little Knife, or Upper Knife River, to be carefully distinguished from that Knife River at the mouth of which were the Minnetaree villages. It falls into the Missouri from the north, in Mountraille Co., 55 miles above the mouth of the Little Missouri. This is probably the stream named Goat-pen Creek by Lewis and Clark : see p. 274 of the edition of 1893. — E. C.

a dangerous chain of rocks extending across the river; we also passed White River;[1] both the streams I have mentioned are insignificant. The weather was warm, and became cloudy, and it is now raining smartly. We have, however, a good quantity of excellent wood, and have made a good run, say sixty miles. We saw what we supposed to be three Grizzly Bears, but could not be sure. We saw on the prairie ahead of us some Indians, and as we neared them, found them to be Assiniboins. There were about ten altogether, men, squaws, and children. The boat was stopped, and a smart-looking, though small-statured man came on board. He had eight plugs of tobacco given him, and was asked to go off; but he talked a vast deal, and wanted powder and ball. He was finally got rid of. During his visit, our Gros Ventre chief and our Sioux were both in my own cabin. The first having killed three of that tribe and scalped them, and the Sioux having a similar record, they had no wish to meet. A few miles above this we stopped to cut wood. Bell and Harris went on shore; and we got a White Wolf, so old and so poor that we threw it over-board. Meantime a fawn Elk was observed crossing the river, coming toward our shore; it was shot at twice, but missed; it swam to the shore, but under such a steep bank that it could not get up. Alexis, who was told of this, ran down the river bank, reached it, and fastened his suspenders around its neck, but could not get it up the bank. Bell had returned, and went to his assistance, but all in vain; the little thing was very strong, and floundered and struggled till it broke the tie, and swam swiftly with the current down the river, and was lost. A slight rope would have secured it to us. This was almost the same spot where the captain caught one alive last season with the yawl; and we could have performed the same

[1] Or White Earth River of some maps, a comparatively small stream, eighteen and one half miles above the mouth of Little Knife River. — E. C.

feat easily, had not the yawl been on deck undergoing
repairs.   We pushed off, and very soon saw more Indians
on the shore, also Assiniboins.   They had crossed the
" Bend " below us, and had brought some trifles to trade
with us; but our captain passed on, and the poor wretches
sat and looked at the " Great Medicine " in astonishment.
Shortly after this, we saw a Wolf attempting to climb a
very steep bank of clay; he fell down thrice, but at last
reached the top and disappeared at once.   On the opposite shore another Wolf was lying down on a sand-bar, like
a dog, and might readily have been taken for one.   We
have stopped for the night at nine o'clock; and I now have
done my day's putting-up of memoranda and sketches,
intending to enlarge upon much after I return home.   I
forgot to say that last evening we saw a large herd of Buffaloes, with many calves among them; they were grazing
quietly on a fine bit of prairie, and we were actually opposite to them and within two hundred yards before they
appeared to notice us.   They stared, and then started at
a handsome canter, suddenly wheeled round, stopped,
closed up their ranks, and then passed over a slight knoll,
producing a beautiful picturesque view.   Another thing I
forgot to speak of is a place not far below the Little Missouri, where Mr. Kipp assured us we should find the remains of a petrified forest, which we hope to see later.

June 11, Sunday.   This day has been tolerably fine,
though windy.   We have seen an abundance of game, a
great number of Elks, common Virginian Deer, Mountain Rams in two places, and a fine flock of Sharp-tailed
Grouse, that, when they flew off from the ground near us,
looked very much like large Meadow Larks.   They
were on a prairie bordering a large patch of Artemisia,
which in the distance presents the appearance of acres of
cabbages.   We have seen many Wolves and some Buffaloes.   One young bull stood on the brink of a bluff, looking at the boat steadfastly for full five minutes; and as

we neared the spot, he waved his tail, and moved off briskly. On another occasion, a young bull that had just landed at the foot of a very steep bluff was slaughtered without difficulty; two shots were fired at it, and the poor thing was killed by a rifle bullet. I was sorry, for we did not stop for it, and its happy life was needlessly ended. I saw near that spot a large Hawk, and also a very small Tamias, or Ground Squirrel. Harris saw a Spermophile, of what species none of us could tell. We have seen many Elks swimming the river, and they look almost the size of a well-grown mule. They stared at us, were fired at, at an enormous distance, it is true, and yet stood still. These animals are abundant beyond belief hereabouts. We have seen much remarkably handsome scenery, but nothing at all comparing with Catlin's descriptions; his book must, after all, be altogether a humbug. Poor devil! I pity him from the bottom of my soul; had he studied, and kept up to the old French proverb that says, "Bon renommé vaut mieux que ceinture doré," he might have become an "honest man" — the quintessence of God's works. We did hope to have reached L'Eau Bourbeux (the Muddy River [1]) this evening, but we are now fast ashore, about six miles below it, about the same distance that we have been told we were ever since shortly after dinner. We have had one event: our boat caught fire, and burned for a few moments near the stern, the effects of the large, hot cinders coming from the chimney; but it was almost immediately put out, thank God! Any inattention, with about 10,000 lbs. of powder on board, might have resulted in a sad accident. We have decided to write a short letter of thanks to our truly gentlemanly captain, and to present him with a handsome six-barrelled

[1] Present name of the stream which flows into the Missouri from the north, in Puford Co. This is the last considerable affluent below the mouth of the Yellowstone, and the one which Lewis and Clark called White Earth River, by mistake. See last note. — E. C.

pistol, the only thing we have that may prove of service to him, although I hope he may never need it.　Sprague drew four figures of the Buffalo's foot; and Bell and I have packed the whole of our skins.　We ran to-day all round the compass, touching every point.　The following is a copy of the letter to Captain Sire, signed by all of us.

Fort Union, Mouth of Yellowstone,
Upper Missouri, *June 11th, 1843.*

Dear Sir,—We cannot part with you previous to your return to St. Louis, without offering to you our best wishes, and our thanks for your great courtesy, assuring you how highly we appreciate, and feel grateful for, your uniform kindness and gentlemanly deportment to each and all of us.　We are most happy to add that our passage to the Yellowstone River has been devoid of any material accident, which we can only attribute to the great regularity and constant care with which you have discharged your arduous duties in the difficult navigation of the river.

We regret that it is not in our power, at this moment, to offer you a suitable token of our esteem, but hope you will confer on us the favor of accepting at our hands a six-barrelled, silver-mounted pistol, which we sincerely hope and trust you may never have occasion to use in defence of your person.　We beg you to consider us,

Your well-wishers and friends, etc.,

Fort Union, June 12, Monday.　We had a cloudy and showery day, and a high wind besides.　We saw many Wild Geese and Ducks with their young.　We took in wood at two places, but shot nothing.　I saw a Wolf giving chase, or driving away four Ravens from a sand-bar; but the finest sight of all took place shortly before we came to the mouth of the Yellowstone, and that was no less than twenty-two Mountain Rams and Ewes mixed, and amid them one young one only.　We came in sight of the fort at five o'clock, and reached it at seven.　We passed the Opposition fort three miles below this; their flags were hoisted, and ours also.　We were saluted from

Fort Union, and we fired guns in return, six in number. The moment we had arrived, the gentlemen of the fort came down on horseback, and appeared quite a cavalcade. I was introduced to Mr. Culbertson and others, and, of course, the introduction went the rounds. We walked to the fort and drank some first-rate port wine, and returned to the boat at half-past nine o'clock. Our captain was pleased with the letter and the pistol. Our trip to the this place has been the quickest on record, though our boat is the slowest that ever undertook to reach the Yellowstone. Including all stoppages and detentions, we have made the trip in forty-eight days and seven hours from St. Louis. We left St. Louis April 25th, at noon; reaching Fort Union June 12th, at seven in the evening.

June 13, Tuesday. We had a remarkably busy day on board and on shore, but spent much of our time writing letters. I wrote home at great length to John Bachman, N. Berthoud, and Gideon B. Smith. We walked to the fort once and back again, and dined on board with our captain and the gentlemen of the fort. We took a ride also in an old wagon, somewhat at the risk of our necks, for we travelled too fast for the nature of what I was told was the road. We slept on board the " Omega," probably for the last time.

We have been in a complete state of excitement unloading the boat, reloading her with a new cargo, and we were all packing and arranging our effects, as well as writing letters. After dinner our belongings were taken to the landing of the fort in a large keel-boat, with the last of the cargo. The room which we are to occupy during our stay at this place is rather small and low, with only one window, on the west side. However, we shall manage well enough, I dare say, for the few weeks we are to be here. This afternoon I had a good deal of conversation with Mr. Culbertson, and found him well disposed to do all he can for us; and no one can ask for more politeness than is shown us. Our captain having invited us to remain with him to-night, we have done so, and will breakfast with him to-morrow morning. It is his intention to leave as early as he can settle his business here. All the trappers are gone to the fort, and in a few weeks will be dispersed over different and distant parts of the wilderness. The filth they had left below has been scraped and washed off, as well indeed as the whole boat, of which there was need enough. I have copied this journal and send it to St. Louis by our good captain; also one box of skins, one pair Elk horns, and one bundle of Wolf and other skins.

June 14, Wednesday. At six this morning all hands rose early; the residue of the cargo for St. Louis was placed on board. Our captain told us time was up, and we all started for the fort on foot, quite a short distance. Having deposited our guns there, Bell, Squires, and I walked off to the wooding-place, where our captain was to remain a good while, and it was there we should bid him adieu. We found this walk one of the worst, the very worst, upon which we ever trod; full of wild rose-bushes, tangled and matted with vines, burs, and thorns of all sorts, and encumbered by thousands of pieces of driftwood, some decayed, some sunk in the earth, while others were entangled with the innumerable roots exposed by floods and rains. We saw nothing but a few Ravens. When nearly half way, we heard the trampling of galloping horses, and loud hallooings, which we found to proceed from the wagon of which we have spoken, which, loaded with men, passed us at a speed one would have thought impossible over such ground. Soon after we had a heavy shower of rain, but reached the boat in good order. Harris and Sprague, who had followed us, came afterwards. I was pretty hot, and rather tired. The boat took on wood for half an hour after we arrived; then the captain shook us all by the hand most heartily, and we bade him God speed.

I parted from him really with sorrow, for I have found
him all I could wish during the whole passage; and his
position is no sinecure, to say naught of the rabble under
his control. All the wood-cutters who remained walked
off by the road; and we went back in the wagon over a
bad piece of ground — much easier, however, than returning on foot. As we reached the prairies, we travelled
faster, and passed by the late garden of the fort, which
had been abandoned on account of the thieving of the
men attached to the Opposition Company, at Fort Mortimer. Harris caught a handsome snake, now in spirits.
We saw Lazuli Finches and several other sorts of small
birds. Upon reaching the fort, from which many great
guns were fired as salutes to the steamer, which were
loudly returned, I was amused at the terror the firing
occasioned to the squaws and their children, who had
arrived in great numbers the previous evening; they
howled, fell down on the earth, or ran in every direction. All the dogs started off, equally frightened, and
made for the distant hills. Dinner not being ready,
three of us took a walk, and saw a good number of
Tamias holes, many cacti of two sorts, and some plants
hitherto uncollected by us. We saw a few Arctic Ground
Finches and two Wolves. After dinner Mr. Culbertson
told us that if a Wolf made its appearance on the
prairie near the fort, he would give it chase on horseback, and bring it to us, alive or dead; and he was as
good as his word. It was so handsomely executed, that
I will relate the whole affair. When I saw the Wolf
(a white one), it was about a quarter of a mile off,
alternately standing and trotting; the horses were about
one-half the distance off. A man was started to drive
these in; and I thought the coursers never would reach
the fort, much less become equipped so as to overhaul
the Wolf. We were all standing on the platform of the
fort, with our heads only above the palisades; and I

was so fidgety that I ran down twice to tell the hunters
that the Wolf was making off.   Mr. Culbertson, however,
told me he would see it did not make off; and in a few
moments he rode out of the fort, gun in hand, dressed
only in shirt and breeches.   He threw his cap off within
a few yards, and suddenly went off with the swiftness of
a jockey bent on winning a race.   The Wolf trotted on,
and ever and anon stopped to gaze at the rider and the
horse; till, finding out the meaning (too late, alas! for
him), he galloped off with all his might; but the horse
was too swift for the poor cur, as we saw the rider gaining ground rapidly.   Mr. Culbertson fired his gun off as
a signal, I was told, that the Wolf would be brought in;
and the horse, one would think, must have been of the
same opinion, for although the Wolf had now reached the
hills, and turned into a small ravine, the moment it had
entered it, the horse dashed after, the sound of the gun
came on the ear, the Wolf was picked up by Mr. Culbertson without dismounting, hardly slackening his pace,
and thrown across the saddle.   The rider returned as
swiftly as he had gone, wet through with a smart shower
that had fallen meantime; and the poor Wolf was placed
at my disposal.   The time taken from the start to the return in the yard did not exceed twenty minutes, possibly
something less.   Two other men who had started at the
same time rode very swiftly also, and skirted the hills to
prevent the Wolf's escape; and one of them brought in
Mr. C.'s gun, which he had thrown on the ground as he
picked up the Wolf to place it on the saddle.   The beast
was not quite dead when it arrived, and its jaws told of
its dying agonies; it scratched one of Mr. C.'s fingers
sorely; but we are assured that such things so often occur
that nothing is thought of it.

   And now a kind of sham Buffalo hunt was proposed,
accompanied by a bet of a suit of clothes, to be given to
the rider who would load and fire the greatest number of

shots in a given distance. The horses were mounted as another Wolf was seen trotting off towards the hills, and Mr. Culbertson again told us he would bring it in. This time, however, he was mistaken; the Wolf was too far off to be overtaken, and it reached the hill-tops, made its way through a deep ravine full of large rocks, and was then given up. Mr. Culbertson was seen coming down without his quarry. He joined the riders, started with his gun empty, loaded in a trice, and fired the first shot; then the three riders came on at full speed, loading and firing first on one side, then on the other of the horse, as if after Buffaloes. Mr. C. fired eleven times before he reached the fort, and within less than half a mile's run; the others fired once less, each. We were all delighted to see these feats. No one was thrown off, though the bridles hung loose, and the horses were under full gallop all the time. Mr. Culbertson's mare, which is of the full Blackfoot Indian breed, is about five years old, and could not be bought for four hundred dollars. I should like to see some of the best English hunting gentlemen hunt in the like manner. We are assured that after dusk, or as soon as the gates of the fort are shut, the Wolves come near enough to be killed from the platform, as these beasts oftentimes come to the trough where the hogs are fed daily. We have seen no less than eight this day from the fort, moving as leisurely as if a hundred miles off. A heavy shower put off running a race; but we are to have a regular Buffalo hunt, where I must act only as a spectator; for, alas! I am now too near seventy to run and load whilst going at full gallop. Two gentlemen arrived this evening from the Crow Indian Nation; they crossed to our side of the river, and were introduced at once. One is Mr. Chouteau, son of Auguste Chouteau, and the other a Scotchman, Mr. James Murray, at whose father's farm, on the Tweed, we all stopped on our return from the Highlands of Scotland. They told us that the snow and ice was yet three feet deep near the mountains, and an abundance over the whole of the mountains themselves. They say they have made a good collection of robes, but that Beavers are very scarce. This day has been spent altogether in talking, sight-seeing, and enjoyment. Our room was small, dark, and dirty, and crammed with our effects. Mr. Culbertson saw this, and told me that to-morrow he would remove us to a larger, quieter, and better one. I was glad to hear this, as it would have been very difficult to draw, write, or work in; and yet it is the very room where the Prince de Neuwied resided for two months, with his secretary and bird-preserver. The evening was cloudy and cold; we had had several showers of rain since our bath in the bushes this morning, and I felt somewhat fatigued. Harris and I made our beds up; Squires fixed some Buffalo robes, of which nine had been given us, on a long old bedstead, never knowing it had been the couch of a foreign prince;[1] Bell and Sprague settled themselves opposite to us on more Buffalo skins, and night closed in. But although we had lain down, it was impossible for us to sleep; for above us was a drunken man affected with a *goître*, and not only was his voice rough and loud, but his words were continuous. His oaths, both in French and English, were better fitted for the Five Points in New York, or St. Giles of London, than anywhere among Christians. He roared, laughed like a maniac, and damned himself and the whole creation. I thought that time would quiet him, but, no! for now clarionets, fiddles, and a drum were heard in the dining-room, where indeed they had been playing at different times during the afternoon, and our friend above began swearing at this as if quite fresh. We had retired for the night; but an invitation was sent us to join the party in the dining-room. Squires was up in a moment, and returned to say that a ball was on foot, and that "all

[1] Maximilian, Prince of Wied.

the beauty and fashion" would be skipping about in less than no time. There was no alternative; we all got up, and in a short time were amid the *beau monde* of these parts. Several squaws, attired in their best, were present, with all the guests, *engagés*, clerks, etc. Mr. Culbertson played the fiddle very fairly; Mr. Guèpe the clarionet, and Mr. Chouteau the drum, as if brought up in the army of the great Napoleon. Cotillions and reels were danced with much energy and apparent enjoyment, and the company dispersed about one o'clock. We retired for the second time, and now occurred a dispute between the drunkard and another man; but, notwithstanding this, I was so wearied that I fell asleep.

June 15, Thursday. We all rose late, as one might expect; the weather was quite cool for the season, and it was cloudy besides. We did nothing else than move our effects to an upstairs room. The Mackinaw boats arrived at the fort about noon, and were unloaded in a precious short time; and all hands being called forth, the empty boats themselves were dragged to a ravine, turned over, and prepared for calking previous to their next voyage up or down, as the case might be. The gentlemen from these boats gave me a fine pair of Deer's horns; and to Mr. Culbertson a young Gray Wolf, and also a young Badger, which they had brought in. It snarled and snapped, and sometimes grunted not unlike a small pig, but did not bite. It moved somewhat slowly, and its body looked flattish all the time; the head has all the markings of an adult, though it is a young of the present spring. Bell and Harris hunted a good while, but procured only a Lazuli Finch and a few other birds. Bell skinned the Wolf, and we put its hide in the barrel with the head of the Buffalo cow, etc. I showed the plates of the quadrupeds to many persons, and I hope with success, as they were pleased and promised me much. To-morrow morning a man called Black Harris

is to go off after Antelopes for me; and the hunters for
the men of the fort and themselves; and perhaps some
of the young men may go with one or both parties.   I
heard many stories about Wolves; particularly I was interested in one told by Mr. Kipp, who assured us he had
caught upwards of one hundred with baited fish-hooks.
Many other tales were told us; but I shall not forget
them, so will not write them down here, but wait till
hereafter.   After shooting at a mark with a bow made of
Elk horn, Mr. Kipp presented it to me.   We saw several
Wolves, but none close to the fort.   Both the common
Crow and Raven are found here; Bell killed one of the
former.

June 16, Friday.   The weather was cool this morning,
with the wind due east.   I drew the young Gray Wolf,
and Sprague made an outline of it.   Bell, Provost, Alexis,
and Black Harris went over the river to try to procure
Antelopes; Bell and Alexis returned to dinner without
any game, although they had seen dozens of the animals
wanted, and also some Common Deer.   The two others,
who travelled much farther, returned at dusk with empty
stomachs and a young fawn of the Common Deer.   Harris
and I took a long walk after my drawing was well towards
completion, and shot a few birds.   The Buffalo, old and
young, are fond of rolling on the ground in the manner of
horses, and turn quite over; this is done not only to clean
themselves, but also to rub off the loose old coat of hair
and wool that hangs about their body like so many large,
dirty rags.   Those about the fort are gentle, but will not
allow a person to touch their bodies, not even the young
calves of the last spring.   Our young Badger is quite fond
of lying on his back, and then sleeps.   His general appearance and gait remind me of certain species of Arma-
dillo.   There was a good deal of talking and jarring about
the fort; some five or six men came from the Opposition
Company, and would have been roughly handled had they

not cleared off at the beginning of trouble.   Arrangements
were made for loading the Mackinaw barges, and it is intended that they shall depart for St. Louis, leaving on
Sunday morning.   We shall all be glad when these boats
with their men are gone, as we are now full to the brim.
Harris has a new batch of patients, and enjoys the work
of physician.

June 17, Saturday.   Warm and fair, with the river rising fast.   The young fawn was hung up, and I drew it.
By dinner-time Sprague had well prepared the Gray Wolf,
and I put him to work at the fawn.   Bell went shooting,
and brought five or six good birds.   The song of the
Lazuli Finch so much resembles that of the Indigo Bird
that it would be difficult to distinguish them by the note
alone.   They keep indifferently among the low bushes
and high trees.   He also brought a few specimens of
Spermophilus hoodii of Richardson,[1] of which the measurements were taken.   Wolves often retreat into holes
made by the sinking of the earth near ravines, burrow-
ing in different directions at the bottoms of these.   I
sent Provost early this morning to the Opposition fort,
to inquire whether Mr. Cutting had written letters
about us, and also to see a fine Kit Fox, brought in one
of their boats from the Yellowstone.   Much has been
done in the way of loading the Mackinaw boats.   Bell
has skinned the young Wolf, and Sprague will perhaps
finish preparing the fawn.   The hunters who went out
yesterday morning have returned, and brought back a
quantity of fresh Buffalo meat.   Squires brought many
fragments of a petrified tree.   No Antelopes were shot,
and I feel uneasy on this score.   Provost returned and
told me Mr. Cutting's men with the letters had not arrived, but that they were expected hourly.   The Kit Fox

[1] This is a synonym of *Spermophilus tridecem-lineatus*, the Thirteen-lined,
or Federation Sphermophile, the variety that is found about Fort Union
being *S. t. pallidus.* — E. C.

had been suffocated to death by some dozens of bundles of Buffalo robes falling on it, while attached to a ladder, and had been thrown out and eaten by the Wolves or the dogs. This evening, quite late, I shot a fine large Gray Wolf. I sincerely hope to see some Antelopes to-morrow, as well as other animals.

June 18, Sunday. This day has been a beautiful, as well as a prosperous one to us. At daylight Provost and Alexis went off hunting across the river. Immediately after an early breakfast, Mr. Murray and three Mackinaw boats started for St. Louis. After the boats were fairly out of sight, and the six-pounders had been twice fired, and the great flag floated in the stiff southwesterly breeze, four other hunters went off over the river, and Squires was one of them. I took a walk with Mr. Culbertson and Mr. Chardon, to look at some old, decaying, and simply constructed coffins, placed on trees about ten feet above ground, for the purpose of finding out in what manner, and when it would be best for us to take away the skulls, some six or seven in number, all Assiniboin Indians. It was decided that we would do so at dusk, or nearly at dark. My two companions assured me that they never had walked so far from the fort unarmed as on this occasion, and said that even a *single* Indian with a gun and a bow might have attacked us; but if several were together, they would pay no attention to us, as that might be construed to mean war. This is a good lesson, however, and one I shall not forget. About ten o'clock Alexis came to me and said that he had killed two male Antelopes, and Provost one Deer, and that he must have a cart to bring the whole in. This was arranged in a few minutes; and Harris and I went across the river on a ferry flat, taking with us a cart and a most excellent mule. Alexis' wife went across also to gather gooseberries. The cart being made ready, we mounted it, I sitting down, and Harris standing up. We took an old abandoned road, filled with fallen timber and bushes innumerable; but Alexis proved to be an excellent driver, and the mule the most active and the strongest I ever saw. We jogged on through thick and thin for about two miles, when we reached a prairie covered with large bushes of Artemisia (called here " Herbe Sainte "), and presently, cutting down a slope, came to where lay our Antelope, a young male, and the skin of the Deer, while its carcass hung on a tree. These were placed in the cart, and we proceeded across the prairie for the other Antelope, which had been tied by the horns to a large bush of Artemisia, being alive when Alexis left it; but it was now dead and stiff. I looked at its eyes at once. This was a fine old male with its coat half shed. I was sorry enough it was dead. We placed it by its relation in the cart, jumped in, and off we went at a good round trot, not returning to the road, but across the prairie and immediately under the clay hills where the Antelope go after they have fed in the prairie below from early dawn until about eight o'clock; there are of course exceptions to the contrary. Part of the way we travelled between ponds made by the melting of the snows, and having on them a few Ducks and a Black Tern, all of which no doubt breed here. After we had passed the last pond, we saw three Antelopes several hundred yards to the lee of us; the moment they perceived us Alexis said they would be off; and so they were, scampering towards the hills until out of sight. We now entered the woods, and almost immediately Harris saw the head of a Deer about fifty yards distant. Alexis, who had only a rifle, would have shot him from the cart, had the mule stood still; but as this was not the case, Alexis jumped down, took a long, deliberate aim, the gun went off, and the Deer fell dead in its tracks. It proved to be a doe with very large milk-bags, and doubtless her fawn or fawns were in the vicinity; but Alexis could not find them in the dense bush. He and Harris dragged her to the

cart, where I stood holding the mule. We reached the
ferry, where the boat had awaited our return, placed the
cart on board without touching the game; and, on landing
at the fort, the good mule pulled it up the steep bank
into the yard. We now had two Antelopes and two Deer
that had been killed before noon. Immediately after
dinner, the head of the old male was cut off, and I went
to work outlining it; first small, with the camera, and
then by squares. Bell was engaged in skinning both the
bodies; but I felt vexed that he had carelessly suffered
the Gray Wolf to be thrown into the river. I spoke to
him on the subject of never losing a specimen till we
were quite sure it would not be needed; and I feel well
assured he is so honest a man and so good a worker that
what I said will last for all time. While looking at the
Deer shot this day, Harris and I thought that their tails
were very long, and that the animals themselves were very
much larger than those we have to the eastward; and we
all concluded to have more killed, and examine and measure closely, as this one may be an exception. It was unfortunate we did not speak of this an hour sooner, as two
Deer had been killed on this side the river by a hunter
belonging to the fort; but Mr. Culbertson assured me
that we should have enough of them in a few days. I am
told that the Rocky Mountain Rams lost most of their
young during the hard frosts of the early spring; for, like
those of the common sheep, the lambs are born as early
as the 1st of March, and hence their comparative scarcity.
Harris and Bell have shot a handsome White Wolf, a
female, from the ramparts; having both fired together, it
is not known which shot was the fatal one. Bell wounded
another in the leg, as there were several marauders about;
but the rascal made off.

June 19, Monday. It began raining early this morning; by "early," I mean fully two hours before daylight.
The first news I heard was from Mr. Chardon, who told

me he had left a Wolf feeding out of the pig's trough, which is immediately under the side of the fort. The next was from Mr. Larpenteur,[1] who opens the gates when the bell rings at sunrise, who told us he saw seven Wolves within thirty yards, or less, of the fort. I have told him since, with Mr. Chardon's permission, to call upon us before he opens these mighty portals, whenever he espies Wolves from the gallery above, and I hope that to-morrow morning we may shoot one or more of these bold marauders. Sprague has been drawing all day, and I a good part of it; and it has been so chilly and cold that we have had fires in several parts of the fort. Bell and Harris have gone shooting this afternoon, and have not yet returned. Bell cleaned the Wolf shot last night, and the two Antelopes; old Provost boiled brine, and the whole of them are now in pickle. There are some notions that two kinds of Deer are found hereabouts, one quite small, the other quite large; but of this I have no proof at present. The weather was too bad for Alexis to go hunting. Young Mr. McKenzie and a companion went across the river, but returned soon afterwards, having seen nothing but one Grizzly Bear. The water is either at a stand, or falling a little. — *Later.* Harris and Bell have returned, and, to my delight and utter astonishment, have brought two new birds: one a Lark,[2] small and beautiful; the other like our common Golden-winged Woodpecker, but with a red mark instead of a black one along the lower mandible running backward.[3] I am quite

---

[1] Charles Larpenteur, whose MS. autobiography I possess. — E. C.

[2] This is the first intimation we have of the discovery of the Missouri Titlark, which Audubon dedicated to Mr. Sprague under the name of *Alauda spragueii*, B. of Am. vii., 1844, p. 334, pl. 486. It is now well known as *Anthus (Neocorys) spraguei.* — E. C.

[3] Here is the original indication of the curious Flicker of the Upper Missouri region, which Audubon named *Picus ayresii*, B. of Am. vii., 1844, p. 348, pl. 494, after W. O. Ayres. It is the *Colaptes hybridus* of Baird, and the *C. aurato-mexicanus* of Hartlaub; in which the specific characters of the

amazed at the differences of opinion respecting the shedding — or not shedding — of the horns of the Antelope;[1] and this must be looked to with the greatest severity, for if these animals *do* shed their horns, they are no longer *Antelopes*. We are about having quite a ball in honor of Mr. Chardon, who leaves shortly for the Blackfoot Fort.

June 20, Tuesday. It rained nearly all night; and though the ball was given, I saw nothing of it, and heard but little, for I went to bed and to sleep. Sprague finished the drawing of the old male Antelope, and I mine, taking besides the measurements, etc., which I give here. . . . Bell has skinned the head and put it in pickle. The weather was bad, yet old Provost, Alexis, and Mr. Bonaventure, a good hunter and a first-rate shot, went over the river to hunt. They returned, however, without anything, though they saw three or four Deer, and a Wolf almost black, with very long hair, which Provost followed for more than a mile, but uselessly, as the rascal outwitted him after all. Harris and Bell are gone too, and I hope they will bring some more specimens of Sprague's Lark and the new Golden-winged Woodpecker.

To fill the time on this dreary day, I asked Mr. Chardon to come up to our room and give us an account of the small-pox among the Indians, especially among the Mandans and Riccarees, and he related as follows : Early in the month of July, 1837, the steamer " Assiniboin " arrived at Fort Clark with many cases of small-pox on board.

Golden-winged and Red-shafted Flickers are mixed and obscured in every conceivable degree. We presently find Audubon puzzled by the curious birds, whose peculiarities have never been satisfactorily explained. — E. C.

[1] The fact that the *Antilocapra americana* does shed its horns was not satisfactorily established till several years after 1843. It was first brought to the notice of naturalists by Dr. C. A. Canfield of California, April 10, 1858, and soon afterward became generally known. (See Proc. Zoöl. Soc. Lond. 1865, p. 718, and 1866, p. 105.) Thereupon it became evident that, as Audubon says, these animals are not true Antelopes, and the family *Antilocapridæ* was established for their reception. On the whole subject see article in Encycl. Amer. i., 1883, pp. 237-242, figs. 1-5. — E. C.

Mr. Chardon, having a young son on the boat, went thirty miles to meet her, and took his son away. The pestilence, however, had many victims on the steamboat, and seemed destined to find many more among the helpless tribes of the wilderness. An Indian stole the blanket of one of the steamboat's watchmen (who lay at the point of death, if not already dead), wrapped himself in it, and carried it off, unaware of the disease that was to cost him his life, and that of many of his tribe — thousands, indeed. Mr. Chardon offered a reward immediately for the return of the blanket, as well as a new one in its stead, and promised that no punishment should be inflicted. But the robber was a great chief; through shame, or some other motive, he never came forward, and, before many days, was a corpse. Most of the Riccarees and Mandans were some eighty miles in the prairies, hunting Buffaloes and saving meat for the winter. Mr. Chardon despatched an express to acquaint them all of the awful calamity, enjoining them to keep far off, for that death would await them in their villages. They sent word in return, that their corn was suffering for want of work, that they were not afraid, and would return; the danger to them, poor things, seemed fabulous, and doubtless they thought other reasons existed, for which this was an excuse. Mr. Chardon sent the man back again, and told them their crop of corn was nothing compared to their lives; but Indians are Indians, and, in spite of all entreaties, they moved *en masse*, to confront the awful catastrophe that was about to follow. When they reached the villages, they thought the whites had saved the Riccarees, and put the plague on them alone (they were Mandans). Moreover, they thought, and said, that the whites had a preventive medicine, which the whites would not give them. Again and again it was explained to them that this was not the case, but all to no purpose; the small-pox had taken such a hold upon the poor Indians, and in such

malignant form, that they died oftentimes within the rising and setting of a day's sun.   They died by hundreds
daily; their bodies were thrown down beneath the high
bluff, and soon produced a stench beyond description.
Men shot their wives and children, and afterwards, driving several balls in their guns, would place the muzzle
in their mouths, and, touching the trigger with their feet,
blow their brains out.   About this time Mr. Chardon was
informed that one of the young Mandan chiefs was bent on
shooting him, believing he had brought the pestilence
upon the Indians.   One of Mr. Chardon's clerks heard of
this plot, and begged him to remain in the store; at first
Mr. Chardon did not place any faith in the tale, but later
was compelled to do so, and followed his clerk's advice.
The young chief, a short time afterwards, fell a victim to
this fearful malady; but probably others would have taken
his life had it not been for one of those strange incidents
which come, we know not why, nor can we explain them.
A number of the chiefs came that day to confer with Mr.
Chardon, and while they were talking angrily with him,
he sitting with his arms on a table between them, a
Dove, being pursued by a Hawk, flew in through the open
door, and sat panting and worn out·on Mr. Chardon's arm
for more than a minute, when it flew off.   The Indians,
who were quite numerous, clustered about him, and asked
him what the bird came to him for?   After a moment's
thought, he told them that the bird had been sent by the
white men, his friends, to see if it was true that the Mandans had killed him, and that it must return with the answer as soon as possible; he added he had told the Dove
to say that the Mandans were his friends, and would
never kill him, but would do all they could for him.
The superstitious redmen believed this story implicitly;
thenceforth they looked on Mr. Chardon as one of the
Great Spirit's sons, and believed he alone could help
them.   Little, however, could be done; the small-pox

continued its fearful ravages, and the Indians grew fewer
and fewer day by day. For a long time the Riccarees
did not suffer; the Mandans became more and more as-
tounded at this, and became exasperated against both
whites and Indians. The disease was of the most viru-
lent type, so that within a few hours after death the
bodies were a mass of rottenness. Men killed themselves,
to die a nobler death than that brought by the dreaded
plague. One young warrior sent his wife to dig his
grave; and she went, of course, for no Indian woman
dares disobey her lord. The grave was dug, and the warrior, dressed in his most superb apparel, with lance and
shield in hand, walked towards it singing his own death
song, and, finding the grave finished, threw down all
his garments and arms, and leaped into it, drawing his
knife as he did so, and cutting his body almost asunder.
This done, the earth was thrown over him, the grave filled
up, and the woman returned to her lodge to live with her
children, perhaps only another day. A great chief, who
had been a constant friend to the whites, having caught
the pest, and being almost at the last extremity, dressed
himself in his fineries, mounted his war-steed, and, fevered
and in agony, rode among the villages, speaking against
the whites, urging the young warriors to charge upon
them and destroy them all. The harangue over, he went
home, and died not many hours afterward. The exposure
and exertion brought on great pains, and one of the men
from the fort went to him with something that gave him
temporary relief; before he died, he acknowledged his
error in trying to create trouble between the whites and
Indians, and it was his wish to be buried in front of the
gate of the fort, with all his trophies around and above
his body; the promise was given him that this should be
done, and he died in the belief that the white man, as he
trod on his grave, would see that he was humbled before
him, and would forgive him. Two young men, just sick-

ening with the disease, began to talk of the dreadful death that awaited them, and resolved not to wait for the natural close of the malady, the effects of which they had seen among their friends and relatives. One said the knife was the surest and swiftest weapon to carry into effect their proposed self-destruction; the other contended that placing an arrow in the throat and forcing it into the lungs was preferable. After a long debate they calmly rose, and each adopted his own method; in an instant the knife was driven into the heart of one, the arrow into the throat of the other, and they fell dead almost at the same instant. Another story was of an extremely handsome and powerful Indian who lost an only son, a beautiful boy, upon whom all his hopes and affections were placed. The loss proved too much for him; he called his wife, and, after telling her what a faithful husband he had been, said to her, "Why should we live? all we cared for is taken from us, and why not at once join our child in the land of the Great Spirit?" She consented; in an instant he shot her dead on the spot, reloaded his gun, put the muzzle in his mouth, touched the trigger, and fell back dead. On the same day another curious incident occurred; a young man, covered with the eruption, and apparently on the eve of death, managed to get to a deep puddle of mire or mud, threw himself in it, and rolled over and over as a Buffalo is wont to do. The sun was scorching hot, and the poor fellow got out of the mire covered with a coating of clay fully half an inch thick and laid himself down; the sun's heat soon dried the clay, so as to render it like unburnt bricks, and as he walked or crawled along towards the village, the mud drying and falling from him, taking the skin with it, and leaving the flesh raw and bleeding, he was in agony, and besought those who passed to kill him; but, strange to say, after enduring tortures, the fever left him, he recovered, and is still living, though badly scarred. Many ran to the river, in the delirium of the burning fever, plunged in the stream, and rose no more. The whites in the fort, as well as the Riccarees, took the disease after all. The Indians, with few exceptions, died, and three of the whites. The latter had no food in the way of bread, flour, sugar, or coffee, and they had to go stealthily by night to steal small pumpkins, about the size of a man's fist, to subsist upon — and this amid a large number of wild, raving, mad Indians, who swore revenge against them all the while. This is a mere sketch of the terrible scourge which virtually annihilated two powerful tribes of Indians, and of the trials of the traders attached to the Fur Companies on these wild prairies, and I can tell you of many more equally strange. The mortality, as taken down by Major Mitchell, was estimated by that gentleman at 150,000 Indians, including those from the tribes of the Riccarees, Mandans, Sioux, and Blackfeet. The small-pox was in the very fort from which I am now writing this account, and its ravages here were as awful as elsewhere. Mr. Chardon had the disease, and was left for dead; but one of his clerks saw signs of life, and forced him to drink a quantity of hot whiskey mixed with water and nutmeg; he fell into a sound sleep, and his recovery began from that hour. He says that with him the pains began in the small of the back, and on the back part of his head, and were intense. He concluded by assuring us all that the small-pox had never been known in the civilized world, as it had been among the poor Mandans and other Indians. Only *twenty-seven* Mandans were left to tell the tale; they have now augmented to ten or twelve lodges in the six years that have nearly elapsed since the pestilence.[1]

[1] That the account given by Audubon is not exaggerated may be seen from the two accounts following; the first from Lewis and Clark, the second from the Prince of Wied : —

"The ancient Maha village had once consisted of 300 cabins, but was burnt about four years ago (1800), soon after the small-pox had destroyed four hundred men, and a proportion of women and children. . . . The

Harris and Bell came back bringing several small birds,
among which three or four proved to be a Blackbird[1]

accounts we have had of the effects of the small-pox are most distressing;
. . . when these warriors saw their strength wasting before a malady which
they could not resist, their frenzy was extreme; they burnt their village, and
many of them put to death their wives and children, to save them from so
cruel an affliction, and that they might go together to some better country."

"New Orleans, June 6, 1838. We have from the trading posts on the
western frontier of Missouri the most frightful accounts of the ravages of
small-pox among the Indians. . . . The number of victims within a few
months is estimated at 30,000, and the pestilence is still spreading. . . .
The small-pox was communicated to the Indians by a person who was on
board the steamboat which went last summer to the mouth of the Yellowstone, to convey both the government presents for the Indians, and the
goods for the barter trade of the fur-dealers. . . . The officers gave notice of
it to the Indians, and exerted themselves to the utmost to prevent any intercourse between them and the vessel; but this was a vain attempt. . . . The
disease first broke out about the 15th of June, 1837, in the village of the
Mandans, from which it spread in all directions with unexampled fury. . . .
Among the remotest tribes of the Assiniboins from fifty to one hundred
died daily. . . . The ravages of the disorder were most frightful among the
Mandans. That once powerful tribe was exterminated, with the exception
of thirty persons. Their neighbors, the Gros Ventres and the Riccarees,
were out on a hunting excursion at the time the disorder broke out, so that
it did not reach them till a month later; yet half the tribe were destroyed
by October 1. Very few of those who were attacked recovered. . . . Many
put an end to their lives with knives or muskets, or by precipitating themselves from the summit of the rock near the settlement. The prairie all
around is a vast field of death, covered with unburied corpses. The Gros
Ventres and the Riccarees, lately amounting to 4,000 souls, were reduced
to less than one half. The Assiniboins, 9,000 in number, are nearly exterminated. They, as well as the Crows and Blackfeet, endeavored to fly in
all directions; but the disease pursued them. . . . The accounts of the
Blackfeet are awful. The inmates of above 1,000 of their tents are already
swept away. No language can picture the scene of desolation which the
country presents. The above does not complete the terrible intelligence
which we receive. . . . According to the most recent accounts, the number
of Indians who have been swept away by the small-pox, on the Western
frontier of the United States, amounts to more than 60,000."

[1] *Quiscalus brewerii* of Audubon, B. of Am. vii., 1844, p. 345, pl. 492, now
known as *Scolecophagus cyanocephalus*. It was new to our fauna when thus
dedicated by Audubon to his friend Dr. Thomas M. Brewer of Boston, but
had already been described by Wagler from Mexico as *Psarocolius cyanocephalus*. It is an abundant bird in the West, where it replaces its near
ally, *Scolecophagus carolinus*. — E. C.

nearly allied to the Rusty Grakle, but with evidently a
much shorter and straighter bill. Its measurements will
be given, of course. The weather is still lowering and
cold, and it rains at intervals. We are now out of specimens of quadrupeds to draw from. Our gentlemen seem
to remember the ball of last night, and I doubt not will
go early to bed, as I shall.

June 21, Wednesday. Cloudy and lowering weather;
however, Provost went off over the river, before daylight,
and shot a Deer, of what kind we do not know; he returned about noon, very hungry. The mud was dreadful
in the bottoms. Bell and young McKenzie went off after
breakfast, but brought nothing but a Sharp-tailed Grouse,
though McKenzie shot two Wolves. The one Harris shot
last night proved to be an old female not worth keeping;
her companions had seamed her jaws, for in this part of
the world Wolves feed upon Wolves, and no mistake.
This evening I hauled the beast under the ramparts, cut
her body open, and had a stake driven quite fast through
it, to hold it as a bait. Harris and Bell are this moment
on the lookout for the rascals. Wolves here not only eat
their own kind, but are the most mischievous animals in
the country; they eat the young Buffalo calves, the young
Antelopes, and the young of the Bighorn on all occasions, besides Hares of different sorts, etc. Buffaloes
never scrape the snow with their feet, but with their
noses, notwithstanding all that has been said to the contrary, even by Mr. Catlin. Bell brought home the hind
parts, the head, and one forefoot of a new species of small
Hare.[1]

We are told these Hares are very plentiful, and yet
this is the first specimen we have seen, and sorry am I

[1] This is no doubt the *Lepus artemisia* of Bachman, Journ. Philad. Acad.
viii., 1839, p. 94, later described and figured by Aud. and Bach., Quad. N.
Am. ii., 1851, p. 272, pl. 88. It is now generally rated as a subspecies of the
common Cottontail, *L. sylvaticus.* Compare also *L. nuttalli,* Aud. and Bach.
ii., 1851, p. 300, pl. 94. — E. C.

that it amounts to no specimen at all. Harris and I walked several miles, but killed nothing; we found the nest of a Sparrow-hawk, and Harris, assisted by my shoulders, reached the nest, and drew out two eggs. Sprague went across the hills eastward, and was fortunate enough to shoot a superb specimen of the Arctic Bluebird. This evening, Mr. Culbertson having told me the Rabbits, such as Bell had brought, were plentiful on the road to the steamboat landing, Harris, Bell, and I walked there; but although we were very cautious, we saw none, and only procured a Black-headed Grosbeak, which was shot whilst singing delightfully. To-morrow morning Mr. Chardon leaves us in the keel-boat for the Blackfoot Fort, and Mr. Kipp will leave for the Crows early next week.

June 22, Thursday. We rose very late this morning, with the exception of Provost who went out shooting quite early; but he saw nothing fit for his rifle. All was bustle after breakfast, as Mr. Chardon's boat was loading, the rigging being put in order, the men moving their effects, etc., and a number of squaws, the wives of the men, were moving to and fro for hours before the ultimate departure of the boat, which is called the "Bee." The cargo being arranged, thirty men went on board, including the commander, friend Chardon, thirteen squaws, and a number of children, all more or less half-breeds. The flag of Fort Union was hoisted, the four-pounder run out of the front gate, and by eleven o'clock all was ready. The keel-boat had a brass swivel on her bows, and fired first, then off went the larger gun, and many an Antelope and Deer were doubtless frightened at the report that echoed through the hills far and near. We bid adieu to our good friend Chardon; and his numerous and willing crew, taking the cordelle to their shoulders, moved the boat against a strong current in good style. Harris and Bell had gone shooting and returned with several birds, among which was a female Red-patched Woodpecker,[1] and a Lazuli Finch. Dinner over, I went off with young McKenzie after Hares; found none, but started a Grizzly Bear from her lair. Owen McKenzie followed the Bear and I continued after Hares; he saw no more of Bruin, and I not a Hare, and we both returned to the fort after a tramp of three hours. As I was walking over the prairie, I found an Indian's skull (an Assiniboin) and put it in my game pouch. Provost made a whistle to imitate the noise made by the fawns at this season, which is used to great advantage to decoy the female Deer; shortly afterward Mr. Bonaventure returned, and a cart was sent off at once to bring in a doe which he had killed below. This species of Deer is much larger than the one we have in Virginia, but perhaps no more so than those in Maine; and as yet we cannot tell whether it may, or may not, prove a distinct species. We took all its measurements, and Bell and Provost are now skinning it. Its gross weight is 140 lbs., which I think is heavier than any doe I have seen before. The animal is very poor and evidently has fawns in the woods. The little new Lark that I have named after Sprague has almost all the habits of the Skylark of Europe. Whilst looking anxiously after it, on the ground where we supposed it to be singing, we discovered it was high over our heads, and that sometimes it went too high for us to see it at all. We have not yet been able to discover its nest. Bell is of opinion that the Red-collared Ground Finch[2] has its nest in the deserted holes of the Ground Squirrel,

---

[1] This is the same hybrid Woodpecker which has been already noted on p. 14. — E. C.

[2] That is, the Chestnut-collared Longspur, *Calcarius ornatus*, which Mr. Bell was mistaken in supposing to breed in holes of the Ground Squirrels, or Spermophiles, as it nests on the open ground, like Sprague's Lark, McCown's Longspur, and most other small birds of the Western plains. But the surmise regarding the nesting of Say's Flycatcher is correct. This is a near relative of the common Pewit Flycatcher, *S. phœbe*, and its nesting places are similar. — E. C.

and we intend to investigate this. He also believes that Say's Flycatcher builds in rocky caverns or fissures, as he found the nest of a bird in some such place, after having wounded one of this species, which retired into the fissures of the rock, which he examined in pursuit of the wounded bird. The nest had no eggs; we are going to pay it a visit. Bell was busy most of the day skinning birds, and Sprague drew a beautiful plant. I found a number of wild roses in bloom, quite sweet-scented, though single, and of a very pale rose-color.

June 23, Friday. We have had a fine, warm day. The hunters of Buffaloes started before daylight, and Squires accompanied them; they are not expected back till some-time to-morrow. Provost went across the river with them, and with the assistance of his bleating whistle, brought several does round him, and a good many Wolves. He killed two does, drew them to a tree, and hung his coat near them while he returned for help to bring them to the fort. The hunters have a belief that a garment hung near game freshly killed will keep the Wolves at bay for a time; but there are exceptions to all rules, as when he returned with the cart, a dozen hungry rascals of Wolves had completely devoured one doe and all but one ham of the other; this he brought to the fort. The does at this season, on hearing the "bleat," run to the spot, suppos-ing, no doubt, that the Wolves have attacked their fawns, and in rushing to the rescue, run towards the hunter, who despatches them without much trouble, unless the woods are thickly overgrown with bushes and brush, when more difficulty is experienced in seeing them, although one may hear them close by; but it is a cruel, deceitful, and un-sportsmanlike method, of which I can never avail myself, and which I try to discountenance. Bell was busy all day with skins, and Sprague with flowers, which he de-lineates finely. Mr. Kipp presented me with a complete dress of a Blackfoot warrior, ornamented with many tufts of Indian hair from scalps, and also with a saddle. After dinner, Harris, who felt poorly all morning, was better, and we went to pay a visit at the Opposition fort. We started in a wagon with an old horse called Peter, which stands fire like a stump. In going, we found we could approach the birds with comparative ease, and we had the good fortune to shoot three of the new Larks. I killed two, and Harris one. When this species starts from the ground, they fly in a succession of undulations, which renders aim at them quite difficult; after this, and in the same manner, they elevate themselves to some considerable height, as if about to sing, and presently pitch towards the ground, where they run prettily, and at times stand still and quite erect for a few minutes; we hope to discover their nests soon. Young Meadow Larks, Red-shafted Woodpeckers, and the Red-cheeked ditto,[1] are abundant. We reached Fort Mortimer in due time; passed first between several sulky, half-starved looking Indians, and came to the gate, where we were received by the "bourgeois,"[2] a young man by the name of Collins, from Hopkinsville, Ky. We found the place in a most miserable condition, and about to be carried away by the falling in of the banks on account of the great rise of water in the Yellowstone, that has actually dammed the Missouri. The current ran directly across, and the banks gave way at such a rate that the men had been obliged already to tear up the front of the fort and remove it to the rear. To-morrow they are to remove the houses themselves, should they stand the coming night, which appeared to me somewhat dubious. We

[1] This passage shows that Audubon observed individuals of the hybrid Woodpecker which he considered identical with *Colaptes cafer*, and also others which he regarded as belonging to the supposed new species — his *C. ayresii.* — E. C.

[2] The usual title or designation of the chief trader or person in charge of any establishment of a fur company. — E. C.

saw a large athletic man who has crossed the mountains twice to the Pacific; he is a Philadelphian, named Wallis, who had been a cook at Fort Union four years, but who had finally deserted, lived for a time with the Crows, and then joined the Opposition. These persons were very polite to us, and invited us to remain and take supper with them; but as I knew they were short of provisions, I would not impose myself upon them, and so, with thanks for their hospitality, we excused ourselves and returned to Fort Union. As we were in search of birds, we saw a small, whitish-colored Wolf trotting across the prairie, which hereabouts is very extensive and looks well, though the soil is poor. We put Peter to a trot and gained on the Wolf, which did not see us until we were about one hundred yards off; he stopped suddenly, and then went off at a canter. Harris gave the whip to Peter, and off we went, evidently gaining rapidly on the beast, when it saw an Indian in its road; taking fright, it dashed to one side, and was soon lost in a ravine. We congratulated ourselves, on reaching the fort, that we had such good fortune as to be able to sup and sleep here, instead of at Fort Mortimer. Bell had taken a walk and brought in a few birds. The prairie is covered with cacti, and Harris and I suffered by them; my feet were badly pricked by the thorns, which penetrated my boots at the junction of the soles with the upper leathers. I have to-day heard several strange stories about Grizzly Bears, all of which I must have corroborated before I fully accept them. The Otters and Musk-rats of this part of the country are smaller than in the States; the first is the worst enemy that the Beaver has.

June 24, Saturday. Bell killed a small Wolf last night, and Harris wounded another. This morning Provost started at daylight, and Bell followed him; but they returned without game. After breakfast Harris went off on horseback, and brought in a Sharp-tailed Grouse. He saw only one

Deer, species not identified. Sprague and I went off last, but brought in nothing new. This afternoon I thought would be a fair opportunity to examine the manners of Sprague's Lark on the wing. Bell drove Peter for me, and I killed four Larks; we then watched the flight of several. The male rises by constant undulations to a great height, say one hundred yards or more; and whilst singing its sweet-sounding notes, beats its wings, poised in the air like a Hawk, without rising at this time; after which, and after each burst of singing, it sails in divers directions, forming three quarters of a circle or thereabouts, then rises again, and again sings; the intervals between the singing are longer than those which the song occupies, and at times the bird remains so long in the air as to render it quite fatiguing to follow it with the eye. Sprague thought one he watched yesterday remained in the air about one hour. Bell and Harris watched one for more than half an hour, and this afternoon I gazed upon one, whilst Bell timed it, for thirty-six minutes. We continued on to Fort Mortimer to see its condition, were received as kindly as yesterday, and saw the same persons. It was four o'clock, and the men were all at dinner, having been obliged to wait until this time because they had no meat in the fort, and their hunters had returned only one hour and a half before. We found that the river had fallen about fourteen inches since last evening, and the men would not remove for the present. On our way homeward Bell shot a fifth Lark, and when we reached the ravine I cut out of a tree-stump the nest of an Arctic Bluebird, with six eggs in it, of almost the same size and color as those of the common Bluebird. Sprague had brought a female of his Lark, and her nest containing five eggs; the measurements of these two species I will write out to-morrow. Our Buffalo hunters are not yet returned, and I think that Squires will feel pretty well fatigued when he reaches the fort. Mr. Culbertson presented me with a pair of stirrups, and a most splendid Blackfoot crupper for my saddle. The day has been warm and clear. We caught seven catfish at the river near the fort, and most excellent eating they are, though quite small when compared with the monsters of this species on the Missouri below.

June 25, Sunday. This day has been warm and the wind high, at first from the south, but this afternoon from the north. Little or nothing has been done in the way of procuring birds or game, except that Harris and Mr. Denig brought in several Arkansas Flycatchers. Not a word from the hunters, and therefore they must have gone far before they met Buffaloes. A few more catfish have been caught, and they are truly excellent.

June 26, Monday. The hunters returned this afternoon about three o'clock; *i. e.*, Squires and McKenzie; but the carts did not reach the fort till after I had gone to bed. They have killed three Antelopes, three bull Buffaloes, and one Townsend's Hare, but the last was lost through carelessness, and I am sorry for it. The men had eaten one of the Antelopes, and the two others are fine males; Bell skinned one, and saved the head and the fore-legs of the other. One of them had the tips of the horns as much crooked inwardly (backwards) as the horns of the European Chamois usually are. This afternoon early Provost brought in a Deer of the large kind, and this also was skinned. After this Harris and Bell went off and brought in several Lazuli Finches, and a black Prairie Lark Finch of the species brought from the Columbia by Townsend and Nuttall. We caught several catfish and a very curious sturgeon, of which Sprague took an outline with the camera, and I here give the measurements. . . . It had run on the shore, and was caught by one of the men. I made a bargain this morning with the hunter Bonaventure Le Brun to procure me ten Bighorns, at $10.00 apiece, or the same price for any number he may get.

Mr. Culbertson lent him old Peter, the horse, and I wrote a *petit billet* to Mr. John Collins, to ask him to have them ferried across the river, as our boat was away on a wood-cutting expedition. As Le Brun did not return, of course he was taken across, and may, perhaps, come back this evening, or early to-morrow morning, with something worth having. At this moment Bell has shot a Wolf from the ramparts, and sadly crippled another, but it made off somehow.

June 27, Tuesday. This morning was quite cool, and the wind from the north. After breakfast Bell and Owen McKenzie went off on horseback on this side of the river, to see how far off the Buffaloes are, and they may probably bring home some game. Sprague and I have been drawing all day yesterday and most of to-day. Provost has been making whistles to call the Deer; later he, Harris, and I, walked to the hills to procure the black root plant which is said to be the best antidote for the bite of the rattlesnake. We found the root and dug one up, but the plant is not yet in bloom. The leaves are long and narrow, and the flowers are said to resemble the dwarf sunflower. Harris shot two of what he calls the Small Shore Lark, male and female; but beyond the size being a little smaller than those found at Labrador, I cannot discover any specific difference. From the top of the hills we saw a grand panorama of a most extensive wilderness, with Fort Union beneath us and far away, as well as the Yellowstone River, and the lake across the river. The hills across the Missouri appeared quite low, and we could see the high prairie beyond, forming the background. Bell and McKenzie returned, having shot a Wolf in a curious manner. On reaching the top of a hill they found themselves close to the Wolf. Bell's horse ran quite past it, but young McKenzie shot and broke one fore-leg, and it fell. Bell then gave his horse to McKenzie, jumped off, ran to the Wolf, and took hold of it by the tail, pulling it towards the horses;

but it got up and ran rapidly. Bell fired two shots in its back with a pistol without stopping it, then he ran as fast as he could, shot it in the side, and it fell. Bell says its tail was longer than usual, but it was not measured, and the Wolf was left on the prairie, as they had no means of bringing it in. They saw an Antelope, some Magpies, and a Swift Fox, but no Buffaloes, though they were fifteen miles from the fort. They ran a Long-tailed Deer, and describe its movements precisely as do Lewis and Clark.[1] Between every three or four short leaps came the long leap of fully twenty-five feet, if not more. The Kit or Swift Fox which they saw stood by a bunch of wormwood, and whilst looking at the hunters, was seen to brush off the flies with his paws.

I am now going to take this book to Lewis Squires and ask him to write in it his account of the Buffalo hunt.

(The following is in Mr. Squires' handwriting:)

"By Mr. Audubon's desire I will relate the adventures that befell me in my first Buffalo hunt, and I am in hopes that among the rubbish a trifle, at least, may be obtained which may be of use or interest to him. On the morning of Friday, the 23d, before daylight, I was up, and in a short time young McKenzie made his appearance. A few minutes sufficed to saddle our horses, and be in readiness for our contemplated hunt. We were accompanied by Mr. Bonaventure the younger, one of the hunters of the fort, and two carts to bring in whatever kind of meat might be procured. We were ferried across the river in a flatboat, and thence took our departure for the Buffalo country. We passed through a wooded bottom for about one mile, and then over a level prairie for about one mile and a half, when we commenced the ascent of the bluffs that bound the western side of the Missouri valley; our

[1] "The black-tailed deer never runs at full speed, but bounds with every foot from the ground at the same time, like the mule-deer." ("Lewis and Clark," ed. 1893.)

course then lay over an undulating prairie, quite rough, and steep hills with small ravines between, and over dry beds of streams that are made by the spring and fall freshets. Occasionally we were favored with a level prairie never exceeding two miles in extent. When the carts overtook us, we exchanged our horses for them, and sat on Buffalo robes on the bottom, our horses following on behind us. As we neared the place where the Buffaloes had been killed on the previous hunt, Bonaventure rode alone to the top of a hill to discover, if possible, their whereabouts; but to our disappointment nothing living was to be seen. We continued on our way watching closely, ahead, right and left. Three o'clock came and as yet nothing had been killed; as none of us had eaten anything since the night before, our appetites admonished us that it was time to pay attention to them. McKenzie and Bonaventure began to look about for Antelopes; but before any were 'comeatable,' I fell asleep, and was awakened by the report of a gun. Before we, in the carts, arrived at the spot from whence this report proceeded, the hunters had killed, skinned, and nearly cleaned the game, which was a fine male Antelope. I regretted exceedingly I was not awake when it was killed, as I might have saved the skin for Mr. Audubon, as well as the head, but I was too late. It was now about five o'clock, and one may well imagine I was *somewhat* hungry. Owen McKenzie commenced eating the raw liver, and offered me a piece. What others can eat, I felt assured I could at least taste. I accordingly took it and ate quite a piece of it; to my utter astonishment, I found it not only palatable but very good; this experience goes far to convince me that our prejudices make things appear more disgusting than fact proves them to be. Our Antelope cut up and in the cart, we proceeded on our 'winding way,' and scarcely had we left the spot where the entrails of the animal remained, before the Wolves and Ravens commenced coming from all quarters, and from places where a minute before there was not a sign of one. We had not proceeded three hundred yards at the utmost, before eight Wolves were about the spot, and others approaching. On our way, both going and returning, we saw a cactus of a conical shape, having a light straw-colored, double flower, differing materially from the flower of the flat cactus, which is quite common; had I had any means of bringing one in, I would most gladly have done so, but I could not depend on the carts, and as they are rather unpleasant companions, I preferred awaiting another opportunity, which I hope may come in a few days. We shot a young of Townsend's Hare, about seven or eight steps from us, with about a dozen shot; I took good care of it until I left the cart on my return to the fort, but when the carts arrived it had carelessly been lost. This I regretted very much, as Mr. Audubon wanted it. It was nearly sunset when Bonaventure discovered a Buffalo bull, so we concluded to encamp for the night, and run the Buffaloes in the morning. We accordingly selected a spot near a pond of water, which in spring and fall is quite a large lake, and near which there was abundance of good pasture; our horses were soon unsaddled and hoppled, a good fire blazing, and some of the Antelope meat roasting on sticks before it. As soon as a bit was done, we commenced operations, and it was soon gone 'the way of all flesh.' I never before ate meat without salt or pepper, and until then never fully appreciated these two *luxuries*, as they now seemed, nor can any one, until deprived of them, and seated on a prairie as we were, or in some similar situation. On the opposite side of the lake we saw a Grizzly Bear, but he was unapproachable. After smoking our pipes we rolled ourselves in our robes, with our saddles for pillows, and were soon lost in a sound, sweet sleep. During the night I was awakened by a crunching sound; the fire had died down, and I sat up and looking about perceived a

Wolf quietly feeding on the remains of our supper. One of the men awoke at the same time and fired at the Wolf, but without effect, and the fellow fled ; we neither saw nor heard more of him during the night. By daylight we were all up, and as our horses had not wandered far, it was the work of a few minutes to catch and saddle them. We rode three or four miles before we discovered anything, but at last saw a group of three Buffaloes some miles from us. We pushed on, and soon neared them; before arriving at their feeding-ground, we saw, scattered about, immense quantities of pumice-stone, in detached pieces of all sizes; several of the hills appeared to be composed wholly of it. As we approached within two hundred yards of the Buffaloes they started, and away went the hunters after them. My first intention of being merely a looker-on continued up to this moment, but it was impossible to resist following; almost unconsciously I commenced urging my horse after them, and was soon rushing up hills and through ravines; but my horse gave out, and disappointment and anger followed, as McKenzie and Bonaventure succeeded in killing two, and wounding a third, which escaped. As soon as they had finished them, they commenced skinning and cutting up one, which was soon in the cart, the offal and useless meat being left on the ground. Again the Wolves made their appearance as we were leaving; they seemed shy, but Owen McKenzie succeeded in killing one, which was old and useless. The other Buffalo was soon skinned and in the cart. In the meantime McKenzie and I started on horseback for water. The man who had charge of the keg had let it all run out, and most fortunately none of us had wanted water until now. We rode to a pond, the water of which was very salt and warm, but we had to drink this or none; we did so, filled our flasks for the rest of the party, and a few minutes afterward rejoined them. We started again for more meat to complete our load. I observed, as we approached the Buf-

faloes, that they stood gazing at us with their heads erect,
lashing their sides with their tails; as soon as they discovered what we were at, with the quickness of thought
they wheeled, and with the most surprising speed, for an
animal apparently so clumsy and awkward, flew before us.
I could hardly imagine that these enormous animals could
move so quickly, or realize that their speed was as great
as it proved to be; and I doubt if in this country one
horse in ten can be found that will keep up with them.
We rode five or six miles before we discovered any more.
At last we saw a single bull, and while approaching him
we started two others; slowly we wended our way towards
them until within a hundred yards, when away they went.
I had now begun to enter into the spirit of the chase, and
off I started, full speed, down a rough hill in swift pursuit;
at the bottom of the hill was a ditch about eight feet wide;
the horse cleared this safely.   I continued, leading the
others by some distance, and rapidly approaching the
Buffaloes.   At this prospect of success my feelings can
better be imagined than described.   I kept the lead of the
others till within thirty or forty yards of the Buffaloes,
when I began making preparations to fire as soon as I was
sufficiently near; imagine, if possible, my disappointment
when I discovered that now, when all my hopes of success
were raised to the highest pitch, I was fated to meet a
reverse as mortifying as success would have been gratifying.   My horse failed, and slackened his pace, despite
every effort of mine to urge him on; the other hunters
rushed by me at full speed, and my horse stopped altogether.   I saw the others fire; the animal swerved a little,
but still kept on.   After breathing my horse a while, I
succeeded in starting him up again, followed after them,
and came up in time to fire one shot ere the animal was
brought down.   I think that I never saw an eye so ferocious in expression as that of the wounded Buffalo; rolling
wildly in its socket, inflamed as the eye was, it had the

most frightful appearance that can be imagined; and in
fact, the picture presented by the Buffalo as a whole is
quite beyond my powers of description. The fierce eyes,
blood streaming from his sides, mouth, and nostrils, he was
the wildest, most unearthly-looking thing it ever fell to my
lot to gaze upon. His sufferings were short; he was soon
cut up and placed in the cart, and we retraced our steps
homeward. Whilst proceeding towards our camping-
ground for the night, two Antelopes were killed, and placed
on our carts. Whenever we approached these animals
they were very curious to see what we were ; they would
run, first to the right, and then to the left, then suddenly
run straight towards us until within gun-shot, or nearly
so. The horse attracted their attention more than the
rider, and if a slight elevation or bush was between us, they
were easily killed. As soon as their curiosity was gratified
they would turn and run, but it was not difficult to shoot
before this occurred. When they turned they would fly
over the prairie for about a mile, when they would again
stop and look at us. During the day we suffered very
much for want of water, and drank anything that had the
appearance of it, and most of the water, in fact all of it,
was either impregnated with salt, sulphur, or magnesia —
most disgusting stuff at any other time, but drinkable now.
The worst of all was some rain-water that we were obliged
to drink, first placing our handkerchiefs over the cup to
strain it, and keep the worms out of our mouths. I drank
it, and right glad was I to get even this. We rode about
five miles to where we encamped for the night, near a little
pond of water. In a few minutes we had a good fire of
Buffalo dung to drive away mosquitoes that were in clouds
about us. The water had taken away our appetites completely, and we went to bed without eating any supper.
Our horses and beds were arranged as on the previous
evening. McKenzie and I intended starting for the fort
early in the morning. We saw a great many Magpies, Cur-

lews, Plovers, Doves, and numbers of Antelopes. About
daylight I awoke and roused McKenzie; a man had gone
for the horses, but after a search of two hours returned
without finding them; all the party now went off except
one man and myself, and all returned without success
except Bonaventure, who found an old horse that had been
lost since April last. He was despatched on this to the
fort to get other horses, as we had concluded that ours
were either lost or stolen. As soon as he had gone, one
of the men started again in search of the runaways, and in
a short time returned with them. McKenzie and I soon
rode off. We saw two Grizzly Bears at the lake again.
Our homeward road we made much shorter by cutting off
several turns; we overtook Bonaventure about four miles
from our encampment, and passed him. We rode forty
miles to the fort in a trifle over six hours. We had travelled in all about one hundred and twenty miles. Bonaventure arrived two hours after we did, and the carts came
in the evening."

Wednesday, June 28. This is an account of Squires' Buffalo hunt, his first one, which he has kindly written in my
journal and which I hope some day to publish. This
morning was very cloudy, and we had some rain, but from
ten o'clock until this moment the weather has been beautiful. Harris shot a handsome though rather small Wolf;
I have made a large drawing, and Sprague a fine diminished one, of the rascal. The first news we had this morning was that the ferry flat had been stolen last night,
probably by the deserters from the fort who have had the
wish to return to St. Louis. Some person outside of the
fort threw a large stone at an Indian woman, and her husband fired in the dark, but no one could be found on
searching. There is much trouble and discomfort to the
managers of such an establishment as this. Provost went
shooting, but saw nothing. Young McKenzie and another
man were sent to find the scow, but in vain. On their re-

turn they said a hunter from Fort Mortimer had brought a Bighorn, and skinned it, and that he would let me have it if I wished. I sent Bell and Squires, and they brought the skin in. It proves to be that of an old female in the act of shedding her winter coat, and I found that she was covered with abundance of downy wool like the Antelopes under similar circumstances. Mr. Larpenteur caught five small catfish, which we ate at breakfast. After dinner Le Brun returned home, but brought only the skin of a young female of the White-tailed Deer, and I was surprised to see that it had the germ of a horn about one inch long; the skin was quite red, and it is saved. A young Elk was brought in good condition, as the hunters here know how to save skins properly; it was too young, however, to take measurements. The horns were in velvet about six inches long. When one sees the powerful bones and muscles of this young animal, one cannot fail to think of the great strength of the creature when mature, and its ability to bear with ease the enormous antlers with which its head is surmounted. The flesh of the Antelope is not comparable with that of the Deer, being dry and usually tough. It is very rarely indeed that a fat Antelope is killed. Bell has been very busy in skinning small birds and animals. We procured a young Red-shafted Woodpecker, killed by an Indian boy with a bow and arrow. Mr. Kipp's " Mackinaw " was launched this evening, and sent across the river with men to relieve the charcoal-burners; she returned immediately and we expect that Mr. Kipp's crew will go off to-morrow about twelve. I was told a curious anecdote connected with a Grizzly Bear, that I will write down; it is as follows: One of the *engagés* of the Company was forced to run away, having killed an Indian woman, and made his way to the Crow Fort, three hundred miles up the Yellowstone River. When he arrived there he was in sad plight, having his own squaw and one or two children along, who had all suffered greatly with hunger,

thirst, and exposure. They were received at the fort, but
in a short time, less than a week afterwards, he again ran
off with his family, and on foot. The discovery was soon
made, and two men were sent after him; but he eluded
their vigilance by keeping close in ravines, etc. The men
returned, and two others with an Indian were despatched
on a second search, and after much travel saw the man
and his family on an island, where he had taken refuge
from his pursuers. The Buffalo-hide canoe in which he
had attempted to cross the river was upset, and it was with
difficulty that he saved his wife and children. They were
now unable to escape, and when talking as to the best way
to secure their return to the fort, the soldiers saw him
walk to the body of a dead Buffalo lying on the shore of
the island, with the evident intention of procuring some of
it for food. As he stooped to cut off a portion, to his
utter horror he saw a small Grizzly Bear crawl out from
the carcass. It attacked him fiercely, and so suddenly
that he was unable to defend himself; the Bear lacerated
his face, arms, and the upper part of his body in a frightful manner, and would have killed him, had not the Indian raised his gun and fired at the Bear, wounding him
severely, while a second shot killed him. The *engagé*
was too much hurt to make further effort to escape, and
one of the Company's boats passing soon after, he and his
family were taken back to the fort, where he was kept to
await his trial.

June 29, Thursday. It rained hard during the night,
but at dawn Provost went shooting and returned to
dinner, having shot a doe, which was skinned and the
meat saved. He saw a Grouse within a few feet of
him, but did not shoot, as he had only a rifle. Bell and
I took a long walk, and shot several birds. We both
were surprised to find a flock of Cliff Swallows endeavoring to build nests beneath the ledges of a clay bank.
Watching the moment when several had alighted against

the bank, I fired, and killed three. Previous to this, as I was walking along a ravine, a White Wolf ran past within fifteen or twenty paces of me, but I had only very small shot, and did not care to wound where I could not kill. The fellow went off at a limping gallop, and Bell after it, squatting whenever the Wolf stopped to look at him; but at last the rascal lost himself in a deep ravine, and a few minutes after we saw him emerge from the shrubs some distance off, and go across the prairie towards the river. Bell saw two others afterwards, and if ever there was a country where Wolves are surpassingly abundant, it is the one we now are in. Wolves are in the habit of often lying down on the prairies, where they form quite a bed, working at bones the while. We found a nest of the Prairie Lark, with four eggs. We saw Arctic Bluebirds, Say's Flycatcher and Lazuli Finches. Say's Flycatcher has a note almost like the common Pewee. They fly over the prairies like Hawks, looking for grasshoppers, upon which they pounce, and if they lose sight of them, they try again at another place. We returned home to dinner, and after this a discussion arose connected with the Red-shafted Woodpecker. We determined to go and procure one of the young, and finding that these have pale-yellow shafts, instead of deep orange-red, such as the old birds have, the matter was tested and settled according to my statement. Harris and I went off after the doe killed this morning, and killed another, but as I have now skins enough, the measurements only were taken, and the head cut off, which I intend drawing to-morrow. Harris shot also a Grouse, and a Woodpecker that will prove a *Canadensis;* he killed the male also, but could not find it, and we found seven young Red-shafted Woodpeckers in one nest. I killed a female Meadow Lark, the first seen in this country by us. Provost told me (and he is a respectable man) that, during the breeding season of the Mountain Ram, the battering of the horns is often heard as far as a mile away, and that at such times they are approached with comparative ease; and there is no doubt that it is during such encounters that the horns are broken and twisted as I have seen them, and not by leaping from high places and falling on their horns, as poetical travellers have asserted. The fact is that when these animals leap from any height they alight firmly on all their four feet. At this season the young are always very difficult to catch, and I have not yet seen one of them. Harris, Bell, and young McKenzie are going Bighorn hunting to-morrow, and I hope they will be successful; I, alas! am no longer young and alert enough for the expedition. We find the mosquitoes very troublesome, and very numerous.

June 30, Friday. The weather was dark, with the wind at the northwest, and looked so like rain that the hunters did not start as they had proposed. Sprague, Harris, and Bell went out, however, after small game. I began drawing at five this morning, and worked almost without cessation till after three, when, becoming fatigued for want of practice, I took a short walk, regretting I could no longer draw twelve or fourteen hours without a pause or thought of weariness. It is now raining quite hard. Mr. Larpenteur went after a large tree to make a ferry-boat, and the new skiff was begun this morning. I sent Provost to Fort Mortimer to see if any one had arrived from below; he found a man had done so last evening and brought letters to Mr. Collins, requesting him to do all he can for us. He also reported that a party of Sioux had had a battle with the Gros Ventres, and had killed three of the latter and a white man who lived with them as a blacksmith. The Gros Ventres, on the other hand, had killed eight of the Sioux and put them to flight. The blacksmith killed two Sioux, and the enemies cut off one leg and one arm, scalped him, and left the mangled body behind them. It is said there is now no person living who can recollect the manner in which the bitter enmity of these two nations originated. The Yellowstone River is again rising fast, and Mr. Kipp will have tough times before he reaches Fort Alexander, which was built by Mr. Alexander Culbertson, our present host, and the Company had it honored by his name. When a herd of Buffaloes is chased, although the bulls themselves run very swiftly off, their speed is not to be compared to that of the cows and yearlings; for these latter are seen in a few minutes to leave the bulls behind them, and as cows and young Buffaloes are preferable to the old males, when the hunters are well mounted they pursue the cows and young ones invariably. Last winter Buffaloes were extremely abundant close to this fort, so much so that while the people were engaged in bringing hay in carts, the Buffaloes during the night came close in, and picked up every wisp that was dropped. An attempt to secure them alive was made by strewing hay in such a manner as to render the bait more and more plentiful near the old fort, which is distant about two hundred yards, and which was once the property of Mr. Sublette and Co.; but as the hogs and common cattle belonging to the fort are put up there regularly at sunset, the Buffaloes ate the hay to the very gates, but would not enter the enclosure, probably on account of the different smells issuing therefrom. At this period large herds slept in front of the fort, but just before dawn would remove across the hills about one mile distant, and return towards night. An attempt was made to shoot them with a cannon — a four-pounder; three were killed and several wounded. Still the Buffaloes came to their sleeping ground at evening, and many were killed during the season. I saw the head of one Mr. Culbertson shot, and the animal must have been of unusual size.

July 1, Saturday. It was still raining when I got up, but a few minutes later the sun was shining through one of our windows, and the wind being at northwest we anticipated a fine day. The ground was extremely wet and muddy, but Harris and Bell went off on horseback, and returned a few minutes after noon. They brought some birds and had killed a rascally Wolf. Bell found the nest of the Arkansas Flycatcher. The nest and eggs, as well as the manners, of this bird resemble in many ways those of our King-bird. The nest was in an elm, twenty or twenty-five feet above the ground, and he saw another in a similar situation. Mr. Culbertson and I walked to the Pilot Knob with a spy-glass, to look at the present condition of Fort Mortimer. This afternoon Squires, Provost, and I walked there, and were kindly received as usual. We found all the people encamped two hundred yards from the river, as they had been obliged to move from the tumbling fort during the rain of last night. Whilst we were there a trapper came in with a horse and told us the following: This man and four others left that fort on the 1st of April last on an expedition after Beavers. They were captured by a party of about four hundred Sioux, who took them prisoners and kept him one day and a half, after which he was released, but his companions were kept prisoners. He crossed the river and found a horse belonging to the Indians, stole it, and reached the fort at last. He looked miserable indeed, almost without a rag of clothing, long hair, filthy beyond description, and having only one very keen, bright eye, which looked as if he was both proud and brave. He had subsisted for the last eleven days on pomme blanche and the thick leaves of the cactus, which he roasted to get rid of the thorns or spines, and thus had fared most miserably; for, previous to the capture of himself and his companions, he had upset his bull canoe and lost his rifle, which to a trapper is, next to life, his dependence. When he was asked if he would have some dinner, he said that he had forgotten the word, but would try the taste of meat again. Mr. Collins was very polite to me, and promised me a hunter for the whole of next week, expressly to shoot Bighorns. I hope this promise may be better kept than that of Mr. Chardon, who told me that should he have one killed within forty miles he would send Alexis back with it at once. We heard some had been killed, but this may not be true; at any rate, men are men all over the world, and a broken promise is not unheard-of. This evening Mr. Culbertson presented me with a splendid dress, as well as one to Harris and one to Bell, and promised one to Sprague, which I have no doubt he will have. Harris and Sprague went off to procure Woodpeckers' nests, and brought the most curious set of five birds that I ever saw, and which I think will puzzle all the naturalists in the world. The first was found near the nest, of which Sprague shot the female, a light-colored Red-shafted Woodpecker. It proved to be of the same color, but had the rudiments of black stripes on the cheeks. Next, Sprague shot an adult yellow-winged male, with the markings principally such as are found in the Eastern States. Harris then shot a young Red-shafted, just fledged, with a black stripe on the cheek. His next shot was a light-colored Red-shafted male, with black cheeks, and another still, a yellow Red-shafted with a red cheek.[1] After all this Mr. Culbertson proposed to run a sham Buffalo hunt again. He, Harris, and Squires started on good horses, went about a mile, and returned full tilt, firing and cracking. Squires fired four times and missed once. Harris did not shoot at all; but Mr. Culbertson fired eleven times, starting at the onset with an empty gun, snapped three times, and reached the fort with his gun loaded. A more wonderful rider I never saw.

July 2, Sunday. The weather was cool and pleasant this morning, with no mosquitoes, which indeed — plentiful and troublesome as they are — Provost tells me are

---

[1] The above is a very good example of the way these Woodpeckers vary in color, presenting a case which, as Audubon justly observes, is a " puzzle to all the naturalists in the world." See note, p. 14. — E. C.

more scarce this season than he ever knew them thus far up the Missouri. Sprague finished his drawing of the doe's head about dinner-time, and it looks well. After dinner he went after the puzzling Woodpeckers, and brought three, all different from each other. Mr. Culbertson, his squaw wife, and I rode to Fort Mortimer, accompanied by young McKenzie, and found Mr. Collins quite ill. We saw the hunters of that fort, and they promised to supply me with Bighorns, at ten dollars apiece in the flesh, and also some Black-tailed Deer, and perhaps a Grizzly Bear. This evening they came to the fort for old Peter and a mule, to bring in their game; and may success attend them! When we returned, Harris started off with Mr. Culbertson and his wife to see the condition of Mr. Collins, to whom he administered some remedies. Harris had an accident that was near being of a serious nature; as he was getting into the wagon, thinking that a man had hold of the reins, which was not the case, his foot was caught between the axle-tree and the wagon, he was thrown down on his arm and side, and hurt to some extent; fortunately he escaped without serious injury, and does not complain much this evening, as he has gone on the ramparts to shoot a Wolf. Sprague saw a Wolf in a hole a few yards from the fort, but said not a word of it till after dinner, when Bell and Harris went there and shot it through the head. It was a poor, miserable, crippled old beast, that could not get out of the hole, which is not more than three or four feet deep. After breakfast we had a hunt after Hares or Rabbits, and Harris saw two of them, but was so near he did not care to shoot at them. Whilst Harris and Mr. Culbertson went off to see Mr. Collins, Mr. Denig and I walked off with a bag and instruments, to take off the head of a three-years-dead Indian chief, called the White Cow. Mr. Denig got upon my shoulders and into the branches near the coffin, which stood about ten feet above ground.

The coffin was lowered, or rather tumbled, down, and the cover was soon hammered off; to my surprise, the feet were placed on the pillow, instead of the head, which lay at the foot of the coffin — if a long box may so be called. Worms innumerable were all about it; the feet were naked, shrunk, and dried up. The head had still the hair on, but was twisted off in a moment, under jaw and all. The body had been first wrapped up in a Buffalo skin without hair, and then in another robe with the hair on, as usual; after this the dead man had been enveloped in an American flag, and over this a superb scarlet blanket. We left all on the ground but the head. Squires, Mr. Denig and young Owen McKenzie went afterwards to try to replace the coffin and contents in the tree, but in vain; the whole affair fell to the ground, and there it lies; but I intend to-morrow to have it covered with earth. The history of this man is short, and I had it from Mr. Larpenteur, who was in the fort at the time of his decease, or self-committed death. He was a good friend to the whites, and knew how to procure many Buffalo robes for them; he was also a famous orator, and never failed to harangue his people on all occasions. He was, however, consumptive, and finding himself about to die, he sent his squaw for water, took an arrow from his quiver, and thursting it into his heart, expired, and was found dead when his squaw returned to the lodge. He was "buried" in the above-mentioned tree by the orders of Mr. McKenzie, who then commanded this fort. Mr. Culbertson drove me so fast, and Harris so much faster, over this rough ground, that I feel quite stiff. I must not forget to say that we had another sham Buffalo chase over the prairie in front of the fort, the riders being Squires, young McKenzie, and Mr. Culbertson; and I was glad and proud to see that Squires, though so inexperienced a hunter, managed to shoot five shots within the mile, McKenzie eleven, and Mr. Culbertson eight. Harris killed an old

Wolf, which he thought was larger and fatter than any killed previously. It was very large, but on examination it was found to be poor and without teeth in the upper jaw.

July 3, Monday. We have had a warm night and day; after breakfast we all six crossed the river in the newly built skiff, and went off in divers directions. Provost and I looked thoroughly through the brushwood, and walked fully six miles from the fort; we saw three Deer, but so far were they that it was useless to shoot. Deer-shooting on the prairies is all hazard; sometimes the animals come tripping along within ten yards of you, and at other times not nearer can you get than one hundred and fifty yards, which was the case this day. The others killed nothing of note, and crossed the river back to the fort two hours at least before us; and we shot and bawled out for nearly an hour, before the skiff was sent for us. I took a swim, found the water very pleasant, and was refreshed by my bath. The Bighorn hunters returned this afternoon with a Bighorn, a female, and also a female Black-tailed Deer. I paid them $15 for the two, and they are to start again to-morrow evening, or the next day.

July 4, Tuesday. Although we had some fireworks going on last evening, after I had laid myself down for the night, the anniversary of the Independence of the United States has been almost the quietest I have ever spent, as far as my recollection goes. I was drawing the whole day, and Sprague was engaged in the same manner, painting a likeness of Mr. Culbertson. Harris and Bell went off to try and procure a buck of the Long White-tailed Deer, and returned after dinner much fatigued and hungry enough. Bell had shot at a Deer and wounded it very severely; the poor thing ran on, but soon lay down, for the blood and froth were gushing out of its mouth. Bell saw the buck lying down, and not being an experienced hunter, thought it was dead, and instead of shooting it again, went back to call Harris; when they returned, the Deer was gone, and although they saw it again and again, the Deer outwitted them, and, as I have said, they returned weary, with no Deer. After dinner I spoke to Mr. Culbertson on the subject, and he told me that the Deer could probably be found, but that most likely the Wolves would devour it. He prepared to send young McKenzie with both my friends; the horses were soon saddled, and the three were off at a gallop. The poor buck's carcass was found, but several Wolves and Turkey Buzzards had fared well upon it; the vertebræ only were left, with a few bits of skin and portions of the horns in velvet. These trophies were all that they brought home. It was a superb and very large animal, and I am very sorry for the loss of it, as I am anxious to draw the head of one of such a size as they represent this to have been. They ran after a Wolf, which gave them leg bail. Meanwhile Squires and Provost started with the skiff in a cart to go up the river two miles, cross, and camp on the opposite shore. The weather became very gloomy and chill. In talking with Mr. Culbertson he told me that no wise man would ever follow a Buffalo bull immediately in his track, even in a hunt, and that no one well initiated would ever run after Buffaloes between the herd and another hunter, as the latter bears on the former ever and anon, and places him in imminent danger. Buffalo cows rarely, if ever, turn on the assailant, but bulls oftentimes will, and are so dangerous that many a fine hunter has been gored and killed, as well as his horse.

July 5, Wednesday. It rained the whole of last night and the weather has been bad all day. I am at the Bighorn's head, and Sprague at Mr. Culbertson. Provost and Squires returned drenched and hungry, before dinner. They had seen several Deer, and fresh tracks of a large Grizzly Bear. They had waded through mud and water enough for one day, and were well fatigued. Harris and Bell both shot at Wolves from the ramparts, and as these things are of such common occurrence I will say no more about them, unless we are in want of one of these beasts. Harris and I went over to see Mr. Collins, who is much better; his hunters had not returned. We found the men there mostly engaged in playing cards and backgammon. The large patches of rose bushes are now in full bloom, and they are so full of sweet fragrance that the air is perfumed by them. The weather looks clear towards the north, and I expect a fine to-morrow. Old Provost has been telling me much of interest about the Beavers, once so plentiful, but now very scarce. It takes about seventy Beaver skins to make a pack of a hundred pounds; in a good market this pack is worth five hundred dollars, and in fortunate seasons a trapper sometimes made the large sum of four thousand dollars. Formerly, when Beavers were abundant, companies were sent with as many as thirty and forty men, each with from eight to a dozen traps, and two horses. When at a propitious spot, they erected a camp, and every man sought his own game; the skins alone were brought to the camp, where a certain number of men always remained to stretch and dry them.

July 6, Thursday. The weather has been pleasant, with the wind at northwest, and the prairies will dry a good deal. After breakfast Harris, Bell, and McKenzie went off on horseback. They saw a Red Fox of the country,[1] which is different from those of the States; they chased it, and though it ran slowly at first, the moment it saw the hunters at full gallop, it ran swiftly from them. McKenzie shot with a rifle and missed it. They saw fresh tracks of the small Hare, but not any of the animals themselves. After dinner I worked at Mr. Culbertson's

---

[1] *Vulpes utah* of Aud. and Bach., Quad. N. Am. iii., 1853, p. 255, pl. 151, or *V. macrourus* of Baird, as already noted. This is the Western variety of the common Red Fox, now usually called *Vulpes fulvus macrourus.* — E. C.

head and dress, and by evening had the portrait nearly finished. At four o'clock Harris, Bell, and Sprague went across the river in the skiff; Sprague to take a view of the fort, the others to hunt. Harris and Bell shot twice at a buck, and killed it, though only one buckshot entered the thigh. Whilst we were sitting at the back gate of the fort, we saw a parcel of Indians coming towards the place, yelling and singing what Mr. Culbertson told me was the song of the scalp dance; we saw through the telescope that they were fourteen in number, with their faces painted black, and that it was a detachment of a war party. When within a hundred yards they all stopped, as if awaiting an invitation; we did not hurry as to this, and they seated themselves on the ground and looked at us, while Mr. Culbertson sent Mr. Denig to ask them to come in by the front gate of the fort, and put them in the Indian house, a sort of camp for the fellows. They all looked miserably poor, filthy beyond description, and their black faces and foully smelling Buffalo robes made them appear to me like so many devils. The leader, who was well known to be a famous rascal, and was painted red, was a tall, well-formed man. The party had only three poor guns, and a few had coarse, common lances; every man had a knife, and the leader was armed with a stick in which were inserted three blades of butcher's-knives; a blow from this weapon would doubtless kill a man. Some of the squaws of the fort, having found that they were Assiniboins, went to meet them; they took one of these, and painted her face black, as a sign of friend-ship. Most of these mighty warriors had a lump of fresh Buffalo meat slung on his back, which was all traded for by Mr. Larpenteur, who gave them in exchange some dried meat, not worth the notice of Harris's dog, and some tobacco. The report of their expedition is as follows: Their party at first consisted of nearly fifty; they trav-elled several hundred miles in search of Blackfeet, and having discovered a small troop of them, they hid till the next morning, when at daylight (this is always the time they prefer for an attack) they rushed upon the enemy, surprised them, killed one at the onset, and the rest took to flight, leaving guns, horses, shields, lances, etc., on the ground. The Assiniboins took several guns and seven horses, and the scalp of the dead Indian. It happened that the man they killed had some time ago killed the father of their chief, and he was full of joy. After eating and resting awhile, they followed the trail of the Blackfeet, hoping to again surprise them; but not seeing them, they separated into small parties, and it is one of these parties that is now with us. The chief, to show his pride and delight at killing his enemy, has borrowed a drum; and the company have nearly ever since been yelling, singing, and beating that beastly tambour. Boucherville came to me, and told me that if the swamp over the river was sufficiently dried by to-morrow morning, he would come early with a companion for two horses, and would go after Bighorns. He returned this afternoon from a Buffalo hunt and had killed six. These six animals, all bulls, will suffice for Fort Mortimer only three days. A rascally Indian had stolen his gun and Bighorn bow; the gun he said he could easily replace, but the loss of the bow he regretted exceedingly.

July 7, Friday. This morning the dirty Indians, who could have washed had they so minded, were beating the tambour and singing their miserable scalp song, until Mr. Culbertson ordered the drum taken away, and gave them more tobacco and some vermilion to bedaub their faces. They were permitted to remain about the fort the remainder of the day, and the night coming they will again be sheltered; but they must depart to-morrow morning. After breakfast Sprague worked on the view of the fort. I went on with the portrait of Mr. Culbertson, who is about as bad a sitter as his wife, whose portrait is very successful, notwithstanding her extreme restlessness. After dinner Harris, Bell, and I started on foot, and walked about four miles from the fort; the day was hot, and horseflies and mosquitoes pretty abundant, but we trudged on, though we saw nothing; we had gone after Rabbits, the tracks of which had been seen previously. We walked immediately near the foot of the clay hills which run from about a mile from and above the fort to the Lord knows where. We first passed one ravine where we saw some very curious sandstone formations, coming straight out horizontally from the clay banks between which we were passing; others lay loose and detached; they had fallen down, or had been washed out some time or other. All were compressed in such a manner that the usual form was an oval somewhat depressed in the centre; but, to give you some idea of these formations, I will send you a rough sketch. Those in the banks extended from five to seven feet, and the largest one on the ground measured a little less than ten feet. Bell thought they would make good sharpening-stones, but I considered them too soft. They were all smooth, and the grain was alike in all. We passed two much depressed and very broken ravines, and at last reached the Rabbit ground. Whilst looking at the wild scenery around, and the clay hills on the other side of the Missouri opposite the fort, I thought that if all these were granite, the formation and general appearance would resemble the country of Labrador, though the grandeur and sublimity of the latter far surpass anything that I have seen since I left them forever. I must not forget to say that on our way we passed through some grasses with bearded shafts, so sharp that they penetrated our moccasins and entered our feet and ankles, and in the shade of a stumpy ash-tree we took off our moccasins and drew the spines out. The Lazuli Finches and Arctic Bluebirds sang in our view; but though we beat all the clumps of low bushes where the Rabbits must go in, whether during night or day, we did not start one. We saw a Wolf which ran close by, reached the brow of the hill, and kept where he could watch our every motion; this they do on all possible occasions. We were all very warm, so we rested awhile, and ate some service-berries, which I found good; the gooseberries were small and green, and almost choked Harris with their sharp acidity. On our return, as we were descending the first deep ravine, a Raven flew off close by; it was so near Bell that he had no time to shoot. I followed it and although loaded with No. 6 shot, I drew my trigger and the bird fell dead; only one shot had touched it, but that had passed through the lungs. After we reached the prairie I shot a Meadow Lark, but lost it, as we had unfortunately not taken Bragg (Harris's dog). We saw a patch of wood called in these regions a "Point;" we walked towards it for the purpose of shooting Deer. I was sent to the lower end, Bell took one side, and Harris the other, and the hound we had with us was sent in; no Deer there, however, and we made for the fort, which we reached hot and thirsty enough after our long walk. As soon as I was cooled I took a good swim. I think the Indians hereabouts poor swimmers; they beat the water with their arms, attempting to "nage à la brasse;" but, alas! it is too bad to mention. I am told, however, that there are no good specimens to judge from at the fort, so this is not much of an opinion. It is strange how very scarce snakes of every description are, as well as insects, except mosquitoes and horseflies. Young McKenzie had been sent to seek for the lost ferry-boat, but returned without success; the new one is expected to be put in the water to-morrow evening. Squires and Provost had the skiff carried overland three miles, and they crossed the river in it with the intention to remain hunting until Sunday night.

July 8, Saturday. Mr. Culbertson told me this morning that last spring early, during a snow-storm, he and Mr. Larpenteur were out in an Indian lodge close by the fort, when they heard the mares which had young colts making much noise; and that on going out they saw a single Wolf that had thrown down one of the colts, and was about doing the same with another. They both made towards the spot with their pistols; and, fearing that the Wolf might kill both the colts, fired before reaching the spot, when too far off to take aim. Master Wolf ran off, but both colts bear evidence of his teeth to this day. When I came down this morning early, I was delighted to see the dirty and rascally Indians walking off to their lodge on the other side of the hills, and before many days they will be at their camp enjoying their merriment (rough and senseless as it seems to me), yelling out their scalp song, and dancing. Now this dance, to commemorate the death of an enemy, is a mere bending and slackening of the body, and patting of the ground with both feet at once, in very tolerable time with their music. Our squaws yesterday joined them in this exemplary ceremony; one was blackened, and all the others painted with vermilion. The art of painting in any color is to mix the color desired with grease of one sort or another; and when well done, it will stick on for a day or two, if not longer. Indians are not equal to the whites in the art of dyeing Porcupine quills; their ingredients are altogether too simple and natural to equal the knowledge of chemicals. Mr. Denig dyed a good quantity to-day for Mrs. Culbertson; he boiled water in a tin kettle with the quills put in when the water boiled, to remove the oil attached naturally to them; next they were thoroughly washed, and fresh water boiled, wherein he placed the color wanted, and boiled the whole for a few minutes, when he looked at them to judge of the color, and so continued until all were dyed. Red, yellow, green, and black quills were the result of his labors. A good deal of vegetable acid is necessary for this purpose, as minerals, so they say here, will not answer. I drew at Mr. Culbertson's portrait till he was tired enough; his wife — a pure Indian — is much interested in my work. Bell and Sprague, after some long talk with Harris about geological matters, of which valuable science he knows a good deal, went off to seek a Wolf's hole that Sprague had seen some days before, but of which, with his usual reticence, he had not spoken. Sprague returned with a specimen of rattle-snake root, which he has already drawn. Bell saw a Wolf munching a bone, approached it and shot at it. The Wolf had been wounded before and ran off slowly, and Bell after it. Mr. Culbertson and I saw the race; Bell gained on the Wolf until within thirty steps when he fired again; the Wolf ran some distance further, and then fell; but Bell was now exhausted by the heat, which was intense, and left the animal where it lay without attempting to skin it. Squires and Provost returned this afternoon about three o'clock, but the first alone had killed a doe. It was the first one he had ever shot, and he placed seven buckshot in her body. Owen went off one way, and Harris and Bell another, but brought in nothing. Provost went off to the Opposition camp, and when he returned told me that a Porcupine was there, and would be kept until I saw it; so Harris drove me over, at the usual breakneck pace, and I bought the animal. Mr. Collins is yet poorly, their hunters have not returned, and they are destitute of everything, not having even a medicine chest. We told him to send a man back with us, which he did, and we sent him some medicine, rice, and two bottles of claret. The weather has been much cooler and pleasanter than yesterday.

July 9, Sunday. I drew at a Wolf's head, and Sprague worked at a view of the fort for Mr. Culbertson. I also worked on Mr. Culbertson's portrait about an hour. I then worked at the Porcupine, which is an animal such as

I never saw or Bell either. Its measurements are: from nose to anterior canthus of the eye, $1\frac{5}{8}$ in., posterior ditto, $2\frac{1}{8}$; conch of ear, $3\frac{1}{2}$; distances from eyes posteriorly, $2\frac{1}{4}$; fore feet stretched beyond nose, $3\frac{1}{2}$; length of head around, $4\frac{1}{8}$; nose to root of tail, $18\frac{1}{2}$; length of tail vertebræ, $6\frac{3}{8}$; to end of hair, $7\frac{3}{4}$; hind claws when stretched equal to end of tail; greatest breadth of palm, $1\frac{1}{4}$; of sole, $1\frac{3}{8}$; outward width of tail at base, $3\frac{5}{8}$; depth of ditto, $3\frac{1}{8}$; length of palm, $1\frac{1}{2}$; ditto of sole, $1\frac{7}{8}$; height at shoulder, 11; at rump, $10\frac{1}{4}$; longest hair on the back, $8\frac{7}{8}$; breadth between ears, $2\frac{1}{4}$; from nostril to split of upper lip, $\frac{3}{4}$; upper incisors, $\frac{5}{8}$; lower ditto, $\frac{3}{4}$; tongue quite smooth; weight 11 lbs. The habits of this animal are somewhat different from those of the Canadian Porcupine. The one of this country often goes in crevices or holes, and young McKenzie caught one in a Wolf's den, along with the old Wolf and seven young; they climb trees, however.

Provost tells me that Wolves are oftentimes destroyed by wild horses, which he has seen run at the Wolves head down, and when at a proper distance take them by the middle of the back with their teeth, and throw them several feet in the air, after which they stamp upon their bodies with the fore feet until quite dead. I have a bad blister on the heel of my right foot, and cannot walk without considerable pain.

July 10, Monday. Squires, Owen, McKenzie, and Provost, with a mule, a cart, and Peter the horse, went off at seven this morning for Antelopes. Bell did not feel well enough to go with them, and was unable to eat his usual meal, but I made him some good gruel, and he is better now. This afternoon Harris went off on horseback after Rabbits, and he will, I hope, have success. The day has been fine, and cool compared with others. I took a walk, and made a drawing of the beautiful sugar-loaf cactus; it does not open its blossoms until after the middle of the day, and closes immediately on being placed in the shade.

July 11, Tuesday. Harris returned about ten o'clock last night, but saw no Hares; how we are to procure any is more than I can tell. Mr. Culbertson says that it was dangerous for Harris to go so far as he did alone up the country, and he must not try it again. The hunters returned this afternoon, but brought only one buck, which is, however, beautiful, and the horns in velvet so remarkable that I can hardly wait for daylight to begin drawing it. I have taken all the measurements of this perfect animal; it was shot by old Provost. Mr. Culbertson — whose portrait is nearly finished — his wife, and I took a ride to look at some grass for hay, and found it beautiful and plentiful. We saw two Wolves, a common one and a prairie one. Bell is better. Sprague has drawn another cactus; Provost and I have now skinned the buck, and it hangs in the ice-house; the head, however, is untouched.

July 12, Wednesday. I rose before three, and began at once to draw the buck's head. Bell assisted me to place it in the position I wanted, and as he felt somewhat better, while I drew, he finished the skin of the Porcupine; so that is saved. Sprague continued his painting of the fort. Just after dinner a Wolf was seen leisurely walking within one hundred yards of the fort. Bell took the repeating rifle, went on the ramparts, fired, and missed it. Mr. Culbertson sent word to young Owen McKenzie to get a horse and give it chase. All was ready in a few minutes, and off went the young fellow after the beast. I left my drawing long enough to see the pursuit, and was surprised to see that the Wolf did not start off on a gallop till his pursuer was within one hundred yards or so of him, and who then gained rapidly. Suddenly the old sinner turned, and the horse went past him some little distance. As soon as he could be turned about McKenzie closed upon him, his gun flashed twice; but now he was almost *à bon touchant*, the gun went off — the Wolf was dead. I walked out to meet Owen with the beast; it was very poor, very old, and good

AUDUBON.

From the pencil sketch by Isaac Sprague, 1842.   In the possession of the Sprague family,
Wellesley Hills, Mass.

for nothing as a specimen. Harris, who had shot at one last night in the late twilight, had killed it, but was not aware of it till I found the villain this morning. It had evidently been dragged at by its brothers, who, however, had not torn it. Provost went over to the other fort to find out where the Buffaloes are most abundant, and did not return till late, so did no hunting. A young dog of this country's breed ate up all the berries collected by Mrs. Culbertson, and her lord had it killed for our supper this evening. The poor thing was stuck with a knife in the throat, after which it was placed over a hot fire outside of the fort, singed, and the hair scraped off, as I myself have treated Raccoons and Opossums. Then the animal was boiled, and I intend to taste one mouthful of it, for I cannot say that just now I should relish an entire meal from such peculiar fare. There are men, however, who much prefer the flesh to Buffalo meat, or even venison. An ox was broken to work this day, and worked far better than I expected. I finished at last Mr. Culbertson's portrait, and it now hangs in a frame. He and his wife are much pleased with it, and I am heartily glad they are, for in conscience I am not; however, it is all I could do, especially with a man who is never in the same position for one whole minute; so no more can be expected. The dog was duly cooked and brought into Mr. Culbertson's room; he served it out to Squires, Mr. Denig, and myself, and I was astonished when I tasted it. With great care and some repugnance I put a very small piece in my mouth; but no sooner had the taste touched my palate than I changed my dislike to liking, and found this victim of the canine order most excellent, and made a good meal, finding it fully equal to any meat I ever tasted. Old Provost had told me he preferred it to any meat, and his subsequent actions proved the truth of his words. We are having some music this evening, and Harris alone is absent, being at his favorite evening occupation, namely, shooting at Wolves from the ramparts.

July 13, Thursday. This has been a cloudy and a sultry day. Sprague finished his drawing and I mine. After dinner Mr. Culbertson, Squires, and myself went off nine miles over the prairies to look at the "meadows," as they are called, where Mr. Culbertson has heretofore cut his winter crop of hay, but we found it indifferent compared with that above the fort. We saw Sharp-tailed Grouse, and what we thought a new species of Lark, which we shot at no less than ten times before it was killed by Mr. Culbertson, but not found. I caught one of its young, but it proved to be only the Shore Lark. Before we reached the meadows we saw a flock of fifteen or twenty Bob-o-link, *Emberiza orizivora*, and on our return shot one of them (a male) on the wing. It is the first seen since we left St. Louis. We reached the meadows at last, and tied our nag to a tree, with the privilege of feeding. Mr. Culbertson and Squires went in the "meadows," and I walked round the so-called patch. I shot seven Arkansas Flycatchers on the wing. After an hour's walking, my companions returned, but had seen nothing except the fresh tracks of a Grizzly Bear. I shot at one of the White-rumped Hawks, of which I have several times spoken, but although it dropped its quarry and flew very wildly afterwards, it went out of my sight. We found the beds of Elks and their fresh dung, but saw none of these animals. I have forgotten to say that immediately after breakfast this morning I drove with Squires to Fort Mortimer, and asked Mr. Collins to let me have his hunter, Boucherville, to go after Mountain Rams for me, which he promised to do. In the afternoon he sent a man over to ask for some flour, which Mr. Culbertson sent him. They are there in the utmost state of destitution, almost of starvation, awaiting the arrival of the hunters like so many famished Wolves. Harris and Bell went across the river and shot a Wolf under the river bank, and afterwards a Duck, but saw nothing else. But during their absence we have had a fine opportunity of witnessing the agility and extreme strength of a year-old Buffalo bull belonging to the fort. Our cook, who is an old Spaniard, threw his lasso over the Buffalo's horns, and all the men in the fort at the time, hauled and pulled the beast about, trying to get him close to a post. He kicked, pulled, leaped sideways, and up and down, snorting and pawing until he broke loose, and ran, as if quite wild, about the enclosure. He was tied again and again, without any success, and at last got out of the fort, but was soon retaken, the rope being thrown round his horns, and he was brought to the main post of the Buffalo-robe press. There he was brought to a standstill, at the risk of breaking his neck, and the last remnant of his winter coat was removed by main strength, which was the object for which the poor animal had undergone all this trouble. After Harris returned to the fort he saw six Sharp-tailed Grouse. At this season this species have no particular spot where you may rely upon finding them, and at times they fly through the woods, and for a great distance, too, where they alight on trees; when, unless you accidentally see them, you pass by without their moving. After we passed Fort Mortimer on our return we saw coming from the banks of the river no less than eighteen Wolves, which altogether did not cover a space of more than three or four yards, they were so crowded. Among them were two Prairie Wolves. Had we had a good running horse some could have been shot; but old Peter is long past his running days. The Wolves had evidently been feeding on some carcass along the banks, and all moved very slowly. Mr. Culbertson gave me a grand pair of leather breeches and a very handsome knife-case, all manufactured by the Blackfeet Indians.

July 14, Friday. Thermometer 70°–95°. Young McKenzie went off after Antelopes across the river alone, but saw only one, which he could not get near. After breakfast Harris, Squires, and I started after birds of all

sorts, with the wagon, and proceeded about six miles on
the road we had travelled yesterday.   We met the hunter
from Fort Mortimer going for Bighorns for me, and Mr.
Culbertson lent him a horse and a mule.   We caught two
young of the Shore Lark, killed seven of Sprague's Lark,
but by bad management lost two, either from the wagon,
my hat, or Harris's pockets.   The weather was exceedingly hot.   We hunted for Grouse in the wormwood
bushes, and after despairing of finding any, we started up
three from the plain, and they flew not many yards to the
river.   We got out of the wagon and pushed for them;
one rose, and Harris shot it, though it flew some yards
before he picked it up.   He started another, and just as
he was about to fire, his gunlock caught on his coat, and
off went Mr. Grouse, over and through the woods until out
of sight, and we returned slowly home.   We saw ten
Wolves this morning.   After dinner we had a curious sight.
Squires put on my Indian dress.   McKenzie put on one of
Mr. Culbertson's, Mrs. Culbertson put on her own *superb*
dress, and the cook's wife put on the one Mrs. Culbertson
had given me.   Squires and Owen were painted in an
awful manner by Mrs. Culbertson, the *Ladies* had their
hair loose, and flying in the breeze, and then all mounted
on horses with Indian saddles and trappings.   Mrs. Culbertson and her maid rode astride like men, and all rode
a furious race, under whip the whole way, for more than
one mile on the prairie; and how amazed would have been
any European lady, or some of our modern belles who
boast their equestrian skill, at seeing the magnificent riding
of this Indian princess — for that is Mrs. Culbertson's rank
— and her servant.   Mr. Culbertson rode with them, the
horses running as if wild, with these extraordinary Indian
riders, Mrs. Culbertson's magnificent black hair floating like
a banner behind her.   As to the men (for two others had
joined Squires and McKenzie), I cannot compare them to
anything in the whole creation.   They ran like wild crea-

tures of unearthly compound.   Hither and thither they dashed, and when the whole party had crossed the ravine below, they saw a fine Wolf and gave the whip to their horses, and though the Wolf cut to right and left Owen shot at him with an arrow and missed, but Mr. Culbertson gave it chase, overtook it, his gun flashed, and the Wolf lay dead.   They then ascended the hills and away they went, with our princess and her faithful attendant in the van, and by and by the group returned to the camp, running full speed till they entered the fort, and all this in the intense heat of this July afternoon.   Mrs. Culbertson, herself a wonderful rider, possessed of both strength and grace in a marked degree, assured me that Squires was equal to any man in the country as a rider, and I saw for myself that he managed his horse as well as any of the party, and I was pleased to see him in his dress, ornaments, etc., looking, however, I must confess, after Mrs. Culbertson's painting his face, like a being from the infernal regions.   Mr. Culbertson presented Harris with a superb dress of the Blackfoot Indians, and also with a Buffalo bull's head, for which Harris had in turn presented him with a gun-barrel of the short kind, and well fitted to shoot Buffaloes.   Harris shot a very young one of Townsend's Hare, Mr. Denig gave Bell a Mouse, which, although it resembles *Mus leucopus* greatly, is much larger, and has a short, thick, round tail, somewhat blunted.

July 15, Saturday.   We were all up pretty early, for we propose going up the Yellowstone with a wagon, and the skiff on a cart, should we wish to cross.   After breakfast all of us except Sprague, who did not wish to go, were ready, and along with two extra men, the wagon, and the cart, we crossed the Missouri at the fort, and at nine were fairly under way — Harris, Bell, Mr. Culbertson, and myself in the wagon, Squires, Provost, and Owen on horseback.   We travelled rather slowly, until we had crossed the point, and headed the ponds on the prairie that run at the foot of the hills opposite. We saw one Grouse, but it could not be started, though Harris searched for it. We ran the wagon into a rut, but got out unhurt; however, I decided to walk for a while, and did so for about two miles, to the turning point of the hills. The wheels of our vehicle were very shackling, and had to be somewhat repaired, and though I expected they would fall to pieces, in some manner or other we proceeded on. We saw several Antelopes, some on the prairie which we now travelled on, and many more on the tops of the hills, bounding westward. We stopped to water the horses at a saline spring, where I saw that Buffaloes, Antelopes, and other animals come to allay their thirst, and repose on the grassy margin. The water was too hot for us to drink, and we awaited the arrival of the cart, when we all took a good drink of the river water we had brought with us. After waiting for nearly an hour to allow the horses to bait and cool themselves, for it was very warm, we proceeded on, until we came to another watering-place, a river, in fact, which during spring overflows its banks, but now has only pools of water here and there. We soaked our wheels again, and again drank ourselves. Squires, Provost, and Owen had left sometime before us, but were not out of our sight, when we started, and as we had been, and were yet, travelling a good track, we soon caught up with them. We shot a common Red-winged Starling, and heard the notes of what was supposed to be a new bird by my companions, but which to my ears was nothing more than the Short-billed Marsh Wren of Nuttall. We reached our camping-place, say perhaps twenty miles' distance, by four o'clock, and all things were unloaded, the horses put to grass, and two or three of the party went in " the point " above, to shoot something for supper. I was hungry myself, and taking the Red-wing and the fishing-line, I went to the river close by, and had the good fortune to catch four fine catfish, when, my bait giving out, I was obliged to desist, as I found that these catfish will not take parts of their own kind as food. Provost had taken a bath, and rowed the skiff (which we had brought this whole distance on the cart, dragged by a mule) along with two men, across the river to seek for game on the point opposite our encampment. They returned, however, without having shot anything, and my four catfish were all the fresh provisions that we had, and ten of us partook of them with biscuit, coffee, and claret. Dusk coming on, the tent was pitched, and preparations to rest made. Some chose one spot and some another, and after a while we were settled. Mr. Culbertson and I lay together on the outside of the tent, and all the party were more or less drowsy. About this time we saw a large black cloud rising in the west; it was heavy and lowering, and about ten o'clock, when most of us were pretty nearly sound asleep, the distant thunder was heard, the wind rose to a gale, and the rain began falling in torrents. All were on foot in a few moments, and considerable confusion ensued. Our guns, all loaded with balls, were hurriedly placed under the tent, our beds also, and we all crawled in, in the space of a very few minutes. The wind blew so hard that Harris was obliged to hold the flappers of the tent with both hands, and sat in the water a considerable time to do this. Old Provost alone did not come in, he sat under the shelving bank of the river, and kept dry. After the gale was over, he calmly lay down in front of the tent on the saturated ground, and was soon asleep. During the gale, our fire, which we had built to keep off the myriads of mosquitoes, blew in every direction, and we had to watch the embers to keep them from burning the tent. After all was over, we snugged ourselves the best way we could in our small tent and under the wagon, and slept soundly till daylight. Mr. Culbertson had fixed himself pretty well, but on arising at daylight to smoke his pipe, Squires immediately crept into his comfortable corner, and snored there till the day was well begun. Mr. Culbertson had my knees for a pillow, and also my hat, I believe, for in the morning, although the first were not hurt, the latter was sadly out of shape in all parts. We had nothing for our breakfast except some vile coffee, and about three quarters of a sea-biscuit, which was soon settled among us. The men, poor fellows, had nothing at all. Provost had seen two Deer, but had had no shot, so of course we were in a quandary, but it is now —

July 16, Sunday. The weather pleasant with a fine breeze from the westward, and all eyes were bent upon the hills and prairie, which is here of great breadth, to spy if possible some object that might be killed and eaten. Presently a Wolf was seen, and Owen went after it, and it was not until he had disappeared below the first low range of hills, and Owen also, that the latter came within shot of the rascal, which dodged in all sorts of manners; but Owen would not give up, and after shooting more than once, he killed the beast. A man had followed him to help bring in the Wolf, and when near the river he saw a Buffalo, about two miles off, grazing peaceably, as he perhaps thought, safe in his own dominions; but, alas! white hunters had fixed their eyes upon him, and from that moment his doom was pronounced. Mr. Culbertson threw down his hat, bound his head with a handkerchief, his saddle was on his mare, he was mounted and off and away at a swift gallop, more quickly than I can describe, not towards the Buffalo, but towards the place where Owen had killed the Wolf. The man brought the Wolf on old Peter, and Owen, who was returning to the camp, heard the signal gun fired by Mr. Culbertson, and at once altered his course; his mare was evidently a little heated and blown by the Wolf chase, but both hunters went after the Buffalo, slowly at first, to rest Owen's steed, but soon, when getting within running distance, they gave whip, overhauled the Bison, and shot at it twice with balls; this halted the animal; the hunters had no more balls, and now loaded with pebbles, with which the poor beast was finally killed. The wagon had been sent from the camp. Harris, Bell, and Squires mounted on horseback, and travelled to the scene of action. They met Mr. Culbertson returning to camp, and he told Bell the Buffalo was a superb one, and had better be skinned. A man was sent to assist in the skinning who had been preparing the Wolf which was now cooking, as we had expected to dine upon its flesh; but when Mr. Culbertson returned, covered with blood and looking like a wild Indian, it was decided to throw it away; so I cut out the liver, and old Provost and I went fishing and caught eighteen catfish. I hooked two tortoises, but put them back in the river. I took a good swim, which refreshed me much, and I came to dinner with a fine appetite. This meal consisted wholly of fish, and we were all fairly satisfied. Before long the flesh of the Buffalo reached the camp, as well as the hide. The animal was very fat, and we have meat for some days. It was now decided that Squires, Provost, and Basil (one of the men) should proceed down the river to the Charbonneau, and there try their luck at Otters and Beavers, and the rest of us, with the cart, would make our way back to the fort. All was arranged, and at half-past three this afternoon we were travelling towards Fort Union. But hours previous to this, and before our scanty dinner, Owen had seen another bull, and Harris and Bell joined us in the hunt. The bull was shot at by McKenzie, who stopped its career, but as friend Harris pursued it with two of the hunters and finished it I was about to return, and thought sport over for the day. However, at this stage of the proceedings Owen discovered another bull making his way slowly over the prairie towards us. I was the only one who had balls, and would gladly have claimed the privilege of running him, but fearing I might make out badly on my slower steed, and so lose meat which we really needed, I handed my gun and balls to Owen McKenzie, and Bell and I went to an eminence to view the chase. Owen approached the bull, which continued to advance, and was now less than a quarter of a mile distant; either it did not see, or did not heed him, and they came directly towards each other, until they were about seventy or eighty yards apart, when the Buffalo started at a good run, and Owen's mare, which had already had two hard runs this morning, had great difficulty in preserving her distance. Owen, perceiving this, breathed her a minute, and then applying the whip was soon within shooting distance, and fired a shot which visibly checked the progress of the bull, and enabled Owen to soon be alongside of him, when the contents of the second barrel were discharged into the lungs, passing through the shoulder blade. This brought him to a stand. Bell and I now started at full speed, and as soon as we were within speaking distance, called to Owen not to shoot again. The bull did not appear to be much exhausted, but he was so stiffened by the shot on the shoulder that he could not turn quickly, and taking advantage of this we approached him; as we came near he worked himself slowly round to face us, and then made a lunge at us; we then stopped on one side and commenced discharging our pistols with little or no effect, except to increase his fury with every shot. His appearance was now one to inspire terror had we not felt satisfied of our ability to avoid him. However, even so, I came very near being overtaken by him. Through my own imprudence, I placed myself directly in front of him, and as he advanced I fired at his head, and then ran *ahead* of him, instead of veering to one side, not supposing that he was able to overtake me; but turning my head over my shoulder, I saw to my horror, Mr. Bull within three feet of me, prepared to give me a taste of his horns. The next instant I turned sharply off, and the Buffalo being unable to turn quickly enough to follow me, Bell took the gun from

Owen and shot him directly behind the shoulder blade. He tottered for a moment, with an increased jet of blood from the mouth and nostrils, fell forward on his horns, then rolled over on his side, and was dead. He was a very old animal, in poor case, and only part of him was worth taking to the fort. Provost, Squires, and Basil were left at the camp preparing for their departure after Otter and Beaver as decided. We left them eight or nine catfish and a quantity of meat, of which they took care to secure the best, namely the boss or hump. On our homeward way we saw several Antelopes, some quite in the prairie, others far away on the hills, but all of them on the alert. Owen tried unsuccessfully to approach several of them at different times. At one place where two were seen he dismounted, and went round a small hill (for these animals when startled or suddenly alarmed always make to these places), and we hoped would have had a shot; but alas! no! One of the Antelopes ran off to the top of another hill, and the other stood looking at him, and us perhaps, till Owen (who had been re-mounted) galloped off towards us. My surprise was great when I saw the other Antelope following him at a good pace (but not by bounds or leaps, as I had been told by a former traveller they sometimes did), until it either smelt him, or found out he was no friend, and turning round galloped speedily off to join the one on the lookout. We saw seven or eight Grouse, and Bell killed one on the ground. We saw a Sand-hill Crane about two years old, looking quite majestic in a grassy bottom, but it flew away before we were near enough to get a shot. We passed a fine pond or small lake, but no bird was there. We saw several parcels of Ducks in sundry places, all of which no doubt had young near. When we turned the corner of the great prairie we found Owen's mare close by us. She had run away while he was after Antelopes. We tied her to a log to be ready for him when he should reach the spot. He had to walk about three miles before he did this. However, to one as young and alert as Owen, such things are nothing. Once they were not to me. We saw more Antelope at a distance, here called " Cabris," and after a while we reached the wood near the river, and finding abundance of service-berries, we all got out to break branches of these plants, Mr. Culbertson alone remaining in the wagon; he pushed on for the landing. We walked after him munching our berries, which we found very good, and reached the landing as the sun was going down behind the hills. Young McKenzie was already there, having cut across the point. We decided on crossing the river ourselves, and leaving all behind us except our guns. We took to the ferry-boat, cordelled it up the river for a while, then took to the nearest sand-bar, and leaping into the mud and water, hauled the heavy boat, Bell and Harris steering and poling the while. I had pulled off my shoes and socks, and when we reached the shore walked up to the fort barefooted, and made my feet quite sore again; but we have had a rest and a good supper, and I am writing in Mr. Culbertson's room, thinking over all God's blessings on this delightful day.

July 17, Monday. A beautiful day, with a west wind. Sprague, who is very industrious at all times, drew some flowers, and I have been busy both writing and drawing. In the afternoon Bell went after Rabbits, but saw one only, which he could not get, and Sprague walked to the hills about two miles off, but could not see any portion of the Yellowstone River, which Mr. Catlin has given in his view, as if he had been in a balloon some thousands of feet above the earth. Two men arrived last evening by land from Fort Pierre, and brought a letter, but no news of any importance; one is a cook as well as a hunter, the other named Wolff, a German, and a tinsmith by trade, though now a trapper.

July 18, Tuesday. When I went to bed last night the

mosquitoes were so numerous downstairs that I took my
bed under my arm and went to a room above, where I
slept well.   On going down this morning, I found two
other persons from Fort Pierre, and Mr. Culbertson very
busy reading and writing letters.   Immediately after
breakfast young McKenzie and another man were despatched on mules, with a letter for Mr. Kipp, and Owen
expects to overtake the boat in three or four days.   An
Indian arrived with a stolen squaw, both Assiniboins;
and I am told such things are of frequent occurrence
among these sons of nature.   Mr. Culbertson proposed
that we should take a ride to see the mowers, and Harris
and I joined him.   We found the men at work, among
them one called Bernard Adams, of Charleston, S. C.,
who knew the Bachmans quite well, and who had read
the whole of the " Biographies of Birds."   Leaving the
men, we entered a ravine in search of plants, etc., and
having started an Owl, which I took for the barred one, I
left my horse and went in search of it, but could not
see it, and hearing a new note soon saw a bird not to be
mistaken, and killed it, when it proved, as I expected, to
be the Rock Wren; then I shot another sitting by the
mouth of a hole.   The bird did not fly off; Mr. Culbertson watched it closely, but when the hole was demolished
no bird was to be found.   Harris saw a Shrike, but of
what species he could not tell, and he also found some
Rock Wrens in another ravine.   We returned to the fort
and promised to visit the place this afternoon, which we
have done, and procured three more Wrens, and killed the
Owl, which proves to be precisely the resemblance of the
Northern specimen of the Great Horned Owl, which we
published under another name.   The Rock Wren, which
might as well be called the Ground Wren, builds its nest
in holes, and now the young are well able to fly, and we
procured one in the act.   In two instances we saw these
birds enter a hole here, and an investigation showed a

passage or communication, and on my pointing out a hole to Bell where one had entered, he pushed his arm in and touched the little fellow, but it escaped by running up his arm and away it flew. Black clouds now arose in the west, and we moved homewards. Harris and Bell went to the mowers to get a drink of water, and we reached home without getting wet, though it rained violently for some time, and the weather is much cooler. Not a word yet from Provost and Squires.

July 19, Wednesday. Squires and Provost returned early this morning, and again I give the former my journal that I may have the account of the hunt in his own words. "As Mr. Audubon has said, he left Provost, Basil, and myself making ready for our voyage down the Yellowstone. The party for the fort were far in the blue distance ere we bid adieu to our camping-ground. We had wished the return party a pleasant ride and safe arrival at the fort as they left us, looking forward to a good supper, and what I *now* call a comfortable bed. We seated ourselves around some boiled Buffalo hump, which, as has been before said, we took good care to appropriate to ourselves according to the established rule of this country, which is, ' When you can, take the best,' and we had done so in this case, more to our satisfaction than to that of the hunters. Our meal finished, we packed everything we had in the skiff, and were soon on our way down the Yellowstone, happy as could be; Provost acting pilot, Basil oarsman, and your humble servant seated on a Buffalo robe, quietly smoking, and looking on the things around. We found the general appearance of the Yellowstone much like the Missouri, but with a stronger current, and the water more muddy. After a voyage of two hours Charbonneau River made its appearance, issuing from a clump of willows; the mouth of this river we found to be about ten feet wide, and so shallow that we were obliged to push our boat over the slippery mud for about forty feet. This passed, we entered a pond formed by the contraction of the mouth and the collection of mud and sticks thereabouts, the pond so formed being six or eight feet deep, and about fifty feet wide, extending about a mile up the river, which is very crooked indeed. For about half a mile from the Yellowstone the shore is lined with willows, beyond which is a level prairie, and on the shores of the stream just beyond the willows are a few scattered trees. About a quarter of a mile from the mouth of the river, we discovered what we were in search of, the Beaver lodge. To measure it was impossible, as it was not perfect, in the first place, in the next it was so muddy that we could not get ashore, but as well as I can I will describe it. The lodge is what is called the summer lodge; it was comprised wholly of brush, willow chiefly, with a single hole for the entrance and exit of the Beaver. The pile resembled, as much as anything to which I can compare it, a brush heap about six feet high, and about ten or fifteen feet base, and standing seven or eight feet from the water. There were a few Beaver tracks about, which gave us some encouragement. We proceeded to our camping-ground on the edge of the prairie; here we landed all our baggage; while Basil made a fire, Provost and I started to set our traps — the two extremes of hunters, the skilful old one, and the ignorant pupil; but I was soon initiated in the art of setting Beaver traps, and to the uninitiated let me say, '*First*, find your game, *then* catch it,' if you can. The first we did, the latter we tried to do. We proceeded to the place where the greatest number of tracks were seen, and commenced operations. At the place where the path enters the water, and about four inches beneath the surface, a level place is made in the mud, upon which the trap is placed, the chain is then fastened to a stake which is firmly driven in the ground under water. The end of a willow twig is then chewed and dipped in the ' Medicine Horn,' which contains the bait; this consists of castoreum mixed with spices; a quantity is collected on the chewed end of the twig, the stick is then placed or stuck in the mud on the edge of the water, leaving the part with the bait about two inches above the surface and in front of the trap; on each side the bait and about six inches from it, two dried twigs are placed in the ground; this done, all's done, and we are ready for the visit of Monsieur Castor. We set two traps, and returned to our camp, where we had supper, then pitched our tent and soon were sound asleep, but before we were asleep we heard a Beaver dive, and slap his tail, which sounded like the falling of a round stone in the water; here was encouragement again. In the morning (Monday) we examined our traps and found — nothing. We did not therefore disturb the traps, but examined farther up the river, where we discovered other tracks and resolved to set our traps there, as Provost concluded that there was but one Beaver, and that a male. We returned to camp and made a good breakfast on Buffalo meat and coffee, *sans* salt, *sans* pepper, *sans* sugar, *sans* anything else of any kind. After breakfast Provost shot a doe.   In the afternoon we removed one trap, Basil and I gathered some wild-gooseberries which I stewed for supper, and made a sauce, which, though *rather acid*, was very good with our meat. The next morning, after again examining our traps and finding nothing, we decided to raise camp, which was accordingly done; everything was packed in the skiff, and we proceeded to the mouth of the river. The water had fallen so much since we had entered, as to oblige us to strip, jump in the mud, and haul the skiff over; rich and rare was the job; the mud was about half thigh deep, and a kind of greasy, sticky, black stuff, with a something about it so very peculiar as to be *rather* unpleasant; however, we did not mind much, and at last got into the Yellowstone, scraped and washed the mud off, and encamped on a prairie about one hundred yards below the Charbonneau. It was near sunset; Provost commenced fishing; we joined him, and in half an hour we caught sixteen catfish, quite large ones. During the day Provost started to the Mauvaises Terres to hunt Bighorns, but returned unsuccessful. He baited his traps for the last time. During his absence thunder clouds were observed rising all around us; we stretched our tent, removed everything inside it, ate our supper of meat and coffee, and then went to bed. It rained some part of the night, but not enough to wet through the tent. The next morning (Tuesday) at daylight, Provost started to examine his traps, while we at the camp put everything in the boat, and sat down to await his return, when we proceeded on our voyage down the Yellowstone to Fort Mortimer, and from thence by land to Fort Union. Nothing of any interest occurred except that we saw two does, one young and one buck of the Bighorns; I fired at the buck which was on a high cliff about a hundred and fifty yards from us; I fired above it to allow for the falling of the ball, but the gun shot so well as to carry where I aimed. The animal was a very large buck; Provost says one of the largest he had seen. As soon as I fired he started and ran along the side of the hill which looked almost perpendicular, and I was much astonished, not only at the feat, but at the surprising quickness with which he moved along, with no apparent foothold. We reached Fort Mortimer about seven o'clock; I left Basil and Provost with the skiff, and I started for Fort Union on foot to send a cart for them. On my way I met Mr. Audubon about to pay a visit to Fort Mortimer; I found all well, despatched the cart, changed my clothes, and feel none the worse for my five days' camping, and quite ready for a dance I hear we are to have to-night."

This morning as I walked to Fort Mortimer, meeting Squires as he has said, well and happy as a Lark, I was surprised to see a good number of horses saddled, and packed in different ways, and I hastened on to find what might be the matter. When I entered the miserable house in which Mr. Collins sleeps and spends his time when not occupied out of doors, he told me thirteen men and seven squaws were about to start for the lakes, thirty-five miles off, to kill Buffaloes and dry their meat, as the last his hunters brought in was already putrid. I saw the cavalcade depart in an E. N. E. direction, remained a while, and then walked back. Mr. Collins promised me half a dozen balls from young animals. Provost was discomfited and crestfallen at the failure of the Beaver hunt; he brought half a doe and about a dozen fine catfish. Mr. Culbertson and I are going to see the mowers, and to-morrow we start on a grand Buffalo hunt, and hope for Antelopes, Wolves, and Foxes.

July 20, Thursday. We were up early, and had our breakfast shortly after four o'clock, and before eight had left the landing of the fort, and were fairly under way for the prairies. Our equipment was much the same as before, except that we had two carts this time. Mr. C. drove Harris, Bell, and myself, and the others rode on the carts and led the hunting horses, or runners, as they are called here. I observed a Rabbit running across the road, and saw some flowers different from any I had ever seen. After we had crossed a bottom prairie, we ascended between the high and rough ravines until we were on the rolling grounds of the plains. The fort showed well from this point, and we also saw a good number of Antelopes, and some young ones. These small things run even faster than the old ones. As we neared the Fox River some one espied four Buffaloes, and Mr. C., taking the telescope, showed them to me, lying on the ground. Our heads and carts were soon turned towards them, and we travelled within half a mile of them, concealed by a ridge or hill which separated them from us. The wind was favorable, and we moved on slowly round the hill, the hunters being now mounted. Harris and Bell had their hats on, but Owen and Mr. Culbertson had their heads bound with handkerchiefs. With the rest of the party I crawled on the ridge, and saw the bulls running away, but in a direction favorable for us to see the chase. On the word of command the horses were let loose, and away went the hunters, who soon were seen to gain on the game; two bulls ran together and Mr. C. and Bell followed after them, and presently one after another of the hunters followed them. Mr. C. shot first, and his bull stopped at the fire, walked towards where I was, and halted about sixty yards from me. His nose was within a few inches of the ground; the blood poured from his mouth, nose, and side, his tail hung down, but his legs looked as firm as ever, but in less than two minutes the poor beast fell on his side, and lay quite dead. Bell and Mr. Culbertson went after the second. Harris took the third, and Squires the fourth. Bell's shot took effect in the buttock, and Mr. Culbertson shot, placing his ball a few inches above or below Bell's; after this Mr. Culbertson ran no more. At this moment Squires's horse threw him over his head, fully ten feet; he fell on his powder-horn and was severely bruised; he cried to Harris to catch his horse, and was on his legs at once, but felt sick for a few minutes. Harris, who was as cool as a cucumber, neared his bull, shot it through the lungs, and it fell dead on the spot. Bell was now seen in full pursuit of his game, and Harris joined Squires, and followed the fourth, which, however, was soon out of my sight. I saw Bell shooting two or three times, and I heard the firing of Squires and perhaps Harris, but the weather was hot, and being afraid of injuring their horses, they let the fourth bull make his escape. Bell's bull fell on his knees, got up again, and rushed on Bell, and was shot again. The animal stood a minute with his tail partially elevated, and then fell dead;

through some mishap Bell had no knife with him, so did not bring the tongue, as is customary. Mr. Culbertson walked towards the first bull and I joined him. It was a fine animal about seven years old; Harris's and Bell's were younger. The first was fat, and was soon skinned and cut up for meat. Mr. Culbertson insisted on calling it my bull, so I cut off the brush of the tail and placed it in my hat-band. We then walked towards Harris, who was seated on his bull, and the same ceremony took place, and while they were cutting the animal up for meat, Bell, who said he thought his bull was about three quarters of a mile distant, went off with me to see it; we walked at least a mile and a half, and at last came to it. It was a poor one, and the tongue and tail were all we took away, and we rejoined the party, who had already started the cart with Mr. Pike, who was told to fall to the rear, and reach the fort before sundown; this he could do readily, as we were not more than six miles distant. Mr. Culbertson broke open the head of "my" bull, and ate part of the brains raw, and yet warm, and so did many of the others, even Squires. The very sight of this turned my stomach, but I am told that were I to hunt Buffalo one year, I should like it "even better than dog meat." Mr. Pike did not reach the fort till the next morning about ten, I will say *en passant*. We continued our route, passing over the same road on which we had come, and about midway between the Missouri and Yellowstone Rivers. We saw more Antelopes, but not one Wolf; these rascals are never abundant where game is scarce, but where game is, there too are the Wolves. When we had travelled about ten miles further we saw seven Buffaloes grazing on a hill, but as the sun was about one hour high, we drove to one side of the road where there was a pond of water, and there stopped for the night; while the hunters were soon mounted, and with Squires they went off, leaving the men to arrange the camp. I crossed the pond, and having ascended the opposite bank, saw the bulls grazing as leisurely as usual. The hunters near them, they started down the hill, and the chase immediately began. One broke from the rest and was followed by Mr. C. who shot it, and then abandoned the hunt, his horse being much fatigued. I now counted ten shots, but all was out of my sight, and I seated myself near a Fox hole, longing for him. The hunters returned in time; Bell and Harris had killed one, but Squires had no luck, owing to his being unable to continue the chase on account of the injury he had received from his fall. We had a good supper, having brought abundance of eatables and drinkables. The tent was pitched; I put up my mosquito-bar under the wagon, and there slept very soundly till sunrise. Harris and Bell wedged together under another bar, Mr. C. went into the tent, and Squires, who is tough and likes to rough it with the hunters, slept on a Buffalo hide somewhere with Moncrévier, one of the most skilful of the hunters. The horses were all hoppled and turned to grass; they, however, went off too far, and had to be sent after, but I heard nothing of all this. As there is no wood on the prairies proper, our fire was made of Buffalo dung, which is so abundant that one meets these deposits at every few feet and in all directions.

July 21, Friday. We were up at sunrise, and had our coffee, after which Lafleur a mulatto, Harris, and Bell went off after Antelopes, for we cared no more about bulls; where the cows are, we cannot tell. Cows run faster than bulls, yearlings faster than cows, and calves faster than any of these. Squires felt sore, and his side was very black, so we took our guns and went after Black-breasted Lark Buntings, of which we saw many, but could not near them. I found a nest of them, however, with five eggs. The nest is planted in the ground, deep enough to sink the edges of it. It is formed of dried fine grasses and roots, without any lining of hair or wool. By and by we saw Harris sitting on a high hill about one mile off, and joined him; he said the bulls they had killed last evening were close by, and I offered to go and see the bones, for I expected that the Wolves had devoured it during the night. We travelled on, and Squires returned to the camp. After about two miles of walking against a delightful strong breeze, we reached the animals; Ravens or Buzzards had worked at the eyes, but only one Wolf, apparently, had been there. They were bloated, and smelt quite unpleasant. We returned to the camp and saw a Wolf cross our path, and an Antelope looking at us. We determined to stop and try to bring him to us; I lay on my back and threw my legs up, kicking first one and then the other foot, and sure enough the Antelope walked towards us, slowly and carefully, however. In about twenty minutes he had come two or three hundred yards; he was a superb male, and I looked at him for some minutes; when about sixty yards off I could see his eyes, and being loaded with buck-shot pulled the trigger without rising from my awkward position. Off he went; Harris fired, but he only ran the faster for some hundred yards, when he turned, looked at us again, and was off. When we reached camp we found Bell there; he had shot three times at Antelopes without killing; Lafleur had also returned, and had broken the foreleg of one, but an Antelope can run fast enough with three legs, and he saw no more of it. We now broke camp, arranged the horses and turned our heads towards the Missouri, and in four and three-quarter hours reached the landing. On entering the wood we again broke branches of service-berries, and carried a great quantity over the river. I much enjoyed the trip; we had our supper, and soon to bed in our hot room, where Sprague says the thermometer has been at 99° most of the day. I noticed it was warm when walking. I must not forget to notice some things which happened on our return. First, as we came near Fox River,

we thought of the horns of our bulls, and Mr. Culbertson, who knows the country like a book, drove us first to
Bell's, who knocked the horns off, then to Harris's, which
was served in the same manner; this bull had been eaten
entirely except the head, and a good portion of mine had
been devoured also; it lay immediately under "Audubon's Bluff" (the name Mr. Culbertson gave the ridge on
which I stood to see the chase), and we could see it when
nearly a mile distant.   Bell's horns were the handsomest
and largest, mine next best, and Harris's the smallest,
but we are all contented.   Mr. Culbertson tells me that
Harris and Bell have done wonders, for persons who have
never shot at Buffaloes from on horseback.   Harris had a
fall too, during his second chase, and was bruised in the
manner of Squires, but not so badly.   I have but little
doubt that Squires killed his bull, as he says he shot it
three times, and Mr. Culbertson's must have died also.
What a terrible destruction of life, as it were for nothing, or next to it, as the tongues only were brought in,
and the flesh of these fine animals was left to beasts and
birds of prey, or to rot on the spots where they fell.   The
prairies are literally *covered* with the skulls of the victims, and the roads the Buffalo make in crossing the
prairies have all the appearance of heavy wagon tracks.
We saw young Golden Eagles, Ravens, and Buzzards.   I
found the Short-billed Marsh Wren quite abundant, and
in such localities as it is found eastward.   The Black-
breasted Prairie-bunting flies much like a Lark, hovering while singing, and sweeping round and round, over
and above its female while she sits on the eggs on the
prairie below. I saw only one Gadwall Duck; these
birds are found in abundance on the plains where
water and rushes are to be found.   Alas! alas! eighteen
Assiniboins have reached the fort this evening in two
groups; they are better-looking than those previously
seen by us.

July 22, Saturday. Thermometer 99°–102°. This day
has been the hottest of the season, and we all felt the influence of this densely oppressive atmosphere, not a breath
of air stirring. Immediately after breakfast Provost and
Lafleur went across the river in search of Antelopes, and
we remained looking at the Indians, all Assiniboins, and
very dirty. When and where Mr. Catlin saw these Indians as he has represented them, dressed in magnificent
attire, with all sorts of extravagant accoutrements, is more
than I can divine, or Mr. Culbertson tell me. The evening was so hot and sultry that Mr. C. and I went into
the river, which is now very low, and remained in the
water over an hour. A dozen catfish were caught in the
main channel, and we have had a good supper from part
of them. Finding the weather so warm I have had my
bed brought out on the gallery below, and so has Squires.
The Indians are, as usual, shut *out* of the fort, all the
horses, young Buffaloes, etc., shut *in ;* and much refreshed
by my bath, I say God bless you, and good-night.

July 23, Sunday. Thermometer 84°. I had a very
pleasant night, and no mosquitoes, as the breeze rose a
little before I lay down; and I anticipated a heavy thunder storm, but we had only a few drops of rain. About
one o'clock Harris was called to see one of the Indians,
who was bleeding at the nose profusely, and I too went
to see the poor devil. He had bled quite enough, and
Harris stopped his nostrils with cotton, put cold water on
his neck and head — God knows when they had felt it
before — and the bleeding stopped. These dirty fellows
had made a large fire between the walls of the fort, but
outside the inner gates, and it was a wonder that the
whole establishment was not destroyed by fire. Before
sunrise they were pounding at the gate to be allowed to
enter, but, of course, this was not permitted. When the
sun had fairly risen, some one came and told me the hill-
tops were covered with Indians, probably Blackfeet. I

walked to the back gate, and the number had dwindled, or the account been greatly exaggerated, for there seemed only fifty or sixty, and when, later, they were counted, there were found to be exactly seventy. They remained a long time on the hill, and sent a youth to ask for whiskey. But whiskey there is none for them, and very little for any one. By and by they came down the hill leading four horses, and armed principally with bows and arrows, spears, tomahawks, and a few guns. They have proved to be a party of Crees from the British dominions on the Saskatchewan River, and have been fifteen days in travelling here. They had seen few Buffaloes, and were hungry and thirsty enough. They assured Mr. Culbertson that the Hudson's Bay Company supplied them all with abundance of spirituous liquors, and as the white traders on the Missouri had none for them, they would hereafter travel with the English. Now ought not this subject to be brought before the press in our country and forwarded to England? If our Congress will not allow our traders to sell whiskey or rum to the Indians, why should not the British follow the same rule? Surely the British, who are so anxious about the emancipation of the blacks, might as well take care of the souls and bodies of the redskins. After a long talk and smoking of pipes, tobacco, flints, powder, gun-screws and vermilion were placed before their great chief (who is tattooed and has a most rascally look), who examined everything minutely, counting over the packets of vermilion; more tobacco was added, a file, and a piece of white cotton with which to adorn his head; then he walked off, followed by his son, and the whole posse left the fort. They passed by the garden, pulled up a few squash vines and some turnips, and tore down a few of the pickets on their way elsewhere. We all turned to, and picked a quantity of peas, which with a fine roast pig, made us a capital dinner. After this, seeing the Assiniboins loitering about the fort, we had some tobacco put up as a target, and many arrows were sent to enter the prize, but I never saw Indians — usually so skilful with their bows — shoot worse in my life.   Presently some one cried there were Buffaloes on the hill, and going to see we found that four bulls were on the highest ridge standing still.   The horses being got in the yard, the guns were gathered, saddles placed, and the riders mounted, Mr. C., Harris, and Bell; Squires declined going, not having recovered from his fall, Mr. C. led his followers round the hills by the ravines, and approached the bulls quite near, when the affrighted cattle ran down the hills and over the broken grounds, out of our sight, followed by the hunters. When I see game chased by Mr. Culbertson, I feel confident of its being killed, and in less than one hour he had killed two bulls, Harris and Bell each one.   Thus these poor animals which two hours before were tranquilly feeding are now dead; short work this.   Harris and Bell remained on the hills to watch the Wolves, and carts being ordered, Mr. C. and I went off on horseback to the second one he had killed.   We found it entire, and I began to operate upon it at once; after making what measurements and investigations I desired, I saved the head, the tail, and a large piece of the silky skin from the rump.   The meat of three of the bulls was brought to the fort, the fourth was left to rot on the ground.   Mr. C. cut his finger severely, but paid no attention to that; I, however, tore a strip off my shirt and bound it up for him.   It is so hot I am going to sleep on the gallery again; the thermometer this evening is 89°.

July 24, Monday.   I had a fine sleep last night, and this morning early a slight sprinkling of rain somewhat refreshed the earth.   After breakfast we talked of going to see if Mr. Culbertson's bull had been injured by the Wolves.   Mr. C., Harris, and I went off to the spot by a roundabout way, and when we reached the animal it was somewhat swollen, but untouched, but we made up our minds to have it weighed, *coute qui coute*. Harris proposed to remain and watch it, looking for Hares meantime, but saw none. The Wolves must be migratory at this season, or so starved out that they have gone elsewhere, as we now see but few. We returned first to the fort, and mustered three men and Bell, for Sprague would not go, being busy drawing a plant, and finding the heat almost insupportable. We carried all the necessary implements, and found Harris quite ready to drink some claret and water which we took for him. To cut up so large a bull, and one now with so dreadful an odor, was no joke; but with the will follows the success, and in about one hour the poor beast had been measured and weighed, and we were once more *en route* for the fort. This bull measured as follows: from end of nose to root of tail, 131 inches; height at shoulder, 67 inches; at rump, 57 inches; tail vertebræ, 15½ inches, hair in length beyond it 11 inches. We weighed the whole animal by cutting it in parts and then by addition found that this Buffalo, which was an old bull, weighed 1777 lbs. avoirdupois. The flesh was all tainted, and was therefore left for the beasts of prey. Our road was over high hills, and presented to our searching eyes a great extent of broken ground, and here and there groups of Buffaloes grazing. This afternoon we are going to bring in the skeleton of Mr. Culbertson's second bull. I lost the head of my first bull because I forgot to tell Mrs. Culbertson that I wished to save it, and the princess had its skull broken open to enjoy its brains. Handsome, and really courteous and refined in many ways, I cannot reconcile to myself the fact that she partakes of raw animal food with such evident relish. Before our departure, in came six half-breeds, belonging, or attached to Fort Mortimer; and understanding that they were first-rate hunters, I offered them ten dollars in goods for each Bighorn up to eight

or ten in number. They have promised to go to-morrow,
but, alas! the half-breeds are so uncertain I cannot tell
whether they will move a step or not. Mrs. Culbertson,
who has great pride in her pure Indian blood, told me
with scorn that "all such no-color fellows are lazy." We
were delayed in starting by a very heavy gale of wind and
hard rain, which cooled the weather considerably; but we
finally got off in the wagon, the cart with three mules
following, to bring in the skeleton of the Buffalo which
Mr. Culbertson had killed; but we were defeated, for
some Wolves had been to it, dragged it about twenty-five
feet, and gnawed the ends of the ribs and the backbone.
The head of Harris's bull was brought in, but it was
smaller; the horns alone were pretty good, and they were
given to Sprague. On our return Mrs. Culbertson was
good enough to give me six young Mallards, which she
had caught by swimming after them in the Missouri; she
is a most expert and graceful swimmer, besides being
capable of remaining under water a long time; all the
Blackfoot Indians excel in swimming and take great pride
in the accomplishment. We found three of the Assiniboins had remained, one of whom wanted to carry off a
squaw, and probably a couple of horses too. He strutted
about the fort in such a manner that we watched him
pretty closely. Mr. Culbertson took his gun, and a six-
barrelled pistol in his pocket; I, my double-barrelled
gun, and we stood at the back gate. The fellow had a
spear made of a cut-and-thrust sword, planted in a good
stick covered with red cloth, and this he never put down
at any time; but no more, indeed, do any Indians, who
carry all their goods and chattels forever about their persons. The three gentlemen, however, went off about
dusk, and took the road to Fort Mortimer, where six half-
breeds from the Northeast brought to Fort Mortimer
eleven head of cattle, and came to pay a visit to their
friends here. All these men know Provost, and have

inquired for him. I feel somewhat uneasy about Provost and La Fleur, who have now been gone four full days. The prairie is wet and damp, so I must sleep indoors. The bull we cut up was not a fat one; I think in good condition it would have weighed 2000 lbs.

July 25, Tuesday. We were all rather lazy this morning, but about dinner-time Owen and his man arrived, and told us they had reached Mr. Kipp and his boat at the crossings within about half a mile of Fort Alexander; that his men were all broken down with drawing the cordelle through mud and water, and that they had lost a white horse, which, however, Owen saw on his way, and on the morning of his start from this fort. About the same time he shot a large Porcupine, and killed four bulls and one cow to feed upon, as well as three rattlesnakes. They saw a large number of Buffalo cows, and we are going after them to-morrow morning bright and early. About two hours later Provost and La Fleur, about whom I had felt some uneasiness, came to the landing, and brought the heads and skins attached to two female Antelopes. Both had been killed by one shot from La Fleur, and his ball broke the leg of a third. Provost was made quite sick by the salt water he had drunk; he killed one doe, on which they fed as well as on the flesh of the "Cabris." Whilst following the Mauvaises Terres (broken lands), they saw about twenty Bighorns, and had not the horse on which Provost rode been frightened at the sight of a monstrous buck of these animals, he would have shot it down within twenty yards. They saw from fifteen to twenty Buffalo cows, and we hope some of the hunters will come up with them to-morrow. I have been drawing the head of one of these beautiful female Antelopes; but their horns puzzle me, and all of us; they seem to me as if they were *new* horns, soft and short; time, however, will prove whether they shed them or not. Our preparations are already made for preserving the skins of the Antelopes, and Sprague is making an outline which I hope will be finished before the muscles of the head begin to soften. Not a word from the six hunters who promised to go after Bighorns on the Yellowstone.

July 26, Wednesday. We were all on foot before daybreak and had our breakfast by an early hour, and left on our trip for Buffalo cows. The wagon was sent across by hauling it through the east channel, which is now quite low, and across the sand-bars, which now reach seven-eighths of the distance across the river. We crossed in the skiff, and walked to the ferry-boat — I barefooted, as well as Mr. Culbertson; others wore boots or moccasins, but my feet have been tender of late, and this is the best cure. Whilst looking about for sticks to support our mosquito bars, I saw a Rabbit standing before me, within a few steps, but I was loaded with balls, and should have torn the poor thing so badly that it would have been useless as a specimen, so let it live. We left the ferry before six, and went on as usual. We saw two Antelopes on entering the bottom prairie, but they had the wind of us, and scampered off to the hills. We saw two Grouse, one of which Bell killed, and we found it very good this evening for our supper. Twelve bulls were seen, but we paid no attention to them. We saw a fine large Hawk, apparently the size of a Red-tailed Hawk, but with the whole head white. It had alighted on a clay hill or bank, but, on being approached, flew off to another, was pursued and again flew away, so that we could not procure it, but I have no doubt that it is a species not yet described. We now crossed Blackfoot River, and saw great numbers of Antelopes. Their play and tricks are curious; I watched many of the groups a long time, and will not soon forget them. At last, seeing we should have no meat for supper, and being a party of nine, it was determined that the first animal seen should be run down and killed. We soon saw a bull, and all agreed to give every

chance possible to Squires. Mr. C., Owen, and Squires
started, and Harris followed without a gun, to see the
chase. The bull was wounded twice by Squires, but no
blood came from the mouth, and now all three shot at it,
but the bull was not apparently hurt seriously; he became
more and more furious, and began charging upon them.
Unfortunately, Squires ran between the bull and a ravine
quite close to the animal, and it suddenly turned on him;
his horse became frightened and jumped into the ravine,
the bull followed, and now Squires lost his balance;
however, he threw his gun down, and fortunately clung
to the mane of his horse and recovered his seat. The
horse got away and saved his life, for, from what Mr. C.
told me, had he fallen, the bull would have killed him in
a few minutes, and no assistance could be afforded him,
as Mr. C. and Owen had, at that moment, empty guns.
Squires told us all; he had never been so bewildered and
terrified before. The bull kept on running, and was shot
at perhaps twenty times, for when he fell he had *twelve
balls* in his side, and had been shot twice in the head.
Another bull was now seen close by us, and Owen killed
it after four shots. Whilst we were cutting up this one,
La Fleur and some one else went to the other, which was
found to be very poor, and, at this season smelling very
rank and disagreeable. A few of the best pieces were
cut away, and, as usual, the hunters ate the liver and fat
quite raw, like Wolves, and we were now on the move
again. Presently we saw seven animals coming towards
us, and with the glass discovered there were six bulls
and one cow. The hunters mounted in quick time, and
away after the cow, which Owen killed very soon. To
my surprise the bulls did not leave her, but stood about
one hundred yards from the hunters, who were cutting
her in pieces; the best parts were taken for dried meat.
Had we not been so many, the bulls would, in all proba
bility, have charged upon the butchers, but after a time

they went off at a slow canter. At this moment Harris and I were going towards the party thus engaged, when a Swift Fox started from a hole under the feet of Harris' horse. I was loaded with balls, and he also; he gave chase and gained upon the beautiful animal with remarkable quickness. Bell saw this, and joined Harris, whilst I walked towards the butchering party. The Fox was overtaken by Harris, who took aim at it several times, but could not get sight on him, and the little fellow doubled and cut about in such a manner that it escaped into a ravine, and was seen no more. Now who will tell me that no animal can compete with this Fox in speed, when Harris, mounted on an Indian horse, overtook it in a few minutes? We were now in sight of a large band of cows and bulls, but the sun was low, and we left them to make our way to the camping-place, which we reached just before the setting of the sun. We found plenty of water, and a delightful spot, where we were all soon at work unsaddling our horses and mules, bringing wood for fires, and picking service-berries, which we found in great quantities and very good. We were thirty miles from Fort Union, close to the three Mamelles, but must have travelled near fifty, searching for and running down the game. All slept well, some outside and others inside the tent, after our good supper. We had a clear, bright day, with the wind from the westward.

July 27, Thursday. This morning was beautiful, the birds singing all around us, and after our early breakfast, Harris, with La Fleur and Mr. Culbertson, walked to the top of the highest of the three Mamelles; Bell went to skinning the birds shot yesterday,[1] among which was a

---

[1] Among the "birds shot yesterday," July 26, when Audubon was too full of his Buffalo hunt to notice them in his Journal, were two, a male and a female, killed by Mr. Bell, which turned out to be new to science. For these were no other than Baird's Bunting, *Emberiza bairdii* of Audubon, B. Amer. vii., 1844, p. 359, pl. 500. Audubon there says it was "during one of our Buffalo hunts, on the 26th July, 1843," and adds: "I have named this

large Titmouse of the Eastern States, while I walked off a
short distance, and made a sketch of the camp and the
three Mamelles. I hope to see a fair picture from this,
painted by Victor, this next winter, God willing. During the night the bulls were heard bellowing, and the
Wolves howling, all around us. Bell had seen evidences
of Grizzly Bears close by, but we saw none of the animals.
An Antelope was heard snorting early this morning, and
seen for a while, but La Fleur could not get it. The
snorting of the Antelope is more like a whistling, sneez-
ing sound, than like the long, clear snorting of our common Deer, and it is also very frequently repeated, say
every few minutes, when in sight of an object of which
the animal does not yet know the nature; for the moment
it is assured of danger, it bounds three or four times like
a sheep, and then either trots off or gallops like a horse.
On the return of the gentlemen from the eminence, from
which they had seen nothing but a Hawk, and heard the
notes of the Rock Wren, the horses were gathered, and
preparations made to go in search of cows. I took my
gun and walked off ahead, and on ascending the first hill
saw an Antelope, which, at first sight, I thought was an
Indian. It stood still, gazing at me about five hundred
yards off; I never stirred, and presently it walked towards
me; I lay down and lowered my rifle; the animal could
not now see my body; I showed it my feet a few times, at
intervals. Presently I saw it coming full trot towards
me; I cocked my gun, loaded with buck-shot in one bar-

species after my young friend Spencer F. Baird, of Carlisle, Pennsylvania."
Special interest attaches to this case; for the bird was not only the first one
ever dedicated to Baird, but the last one ever named, described, and figured
by Audubon; and the plate of it completes the series of exactly 500 plates
which the octavo edition of the " Birds of America" contains. This bird
became the *Centronyx bairdii* of Baird, the *Passerculus bairdi* of Coues, and
the *Ammodramus bairdi* of some other ornithologists. See " Birds of the
Colorado Valley," i., 1878, p. 630. One of Audubon's specimens shot this
day is catalogued in Baird's Birds of N. Am., 1858, p. 441. — E. C.

rel and ball in the other. He came within thirty yards of
me and stopped suddenly, then turned broadside towards
me.   I could see his very eyes, his beautiful form, and
his fine horns, for it was a buck.   I pulled one trigger —
it snapped, the animal moved not; I pulled the other,
snapped again, and away the Antelope bounded, and ran
swiftly from me.   I put on fresh caps, and saw it stop
after going a few hundred yards, and presently it came
towards me again, but not within one hundred and fifty
yards, when seeing that it would not come nearer I pulled
the trigger with the ball; off it went, and so did the Antelope, which this time went quite out of my sight.   I returned to camp and found all ready for a move.   Owen
went up a hill to reconnoitre for Antelopes and cows; seeing one of the former he crept after it.   Bell followed,
and at this moment a Hare leaped from the path before
us, and stopped within twenty paces.   Harris was not
loaded with shot, and I only with buck-shot; however, I
fired and killed it; it proved to be a large female, and
after measuring, we skinned it, and I put on a label
"Townsend's Hare, killed a few miles from the three
Mamelles, July 27, 1843."   After travelling for a good
while, Owen, who kept ahead of us, made signs from the
top of a high hill that Buffaloes were in sight.   This
signal is made by walking the rider's horse backwards
and forwards several times.   We hurried on towards him,
and when we reached the place, he pointed to the spot
where he had seen them, and said they were travelling
fast, being a band of both cows and bulls.   The hunters
were mounted at once, and on account of Squires' sore-
ness I begged him not to run; so he drove me in the
wagon as fast as possible over hills, through plains and
ravines of all descriptions, at a pace beyond belief.   From
time to time we saw the hunters, and once or twice the
Buffaloes, which were going towards the fort.   At last
we reached an eminence from which we saw both the

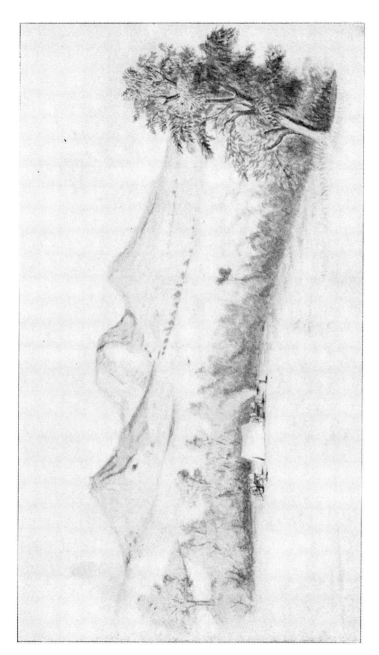

CAMP AT THE THREE MAMELLES.

FROM A DRAWING BY AUDUBON, HITHERTO UNPUBLISHED.

game and the hunters approaching the cattle, preparatory to beginning the chase. It seems there is no etiquette among Buffalo hunters, and this proved a great disappointment to friend Harris, who was as anxious to kill a cow, as he had been to kill a bull. Off went the whole group, but the country was not as advantageous to the pursuers, as to the pursued. The cows separated from the bulls, the latter making their way towards us, and six of them passed within one hundred yards of where I stood; we let them pass, knowing well how savage they are at these times, and turned our eyes again to the hunters. I saw Mr. C. pursuing one cow, Owen another, and Bell a third. Owen shot one and mortally wounded it; it walked up on a hill and stood there for some minutes before falling. Owen killed a second close by the one Mr. C. had now killed, Bell's dropped dead in quite another direction, nearly one mile off. Two bulls we saw coming directly towards us, so La Fleur and I went under cover of the hill to await their approach, and they came within sixty yards of us. I gave La Fleur the choice of shooting first, as he had a rifle; he shot and missed; they turned and ran in an opposite direction, so that I, who had gone some little distance beyond La Fleur, had no chance, and I was sorry enough for my politeness. Owen had shot a third cow, which went part way up a hill, fell, and kicked violently; she, however, rose and again fell, and kept kicking with all her legs in the air. Squires now drove to her, and I walked, followed by Moncrévier, a hunter; seeing Mr. C. and Harris on the bottom below we made signs for them to come up, and they fortunately did, and by galloping to Squires probably saved that young man from more danger; for though I cried to him at the top of my voice, the wind prevented him from hearing me; he now stopped, however, not far from a badly broken piece of ground over which had he driven at his usual speed, which I doubt not he would have attempted,

some accident must have befallen him.   Harris and Mr.
C. rode up to the cow, which expired at that moment.
The cow Mr. C. had killed was much the largest, and we
left a cart and two men to cut up this, and the first two
Owen had killed, and went to the place where the first
lay, to have it skinned for me.   Bell joined us soon, bringing a tongue with him, and he immediately began operations on the cow, which proved a fine one, and I have the
measurements as follows: "Buffalo Cow, killed by Mr.
Alexander Culbertson, July 27, 1843.   Nose to root of
tail, 96 inches.   Height at shoulder, 60; at rump, $55\frac{1}{2}$.
Length of tail vertebræ, 13; to end of hair, 25; from
brisket to bottom of feet, $21\frac{1}{2}$; nose to anterior canthus,
$10\frac{1}{2}$; between horns at root, $11\frac{3}{8}$; between tops of ditto,
$17\frac{1}{8}$; between nostrils, $2\frac{1}{4}$; length of ditto, $2\frac{1}{2}$; height of
nose, $3\frac{1}{8}$; nose to opening of ear, 20; ear from opening to
tip, 5; longest hair on head, 14 inches; from angle of
mouth to end of under lip, $3\frac{1}{2}$."   Whilst we were at this,
Owen and Pike were hacking at their cow.   After awhile
all was ready for departure, and we made for the "coupe"
at two o'clock, and expected to have found water to enable us to water our horses, for we had yet some gallons
of the Missouri water for our own use.   We found the
road to the "coupe," which was seen for many, many miles.
The same general appearance of country shows throughout the whole of these dreary prairies; up one hill and
down on the other side, then across a plain with ravines
of more or less depth.   About two miles west of the
"coupe," Owen and others went in search of water, but
in vain; and we have had to cross the "coupe" and travel
fully two miles east of it, when we came to a mere puddle,
sufficient however, for the night, and we stopped.   The
carts with the meat, and our effects, arrived after a while;
the meat was spread on the grass, the horses and mules
hoppled and let go, to drink and feed.   All hands collected Buffalo dung for fuel, for not a bush was in sight,

and we soon had a large fire.   In the winter season
this prairie fuel is too wet to burn, and oftentimes the
hunters have to eat their meat raw, or go without their
supper.   Ours was cooked however; I made mine chiefly
from the liver, as did Harris; others ate boiled or roasted
meat as they preferred.   The tent was pitched, and I
made a bed for Mr. C. and myself, and guns, etc., were
all under cover; the evening was cool, the wind fresh,
and no mosquitoes.   We had seen plenty of Antelopes;
I shot at one twenty yards from the wagon with small
shot.   Harris killed a Wolf, but we have seen very few,
and now I will wish you all good-night; God bless you!

July 28, Friday.   This morning was cold enough for a
frost, but we all slept soundly until daylight, and about
half-past three we were called for breakfast.   The horses
had all gone but four, and, as usual, Owen was despatched
for them.   The horses were brought back, our coffee
swallowed, and we were off, Mr. C. and I, in the wagon.
We saw few Antelopes, no Buffalo, and   reached   the
ferry opposite the fort at half-past seven.   We found
all well, and about eleven Assiniboins, all young men,
headed by the son of a great chief called " Le mangeur
d'hommes " (the man-eater).   The poor wretched Indian
whom Harris had worked over, died yesterday morning,
and was buried at once.   I had actually felt chilly riding
in the wagon, and much enjoyed a breakfast Mrs. Culbertson had kindly provided for me.   We had passed over
some very rough roads, and at breakneck speed, but I did
not feel stiff as I expected, though somewhat sore, and a
good night's rest is all I need.   This afternoon the cow's
skin and head, and the Hare arrived, and have been preserved.   A half-breed well known to Provost has been
here to make a bargain with me about Bighorns, Grizzly
Bear, etc., and will see what he and his two sons can do;
but I have little or no confidence in these gentry.   I was
told this afternoon that at Mouse River, about two hundred

miles north of this, there are eight hundred carts in one gang, and four hundred in another, with an adequate number of half-breeds and Indians, killing Buffalo and drying their meat for winter provisions, and that the animals are there in millions. When Buffalo bulls are shot from a distance of sixty or seventy yards, they rarely charge on the hunter, and Mr. Culbertson has killed as many as nine bulls from the same spot, when unseen by these terrible beasts. Beavers, when shot swimming, and killed, sink at once to the bottom, but their bodies rise again in from twenty to thirty minutes. Hunters, who frequently shoot and kill them by moonlight, return in the morning from their camping-places, and find them on the margins of the shores where they had shot. Otters do the same, but remain under water for an hour or more.

July 29, Saturday. Cool and pleasant. About one hour after daylight Harris, Bell, and two others, crossed the river, and went in search of Rabbits, but all returned without success. Harris, after breakfast, went off on this side, saw none, but killed a young Raven. During the course of the forenoon he and Bell went off again, and brought home an old and young of the Sharp-tailed Grouse. This afternoon they brought in a Loggerhead Shrike and two Rock Wrens. Bell skinned all these. Sprague made a handsome sketch of the five young Buffaloes belonging to the fort. This evening Moncrévier and Owen went on the other side of the river, but saw nothing. We collected berries of the dwarf cherries of this part, and I bottled some service-berries to carry home.

July 30, Sunday. Weather cool and pleasant. After breakfast we despatched La Fleur and Provost after Antelopes and Bighorns. We then went off and had a battue for Rabbits, and although we were nine in number, and all beat the rose bushes and willows for several hundred yards, not one did we see, although their traces were apparent in several places. We saw tracks of a young Grizzly Bear near the river shore. After a good dinner of Buffalo meat, green peas, and a pudding, Mr. C., Owen, Mr. Pike, and I went off to Fort Mortimer. We had an arrival of five squaws, half-breeds, and a gentleman of the same order, who came to see our fort and our ladies. The princess went out to meet them covered with a fine shawl, and the visitors followed her to her own room. These ladies spoke both the French and Cree languages. At Fort Mortimer we found the hunters from the north, who had returned last evening and told me they had seen nothing. I fear that all my former opinions of the half-breeds are likely to be realized, and that they are all more *au fait* at telling lies, than anything else; and I expect now that we shall have to make a regular turn-out ourselves, to kill both Grizzly Bears and Bighorns. As we were riding along not far from this fort, Mr. Culbertson fired off the gun given him by Harris, and it blew off the stock, lock, and breech, and it was a wonder it did not kill him, or me, as I was sitting by his side. After we had been at home about one hour, we were all called out of a sudden by the news that the *Horse Guards* were coming, full gallop, driving the whole of their charge before them. We saw the horses, and the cloud of dust that they raised on the prairies, and presently, when the Guards reached the gates, they told us that they had seen a party of Indians, which occasioned their hurried return. It is now more than one hour since I wrote this, and the Indians are now in sight, and we think they were frightened by three or four squaws who had left the fort in search of " pommes blanches." Sprague has collected a few seeds, but I intend to have some time devoted to this purpose before we leave on our passage downwards. This evening five Indians arrived, among whom is the brother of the man who died a few days ago; he brought a horse, and an Elk skin, which I bought, and he now considers himself a rich man. He reported Buffaloes very near, and to-morrow morning the hunters will

be after them.   When Buffaloes are about to lie down,
they draw all their four feet together slowly, and balancing
the body for a moment, bend their fore legs, and fall on
their knees first, and the hind ones follow.   In young
animals, some of which we have here, the effect produced
on their tender skin is directly seen, as callous round
patches without hair are found; after the animal is about
one year old, these are seen no more.   I am told that
Wolves have not been known to attack men and horses in
these parts, but they do attack mules and colts, always
making choice of the fattest.   We scarcely see one now-a-
days about the fort, and yet two miles from here, at Fort
Mortimer, Mr. Collins tells me it is impossible to sleep, on
account of their howlings at night.   When Assiniboin
Indians lose a relative by death, they go and cry under
the box which contains the body, which is placed in a tree,
cut their legs and different parts of the body, and moan
miserably for hours at a time.   This performance has been
gone through with by the brother of the Indian who died
here.

July 31, Monday.   Weather rather warmer.   Mr. Larpenteur went after Rabbits, saw none, but found a horse,
which was brought home this afternoon.   Mr. C., Harris,
Bell, and Owen went after Buffaloes over the hills, saw
none, so that all this day has been disappointment to us.
Owen caught a *Spermophilus hoodii.*   The brother of
the dead Indian, who gashed his legs fearfully this morning,
went off with his wife and children and six others, who had
come here to beg.   One of them had for *a letter of recommendation* one of the advertisements of the steamer
"Trapper," which will be kept by his chief for time imme-
morial to serve as a pass for begging.   He received from
us ammunition and tobacco.   Sprague collected seeds this
morning, and this afternoon copied my sketch of the three
Mamelles.   Towards sunset I intend to go myself after
Rabbits, along the margins of the bushes and the shore.

We have returned from my search after Rabbits; Harris and I each shot one. We saw five Wild Geese. Harris lost his snuff-box, which he valued, and which I fear will never be found. Squires to-day proposed to me to let him remain here this winter to procure birds and quadrupeds, and I would have said "yes" at once, did he understand either or both these subjects, or could draw; but as he does not, it would be useless.

August 1, Tuesday. The weather fine, and warmer than yesterday. We sent off four Indians after Rabbits, but as we foolishly gave them powder and shot, they returned without any very soon, having, of course, hidden the ammunition. After breakfast Mr. C. had a horse put in the cart, and three squaws went off after "pommes blanches," and Sprague and I followed in the wagon, driven by Owen. These women carried sticks pointed at one end, and blunt at the other, and I was perfectly astonished at the dexterity and rapidity with which they worked. They place the pointed end within six inches of the plant, where the stem enters the earth, and bear down upon the other end with all their weight and move about to the right and left of the plant until the point of the stick is thrust in the ground to the depth of about seven inches, when acting upon it in the manner of a lever, the plant is fairly thrown out, and the root procured. Sprague and I, who had taken with us an instrument resembling a very narrow hoe, and a spade, having rather despised the simple instruments of the squaws, soon found out that these damsels could dig six or seven, and in some cases a dozen, to our *one*. We collected some seeds of these plants as well as those of some others, and walked fully six miles, which has rendered my feet quite tender again. Owen told me that he had seen, on his late journey up the Yellowstone, Grouse, both old and young, with a black breast and with a broad tail; they were usually near the margin of a wood. What they are I cannot tell, but he and Bell

are going after them to-morrow morning. Just after dinner
Provost and La Fleur returned with two male Antelopes,
skinned, one of them a remarkably large buck, the other
less in size, both skins in capital order. We have taken
the measurements of the head of the larger. The timber
for our boat has been hauling across the sand-bar ever
since daylight, and of course the work will proceed pretty
fast. The weather is delightful, and at night, indeed, quite
cool enough. I spoke to Sprague last night about remaining here next winter, as he had mentioned his wish to do
so to Bell some time ago, but he was very undecided.
My regrets that I promised you all so faithfully that I
would return this fall are beyond description. I am, as
years go, an old man, but I do not feel old, and there is
so much of interest here that I forget oftentimes that I am
not as young as Owen.

August 2, Wednesday. Bell and Owen started on their
tour up the Yellowstone[1] after Cocks of the Plain [Sage
Grouse, *Centrocercus urophasianus*]. Provost and Moncrévier went in the timber below after Deer, but saw none.
We had an arrival of six Chippeway Indians, and afterwards
about a dozen Assiniboins. Both these parties were better
dressed, and looked better off than any previous groups that
we have seen at this fort. They brought some few robes to
barter, and the traffic was carried on by Mr. Larpenteur in
his little shop, through a wicket. On the arrival of the
Assiniboins, who were headed by an old man, one of the
Chippeways discovered a horse, which he at once not only
claimed, but tied; he threw down his new blanket on the
ground, and was leading off the horse, when the other Indian
caught hold of it, and said that he had fairly bought it, etc.
The Chippeway now gave him his gun, powder, and ball, as
well as his *looking-glass*, the most prized of all his posses-
sions, and the Assiniboin, now apparently satisfied, gave
up the horse, which was led away by the new (or old)

[1] See Bell's account of the trip, page 176.

owner. We thought the matter was ended, but Mr. Culbertson told us that either the horse or the Chippeway would be caught and brought back. The latter had mounted a fine horse which he had brought with him, and was leading the other away, when presently a gun was heard out of the fort, and Mr. C. ran to tell us that the horse of the Chippeway had been shot, and that the rider was running as fast as he could to Fort Mortimer. Upon going out we found the horse standing still, and the man running; we went to the poor animal, and found that the ball had passed through the thigh, and entered the belly. The poor horse was trembling like an aspen; he at last moved, walked about, and went to the river, where he died. Now it is curious that it was not the same Assiniboin who had sold the horse that had shot, but another of their party; and we understand that it was on account of an old grudge against the Chippeway, who, by the way, was a surly-looking rascal. The Assiniboins brought eight or ten horses and colts, and a number of dogs. One of the colts had a necklace of " pommes blanches," at the end of which hung a handful of Buffalo calves' hoofs, not more than ¾ inch long, and taken from the calves before birth, when the mothers had been killed. Harris and I took a ride in the wagon over the Mauvaises Terres above the fort, in search of petrified wood, but though we found many specimens, they were of such indifferent quality that we brought home but one. On returning we followed a Wolf path, of which there are hundreds through the surrounding hills, all leading to the fort. It is curious to see how well they understand the best and shortest roads. From what had happened, we anticipated a row among the Indians, but all seemed quiet. Mr. C. gave us a good account of Fort McKenzie. I have been examining the fawn of the Long-tailed Deer of this country, belonging to old Baptiste; the man feeds it regularly, and the fawn follows him everywhere. It will race backwards and forwards over the prairie back of the fort, for a mile or more, running at the very top of its speed; suddenly it will make for the gate, rush through and overwhelm Baptiste with caresses, as if it had actually lost him for some time. If Baptiste lies on the ground pretending to sleep, the fawn pushes with its nose, and licks his face as a dog would, till he awakens.

August 3, Thursday. We observed yesterday that the atmosphere was thick, and indicated the first appearance of the close of summer, which here is brief. The nights and mornings have already become cool, and summer clothes will not be needed much longer, except occasionally. Harris and Sprague went to the hills so much encrusted with shells. We have had some talk about going to meet Bell and Owen, but the distance is too great, and Mr. C. told me he was not acquainted with the road beyond the first twenty-five or thirty miles. We have had a slight shower, and Mr. C. and I walked across the bar to see the progress of the boat. The horse that died near the river was hauled across to the sand-bar, and will make good cat-fish bate for our fishers. This morning we had another visitation of Indians, seven in number; they were very dirty, wrapped in disgusting Buffalo robes, and were not allowed inside the inner gate, on account of their filthy condition.

August 4, Friday. We were all under way this morning at half-past five, on a Buffalo hunt, that is to say, the residue of *us*, Harris and I, for Bell was away with Owen, and Squires with Provost after Bighorns, and Sprague at Fort Mortimer. Tobacco and matches had been forgotten, and that detained us for half an hour; but at last we started in good order, with only one cart following us, which carried Pike and Moncrévier. We saw, after we had travelled ten miles, some Buffalo bulls; some alone, others in groups of four or five, a few Antelopes, but more shy than ever before. I was surprised to see how careless the bulls were of us, as some actually gave us chances to approach them within a hundred yards, looking steadfastly, as if not caring a bit for us. At last we saw one lying down immediately in our road, and determined to give him a chance for his life. Mr. C. had a white horse, a runaway, in which he placed a good deal of confidence; he mounted it, and we looked after him. The bull did not start till Mr. C. was within a hundred yards, and then at a gentle and slow gallop. The horse galloped too, but only at the same rate. Mr. C. thrashed him until his hands were sore, for he had no whip, the bull went off without even a shot being fired, and the horse is now looked upon as forever disgraced. About two miles farther another bull was observed lying down in our way, and it was concluded to run him with the white horse, accompanied, however, by Harris. The chase took place, and the bull was killed by Harris, but the white horse is now scorned by every one. A few pieces of meat, the tongue, tail, and head, were all that was taken from this very large bull. We soon saw that the weather was becoming cloudy, and we were anxious to reach a camping-place; but we continued to cross ranges of hills, and hoped to see a large herd of Buffaloes. The weather was hot " out of mind," and we continued till, reaching a fine hill, we saw in a beautiful valley below us seventy to eighty head, feeding peacefully in groups and singly, as might happen. The bulls were mixed in with the cows, and we saw one or two calves. Many bulls were at various distances from the main group, but as we advanced towards them they galloped off and joined the others. When the chase began it was curious to see how much swifter the cows were than the bulls, and how soon they divided themselves into parties of seven or eight, exerting themselves to escape from their murderous pursuers. All in vain, however; off went the guns and down went the cows, or stood bleeding through the nose, mouth, or bullet holes. Mr. C. killed three, and Harris one in about half an hour. We had quite enough, and the slaughter was ended. We had driven up to the nearest fallen cow, and approached close to her, and found that she was not dead, but trying to rise to her feet. I cannot bear to see an animal suffer unnecessarily, so begged one of the men to take my knife and stab her to the heart, which was done. The animals were cut up and skinned, with considerable fatigue. To skin bulls and cows and cut up their bodies is no joke, even to such as are constantly in the habit of doing it. Whilst Mr. Culbertson and the rest had gone to cut up another at some distance, I remained on guard to save the meat from the Wolves, but none came before my companions returned. We found the last cow quite dead. As we were busy about her the rain fell in torrents, and I found my blanket *capote* of great service. It was now nearly sundown, and we made up our minds to camp close by, although there was no water for our horses, neither any wood. Harris and I began collecting Buffalo-dung from all around, whilst the others attended to various other affairs. The meat was all unloaded and spread on the ground, the horses made fast, the fire burned freely, pieces of liver were soon cooked and devoured, coffee drunk in abundance, and we went to rest.

August 5, Saturday. It rained in the night; but this morning the weather was cool, wind at northwest, and cloudy, but not menacing rain. We made through the road we had come yesterday, and on our way Harris shot a young of the Swift Fox, which we could have caught alive had we not been afraid of running into some hole. We saw only a few bulls and Antelopes, and some Wolves. The white horse, which had gone out as a *hunter*, returned as a *pack-horse*, loaded with the entire flesh of a Buffalo cow; and our two mules drew three more and the heads of all four. This morning at daylight, when we were called to drink our coffee, there was a Buffalo feeding within twenty steps of our tent, and it moved slowly towards the hills as we busied ourselves making preparations for our departure. We reached the fort at noon; Squires, Provost, and La Fleur had returned; they had wounded a Bighorn, but had lost it. Owen and Bell returned this afternoon; they had seen no Cocks of the plains, but brought the skin of a female Elk, a Porcupine, and a young White-headed Eagle. Provost tells me that Buffaloes become so very poor during hard winters, when the snows cover the ground to the depth of two or three feet, that they lose their hair, become covered with scabs, on which the Magpies feed, and the poor beasts die by hundreds. One can hardly conceive how it happens, notwithstanding these many deaths and the immense numbers that are murdered almost daily on these boundless wastes called prairies, besides the hosts that are drowned in the freshets, and the hundreds of young calves who die in early spring, so many are yet to be found. Daily we see so many that we hardly notice them more than the cattle in our pastures about our homes. But this cannot last; even now there is a perceptible difference in the size of the herds, and before many years the Buffalo, like the Great Auk, will have disappeared; surely this should not be permitted. Bell has been relating his adventures, our boat is going on, and I wish I had a couple of Bighorns. God bless you all.

August 6, Sunday. I very nearly lost the skin of the Swift Fox, for Harris supposed the animal rotten with the great heat, which caused it to have an odor almost insupportable, and threw it on the roof of the gallery. Bell was so tired he did not look at it, so I took it down, skinned it, and with the assistance of Squires put the coat into pickle, where I daresay it will keep well enough. The weather is thick, and looks like a thunderstorm. Bell, having awaked refreshed by his night's rest, has given me the measurements of the Elk and the Porcupine. Provost has put the skin of the former in pickle, and has gone to Fort Mortimer to see Boucherville and others, to try if they

would go after Bighorn to-morrow morning. This afternoon we had an arrival of Indians, the same who were here
about two weeks ago. They had been to Fort Clark, and
report that a battle had taken place between the Crees and
Gros Ventres, and that the latter had lost. Antelopes
often die from the severity of the winter weather, and are
found dead and shockingly poor, even in the immediate
vicinity of the forts. These animals are caught in pens
in the manner of Buffaloes, and are despatched with clubs,
principally by the squaws. In 1840, during the winter,
and when the snow was deep on the prairies and in the
ravines by having drifted there, Mr. Laidlow, then at Fort
Union, caught four Antelopes by following them on horseback and forcing them into these drifts, which were in
places ten or twelve feet deep. They were brought home
on a sleigh, and let loose about the rooms. They were so
very gentle that they permitted the children to handle
them, although being loose they could have kept from
them. They were removed to the carpenter's shop, and
there one broke its neck by leaping over a turning-lathe.
The others were all killed in some such way, for they became very wild, and jumped, kicked, etc., till all were dead.
Very young Buffaloes have been caught in the same way,
by the same gentleman, assisted by Le Brun and four
Indians, and thirteen of these he took down the river,
when they became somewhat tamed. The Antelopes cannot be tamed except when caught young, and then they
can rarely be raised. Mr. Wm. Sublette, of St. Louis, had
one however, a female, which grew to maturity, and was
so gentle that it would go all over his house, mounting
and descending steps, and even going on the roof of the
house. It was alive when I first reached St. Louis, but I
was not aware of it, and before I left, it was killed by an
Elk belonging to the same gentleman. Provost returned,
and said that Boucherville would go with him and La Fleur
to-morrow morning early, *but I doubt it.*

August 7, Monday. Provost, Bell, and La Fleur started after breakfast, having waited nearly four hours for Boucherville. They left at seven, and the Indians were curious to know where they were bound, and looked at them with more interest than we all liked. At about nine, we saw Boucherville, accompanied by five men, all mounted, and they were surprised that Provost had not waited for them, or rather that he had left so early. I gave them a bottle of whiskey, and they started under the whip, and must have overtaken the first party in about two hours. To-day has been warmer than any day we have had for two weeks. Sprague has been collecting seeds, and Harris and I searching for stones with impressions of leaves and fern; we found several. Mr. Denig says the Assiniboins killed a Black Bear on White Earth River, about sixty miles from the mouth; they are occasionally killed there, but it is a rare occurrence. Mr. Denig saw the skin of a Bear at their camp last winter, and a Raccoon was also killed on the Cheyenne River by the Sioux, who knew not what to make of it. Mr. Culbertson has given me the following account of a skirmish which took place at Fort McKenzie in the Blackfoot country, which I copy from his manuscript.

"*August 28, 1834.* At the break of day we were aroused from our beds by the report of an enemy being in sight. This unexpected news created naturally a confusion among us all; never was a set of unfortunate beings so surprised as we were. By the time that the alarm had spread through the fort, we were surrounded by the enemy, who proved to be Assiniboins, headed by the chief Gauché (the Antelope). The number, as near as we could judge, was about four hundred. Their first attack was upon a few lodges of Piegans, who were encamped at the fort. They also, being taken by surprise, could not escape. We exerted ourselves, however, to save as many as we could, by getting them into the fort. But the foolish

squaws, when they started from their lodges, each took a
load of old saddles and skins, which they threw in the
door, and stopped it so completely that they could not get
in, and here the enemy massacred several. In the mean
time our men were firing with muskets and shot-guns.
Unfortunately for us, we could not use our cannon, as
there were a great many Piegans standing between us and
the enemy; this prevented us from firing a telling shot on
them at once. The engagement continued nearly an hour,
when the enemy, finding their men drop very fast, retreated
to the bluffs, half a mile distant; there they stood making
signs for us to come on, and give them an equal chance on
the prairie. Although our force was much weaker than
theirs, we determined to give them a trial. At the same
time we despatched an expert runner to an encampment
of Piegans for a reinforcement. We mounted our horses,
and proceeded to the field of battle, which was a perfect
level, where there was no chance to get behind a tree, or
anything else, to keep off a ball. We commenced our fire
at two hundred yards, but soon lessened the distance to
one hundred. Here we kept up a constant fire for two
hours, when, our horses getting fatigued, we concluded to
await the arrival of our reinforcements. As yet none of
us were killed or badly wounded, and nothing lost but one
horse, which was shot under one of our men named Bour-
bon. Of the enemy we cannot tell how many were killed,
for as fast as they fell they were carried off the field.
After the arrival of our reinforcements, which consisted
of one hundred and fifty mounted Piegans, we charged and
fought again for another two hours, and drove them across
the Maria River, where they took another stand; and here
Mr. Mitchell's horse was shot under him and he was
wounded. In this engagement the enemy had a decided
advantage over us, as they were concealed in the bushes,
while we were in the open prairie. However, we succeeded
in making them retreat from this place back on to a high

prairie, but they suddenly rushed upon us and compelled us to retreat across the Maria. Then they had us in their power; but for some reason, either lack of courage or knowledge, they did not avail themselves of their opportunity. They could have killed a great many of us when we rushed into the water, which was almost deep enough to swim our horses; they were close upon us, but we succeeded in crossing before they fired. This foolish move came near being attended with fatal consequences, which we were aware of, but our efforts to stop it were unsuccessful. We, however, did not retreat far before we turned upon them again, with the determination of driving them to the mountains, in which we succeeded. By this time it was so dark that we could see no more, and we concluded to return. During the day we lost seven killed, and twenty wounded. Two of our dead the enemy had scalped. It is impossible to tell how many of the enemy were killed, but their loss must have been much greater than ours, as they had little ammunition, and at the last none. Our Indians took two bodies and burned them, after scalping them. The Indians who were with us in this skirmish deserve but little credit for their bravery, for in every close engagement the whites, who were comparatively few, always were in advance of them. This, however, had one good effect, for it removed the idea they had of our being cowards, and made them believe we were unusually brave. Had it not been for the assistance we gave the Piegans they would have been cut off, for I never saw Indians behave more bravely than the enemy this day; and had they been well supplied with powder and ball they would have done much more execution. But necessity compelled them to spare their ammunition, as they had come a long way, and they must save enough to enable them to return home. And on our side had we been positive they were enemies, even after they had surprised us in the manner they did, we could have killed many of them at first, but thinking that they were a band of Indians coming with this ceremony to trade (which is not uncommon) we did not fire upon them till the balls and arrows came whistling about our heads; then only was the word given, ' Fire ! ' Had they been bold enough at the onset to have rushed into the fort, we could have done nothing but suffer death under their tomahawks."

Mr. Denig gave me the following " Bear Story," as he heard it from the parties concerned : " In the year 1835 two men set out from a trading-post at the head of the Cheyenne, and in the neighborhood of the Black Hills, to trap Beaver ; their names were Michel Carrière and Bernard Le Brun. Carrière was a man about seventy years old, and had passed most of his life in the Indian country, in this dangerous occupation of trapping. One evening as they were setting their traps along the banks of a stream tributary to the Cheyenne, somewhat wooded by bushes and cottonwood trees, their ears were suddenly saluted by a growl, and in a moment a large she Bear rushed upon them. Le Brun, being a young and active man, immediately picked up his gun, and shot the Bear through the bowels. Carrière also fired, but missed. The Bear then pursued them, but as they ran for their lives, their legs did them good service ; they escaped through the bushes, and the Bear lost sight of them. They had concluded the Bear had given up the chase, and were again engaged in setting their traps, when Carrière, who was a short distance from Le Brun, went through a small thicket with a trap and came directly in front of the huge, wounded beast, which, with one spring, bounded upon him and tore him in an awful manner. With one stroke of the paw on his face and forehead he cut his nose in two, and one of the claws reached inward nearly to the brain at the root of the nose ; the same stroke tore out his right eye and most of the flesh from that side of his face. His arm and side were *literally torn to pieces*, and the Bear, after handling him in this gentle manner for two or three minutes, threw him upwards about six feet, when he lodged, to all appearance dead, in the fork of a tree. Le Brun, hearing the noise, ran to his assistance, and again shot the Bear and killed it. He then brought what he at first thought was the dead body of his friend to the ground. Little appearance of a human being was left to the poor man, but Le Brun found life was not wholly extinct. He made a *travaille* and carried him by short stages to the nearest trading-post, where the wounded man slowly recovered, but was, of course, the most mutilated-looking being imaginable. Carrière, in telling the story, says that he fully believes it to have been the Holy Virgin that lifted him up and placed him in the fork of the tree, and thus preserved his life. The Bear is stated to have been as large as a common ox, and must have weighed, therefore, not far from 1500 lbs." Mr. Denig adds that he saw the man about a year after the accident, and some of the wounds were, even then, not healed. Carrière fully recovered, however, lived a few years, and was killed by the Blackfeet near Fort Union.

When Bell was fixing his traps on his horse this morning, I was amused to see Provost and La Fleur laughing outright at him, as he first put on a Buffalo robe under his saddle, a blanket over it, and over that his mosquito bar and his rain protector. These old hunters could not understand why he needed all these things to be comfortable; then, besides, he took a sack of ship-biscuit. Provost took only an old blanket, a few pounds of dried meat, and his tin cup, and rode off in his shirt and dirty breeches. La Fleur was worse off still, for he took no blanket, and said he could borrow Provost's tin cup; but he, being a most temperate man, carried the bottle of whiskey to mix with the brackish water found in the Mauvaises Terres, among which they have to travel till their return. Harris and I contemplated going to a quarry from which the stones of the powder magazine were brought, but it

became too late for us to start in time to see much, and
the wrong horses were brought us, being both *runners;* we
went, however, across the river after Rabbits.   Harris
killed a Red-cheeked Woodpecker and shot at a Rabbit,
which he missed.   We had a sort of show by Moncrévier
which was funny, and well performed; he has much versa-
tility, great powers of mimicry, and is a far better actor than
many who have made names for themselves in that line.
Jean Baptiste told me the following: "About twelve years
ago when Mr. McKenzie was the superintendent of this
fort, at the season when green peas were plenty and good,
Baptiste was sent to the garden about half a mile off, to
gather a quantity.   He was occupied doing this, when, at
the end of a row, to his astonishment, he saw a very large
Bear gathering peas also.   Baptiste dropped his tin bucket,
ran back to the fort as fast as possible, and told Mr.
McKenzie, who immediately summoned several other men
with guns; they mounted their horses, rode off, and killed
the Bear; but, alas! Mr. Bruin had emptied the bucket of
peas."

August 8, Tuesday.   Another sultry day.   Immediately
after breakfast Mr. Larpenteur drove Harris and myself in
search of geological specimens, but we found none worth
having.   We killed a *Spermophilus hoodii*, which, although
fatally wounded, entered its hole, and Harris had to draw
it out by the hind legs.   We saw a family of Rock Wrens,
and killed four of them.   I killed two at one shot; one of
the others must have gone in a hole, for though we saw it
fall we could not find it.   Another, after being shot, found
its way under a flat stone, and was there picked up, quite
dead, Mr. Larpenteur accidentally turning the stone up.
We saw signs of Antelopes and of Hares (Townsend), and
rolled a large rock from the top of a high hill.   The notes
of the Rock Wren are a prolonged cree-è-è-è.   On our
return home we heard that Boucherville and his five hunters
had returned with nothing for me, and they had not met

Bell and his companions. We were told also that a few minutes after our departure the roarings and bellowings of Buffalo were heard across the river, and that Owen and two men had been despatched with a cart to kill three fat cows but *no more;* so my remonstrances about useless slaughter have not been wholly unheeded. Harris was sorry he had missed going, and so was I, as both of us could have done so. The milk of the Buffalo cow is truly good and finely tasted, but the bag is never large as in our common cattle, and this is probably a provision of nature to render the cows more capable to run off, and escape from their pursuers. Bell, Provost, and La Fleur returned just before dinner; they had seen no Bighorns, and only brought the flesh of two Deer killed by La Fleur, and a young Magpie. This afternoon Provost skinned a calf that was found by one of the cows that Owen killed; it was *very* young, only a few hours old, but large, and I have taken its measurements. It is looked upon as a phenomenon, as no Buffalo cow calves at this season. The calving time is from about the 1st of February to the last of May. Owen went six miles from the fort before he saw the cattle; there were more than three hundred in number, and Harris and I regretted the more we had not gone, but had been fruitlessly hunting for stones. It is curious that while Harris was searching for Rabbits early this morning, he heard the bellowing of the bulls, and thought first it was the growling of a Grizzly Bear, and then that it was the fort bulls, so he mentioned it to no one. To-morrow evening La Fleur and two men will go after Bighorns again, and they are not to return before they have killed one male, at least. This evening we went a-fishing across the river, and caught ten good catfish of the upper Missouri species, the sweetest and best fish of the sort that I have eaten in any part of the country. Our boat is going on well, and looks pretty to boot. Her name will be the " Union," in consequence of the united exertions of my companions to do all that could be done, on this costly expedition. The young Buffaloes now about the fort have begun shedding their red coats, the latter-colored hair dropping off in patches about the size of the palm of my hand, and the new hair is dark brownish black.

August 9, Wednesday. The weather is cool and we are looking for rain. Squires, Provost, and La Fleur went off this morning after an early breakfast, across the river for Bighorns with orders not to return without some of these wild animals, which reside in the most inaccessible portions of the broken and lofty clay hills and stones that exist in this region of the country; they never resort to the low lands except when moving from one spot to another; they swim rivers well, as do Antelopes. I have scarcely done anything but write this day, and my memorandum books are now crowded with sketches, measurements, and descriptions. We have nine Indians, all Assiniboins, among whom *five* are chiefs. These nine Indians fed for three days on the flesh of only a single Swan; they saw no Buffaloes, though they report large herds about their village, fully two hundred miles from here. This evening I caught about one dozen catfish, and shot a *Spermophilus hoodii,* an old female, which had her pouches distended and filled with the seeds of the wild sunflower of this region. I am going to follow one of their holes and describe the same.

August 10, Thursday. Bell and I took a walk after Rabbits, but saw none. The nine Indians, having received their presents, went off with apparent reluctance, for when you begin to give them, the more they seem to demand. The horseguards brought in another *Spermophilus hoodii;* after dinner we are going to examine one of their burrows. We have been, and have returned; the three burrows which we dug were as follows: straight downward for three or four inches, and gradually becoming deeper in an oblique slant, to the depth of eight or nine inches, but not more, and none of these holes extended more than six or seven feet beyond this. I was disappointed at not finding nests, or rooms for stores. Although I have said much about Buffalo running, and butchering in general, I have not given the particular manner in which the latter is performed by the hunters of this country, — I mean the white hunters, — and I will now try to do so. The moment that the Buffalo is dead, three or four hunters, their faces and hands often covered with gunpowder, and with pipes lighted, place the animal on its belly, and by drawing out each fore and hind leg, fix the body so that it cannot fall down again; an incision is made near the root of the tail, immediately above the root in fact, and the skin cut to the neck, and taken off in the roughest manner imaginable, downwards and on both sides at the same time. The knives are going in all directions, and many wounds occur to the hands and fingers, but are rarely attended to at this time. The pipe of one man has perhaps given out, and with his bloody hands he takes the one of his nearest companion, who has his own hands equally bloody. Now one breaks in the skull of the bull, and with bloody fingers draws out the hot brains and swallows them with peculiar zest; another has now reached the liver, and is gobbling down enormous pieces of it; whilst, perhaps, a third, who has come to the paunch, is feeding luxuriously on some — to me — disgusting-looking offal. But the main business proceeds. The flesh is taken off from the sides of the boss, or hump bones, from where these bones begin to the very neck, and the hump itself is thus destroyed. The hunters give the name of "hump" to the mere bones when slightly covered by flesh; and it is cooked, and very good when fat, young, and well broiled. The pieces of flesh taken from the sides of these bones are called *filets*, and are the best portion of the animal when properly cooked. The forequarters, or shoulders, are taken off, as well as the hind ones, and the sides, covered by a thin portion of flesh called the *depouille*, are taken out. Then the ribs are broken off at the vertebræ, as well as the boss bones. The marrow-bones, which are those of the fore and hind legs only, are cut out last. The feet usually remain attached to these; the paunch is stripped of its covering of layers of fat, the head and the backbone are left to the Wolves, the pipes are all emptied, the hands, faces, and clothes all bloody, and now a glass of grog is often enjoyed, as the stripping off the skins and flesh of three or four animals is truly very hard work. In some cases when no water was near, our supper was cooked without our being washed, and it was not until we had travelled several miles the next morning that we had any opportunity of cleaning ourselves; and yet, despite everything, we are all hungry, eat heartily, and sleep soundly. When the wind is high and the Buffaloes run towards it, the hunter's guns very often snap, and it is during their exertions to replenish their pans, that the powder flies and sticks to the moisture every moment accumulating on their faces; but nothing stops these daring and usually powerful men, who the moment the chase is ended, leap from their horses, let them graze, and begin their butcher-like work.

August 11, Friday. The weather has been cold and windy, and the day has passed in comparative idleness with me. Squires returned this afternoon alone, having left Provost and La Fleur behind. They have seen only two Bighorns, a female and her young. It was concluded that, if our boat was finished by Tuesday next, we would leave on Wednesday morning, but I am by no means assured of this, and Harris was quite startled at the very idea. Our boat, though forty feet long, is, I fear, too small. *Nous verrons!* Some few preparations for packing have been made, but Owen, Harris, and Bell are going out early to-morrow morning to hunt Buffaloes, and when they return we will talk matters over. The activity of Buffaloes is almost beyond belief; they can climb the steep defiles of the Mauvaises Terres in hundreds of places where men cannot follow them, and it is a fine sight to see a large gang of them proceeding along these defiles four or five hundred feet above the level of the bottoms, and from which pathway if one of the number makes a mis-step or accidentally slips, he goes down rolling over and over, and breaks his neck ere the level ground is reached. Bell and Owen saw a bull about three years old that leaped a ravine filled with mud and water, at least twenty feet wide; it reached the middle at the first bound, and at the second was mounted on the opposite bank, from which it kept on bounding, till it gained the top of quite a high hill. Mr. Culbertson tells me that these animals can endure hunger in a most extraordinary manner. He says that a large bull was seen on a spot half way down a precipice, where it had slid, and from which it could not climb upwards, and either could not or would not descend; at any rate, it did not leave the position in which it found itself. The party who saw it returned to the fort, and, on their way back on the *twenty-fifth* day after, they passed the hill, and saw the bull standing there. The thing that troubles them most is crossing rivers on the ice; their hoofs slip from side to side, they become frightened, and stretch their four legs apart to support the body, and in such situations the Indians and white hunters easily approach, and stab them to the heart, or cut the hamstrings, when they become an easy prey. When in large gangs those in the centre are supported by those on the outposts, and if the stream is not large, reach the shore and readily escape. Indians of different tribes hunt the Buffalo in different ways; some hunt on horseback, and use arrows altogether; they are rarely expert in reloading the gun in the close race. Others hunt on foot, using guns, arrows, or both. Others follow with patient perseverance, and kill them also. But I will give you the manner pursued by the

Mandans. Twenty to fifty men start, as the occasion suits, each provided with two horses, one of which is a pack-horse, the other fit for the chase. They have quivers with from twenty to fifty arrows, according to the wealth of the hunter. They ride the pack horse bareback, and travel on, till they see the game, when they leave the pack-horse, and leap on the hunter, and start at full speed and soon find themselves amid the Buffaloes, on the flanks of the herd, and on both sides. When within a few yards the arrow is sent, they shoot at a Buffalo somewhat ahead of them, and send the arrow in an oblique manner, so as to pass through the lights. If the blood rushes out of the nose and mouth the animal is fatally wounded, and they shoot at it no more; if not, a second, and perhaps a third arrow, is sent before this happens. The Buffaloes on starting carry the tail close in between the legs, but when wounded they switch it about, especially if they wish to fight, and then the hunter's horse shies off and lets the mad animal breathe awhile. If shot through the heart, they occasionally fall dead on the instant; sometimes, if not hit in the right place, a dozen arrows will not stop them. When wounded and mad they turn suddenly round upon the hunter, and rush upon him in such a quick and furious manner that if horse and rider are not both on the alert, the former is overtaken, hooked and overthrown, the hunter pitched off, trampled and gored to death. Although the Buffalo is such a large animal, and to all appearance a clumsy one, it can turn with the quickness of thought, and when once enraged, will rarely give up the chase until avenged for the wound it has received. If, however, the hunter is expert, and the horse fleet, they outrun the bull, and it returns to the herd. Usually the greater number of the gang is killed, but it very rarely happens that some of them do not escape. This however is not the case when the animal is pounded, especially by the Gros Ventres, Black

Feet, and Assiniboins. These pounds are called "parks," and the Buffaloes are made to enter them in the following manner: The park is sometimes round and sometimes square, this depending much on the ground where it is put up; at the end of the park is what is called a *precipice* of some fifteen feet or less, as may be found. It is approached by a funnel-shaped passage, which like the park itself is strongly built of logs, brushwood, and pickets, and when all is ready a young man, very swift of foot, starts at daylight covered over with a Buffalo robe and wearing a Buffalo head-dress. The moment he sees the herd to be taken, he bellows like a young calf, and makes his way slowly towards the contracted part of the funnel, imitating the cry of the calf, at frequent intervals. The Buffaloes advance after the decoy; about a dozen mounted hunters are yelling and galloping behind them, and along both flanks of the herd, forcing them by these means to enter the mouth of the funnel. Women and children are placed behind the fences of the funnel to frighten the cattle, and as soon as the young man who acts as decoy feels assured that the game is in a fair way to follow to the bank or "precipice," he runs or leaps down the bank, over the barricade, and either rests, or joins in the fray. The poor Buffaloes, usually headed by a large bull, proceed, leap down the bank in haste and confusion, the Indians all yelling and pursuing till every bull, cow, and calf is impounded. Although this is done at all seasons, it is more general in October or November, when the hides are good and salable. Now the warriors are all assembled by the pen, calumets are lighted, and the chief smokes to the Great Spirit, the four points of the compass, and lastly to the Buffaloes. The pipe is passed from mouth to mouth in succession, and as soon as this ceremony is ended, the destruction commences. Guns shoot, arrows fly in all directions, and the hunters being on the outside of the enclosure, destroy the whole gang, before they jump over to clean and skin the murdered herd. Even the children shoot small, short arrows to assist in the destruction. It happens sometimes however, that the leader of the herd will be restless at the sight of the precipices, and if the fence is weak will break through it, and all his fellows follow him, and escape. The same thing sometimes takes place in the pen, for so full does this become occasionally that the animals touch each other, and as they cannot move, the very weight against the fence of the pen is quite enough to break it through; the smallest aperture is sufficient, for in a few minutes it becomes wide, and all the beasts are seen scampering over the prairies, leaving the poor Indians starving and discomfited. Mr. Kipp told me that while travelling from Lake Travers to the Mandans, in the month of August, he rode in a heavily laden cart for six successive days through masses of Buffaloes, which divided for the cart, allowing it to pass without opposition. He has seen the immense prairie back of Fort Clark look black to the tops of the hills, though the ground was covered with snow, so crowded was it with these animals; and the masses probably extended much further. In fact it is *impossible to describe or even conceive* the vast multitudes of these animals that exist even now, and feed on these ocean-like prairies.

August 12, Saturday. Harris, Bell, and Owen went after Buffaloes; killed six cows and brought them home. Weather cloudy, and rainy at times. Provost returned with La Fleur this afternoon, had nothing, but had seen a Grizzly Bear. The "Union" was launched this evening and packing, etc., is going on. I gave a memorandum to Jean Baptiste Moncrévier of the animals I wish him to procure for me.

August 13, Sunday. A most beautiful day. About dinner time I had a young Badger brought to me dead; I bought it, and gave in payment two pounds of sugar. The body of these animals is broader than high, the neck is powerfully strong, as well as the fore-arms, and strongly clawed fore-feet. It weighed 8½ lbs. Its measurements were all taken. When the pursuer gets between a Badger and its hole, the animal's hair rises, and it at once shows fight. A half-breed hunter told Provost, who has just returned from Fort Mortimer, that he was anxious to go down the river with me, but I know the man and hardly care to have him. If I decide to take him Mr. Culbertson, to whom I spoke of the matter, told me my only plan was to pay him by the piece for what he killed and brought on board, and that in case he did not turn out well between this place and Fort Clark, to leave him there; so I have sent word to him to this effect by Provost this afternoon. Bell is skinning the Badger, Sprague finishing the map of the river made by Squires, and the latter is writing. The half-breed has been here, and the following is our agreement: "It is understood that François Détaillé will go with me, John J. Audubon, and to secure for me the following quadrupeds — if possible — for which he will receive the prices here mentioned, payable at Fort Union, Fort Clark, or Fort Pierre, as may best suit him.

For each Bighorn male $10.00
For a large Grizzly Bear 20.00
For a large male Elk 6.00
For a Black-tailed Deer, male or female . . . 6.00
For Red Foxes 3.00
For small Gray Foxes 3.00
For Badgers 2.00
For large Porcupine 2.00

Independent of which I agree to furnish him with his passage and food, he to work as a hand on board. Whatever he kills for food will be settled when he leaves us, or, as he says, when he meets the Opposition boat coming up to Fort Mortimer." He will also accompany us in our hunt after Bighorns, which I shall undertake, notwithstanding Mr. Culbertson and Squires, who have been to the Mauvaises Terres, both try to dissuade me from what they fear will prove over-fatiguing; but though my strength is not what it was twenty years ago, I am yet equal to much, and my eyesight far keener than that of many a younger man, though that too tells me I am no longer a youth. . . .

The only idea I can give in *writing* of what are called the "Mauvaises Terres" would be to place some thousands of loaves of sugar of different sizes, from quite small and low, to large and high, all irregularly truncated at top, and placed somewhat apart from each other. No one who has not seen these places can form any idea of these resorts of the Rocky Mountain Rams, or the difficulty of approaching them, putting aside their extreme wildness and their marvellous activity. They form paths around these broken-headed cones (that are from three to fifteen hundred feet high), and run round them at full speed on a track that, to the eye of the hunter, does not appear to be more than a few inches wide, but which is, in fact, from a foot to eighteen inches in width. In some places there are piles of earth from eight to ten feet high, or even more, the tops of which form platforms of a hard and shelly rocky substance, where the Bighorn is often seen looking on the hunter far below, and standing immovable, as if a statue. No one can imagine how they reach these places, and that too with their young, even when the latter are quite small. Hunters say that the young are usually born in such places, the mothers going there to save the helpless little one from the Wolves, which, after men, seem to be their greatest destroyers. The Mauvaises Terres are mostly formed of grayish white clay, very sparsely covered with small patches of thin grass, on which the Bighorns feed, but which, to all appearance, is a very scanty supply, and there, and there only, they feed, as not one has ever been seen on the bottom or prairie land further than the foot of these most extraordinary hills. In wet weather, no man can climb any of them, and at such times they are greasy, muddy, sliding grounds. Oftentimes when a Bighorn is seen on a hill-top, the hunter has to ramble about for three or four miles before he can approach within gun-shot of the game, and if the Bighorn ever sees his enemy, pursuit is useless. The tops of some of these hills, and in some cases whole hills about thirty feet high, are composed of a conglomerated mass of stones, sand, and clay, with earth of various sorts, fused together, and having a brick-like appearance. In this mass pumice-stone of various shapes and sizes is to be found. The whole is evidently the effect of volcanic action. The bases of some of these hills cover an area of twenty acres or more, and the hills rise to the height of three or four hundred feet, sometimes even to eight hundred or a thousand; so high can the hunter ascend that the surrounding country is far, far beneath him. The strata are of different colored clays, coal, etc., and an earth impregnated with a salt which appears to have been formed by internal fire or heat, the earth or stones of which I have first spoken in this account, lava, sulphur, salts of various kinds, oxides and sulphates of iron; and in the sand at the tops of some of the highest hills I have found marine shells, but so soft and crumbling as to fall apart the instant they were exposed to the air. I spent some time over various lumps of sand, hoping to find some perfect ones that would be hard enough to carry back to St. Louis; but 't was "love's labor lost," and I regretted exceedingly that only a few fragments could be gathered. I found globular and oval shaped stones, very heavy, apparently composed mostly of iron, weighing from fifteen to twenty pounds; numbers of petrified stumps from one to three feet in diameter; the

Mauvaises Terres abound with them; they are to be
found in all parts from the valleys to the tops of the hills,
and appear to be principally of cedar.   On the sides of
the hills, at various heights, are shelves of rock or stone
projecting out from two to six, eight, or even ten feet, and
generally square, or nearly so; these are the favorite resorts of the Bighorns during the heat of the day, and
either here or on the tops of the highest hills they are to
be found.   Between the hills there is generally quite a
growth of cedar, but mostly stunted and crowded close
together, with very large stumps, and between the stumps
quite a good display of grass; on the summits, in some
few places, there are table-lands, varying from an area
of one to ten or fifteen acres; these are covered with a
short, dry, wiry grass, and immense quantities of flat
leaved cactus, the spines of which often warn the hunter
of their proximity, and the hostility existing between
them and his feet.   These plains are not more easily
travelled than the hillsides, as every step may lead the
hunter into a bed of these pests of the prairies.   In the
valleys between the hills are ravines, some of which are
not more than ten or fifteen feet wide, while their depth
is beyond the reach of the eye.   Others vary in depth
from ten to fifty feet, while some make one giddy to look
in; they are also of various widths, the widest perhaps
a hundred feet.   The edges, at times, are lined with
bushes, mostly wild cherry; occasionally Buffaloes make
paths across them, but this is rare.   The only safe way to
pass is to follow the ravine to the head, which is usually
at the foot of some hill, and go round.   These ravines are
mostly between every two hills, although like every general rule there are variations and occasionally places
where three or more hills make only one ravine.   These
small ravines all connect with some larger one, the size of
which is in proportion to its tributaries.   The large one
runs to the river, or the water is carried off by a subterra-

nean channel. In these valleys, and sometimes on the
tops of the hills, are holes, called "sink holes;" these
are formed by the water running in a small hole and working away the earth beneath the surface, leaving a crust
incapable of supporting the weight of a man; and if an
unfortunate steps on this crust, he soon finds himself in
rather an unpleasant predicament. This is one of the
dangers that attend the hunter in these lands; these holes
eventually form a ravine such as I have before spoken of.
Through these hills it is almost impossible to travel with
a horse, though it is sometimes done by careful management, and a correct knowledge of the country. The sides
of the hills are very steep, covered with the earth and
stones of which I have spoken, all of which are quite loose
on the surface; occasionally a bunch of wormwood here
and there seems to assist the daring hunter; for it is no
light task to follow the Bighorns through these lands,
and the pursuit is attended with much danger, as the least
slip at times would send one headlong into the ravines
below. On the sides of these high hills the water has
washed away the earth, leaving caves of various sizes;
and, in fact, in some places all manner of fantastic forms
are made by the same process. Occasionally in the valleys are found isolated cones or domes, destitute of vegetation, naked and barren. Throughout the Mauvaises
Terres there are springs of water impregnated with salt,
sulphur, magnesia, and many other salts of all kinds.
Such is the water the hunter is compelled to drink, and
were it not that it is as cold as ice it would be almost impossible to swallow it. As it is, many of these waters
operate as cathartics or emetics; this is one of the most
disagreeable attendants of hunting in these lands. Moreover, venomous snakes of many kinds are also found here.
I saw myself only one copperhead, and a common garter-
snake. Notwithstanding the rough nature of the country, the Buffaloes have paths running in all directions,

and leading from the prairies to the river.   The hunter sometimes, after toiling for an hour or two up the side of one of these hills, trying to reach the top in hopes that when there he will have for a short distance at least, either a level place or good path to walk on, finds to his disappointment that he has secured a point that only affords a place scarcely large enough to stand on, and he has the trouble of descending, perhaps to renew his disappointment in the same way, again and again, such is the deceptive character of the country.   I was thus deceived time and again, while in search of Bighorns.   If the hill does not terminate in a point it is connected with another hill, by a ridge so narrow that nothing but a Bighorn can walk on it.   This is the country that the Mountain Ram inhabits, and if, from this imperfect description, any information can be derived, I shall be more than repaid for the trouble I have had in these tiresome hills. Whether my theory be correct or incorrect, it is this: These hills were at first composed of the clays that I have mentioned, mingled with an immense quantity of combustible material, such as coal, sulphur, bitumen, etc.; these have been destroyed by fire, or (at least the greater part) by volcanic action, as to this day, on the Black Hills and in the hills near where I have been, fire still exists; and from the immense quantities of pumice-stone and melted ores found among the hills, even were there no fire now to be seen, no one could doubt that it had, at some date or other, been there; as soon as this process had ceased, the rains washed out the loose material, and carried it to the rivers, leaving the more solid parts as we now find them; the action of water to this day continues.   As I have said, the Bighorns are very fond of resorting to the shelves, or ledges, on the sides of the hills, during the heat of the day, when these places are shaded; here they lie, but are aroused instantly upon the least appearance of danger, and, as soon as they have discovered the cause of alarm, away they go, over hill and ravine, occasionally stopping to look round, and when ascending the steepest hill, there is no apparent diminution of their speed. They will ascend and descend places, when thus alarmed, so inaccessible that it is almost impossible to conceive how, and where, they find a foothold. When observed before they see the hunter, or while they are looking about when first alarmed, are the only opportunities the hunter has to shoot them; for, as soon as they start there is no hope, as to follow and find them is a task not easily accomplished, for where or how far they go when thus on the alert, heaven only knows, as but few hunters have ever attempted a chase. At all times they have to be approached with the greatest caution, as the least thing renders them on the *qui vive.* When not found on these shelves, they are seen on the tops of the most inaccessible and highest hills, looking down on the hunters, apparently conscious of their security, or else lying down tranquilly in some sunny spot quite out of reach. As I have observed before, the only times that these animals can be shot are when on these ledges, or when moving from one point to another. Sometimes they move only a few hundred yards, but it will take the hunter several hours to approach near enough for a shot, so long are the *détours* he is compelled to make. I have been thus baffled two or three times. The less difficult hills are found cut up by paths made by these animals; these are generally about eighteen inches wide. These animals appear to be quite as agile as the European Chamois, leaping down precipices, across ravines, and running up and down almost perpendicular hills. The only places I could find that seemed to afford food for them, was between the cedars, as I have before mentioned; but the places where they are most frequently found are barren, and without the least vestige of vegetation. From the character of the lands where these animals are found, their own shyness, watchfulness, and agility, it is readily seen what the hunter must endure, and what difficulties he must undergo to near these "Wild Goats." It is one constant time of toil, anxiety, fatigue, and danger. Such the country! Such the animal! Such the hunting!

August 16. Started from Fort Union at 12 M. in the Mackinaw barge "Union." Shot five young Ducks. Camped at the foot of a high bluff. Good supper of Chickens and Ducks.

Thursday, 17th. Started early. Saw three Bighorns, some Antelopes, and many Deer, fully twenty; one Wolf, twenty-two Swans, many Ducks. Stopped a short time on a bar. Mr. Culbertson shot a female Elk, and I killed two bulls. Camped at Buffalo Bluff, where we found Bear tracks.

Friday, 18th. Fine. Bell shot a superb male Elk. The two bulls untouched since killed. Stopped to make an oar, when I caught four catfish. "Kayac" is the French Missourian's name for Buffalo Bluffs, original French for Moose; in Assiniboin "Tah-Tah," in Blackfoot "Sick-e-chi-choo," in Sioux "Tah-Tah." Fifteen to twenty female Elks drinking, tried to approach them, but they broke and ran off to the willows and disappeared. We landed and pursued them. Bell shot at one, but did not find it, though it was badly wounded. These animals are at times unwary, but at others vigilant, suspicious, and well aware of the coming of their enemies.

Saturday, 19th. Wolves howling, and bulls roaring, just like the long continued roll of a hundred drums. Saw large gangs of Buffaloes walking along the river. Headed Knife River one and a half miles. Fresh signs of Indians, burning wood embers, etc. I knocked a cow down with two balls, and Mr. Culbertson killed her. Abundance of Bear tracks. Saw a great number of bushes bearing the berries of which Mrs. Culbertson has given me a necklace. Herds of Buffaloes on the prairies. Mr. Culbertson killed another cow, and in going to see it I had a severe fall over a partially sunken log. Bell killed a doe and wounded the fawn.

Sunday, 20th. *Tamias quadrivittatus* runs up trees; abundance of them in the ravine, and Harris killed one. Bell wounded an Antelope. Thousands upon thousands of Buffaloes; the roaring of these animals resembles the grunting of hogs, with a rolling sound from the throat. Mr. C. killed two cows, Sprague killed one bull, and I made two sketches of it after death. The men killed a cow, and the bull would not leave her although shot four times. Stopped by the high winds all this day. Suffered much from my fall.

Monday, 21st. Buffaloes all over the bars and prairies, and many swimming; the roaring can be heard for miles. The wind stopped us again at eight o'clock; breakfasted near the tracks of Bears surrounded by hundreds of Buffaloes. We left our safe anchorage and good hunting-grounds too soon; the wind blew high, and we were obliged to land again on the opposite shore, where the gale has proved very annoying. Bear tracks led us to search for those animals, but in vain. Collected seeds. Shot at a Rabbit, but have done nothing. Saw many young and old Ducks, — Black Mallards and Gadwalls. I shot a bull and broke his thigh, and then shot at him thirteen times before killing. Camped at the same place.

Tuesday, 22d. Left early and travelled about twelve miles. Went hunting Elks. Mr. Culbertson killed a Deer, and he and Squires brought the meat in on their backs. I saw nothing, but heard shots which I thought were from Harris. I ran for upwards of a mile to look for him, hallooing the whole distance, but saw nothing of him. Sent three men who hallooed also, but came back without further intelligence. Bell shot a female Elk and brought in part of the meat. We walked to the Little Missouri and shot the fourth bull this trip. We saw many Ducks.

In the afternoon we started again, and went below the Little Missouri, returned to the bull and took his horns, etc. Coming back to the boat Sprague saw a Bear; we went towards the spot; the fellow had turned under the high bank and was killed in a few seconds. Mr. Culbertson shot it first through the neck, Bell and I in the body.

Wednesday, 23d. Provost skinned the Bear. No Prairie-Dogs caught. The wind high and cold. Later two Prairie-Dogs were shot; their notes resemble precisely those of the Arkansas Flycatcher. Left this afternoon and travelled about ten miles. Saw another Bear and closely observed its movements. We saw several drowned Buffaloes, and were passed by Wolves and Passenger Pigeons. Camped in a bad place under a sky with every appearance of rain.

Thursday, 24th. A bad night of wind, very cloudy; left early, as the wind lulled and it became calm. Passed "L'Ours qui danse," travelled about twenty miles, when we were again stopped by the wind. Hunted, but found nothing. The fat of our Bear gave us seven bottles of oil. We heard what some thought to be guns, but I believed it to be the falling of the banks. Then the Wolves howled so curiously that it was supposed they were Indian dogs. We went to bed all prepared for action in case of an attack; pistols, knives, etc., but I slept very well, though rather cold.

Friday, 25th. Fair, but foggy, so we did not start early. I found some curious stones with impressions of shells. It was quite calm, and we passed the two Riccaree winter villages. Many Eagles and Peregrine Falcons. Shot another bull. Passed the Gros Ventre village at noon; no game about the place. "La Main Gauche," an Assiniboin chief of great renown, left seventy warriors killed and thirty wounded on the prairie opposite, the year following the small-pox. The Gros Ventres are a courageous tribe. Reached the Mandan village; hundreds of Indians swam to us with handkerchiefs tied on their heads like turbans.

Our old friend " Four Bears " met us on the shore; I gave him eight pounds of tobacco. He came on board and went down with us to Fort Clark, which we reached at four o'clock. Mr. Culbertson and Squires rode out to the Gros Ventre village with " Four Bears " after dark, and returned about eleven; they met with another chief who curiously enough was called " The Iron Bear."

Saturday, 26th. Fine, but a cold, penetrating wind. Started early and landed to breakfast. A canoe passed us with two men from the Opposition. We were stopped by the wind for four hours, but started again at three; passed the Butte Quarré at a quarter past five, followed now by the canoe, as the two fellows are afraid of Indians, and want to come on board our boat; we have not room for them, but will let them travel with us. Landed for the night, and walked to the top of one of the buttes from which we had a fine and very extensive view. Saw a herd of Buffaloes, which we approached, but by accident did not kill a cow. Harris, whom we thought far off, shot too soon and Moncrévier and the rest of us lost our chances. We heard Elks whistling, and saw many Swans. The canoe men camped close to us.

Sunday, 27th. Started early in company with the canoe. Saw four Wolves and six bulls, the latter to our sorrow in a compact group and therefore difficult to attack. They are poor at this season, and the meat very rank, but yet are fresh meat. The wind continued high, but we landed in the weeds assisted by the canoe men, as we saw a gang of cows. We lost them almost immediately though we saw their *wet tracks* and followed them for over a mile, but then gave up the chase. On returning to the river we missed the boat, as she had been removed to a better landing below; so we had quite a search for her. Mrs. Culbertson worked at the *parflèche* with Golden Eagle feathers; she had killed the bird herself. Stopped by the wind at noon. Walked off and saw Buffaloes, but the wind was adverse. Bell and Harris, however, killed a cow, a single one, that had been wounded, whether by shot or by an arrow no one can tell. We saw a bull on a sand-bar; the poor fool took to the water and swam so as to meet us. We shot at him about a dozen times, I shot him through one eye, Bell, Harris, and Sprague about the head, and yet the animal made for our boat and came so close that Mr. Culbertson touched him with a pole, when he turned off and swam across the river, but acted as if wild or crazy; he ran on a sand-bar, and at last swam again to the opposite shore, in my opinion to die, but Mr. Culbertson says he may live for a month. We landed in a good harbor on the east side about an hour before sundown. Moncrévier caught a catfish that weighed sixteen pounds, a fine fish, though the smaller ones are better eating.

Monday, 28th. A gale all night and this morning also. We are in a good place for hunting, and I hope to have more to say anon. The men returned and told us of many Bear tracks, and four of us started off. Such a walk I do not remember; it was awful — mire, willows, vines, holes, fallen logs; we returned much fatigued and having seen nothing. The wind blowing fiercely.

Tuesday, 29th. Heavy wind all night. Bad dreams about my own Lucy. Walked some distance along the shores and caught many catfish. Two Deer on the other shore. Cut a cotton-tree to fasten to the boat to break the force of the waves. The weather has become sultry. Beavers during the winter oftentimes come down amid the ice, but enter any small stream they meet with at once. Apple River, or Creek, was formerly a good place for them, as well as Cannon Ball River. Saw a Musk-rat this morning swimming by our barge. Slept on a muddy bar with abundance of mosquitoes.

Wednesday, 30th. Started at daylight. Mr. Culbertson and I went off to the prairies over the most infernal ground I ever saw, but we reached the high prairies by dint of industry, through swamps and mire. We saw two bulls, two calves, and one cow; we killed the cow and the larger calf, a beautiful young bull; returned to the boat through the most abominable swamp I ever travelled through, and reached the boat at one o'clock, thirsty and hungry enough. Bell and all the men went after the meat and the skin of the young bull. I shot the cow, but missed the calf by shooting above it. We started later and made about ten miles before sunset.

Thursday, 31st. Started early; fine and calm. Saw large flocks of Ducks, Geese, and Swans; also four Wolves. Passed Mr. Primeau's winter trading-house; reached Cannon Ball River at half-past twelve. No game; water good-tasted, but warm. Dinner on shore. Saw a Rock Wren on the bluffs here. Saw the prairie on fire, and signs of Indians on both sides. Weather cloudy and hot. Reached Beaver Creek. Provost went after Beavers, but found none. Caught fourteen catfish. Saw a wonderful example of the power of the Buffalo in working through the heavy, miry bottom lands.

Friday, September 1. Hard rain most of the night, and uncomfortably hot. Left our encampment at eight o'clock. Saw Buffaloes and landed, but on approaching them found only bulls; so returned empty-handed to the boat, and started anew. We landed for the night on a large sand-bar connected with the mainland, and saw a large gang of Buffaloes, and Mr. Culbertson and a man went off; they shot at two cows and killed one, but lost her, as she fell in the river and floated down stream, and it was dusk. A heavy cloud arose in the west, thunder was heard, yet the moon and stars shone brightly. After midnight rain came on. The mosquitoes are far too abundant for comfort.

Saturday, September 2. Fine but windy. Went about ten miles and stopped, for the gale was so severe. No fresh meat on board. Saw eight Wolves, four white ones.

Walked six miles on the prairies, but saw only three bulls. The wind has risen to a gale. Saw abundance of Black-breasted Prairie Larks, and a pond with Black Ducks. Returned to the pond after dinner and killed four Ducks.

Sunday, 3d. Beautiful, calm, and cold. Left early and at noon put ashore to kill a bull, having no fresh meat on board. He took the wind and ran off. Touched on a bar, and I went overboard to assist in pushing off and found the water very pleasant, for our cold morning had turned into a hot day. Harris shot a Prairie Wolf. At half-past four saw ten or twelve Buffaloes. Mr. Culbertson, Bell, a canoe man, and I, went after them; the cattle took to the river, and we went in pursuit; the other canoe man landed, and ran along the shore, but could not head them. He shot, however, and as the cattle reached the bank we gave them a volley, but uselessly, and are again under way. Bell and Mr. C. were well mired and greatly exhausted in consequence. No meat for another day. Stopped for the night at the mouth of the Moreau River. Wild Pigeons, Sandpipers, but no fish.

Monday, 4th. Cool night. Wind rose early, but a fine morning. Stopped by the wind at eleven. Mr. Culbertson, Bell, and Moncrévier gone shooting. Many signs of Elk, etc., and flocks of Wild Pigeons. A bad place for hunting, but good for safety. Found Beaver tracks, and small trees cut down by them. Provost followed the bank and found their lodge, which he says is an old one. It is at present a mass of sticks of different sizes matted together, and fresh tracks are all around it. To dig them out would have proved impossible, and we hope to catch them in traps to-night. Beavers often feed on berries when they can reach them, especially Buffalo berries [*Shepherdia argentea*]. Mr. Culbertson killed a buck, and we have sent men to bring it entire. The Beavers in this lodge are not residents, but vagrant Beavers. The buck was brought in; it is of the same kind as at Fort

CAMP ON THE MISSOURI.

FROM A DRAWING BY ISAAC SPRAGUE.

Union, having a longer tail, we think, than the kind found East. Its horns were very small, but it is skinned and in brine. We removed our camp about a hundred yards lower down, but the place as regards wood is very bad. Provost and I went to set traps for Beaver; he first cut two dry sticks eight or nine feet long; we reached the river by passing through the tangled woods; he then pulled off his breeches and waded about with a pole to find the depth of the water, and having found a fit spot he dug away the mud in the shape of a half circle, placed a bit of willow branch at the bottom and put the trap on that. He had two small willow sticks in his mouth; he split an end of one, dipped it in his horn of castoreum, or "medicine," as he calls his stuff, and left on the end of it a good mass of it, which was placed in front of the jaws of the trap next the shore; he then made the chain of the trap secure, stuck in a few untrimmed branches on each side, and there the business ended. The second one was arranged in the same way, except that there was no bit of willow under it. Beavers when caught in shallow water are often attacked by the Otter, and in doing this the latter sometimes lose their own lives, as they are very frequently caught in the other trap placed close by. Mr. Culbertson and Bell returned without having shot, although we heard one report whilst setting the traps. Elks are very numerous here, but the bushes crack and make so much noise that they hear the hunters and fly before them. Bell shot five Pigeons at once. Harris and Squires are both poorly, having eaten too indulgently of Buffalo brains. We are going to move six or seven hundred yards lower down, to spend the night in a more sheltered place. I hope I may have a large Beaver to-morrow.

Tuesday, 5th. At daylight, after some discussion about Beaver lodges, Harris, Bell, Provost, and I, with two men, went to the traps — nothing caught. We now had the lodge demolished outwardly, namely, all the sticks removed, under which was found a hole about two and a half feet in diameter, through which Harris, Bell, and Moncrévier (who had followed us) entered, but found nothing within, as the Beaver had gone to the river. Harris saw it, and also the people at the boat. I secured some large specimens of the cuttings used to build the lodge, and a pocketful of the chips. Before Beavers fell the tree they long for, they cut down all the small twigs and saplings around. The chips are cut above and below, and then split off by the animal; the felled trees lay about us in every direction. We left our camp at half-past five; I again examined the lodge, which was not finished, though about six feet in diameter. We saw a Pigeon Hawk giving chase to a Spotted Sandpiper on the wing. When the Hawk was about to seize the little fellow it dove under water and escaped. This was repeated five or six times; to my great surprise and pleasure, the Hawk was obliged to relinquish the prey. As the wind blew high, we landed to take breakfast, on a fine beach, portions of which appeared as if paved by the hand of man. The canoe men killed a very poor cow, which had been wounded, and so left alone. The wind fell suddenly, and we proceeded on our route till noon, when it rose, and we stopped again. Mr. Culbertson went hunting, and returned having killed a young buck Elk. Dined, and walked after the meat and skin, and took the measurements. Returning, saw two Elks driven to the hills by Mr. Culbertson and Bell. Met Harris, and started a monstrous buck Elk from its couch in a bunch of willows; shot at it while running about eighty yards off, but it was not touched. Meantime Provost had heard us from our dinner camp; loading his rifle he came within ten paces, when his gun snapped. We yet hope to get this fine animal. Harris found a Dove's nest with one young one, and an egg just cracked by the bird inside; the nest was on the ground. Curious all this at this late late season, and in a woody part of the country. Saw a Bat.

Wednesday, 6th. Wind blowing harder. Ransacked the point and banks both below and above, but saw only two Wolves; one a dark gray, the largest I have yet seen. Harris shot a young of the Sharp-tailed Grouse; Bell, three Pigeons; Provost went off to the second point below, about four miles, after Elks; Sprague found another nest of Doves on the ground, with very small young. The common Bluebird was seen, also a Whip-poor-will and a Night-Hawk. Wind high and from the south.

Thursday, 7th. About eleven o'clock last night the wind shifted *suddenly* to northwest, and blew so violently that we all left the boat in a hurry. Mrs. Culbertson, with her child in her arms, made for the willows, and had a shelter for her babe in a few minutes. Our guns and ammunition were brought on shore, as we were afraid of our boat sinking. We returned on board after a while; but I could not sleep, the motion making me very sea-sick; I went back to the shore and lay down after mending our fire. It rained hard for about two hours; the sky then became clear, and the wind wholly subsided, so I went again to the boat and slept till eight o'clock. A second gale now arose; the sky grew dark; we removed our boat to a more secure position, but I fear we are here for another day. Bell shot a *Caprimulgus*,[1] so small that I have no doubt it is the one found on the Rocky Mountains by Nuttall, after whom I have named it. These birds are now travelling south. Mr. Culbertson and I walked up the highest hills of the prairie, but saw nothing. The river has suddenly risen two feet, the water rises now at the rate of eight inches in two and a half hours, and the wind has somewhat moderated. The little Whip-poor-will proves an old male, but it is now in moult. Left our camp at five, and went down rapidly to an island four miles below. Mr. Culbertson, Bell, Harris, and Provost went off to look for Elks, but I

---

[1] Nuttall's Poor-will, now known as *Phalænoptilus nuttalli*, which has a two-syllabled note, rendered " oh-will " in the text beyond. — E. C.

fear fruitlessly, as I see no tracks, nor do I find any of their beds. About ten o'clock Harris called me to hear the notes of the new Whip-poor-will; we heard two at once, and the sound was thus: "Oh-will, oh-will," repeated often and quickly, as in our common species. The night was beautiful, but cold.

Friday, 8th. Cloudy and remarkably cold; the river has risen 6½ feet since yesterday, and the water is muddy and thick. Started early. The effect of sudden rises in this river is wonderful upon the sand-bars, which are no sooner covered by a foot or so of water than they at once break up, causing very high waves to run, through which no small boat could pass without imminent danger. The swells are felt for many feet as if small waves at sea. Appearances of rain. The current very strong; but we reached Fort Pierre at half-past five, and found all well.

Saturday, 9th. Rain all night. Breakfasted at the fort. Exchanged our boat for a larger one. Orders found here obliged Mr. Culbertson to leave us and go to the Platte River establishment, much to my regret.

Sunday, 10th. Very cloudy. Mr. Culbertson gave me a *parflèche*[1] which had been presented to him by "L'Ours de Fer," the Sioux chief. It is very curiously painted, and is a record of a victory of the Sioux over their enemies, the Gros Ventres. Two rows of horses with Indians dressed in full war rig are rushing onwards; small black marks everywhere represent the horse tracks; round green marks are shields thrown away by the enemy in their flight, and red spots on the horses, like wafers, denote wounds.

Monday, 11th. Cloudy; the men at work fitting up our new boat. Rained nearly all day, and the wind shifted to every point of the compass. Nothing done.

---

[1] A *parflèche* is a hide, usually a Buffalo bull's, denuded of hair, dressed and stretched to the desired shape. All articles made from this hide are also called parflèche, such as wallets, pouches, etc.

Tuesday, 12th. Partially clear this morning early, but rained by ten o'clock. Nothing done.

Wednesday, 13th. Rainy again. Many birds were seen moving southwest. Our boat is getting into travelling shape. I did several drawings of objects in and about the fort.

Thursday, 14th. Cloudy and threatening. Mr. Laidlow making ready to leave for Fort Union, and ourselves for our trip down the river. Mr. Laidlow left at half-past eleven, and we started at two this afternoon; landed at the farm belonging to the fort, and procured a few potatoes, some corn, and a pig.

Friday, 15th. A foggy morning. Reached Fort George. Mr. Illingsworth left at half-past ten. Wind ahead, and we were obliged to stop on this account at two. Fresh signs of both Indians and Buffaloes, but nothing killed.

Saturday, 16th. Windy till near daylight. Started early; passed Ebbett's new island. Bell heard Parrakeets. The day was perfectly calm. Found *Arvicola pennsylvanica.* Landed at the Great Bend for Black-tailed Deer and wood. Have seen nothing worthy our attention. Squires put up a board at our old camp the " Six Trees," which I hope to see again. The Deer are lying down, and we shall not go out to hunt again till near sunset. The note of the Meadow Lark here is now unheard. I saw fully two hundred flying due south. Collected a good deal of the Yucca plant.

Sunday, 17th. We had a hard gale last night with rain for about an hour. This morning was beautiful; we started early, but only ran for two hours, when we were forced to stop by the wind, which blew a gale. Provost saw fresh signs of Indians, and we were told that there were a few lodges at the bottom of the Bend, about two miles below us. The wind is north and quite cold, and the contrast between to-day and yesterday is great. Went shooting, and killed three Sharp-tailed Grouse. Left our camp about three o'clock as the wind abated. Saw ten or twelve

Antelopes on the prairie where the Grouse were. We camped about a mile from the spot where we landed in May last, at the end of the Great Bend. The evening calm and beautiful.

Monday, 18th. The weather cloudy and somewhat windy. Started early; saw a Fish Hawk, two Gulls, two White-headed Eagles and abundance of Golden Plovers. The Sharp-tailed Grouse feeds on rose-berries and the seeds of the wild sunflower and grasshoppers. Stopped at twenty minutes past nine, the wind was so high, and warmed some coffee. Many dead Buffaloes are in the ravines and on the prairies. Harris, Bell, and Sprague went hunting, but had no show with such a wind. Sprague outlined a curious hill. The wind finally shifted, and then lulled down. Saw Say's Flycatcher, with a Grosbeak. Saw two of the common Titlark. Left again at two, with a better prospect. Landed at sunset on the west side. Signs of Indians. Wolves howling, and found one dead on the shore, but too far gone to be skinned; I was sorry, as it was a beautiful gray one. These animals feed on wild plums in great quantities. Tried to shoot some Doves for my Fox and Badger, but without success. Pea-vines very scarce.

Tuesday, 19th. Dark and drizzly. Did not start until six. Reached Cedar Island, and landed for wood to use on the boat. Bell went off hunting. Wind north. Found no fit trees and left. Passed the burning cliffs and got on a bar. The weather fine, and wind behind us. Wolves will even eat the frogs found along the shores of this river. Saw five, all gray. At three o'clock we were obliged to stop on account of the wind, under a poor point. No game.

Wednesday, 20th. Wind very high. Tracks of Wild Cats along the shore. The motion of the boat is so great it makes me sea-sick. Sprague saw a Sharp-tailed Grouse. We left at half-past twelve. Saw immense numbers of

Pin-tailed Ducks, but could not get near them. Stopped
on an island to procure pea-vines for my young Deer, and
found plenty. Our camp of last night was only two miles
and a half below White River. Ran on a bar and were
delayed nearly half an hour. Shot two Blue-winged Teal.
Camped opposite Bijou's Hill.

Thursday, 21st. Wind and rain most of the night.
Started early. Weather cloudy and cold. Landed to examine Burnt Hills, and again on an island for pea-vines.
Fresh signs of Indians. Saw many Antelopes and Mule
Deer. At twelve saw a bull on one side of the river,
and in a few moments after a herd of ten cattle on the other
side. Landed, and Squires, Harris, Bell, and Provost have
gone to try to procure fresh meat; these are the first Buffaloes seen since we left Fort Pierre. The hunters only
killed one bull; no cows among eleven bulls, and this is
strange at this season. Saw three more bulls in a ravine.
Stopped to camp at the lower end of great Cedar Island at
five o'clock. Fresh signs of Buffaloes and Deer. We cut
some timber for oars. Rain set in early in the evening,
and it rained hard all night.

Friday, 22d. Raining; left at a quarter past eight, with
the wind ahead. Distant thunder. Everything wet and
dirty after a very uncomfortable night. We went down
the river about a mile, when we were forced to come to on
the opposite side by the wind and the rain. Played cards
for a couple of hours. No chance to cook or get hot
coffee, on account of the heavy storm. We dropped down
a few miles and finally camped till next day in the mud,
but managed to make a roaring fire. Wolves in numbers
howling all about us, and Owls hooting also. Still raining
heavily. We played cards till nine o'clock to kill time.
Our boat a quagmire.

Saturday, 23d. A cloudy morning; we left at six o'clock.
Five Wolves were on a sand-bar very near us. Saw Red-
shafted Woodpeckers, and two House Swallows. Have

made a good run of about sixty miles. At four this afternoon we took in three men of the steamer "New Haven"
belonging to the Opposition, which was fast on the bar,
eight miles below. We reached Ponca Island and landed
for the night. At dusk the steamer came up, and landed
above us, and we found Messrs. Cutting and Taylor, and
I had the gratification of a letter from Victor and Johnny,
of July 22d.

Sunday, 24th. Cloudy, windy, and cold. Both the steamer
and ourselves left as soon as we could see. Saw a Wolf on
a bar, and a large flock of White Pelicans, which we took
at first for a keel-boat. Passed the Poncas, L'Eau qui Court,
Manuel, and Basil rivers by ten o'clock.[1] Landed just
below Basil River, stopped by wind. Hunted and shot one
Raven, one Turkey Buzzard, and four Wood-ducks. Ripe
plums abound, and there are garfish in the creek. Found
feathers of the Wild Turkey. Signs of Indians, Elks, and
Deer. Provost and the men made four new oars. Went
to bed early.

Monday, 25th. Blowing hard all night, and began raining
before day. Cold, wet, and misty. Started at a quarter
past ten, passed Bonhomme Island at four, and landed for
the night at five, fifteen miles below.

Tuesday, 26th. Cold and cloudy; started early. Shot a
Pelican. Passed Jack's River at eleven. Abundance of
Wild Geese. Bell killed a young White Pelican. Weather
fairer but coldish. Sprague killed a Goose, but it was lost.
Camped a few miles above the Vermilion River. Harris
saw Raccoon tracks on Basil River.

Wednesday, 27th. Cloudy but calm. Many Wood-ducks,
and saw Raccoon tracks again this morning. Passed the
Vermilion River at half-past seven. My Badger got out
of his cage last night, and we had to light a candle to secure
it. We reached the Fort of Vermilion at twelve, and met

---

[1] Niobrara River; for which, and for others here named, see the previous
note, date of May 20.

with a kind reception from Mr. Pascal. Previous to this
we met a barge going up, owned and commanded by Mr.
Tybell, and found our good hunter Michaux. He asked me
to take him down, and I promised him $20 per month to
St. Louis. We bought two barrels of superb potatoes, two
of corn, and a good fat cow. For the corn and potatoes I
paid no less than $16.00.

Thursday, 28th. A beautiful morning, and we left at
eight. The young man who brought me the calf at Fort
George has married a squaw, a handsome girl, and she is
here with him. Antelopes are found about twenty-five
miles from this fort, but not frequently. Landed fifteen
miles below on Elk Point. Cut up and salted the cow.
Provost and I went hunting, and saw three female Elks, but
the order was to shoot only bucks; a large one started
below us, jumped into the river, and swam across, carrying
his horns flat down and spread on each side of his back;
the neck looked to me about the size of a flour-barrel.
Harris killed a hen Turkey, and Bell and the others saw
plenty but did not shoot, as Elks were the order of the
day. I cannot eat beef after being fed on Buffaloes. I am
getting an old man, for this evening I missed my footing
on getting into the boat, and bruised my knee and my
elbow, but at seventy and over I cannot have the spring of
seventeen.

Friday, 29th. Rained most of the night, and it is
raining and blowing at present. Crossed the river and
have encamped at the mouth of the Iowa River,[1] the
boundary line of the Sioux and Omahas. Harris shot a
Wolf. My knee too sore to allow me to walk. Stormy
all day.

Saturday, 30th. Hard rain all night, the water rose four

[1] On the south side of the Missouri, in present Nebraska, a short distance above the mouth of the Big Sioux. This small stream is Roloje Creek
of Lewis and Clark, Ayoway River of Nicollet, appearing by error as "Nor-
way" and "Nioway" Creek on General Land Office maps. — E. C.

inches. Found a new species of large bean in the Wild
Turkey. Mosquitoes rather troublesome. The sun shining
by eight o'clock, and we hope for a good dry day. Whip-
poor-wills heard last night, and Night-hawks seen flying.
Saw a Long-tailed Squirrel that ran on the shore at the
cry of our Badger. Michaux had the boat landed to bring
on a superb set of Elk-horns that he secured last week.
Abundance of Geese and Ducks. Weather clouding over
again, and at two we were struck by a heavy gale of wind,
and were obliged to land on the weather shore; the wind
continued heavy, and the motion of the boat was too much
for me, so I slipped on shore and with Michaux made a
good camp, where we rolled ourselves in our blankets and
slept soundly.

Sunday, October 1. The wind changed, and lulled before
morning, so we left at a quarter past six. The skies looked
rather better, nevertheless we had several showers. Passed
the [Big] Sioux River at twenty minutes past eleven.
Heard a Pileated Woodpecker, and saw Fish Crows. Geese
very abundant. Landed below the Sioux River to shoot
Turkeys, having seen a large male on the bluffs. Bell
killed a hen, and Harris two young birds; these will keep
us going some days. Stopped again by the wind opposite
Floyd's grave; started again and ran about four miles,
when we were obliged to land in a rascally place at twelve
o'clock. Had hail and rain at intervals. Camped at the
mouth of the Omaha River, six miles from the village.
The wild Geese are innumerable. The wind has ceased
and stars are shining.

Monday, 2d. Beautiful but *cold.* The water has risen
nine inches, and we travel well. Started early. Stopped
at eight by the wind at a vile place, but plenty of Jerusalem
artichokes, which we tried and found very good. Started
again at three, and made a good run till sundown, when
we found a fair camping-place and made our supper from
excellent young Geese.

Tuesday, 3d. A beautiful, calm morning; we started early. Saw three Deer on the bank. A Prairie Wolf travelled on the shore beside us for a long time before he found a place to get up on the prairie. Plenty of Sand-hill Cranes were seen as we passed the Little Sioux River. Saw three more Deer, another Wolf, two Swans, several Pelicans, and abundance of Geese and Ducks. Passed Soldier River at two o'clock. We were caught by a snag that scraped and tore us a little. Had we been two feet nearer, it would have ruined our barge. We passed through a very swift cut-off, most difficult of entrance. We have run eighty-two miles and encamped at the mouth of the cut-off, near the old bluffs. Killed two Mallards; the Geese and Ducks are abundant beyond description. Brag, Harris' dog, stole and hid all the meat that had been cooked for our supper.

Wednesday, 4th. Cloudy and coldish. Left early and can't find my pocket knife, which I fear I have lost. We were stopped by the wind at Cabané Bluffs, about twenty miles above Fort Croghan; we all hunted, with only fair results. Saw some hazel bushes, and some black walnuts. Wind-bound till night, and nothing done.

Thursday, 5th. Blew hard all night, but a clear and beautiful sunrise. Started early, but stopped by the wind at eight. Bell, Harris, and Squires have started off for Fort Croghan. As there was every appearance of rain we left at three and reached the fort about half-past four. Found all well, and were most kindly received. We were presented with some green corn, and had a quantity of bread made, also bought thirteen eggs from an Indian for twenty-five cents. Honey bees are found here, and do well, but none are seen above this place. I had an unex-pected slide on the bank, as it had rained this afternoon; and Squires had also one at twelve in the night, when he and Harris with Sprague came to the boat after having played whist up to that hour.

Friday, 6th. Some rain and thunder last night. A tolerable day. Breakfast at the camp, and left at half-past eight. Our man Michaux was passed over to the officer's boat, to steer them down to Fort Leavenworth, where they are ordered, but we are to keep in company, and he is to cook for us at night. The whole station here is broken up, and Captain Burgwin[1] leaves in a few hours by land with the dragoons, horses, etc. Stopped at Belle Vue at nine, and had a kind reception; bought 6 lbs. coffee, 13 eggs, 2 lbs. butter, and some black pepper. Abundance of Indians, of four different nations. Major Miller, the agent, is a good man for this place. Left again at eleven. A fine day. Passed the Platte and its hundreds of snags, at a quarter past one, and stopped for the men to dine. The stream quite full, and we saw some squaws on the bar, the village was in sight. Killed two Pelicans, but only got one. Encamped about thirty miles below Fort Croghan. Lieutenant Carleton supped with us, and we had a rubber of whist.

Saturday, 7th. Fine night, and fine morning. Started too early, while yet dark, and got on a bar. Passed McPherson's, the first house in the State of Missouri, at eight o'clock. Bell skinned the young of *Fringilla harrisi.* Lieutenant Carleton came on board to breakfast with us — a fine companion and a perfect gentleman. Indian war-whoops were heard by him and his men whilst embarking this morning after we left. We encamped at the mouth of Nishnebottana, a fine, clear stream. Went to the house of Mr. Beaumont, who has a pretty wife. We made a fine run of sixty or seventy miles.

Sunday, 8th. Cloudy, started early, and had rain by eight o'clock. Stopped twice by the storm, and played cards to relieve the dulness. Started at noon, and ran till half-past four. The wind blowing hard we stopped at a good place for our encampment. Presented a plate

[1] J. H. K. Burgwin. See a previous note, date of May 10.

of the quadrupeds to Lieut. James Henry Carleton,[2] and he gave me a fine Black Bear skin, and has promised me a set of Elk horns. Stopped on the east side of the river in the evening. Saw a remarkably large flock of Geese passing southward.

Monday, 9th. Beautiful and calm; started early. Bell shot a Gray Squirrel, which was divided and given to my Fox and my Badger. Squires, Carleton, Harris, Bell, and Sprague walked across the Bend to the Black Snake Hills, and killed six Gray Squirrels, four Parrakeets, and two Partridges. Bought butter, eggs, and some whiskey for the men; exchanged knives with the lieutenant. Started and ran twelve miles to a good camp on the Indian side.

Tuesday, 10th. Beautiful morning, rather windy; started early. Great flocks of Geese and Pelicans; killed two of the latter. Reached Fort Leavenworth at four, and, as usual everywhere, received most kindly treatment and reception from Major Morton. Lieutenant Carleton gave me the Elk horns. Wrote to John Bachman, Gideon B. Smith, and a long letter home.

Wednesday, 11th. Received a most welcome present of melons, chickens, bread, and butter from the generous major. Lieutenant Carleton came to see me off, and we parted reluctantly. Left at half-past six; weather calm and beautiful. Game scarce, paw-paws plentiful. Stopped at Madame Chouteau's, where I bought three pumpkins. Stopped at Liberty Landing and delivered the letters of Laidlow to Black Harris. Reached Independence Landing at sundown; have run sixty miles. Found no letters. Steamer " Lebanon " passed upwards at half-past eight.

Thursday, 12th. Beautiful and calm; stopped and bought eggs, etc., at a Mr. Shivers', from Kentucky. Ran

---

[1] Of Maine; in 1843 a second lieutenant of the First Dragoons. He rose during the Civil War to be lieutenant-colonel of the Fourth Cavalry, and Brevet Major-General of Volunteers; died Jan. 7, 1873.

well to Lexington, where we again stopped for provisions;
ran sixty miles to-day.

Friday, 13th. Heavy white frost, and very foggy.
Started early and ran well. Tried to buy butter at several places, but in vain. At Greenville bought coffee.
Abundance of Geese and White Pelicans; many Sand-
hill Cranes. Harris killed a Wood-duck. Passed Grand
River; stopped at New Brunswick, where we bought excellent beef at $2\frac{1}{2}$ cents a pound, but very inferior to Buffalo. Camped at a deserted wood yard, after running
between sixty and seventy miles.

Saturday, 14th. A windy night, and after eight days'
good run, I fear we shall be delayed to-day. Stopped by
a high wind at twelve o'clock. We ran ashore, and I
undertook to push the boat afloat, and undressing for the
purpose got so deep in the mud that I had to spend a
much longer time than I desired in very cold water.
Visited two farm houses, and bought chickens, eggs, and
butter; very little of this last. At one place we procured corn bread. The squatter visited our boat, and we
camped near him. He seemed a good man; was from
North Carolina, and had a fine family. Michaux killed
two Hutchins' Geese,[1] the first I ever saw in the flesh.
Ran about twenty miles; steamer "Lebanon" passed us
going downwards, one hour before sunset. Turkeys and
Long-tailed Squirrels very abundant.

Sunday, 15th. Cold, foggy, and cloudy; started early.
Passed Chariton River and village, and Glasgow; bought
bread, and oats for my Deer. Abundance of Geese and
Ducks. Passed Arrow Rock at eleven. Passed Boones-
ville, the finest country on this river; Rocheport, with
high, rocky cliffs; six miles below which we encamped,
having run sixty miles.

Monday, 16th. Beautiful autumnal morning, a heavy
white frost and no wind. Started early, before six. The

[1] *Branta hutchinsi.*

current very strong. Passed Nashville, Marion, and steamer " Lexington" going up. Jefferson City at twelve. Passed the Osage River and saw twenty-four Deer opposite Smith Landing; camped at sundown, and found Giraud, the "strong man." Ran sixty-one miles. Met the steamer " Satan," badly steered. Abundance of Geese and Ducks everywhere.

Tuesday, 17th. Calm and very foggy. Started early and floated a good deal with the strong current. Saw two Deer. The fog cleared off by nine o'clock. Passed the Gasconade River at half-past nine. Landed at Pinckney to buy bread, etc. Buffaloes have been seen mired, and unable to defend themselves, and the Wolves actually eating their noses while they struggled, but were eventually killed by the Wolves. Passed Washington and encamped below it at sundown; a good run.

Wednesday, 18th. Fine and calm; started very early. Passed Mount Pleasant. Landed at St. Charles to purchase bread, etc. Provost became extremely drunk, and went off by land to St. Louis. Passed the Charbonnière River, and encamped about one mile below. The steamer "Tobacco Plant" landed on the shore opposite. Bell and Harris killed a number of Gray Squirrels.

Thursday, 19th. A heavy white frost, foggy, but calm. We started early, the steamer after us. Forced by the fog to stop on a bar, but reached St. Louis at three in the afternoon. Unloaded and sent all the things to Nicholas Berthoud's warehouse. Wrote home.

Left St. Louis October 22, in steamer " Nautilus" for Cincinnati.

Reached home at 3 P. M., November 6th, 1843, and thank God, found all my family quite well.[1]

---

[1] Audubon's daughter-in-law, Mrs. V. G. Audubon, writes : " He returned on the 6th of November, 1843. It was a bright day, and the whole family, with his old friend Captain Cummings, were on the piazza waiting for the carriage to come from Harlem [then the only way of reaching New York by

[Copied from Bell's Journal.[1]]

"*August 2.* Started at half-past seven this morning; saw several Yellow-legs (Godwits), and some young Blue-winged Teal in the pond in the first prairie. Shot two Curlews; saw two very fine male Elks; they were lying down quite near us, under a bank where they got the wind of us. The Sharp-tailed Grouse are first-rate eating now, as they feed entirely on grasshoppers, and berries of different kinds. Owen climbed a tree to a White-headed Eagle's nest, and drove a young one out, which fell to the ground and was caught alive, and brought to the fort. Is it not very remarkable that Eagles of this species should have their young in the nest at this late season, when in the Floridas I have shot them of the same size in February? Shot at a Wolf, which being wounded, went off about one hundred yards, and yelled like a dog; a very remarkable instance, as all we have killed or wounded, and they have been many, rarely make any sound, and if they do it is simply a snapping at their pursuer. As we went up the Missouri on the 7th instant, I found numbers of Cliff Swallow's nests, with the old ones feeding their young. This is also very late and uncommon at this season. Saw a Peregrine Falcon feeding its young. La Fleur shot two bucks of the White-tailed Deer with two shots, and the meat, which we brought home, proved fat and good. Saw Beaver tracks, and young Green-winged Teals. We saw hills impregnated with sulphur and coal, some of them

---

rail]. There were two roads, and hearing wheels, some ran one way and some another, each hoping to be the first to see him; but he had left the carriage at the top of the hill, and came on foot straight down the steepest part, so that those who remained on the piazza had his first kiss. He kissed his sons as well as the ladies of the party. He had on a green blanket coat with fur collar and cuffs; his hair and beard were very long, and he made a fine and striking appearance. In this dress his son John painted his portrait."

[1] See page 126.

MRS. AUDUBON, 1854.

FROM A DAGUERREOTYPE.

on fire, and now and then portions of them gave way, by hundreds of tons at a time. In one place I saw a vein of coal on fire; we were following a path close to the foot of a high hill, and at a turn as we looked ahead, we found the way suddenly blocked by the earth falling down from above us, and looking up saw a line of coal, or other dark substance; it was about two feet thick, and about seventy-five feet from the bottom and forty from the top. It was burning very slowly, and in several places, for about fifty yards, emitting whitish smoke, something like sulphur when burning, and turning the earth or rock above, quite red, or of a brick color. It would undermine the earth above, which then fell in large masses, and this was the cause of the obstruction in the path before us. It must have been burning for a long time, as it had already burned some distance along the hill, and hundreds of tons of earth had fallen. In some places I saw banks of clay twenty feet high, quite red, hard in some parts, and in others very scaly and soft, even crumbling to pieces. Where the fire was burning, the clay was red, varying from one to three feet in thickness; no appearance of coal presented itself where the fire had passed along and was extinguished, but very distinct above the fire, and I have no doubt there is a small quantity of sulphur mixed with this coal, or whatever the substance may be. In another place a short distance from these hills, and in a ravine, I also saw some red stones which looked very much as if the corners of a house which had once been there still remained, with the remnants of two sides yet straight. These stones varied from six to twenty inches in thickness, and many of them were square and about eighteen or twenty feet high; we had not time to remain and examine and measure as carefully as I should have liked to do."

EXTRACTS from Mr. Culbertson's Journal, kept at Fort McKenzie, Blackfeet Indian Country in 1834.[1]

"*Friday, June 13*. Blood Indians started this morning to go to war against the Crows. They had not left long, when the 'Old Bull's Backfat's' son, with his sister, brother, and brother-in-law, returned to the fort, saying they must go back to the camp. After I had given them tobacco and ammunition they all started, but did not get more than two miles from the fort before they were all killed by the Crows, except one, who by some means leaped on one of the Crow horses and fled to the fort. The squaw no doubt was taken prisoner, as in the evening I went out and found the bodies of her husband and brother, but she was not there. On Saturday, the 14th, I went out and brought in the bodies, and had them decently interred. The young man who had escaped was only slightly wounded, and started again for the camp with three Gros Ventres.

"*Tuesday, 24th*. We were all surprised this evening at the arrival of the squaw who had been taken prisoner, and who had been carried to the Crow village where she was kept tied every night until the one in which she made her escape. During the previous day having it in contemplation to escape, she took the precaution of hiding a knife under her garment of skins, but most unfortunately she went out with one of the Crow squaws, and in stooping, the knife fell out; this was reported, and as a punishment she was stripped of every particle of clothing, and when night came was not tied, as it was not imagined she would leave the cover of the tent. However, she decided nothing should keep her from availing herself of the only

[1] These extracts, as well as the descriptions by Mr. Denig and Mr. Culbertson, of Forts Union and McKenzie, which follow, are in Audubon's writing, at the end of one of the Missouri River journals, and are given as descriptions of the life and habitations of those early western pioneers and fur-traders.

opportunity she might ever have; she started with *abso-lutely no covering of any kind*, and in this plight she trav-elled across the prairies, almost without stopping to rest, and with little food, for *four days and three nights ;* unfor-tunately the weather was unusually cold for the season, as well as wet. She arrived at the fort in a most wretched and pitiable condition, but greatly to the joy and consola-tion of her relations and friends. She said that after her arrival at the Crow village, they made her dance with the scalps of her brother and husband tied to her hair, and clothed in the bloody shirt of the latter. On Wednes-day, 25th, a band of four hundred Crows arrived with the intention of taking the fort by stratagem if they could get the opportunity; but they failed in this, as I would not allow one of them inside the fort, or to come within firing distance of their arms. They used every artifice in their power to persuade me to let in a few of them to smoke the pipe of peace, assuring me that their intentions were good, and that they loved the white peo-ple. Finding all this of no avail, they brought their best horses to give to me, for which they did not wish to re-ceive anything more than the privilege of letting some of them come in; but all this was in vain, as I was well aware of their treacherous intentions. I divided my men in the two bastions, with orders to fire upon the first one that might approach during the night, and warned them of my having given such orders, telling them that I did not wish to strike the first blow, but that if they com-menced they would go off with small numbers, and sore hearts. There was an American with them who now told me of their intentions, and that they were deter-mined to take the fort. I sent them word by him that we were ready for them if they thought themselves able to do so, and to come and try; but when they saw our cannon pointed towards them, they were not so anxious to make a rush. On the 26th the Crows made another attempt to get in, but after a long and persuasive talk they found that it would not do. They then crossed the river and came on the high bank opposite to the fort, and fired upon us, and while some of them were yet crossing the river I let loose a cannon ball among them, which, if it did no harm, made them move at a quick pace, and after a while they all went off, leaving us without food of any sort; but fortunately on Monday the 30th, a party of Blood Indians came in from the Crows with fifteen horses and considerable meat. The Crows had taken all our horses shortly before, and promised to return them in a few days if I would let them in. I was also informed that they had even brought pack-horses to carry off the goods from the fort after having accomplished the destruction of the building and the massacre of ourselves."

From these extracts the nature of the Indians of these regions may be exemplified a thousand times better, *because true*, than by all the trashy stuff written and published by Mr. Catlin.

DESCRIPTION OF FORT UNION

By EDWIN T. DENIG. July 30, 1843

"FORT UNION, the principal and handsomest trading-post on the Missouri River, is situated on the north side, about six and a half miles above the mouth of the Yellowstone River; the country around it is beautiful, and well chosen for an establishment of the kind. The front of the fort is but a few steps, say twenty-five, from the bank of the Missouri. Behind the fort is a prairie with an agreeable ascent to the commencement of the bluffs, about one and a half miles in width, and two in length, surrounded at the

borders with high hills, or bluffs. Above and below, at
the distance of two hundred yards commence the points,
or bottoms, of the Missouri, which contain great quantities
of cottonwood, ash, and elm, supplying the fort with fuel,
boat and building timber. The fort itself was begun in
the fall of 1829, under the superintendence of Kenneth
McKenzie, Esq., an enterprising and enlightened Scotchman, and now a well known and successful merchant in
St. Louis. As the immense deal of work about such an
undertaking had but few men to accomplish it, it was not
wholly completed till after the expiration of *four years*,
and indeed since then has been greatly improved by the
other gentlemen who subsequently took charge of the
fort. The plan of the fort is laid nearly due north and
south, fronting 220 feet and running back 240 feet. This
space is enclosed by pickets or palisades of twenty feet
high, made of large hewn cottonwood, and founded upon
stone. The pickets are fitted into an open framework in
the inside, of sufficient strength to counterbalance their
weight, and sustained by braces in the form of an **X**,
which reaches in the inside from the pickets to the frame,
so as to make the whole completely solid and secure,
from either storm or attack. On the southwest and northeast corners, are bastions, built entirely out of stone, and
measuring 24 feet square, over 30 feet high, and the wall
three feet thick; this is whitewashed. Around the tops of
the second stories are balconies with railings, which serve
for observatories, and from the tops of the roofs are two
flag-staffs 25 feet high, on which wave the proud Eagle of
America. Two weathercocks, one a Buffalo bull, the
other an Eagle, complete the outsides. In the interior of
the northeast bastion are placed opposite their port-holes
one three-pounder iron cannon and one brass swivel, both
mounted, and usually kept loaded, together with a dozen
muskets in case of a sudden attack from the Indians.
Balls, cartridges, and other ammunition are always in readi-

ness for the use of the same. The contents of the southeast bastion are similar to those of the other, with the
exception of the cannon, having but one small swivel.
These and other preparations render the place impregnable
to any force without, not furnished with artillery. The principal building in the establishment, and that of the gentleman in charge, or Bourgeois, is now occupied by Mr.
Culbertson, one of the partners of the Company. It is
78 feet front by 24 feet depth, and a story and a half high.
The front has a very imposing appearance, being neatly
weather-boarded, and painted white, and with green win-
dow-shutters; it is roofed with shingle, painted red to preserve the wood. In the roof in front are four dormer
windows, which serve to give light to the attic. The piazza
in front adds much to the comfort and appearance, the
posts are all turned, and painted white. It serves as a
pleasant retreat from the heat of the day, and is a refreshing place to sleep at night when mosquitoes are plenty.
Mr. Audubon, the naturalist, now here upon scientific
researches, together with his secretary, Mr. Squires, prefer
this hard bed to the more luxurious comforts of feathers
and sheets. The interior of this building is handsomely
papered and ornamented with portraits and pictures, and
portioned off in the following manner. Mr. Culbertson
has the principal room, which is large, commodious, and
well-furnished; from it he has a view of all that passes
within the fort. Next to this is the office, which is
devoted exclusively to the business of the Company, which
is immense. This department is now under my super-
vision (viz., E. T. Denig). These two rooms occupy
about one-half the building. In the middle is a hall,
eight feet wide, which separates these rooms from the
other part. In this is the mess-room, which is nearly
equal in size to that of Mr. Culbertson. Here the Bourgeois, taking his seat at the head of the table, attends to
its honors, and serves out the *luxuries* this wilderness

produces to his visitors and clerks, who are seated in their proper order and rank. The mechanics of the fort eat at the second table. Adjoining this room is the residence of Mr. Denig. In the upper story are at present located Mr. Audubon and his suite. Here from the pencils of Mr. Audubon and Mr. Sprague emanate the splendid paintings and drawings of animals and plants, which are the admiration of all; and the Indians regard them as marvellous, and almost to be worshipped. In the room next to this is always kept a selection of saddlery and harness, in readiness for rides of pleasure, or for those rendered necessary for the protection of the horses which are kept on the prairie, and which suffer from frequent depredations on the part of the Indians, which it is the duty of the men at the fort to ward off as far as possible. The next apartment is the tailor's shop, so placed as to be out of the way of the Indian visitors as much as possible, who, were it at all easy of access, would steal some of the goods which it is necessary to have always on hand. So much for the principal house. On the east side of the fort, extending north and south, is a building, on range, all under one roof, 127 ft. long by 25 ft. deep, and used for the following purposes. A small room at the north end for stores and luggage; then the retail store, in which is kept a fair supply of merchandise, and where all white persons buy or sell. The prices of all goods are fixed by a tariff or stationary value, so that no bargaining or cheating is allowed; this department is now in charge of Mr. Larpenteur. Adjoining this is the wholesale warehouse, in which is kept the principal stock of goods intended for the extensive trade; this room is 57 ft. in length. Next is a small room for the storage of meat and other supplies. At the end is the press room, where all robes, furs, and peltries are stored. The dimensions extend to the top of the roof inside, which roof is perfectly waterproof. It will contain from 2800 to 3000 packs of Buffalo robes. All this range is very strongly put together, weather-boarded outside, and lined with plank within. It has also cellar and garret. Opposite this, on the other side of the fort enclosure, is a similar range of buildings 119 ft. long by 21 ft. wide, perhaps not quite so strongly built, but sufficiently so to suit all purposes. The height of the building is in proportion to that of the pickets; it is one large story high, and shingle-roofed. This is partitioned off into six different apartments of nearly equal size. The first two are appropriated to the use of the clerks who may be stationed at the post. The next is the residence of the hunters, and the remaining three the dwellings of the men in the employ of the Company. An ice-house 24 by 21 ft. is detached from this range, and is well filled with ice during the winter, which supply generally lasts till fall. Here is put all fresh meat in the hot weather, and the fort in the summer season is usually provisioned for ten days. The kitchen is behind the Bourgeois' house on the north side, and about two steps from the end of the hall, — so situated for convenience in carrying in the cooked victuals to the mess-room. Two or three cooks are usually employed therein, at busy times more. The inside frame-work of the fort, which sustains the pickets, forms all around a space about eight feet wide described by the braces or X, and about fifteen feet high. A balcony is built on the top of this, having the summit of the X for its basis, and is formed of sawed plank nailed to cross beams from one brace to another. This balcony affords a pleasant walk all round the inside of the fort, within five feet of the top of the pickets; from here also is a good view of the surrounding neighborhood, and it is well calculated for a place of defence. It is a favorite place from which to shoot Wolves after nightfall, and for standing guard in time of danger. The openings that would necessarily follow from such a construction, under the gallery, are fitted in some places with small

huts or houses.   Behind the kitchen there are five of such
houses, leaving at the same time plenty of space between
them and the other buildings.   The first of these is a
stable for Buffalo calves, which are annually raised here,
being caught during the severe storms of winter; the second a hen-house, well lined, plastered, and filled with
chickens; third, a very pleasant room intended as an artist's work-room, fourth, a cooper's shop, and then the
milk house and dairy.   Several houses of the same kind
and construction are also built on the west and south
sides; one contains coal for the blacksmith, and ten
stables, in all 117 ft. long, and 10 ft. wide, with space
enough to quarter fifty horses.   These are very useful, as
the Company have always a number of horses and cattle
here.   These buildings, it will be understood, do not interfere with the Area or Parade of the fort, and are hardly
noticed by a casual observer, but occupy the space under
the balcony that would otherwise be useless and void.
Fifty more of the same kind could be put up without intruding upon any portion of the fort used for other purposes.   On the front side, and west of the gate, is a house
50 by 21 feet, which, being divided into two parts, one half
opening into the fort, is used as a blacksmith's, gun-
smith's, and tinner's shop; the other part is used as a
reception-room for Indians, and opens into the passage,
which is made by the double gate.   There are two large
outside gates to the fort, one each in the middle of the
front and rear, and upon the top of the front one is a
painting of a treaty of peace between the Indians and
whites executed by J. B. Moncrévier, Esq.   These gates
are 12 ft. wide, and 14 ft. high.   At the front there is an
inside gate of the same size at the inner end of the Indian
reception room, which shuts a passage from the outside
gate of 32 ft. in length, and the same width as the gate;
the passage is formed of pickets.   The outside gate can
be left open, and the inside one closed, which permits the

Indians to enter the reception room without their having any communication with the fort. Into this room are brought all trading and war parties, until such time as their business is ascertained; there is also behind this room a trade shop, and leading into it a window through which the Indians usually trade, being secure from rain or accident; there is also another window through the pickets to the outside of the fort, which is used in trading when the Indians are troublesome, or too numerous. The Powder Magazine is perhaps the best piece of work, as regards strength and security, that could be devised for a fort like this. The dimensions are 25 by 18 ft.; it is built out of stone, which is a variety of limestone with a considerable quantity of sand in its composition. The walls are 4 ft. thick at the base, and increasing with the curve of the arch become gradually thicker as they rise, so that near the top they are about 6 ft. in thickness. The inside presents a complete semicircular arch, which is covered on the top with stones and gravel to the depth of 18 inches. The whole is covered with a shingle roof through which fire may burn yet with no danger to the powder within. There are two doors, one on the outside, the other a few feet within; the outer one is covered with tin. There are several other small buildings under the balcony, which are used for harness, tool-houses, meat, etc. The space behind the warehouse between that and the pickets, being free from buildings, affords a good horse yard, and some shelter to the horses in bad weather. The area of the fort within the fronts of the houses is 189 ft. long, and 141 ft. wide. In the centre of this arises a flag-staff 63 ft. high. This is surrounded at the base by a railing and panel work in an octagonal form, enclosing a portion of ground 12 ft. in diameter, in which are planted lettuce, radishes, and cress, and which presents at the same time a useful and handsome appearance. By the side of this stands a mounted four-pounder iron cannon. This flag-staff is the glory of the fort, for on high, seen from far and wide, floats the Star Spangled Banner, an immense flag which once belonged to the United States Navy, and gives the certainty of security from dangers, rest to the weary traveller, peace and plenty to the fatigued and hungry, whose eyes are gladdened by the sight of it on arriving from the long and perilous voyages usual in this far western wild.   It is customary on the arrivals and departures of the Bourgeois, or of the boats of gentlemen of note, to raise the flag, and by the firing of the cannon show them a welcome, or wish them a safe arrival at their point of destination.   When interest and affection are as circumscribed as here, they must necessarily be more intense, and partings are more regretted, being accompanied by dangers to the departing friends, and meetings more cordial, those dangers having been surmounted.   The casualties of the country are common to all, and felt the more by the handful, who, far from civilization, friends, or kindred, are associated in those risks and excitements which accrue from a life among savages.   About two hundred feet east of Fort Union is an enclosure about 150 ft. square, which is used for hay and other purposes.   Two hundred and fifty good cart-loads of hay are procured during the summer and stacked up in this place for winter use of horses and cattle, the winter being so severe and long, and snow so deep that little food is to be found for them on the prairies at that season.   There are, at present, in this place thirty head of cattle, forty horses, besides colts, and a goodly number of hogs.   A garden on a small scale is attached to the ' old fort ' as it is called, which supplies the table with peas, turnips, radishes, lettuce, beets, onions, etc.   The large garden, half a mile off and below the fort, contains one and a half acres, and produces most plentiful and excellent crops of potatoes, corn, and every kind of vegetable, but has not been worked this year.   In the summer

of 1838, Mr. Culbertson had from it 520 bushels of potatoes, and as many other vegetables as he required for the
use of the fort. Rainy seasons prove most favorable in
this climate for vegetation, but they rarely occur. It is
indeed pleasant to know that the enterprising men who
commenced, and have continued with untiring perseverance, the enlargement of the Indian trade, and labored
hard for the subordination, if not civilization, of the Indians, should occasionally sit down under their own vine
and fig-tree, and enjoy at least the semblance of living
like their more quiet, though not more useful brothers in
the United States."

FORT McKENZIE

By ALEXANDER CULBERTSON, Esq. August 7, 1843

"THE American Fur Company, whose untiring perseverance and enterprise have excited the wonder and admiration of many people, both in this and other countries, and
who have already acquired a well-earned fame for their
labors among the aborigines of this wilderness, and who
are now an example of the energy of the American people,
had, until the year 1832, no stations among the Blackfeet,
Piegans, Blood Indians, or Gros Ventres de Prairie, these
tribes being so hostile and bloodthirsty as to make the
trading, or the erecting of a fort among them too dangerous to be attempted. At last, however, these dangers
and difficulties were undertaken, commenced, and surmounted, and Fort McKenzie was erected in the very
heart of these tribes. The fort was begun in 1832, under
the superintendence of David D. Mitchell, then one of the
clerks of the Company, now U. S. Superintendent of
Indian Affairs. The fort was completed by me, Alexander
Culbertson, then a clerk of the Company, now one of the

partners. During the first year, owing to the exigencies of the occasion, a temporary, though substantial fort was erected, which, however, served to protect the daring few who undertook and accomplished the perilous task. To those who are quietly sitting by their firesides in the heart of civilized life, enjoying all its luxuries, pleasures, and comforts, and who are far removed from the prairie land and the red men, the situation of this party can hardly be pictured. They were surrounded by dangers of all kinds, but more especially from the tribes of Indians before mentioned. Two thousand lodges of Blackfeet were near them, waiting only until an opportunity should offer to satisfy their thirst for blood, to fall upon and kill them. Apart from this tribe the others were loitering around them for the same purpose; add to this, privations, fatigues, hardships, and personal ills which have to be encountered in a country like this. All, however, was met courageously; undaunted by appearances, unintimidated by threats, not unmanned by hardships and fatigues, they pushed ahead, completed the fort, and at last accomplished their object of establishing a trade with the tribes above mentioned; and they now enjoy a comparative peace, and are living upon fairly friendly terms with their late most violent enemies. During the following year another fort was commenced and completed, and retained its former name of Fort McKenzie, being named after Kenneth McKenzie, Esq., one of the partners of the Company. The fort is situated on the north side of the Missouri, about six miles above the mouth of the Maria, and about forty miles below the 'Great Falls' of the Missouri, on a beautiful prairie, about fifteen feet above the highest-water mark, and about 225 feet from the river. The prairie rises gradually from the water's edge to the hills in the rear, about half a mile from the river. It is about a mile long, terminating at a 'côte qui trompe de l'eau' on the lower end, and in a point at the upper end,

formerly heavily covered with timber, but now entirely
destitute. Opposite the fort is a high perpendicular bank
of black clay, rising from the river to the height of 150
feet; from this all that takes place within the walls of the
fort can be seen, which would seem to have rendered the
placing of the fort in such a position extremely inju-
dicious. But not through carelessness was this done; it is
simply the *sole place* in this section of country, near the
river, where a fort can be built, as the land is so rough
and uneven as to render the erection of a fort at any
other spot *impossible*. From this bank little or no danger
is apprehended, as the river is about one hundred yards
wide, and a ball fired by the Indians from this height,
and at this distance, with the weapons that they have,
would be incapable of doing any execution. Timber in
this country has become very scarce; points which a few
years ago were covered with heavy forests of the different
kinds of wood of the district have by some law of nature
become entirely destitute, especially a point below the
island called by the voyageurs the 'Grand Isle' (which
is situated at the commencement of the Mauvaises
Terres), where it has dwindled to a few scattering cotton-
woods and box elders; and this is the only wood now to
be found in this section of the country between 'Grand
Isle' and the 'Great Falls' of the Missouri. It is with
the greatest difficulty and economy that from the little
wood to be found the fort is supplied with the necessary
fuel; this is dealt out as a ration, allowing a certain
quantity to each room, sufficient, however, to do the cooking, and warm the inmates. *At all times*, except when
serving the ration, the wood is kept closely locked. This
is one of the privations of the country, and, indeed the
country affords very little which adds to the comfort of
the trader who makes these wilds his home, except such
as can be procured from the wild animals. Three sides
of the fort are built of pickets of hewn cottonwood,

squared, placed close together, eighteen feet long, planted three feet deep in the earth, leaving fifteen feet above ground. The pickets are connected at the top by a strong piece pinned to them. The fourth side, facing the northeast, is built of pickets framed in wooden sills lying in the ground, similar to those at Fort Union. The fort is two hundred feet square, ranging north and south and facing south. On the northeast and southwest corners are bastions built of cottonwood timber, ball proof, rising about eight feet above the pickets, twenty feet square and divided into two stories. In each bastion is a cannon, loaded muskets, cartridges, balls, and every requisite necessary to prevent and repel any attack that may take place, and which is hourly expected, from the surrounding tribes of Indians. In each bastion are port and loop holes for the cannon and muskets, and these command the four sides of pickets, and an extensive range over the prairie. Along the rear line of pickets, and about twenty-five feet from them, is the principal range of buildings in the fort. These are occupied by the Bourgeois, clerks, and interpreters. It is divided into three apartments; the principal room, with every comfort that this dreary place affords, belongs to the Bourgeois and is twenty feet square; and here, to partially remove the *ennui* of dull times, is a library of such books as time and opportunity have permitted the dwellers in the fort to collect; this is at the command of those who choose to 'drive dull care away,' and contains a little of everything, science, history, poetry, and fiction. Adjoining this room is a hall or passage eight feet wide, running from front to rear of the building, with a door opening into the Bourgeois's room, another opening into the clerk's room; the clerk's room is also used as a mess-room and is the same size as that of the Bourgeois. Adjoining the clerk's room is the one belonging to the interpreters; it is twenty-four by twenty feet and is also used as a council room, and reception room for the chiefs that may arrive at the fort. *The chiefs only* are admitted within the walls; not that any danger is apprehended now from them, but to prevent any trouble that might possibly occur were numbers permitted to enter. The house is of cottonwood logs, with a plank roof covered with earth, chimneys of mud, two windows and doors in the Bourgeois's room, one each in the other rooms. The interior is ceiled and walled with plank. In the Bourgeois's room are two doors made of pine plank which was sawed in the Rocky Mountains. The house is 75 by 20 ft. Most of the buildings in the fort are made in a similar manner. Above the three rooms described is a garret extending the whole length of the building. About three feet back of this edifice is the kitchen, a neat building twenty feet square, in which everything belonging to this most important and useful apartment is to be found, always in good order, clean and bright, as it is the imperative duty of the cook, or person in charge, to have all connected with this department in perfect order. From this room *all* persons are excluded, unless duty or business requires them to be there. Adjoining this, on the same line north, is a house of the same dimensions as the kitchen, which is used for salting and preserving tongues, one of the delicacies of the civilized world; when not thus used it answers the purpose of a wash-house. In these buildings are bedrooms occupied by the persons having charge of these departments. Extending along the west line of pickets, and about three feet from them, leaving a space between the range and the Bourgeois's house is a line of buildings divided in four apartments; one used for a blacksmith's and tinner's shop, another for a carpenter's shop, one for the tailor, and the other for the men. In the square formed by the pickets and ends of the Bourgeois's and men's houses, is a yard for sawing timber, a quantity of which is necessarily required about the fort. A house running from the south bastion to the passage, twenty-four feet square, is used as a reception room for war and trading parties; a door leads from this to the passage formed by the double gates, thereby cutting off all communication with the interior of the fort. In this room all parties are received by the interpreter, who is always ready to smoke and talk with the Indians. Next to this room is a passage formed by the double gates, and two parallel lines of pickets extending inwards, making the passage about thirty feet long and twelve wide; at the ends are two large gates, about twelve feet wide and the same height. Opposite the room last described is a similar one 20 by 15 ft., in which the Indians bring their robes to trade. Next this is a trade store, where are kept goods, trinkets, etc., to be traded with the Indians. The trading is done through a window or wicket two feet square, and a foot thick, strongly hinged to the picket; this opening is at the command of the trader, who can open or close it, as the Indians may appear friendly or otherwise, thereby completely cutting off, if necessary, all communication between the Indians and the trade store; and it is through this opening *only* that trade is carried on. Next this is a room twenty-four feet square, where all goods obtained from the Indians are placed as soon as the trade is finished; and adjoining the trade shop is a room, between it and the pickets, about ten feet square, with a window and door opening into the trade shop, with a chimney, fireplace, and stove used only for warming the trader when off duty, or when awaiting the arrival of Indians. Along the east line of pickets, and about forty feet from them, is another range of buildings, about a hundred feet long and twenty deep, divided into five apartments. The first three are for storing packs of robes, furs, peltries, etc., and will hold eighteen hundred packs of robes; the fourth room is a retail store, 15 by 20 ft., in which is always a good assortment of stores, the prices fixed by a regular tariff, so no cheating is possible. All whites buy and sell here.   Fifth, is the wholesale warehouse, in which are boxes, bales, and all goods kept in quantity till required. Within a few feet of this, and northeast, is the meat house, twenty-four feet square, in which all meat traded from the Indians is kept till needed for use.   Near the meat house south is a powder magazine, a hole dug in the ground ten feet square, walled with timber to the surface, covered with a timber roof four feet above the surface in the centre, and this is covered to the depth of three feet with earth; in the roof is an outer door three feet square, opening upon another of the same size; this is so arranged that in case of fire the whole can be covered in a few minutes, and rendered fire-proof.   In the southeast corner is a large barn, 60 by 50 ft., capable of containing sufficient hay for all the cattle and horses during the long, cold, tedious winters of this country.   Adjoining is a range of large and warm stables for the horses of the fort, and some extra ones if required, providing them with a good shelter from the piercing cold and severe storms.   Extending from the stables is a range of small buildings used for keeping saddlery, harness, boat-rigging, tools, etc., thereby providing ' a place for everything,' and it is required that everything shall be in its place.   Over this is a gallery extending along this line of pickets, answering the purposes of a promenade, observatory, guard station, and place of defence.   In the southeast corner in front of the barn is a yard 30 by 60 ft., used for receiving carts, wagons, wood, and so forth.   At the end of the yard in the rear of the dry-goods warehouse is an ice house, that will contain nearly forty loads of ice; meat placed here will keep several days in the heat of summer, and thus save the hunter from a daily ride over the burning prairies.   The stock belonging to the fort consists of thirty to forty horses, ten or twelve cattle, and a number of hogs.   Fort McKenzie boasts of one of the most splendid Durham bulls that can be found in the United States or Territories.   The area in

front of the buildings is about a hundred feet square; from
the centre rises a flag-staff fifty feet high; from this wave
the glorious folds of the starry banner of our native land,
made more beautiful by its situation in the dreary wilderness around it.   The wanderer, as he sees the bright folds
from afar, hails them with gladness, as it means for him a
place of safety.   No sight is more welcome to the voya-
geur, the hunter, or the trapper.   That flag cheers all
who claim it as theirs, and it protects all, white men or
red.   Here in the wilderness all fly to it for refuge, and
depend on it for security.   Upon the arrival or departure
of the Bourgeois, men of note, or arrival and departure of
the boats, the flag is raised, and salutes fired.   Here,
where but few are gathered together, undying attachments
are formed, a unanimity of feeling exists, to be found perhaps only in similar situations.   When the hour of parting
comes it is with regret, for amid the common dangers, so
well known, none know when the meeting again will be,
and when the hour of meeting comes, the joy is honest
and unfeigned that the dangers are safely surmounted.
Such is Fort McKenzie, such are its inmates.   Removed
as they are from civilization and its pleasures, home and
friends, they find in each other friends and brothers:
friends that forsake not in the hour of danger, but cling
through all changes; brothers in feeling and action, and
'though there be many, in heart they are one.'"

EPISODES

EPISODES[1]

THESE Episodes were introduced in the letterpress of the first three volumes of the "Ornithological Biographies," but are not in the octavo edition of the "Birds of America," and I believe no entire reprint of them has been made before. So far as possible they have been arranged chronologically.

[1] One episode has been added, — "My Style of drawing Birds," — and three have been omitted, that on Bewick being in the "Journal of England and France," and the others not of general interest.

EPISODES

LOUISVILLE IN KENTUCKY

L OUISVILLE in Kentucky has always been a favorite place of mine. The beauty of its situation on the banks of *La Belle Rivière*, just at the commencement of the famed rapids, commonly called the Falls of the Ohio, had attracted my notice, and when I removed to it, immediately after my marriage, I found it more agreeable than ever. The prospect from the town is such that it would please even the eye of a Swiss. It extends along the river for seven or eight miles, and is bounded on the opposite side by a fine range of low mountains, known by the name of the Silver Hills. The rumbling sound of the waters as they tumble over the rock-paved bed of the rapids is at all times soothing to the ear. Fish and game are abundant. But, above all, the generous hospitality of the inhabitants, and the urbanity of their manners, had induced me to fix upon it as a place of residence; and I did so with the more pleasure when I found that my wife was as much gratified as myself by the kind attentions which were shown to us, utter strangers as we were, on our arrival.

No sooner had we landed, and made known our intention of remaining, than we were introduced to the principal inhabitants of the place and its vicinity, although we had not brought a single letter of introduction, and could not but see, from their unremitting kindness, that the Virginian spirit of hospitality displayed itself in all the words and actions of our newly formed friends. I wish here to name those persons who so unexpectedly came forward to render our stay among them agreeable, but feel at a loss with whom to begin, so equally deserving are they of our gratitude. The Croghans, the Clarks (our great traveller included), the Berthouds, the Galts, the Maupins, the Tarascons, the Beals, and the Booths, form but a small portion of the long list which I could give. The matrons acted like mothers to my wife, the daughters proved agreeable associates, and the husbands and sons were friends and companions to me. If I absented myself on business, or otherwise, for any length of time, my wife was removed to the hospitable abode of some friend in the neighborhood until my return, and then, kind reader, I was several times obliged to spend a week or more with these good people before they could be prevailed upon to let us return to our own residence. We lived for two years at Louisville, where we enjoyed many of the best pleasures which this life can afford; and whenever we have since chanced to pass that way, we have found the kindness of our former friends unimpaired.

During my residence at Louisville, much of my time was employed in my ever favorite pursuits. I drew and noted the habits of everything which I procured, and my collection was daily augmenting, as every individual who carried a gun always sent me such birds or quadrupeds as he thought might prove useful to me. My portfolios already contained upwards of two hundred drawings. Dr. W. C. Galt being a botanist, was often consulted by me, as well as his friend, Dr. Ferguson. Mr. Gilly drew beautifully, and was fond of my pursuits. So was my friend, and now relative, N. Berthoud. As I have already said, our time was spent in the most agreeable manner, through the hospitable friendship of our acquaintance.

One fair morning I was surprised by the sudden entrance into our counting-room of Mr. Alexander Wilson, the celebrated author of the " American Ornithology," of whose existence I had never until that moment been apprised. This happened in March, 1810. How well do I remember him, as he walked up to me! His long, rather hooked nose, the keenness of his eyes, and his prominent cheek bones, stamped his countenance with a peculiar character. His dress, too, was of a kind not usually seen in that part of the country, — a short coat, trousers, and a waistcoat of gray cloth. His stature was not above the middle size. He had two volumes under his arm, and as he approached the table at which I was working, I thought I discovered something like astonishment in his countenance. He, however, immediately proceeded to disclose the object of his visit, which was to procure subscriptions for his work. He opened his books, explained the nature of his occupations, and requested my patronage.

I felt surprised and gratified at the sight of his volumes, turned over a few of the plates, and had already taken a pen to write my name in his favor, when my partner, rather abruptly, said to me in French, "My dear Audubon, what induces you to subscribe to this work? Your drawings are certainly far better, and again, you must know as much of the habits of American birds as this gentlemen." Whether Mr. Wilson understood French or not, or if the suddenness with which I paused disappointed him, I cannot tell; but I clearly perceived he was not pleased. Vanity and the encomiums of my friend prevented me from subscribing. Mr. Wilson asked me if I had many drawings of birds. I rose, took down a large portfolio, laid it on the table, and showed him, as I would show you, kind reader, or any other person fond of such subjects, the whole of the contents, with the same patience with which he had shown me his own engravings.

His surprise appeared great, as he told me he never had the most distant idea that any other individual than himself had been engaged in forming such a collection. He

asked me if it was my intention to publish, and when I
answered in the negative, his surprise seemed to increase.
And, truly, such was not my intention; for until long after,
when I met the Prince of Musignano in Philadelphia, I had
not the least idea of presenting the fruits of my labors to
the world. Mr. Wilson now examined my drawings with
care, asked if I should have any objections to lending him
a few during his stay, to which I replied that I had none;
he then bade me good-morning, not, however, until I had
made an arrangement to explore the woods in the vicinity
with him, and had promised to procure for him some birds
of which I had drawings in my collection, but which he
had never seen.

It happened that he lodged in the same house with us,
but his retired habits, I thought, exhibited either a strong
feeling of discontent or a decided melancholy. The
Scotch airs which he played sweetly on his flute made me
melancholy too, and I felt for him. I presented him to
my wife and friends, and seeing that he was all enthusiasm,
exerted myself as much as was in my power to procure
for him the specimens which he wanted. We hunted together, and obtained birds which he had never before seen;
but, reader, I did not subscribe to his work, for, even at
that time, my collection was greater than his. Thinking
that perhaps he might be pleased to publish the results of
my researches, I offered them to him, merely on condition
that what I had drawn, or might afterwards draw and send
to him, should be mentioned in his work as coming from
my pencil. I, at the same time, offered to open a corres-
pondence with him, which I thought might prove beneficial
to us both. He made no reply to either proposal, and before many days had elapsed, left Louisville, on his way to
New Orleans, little knowing how much his talents were
appreciated in our little town, at least by myself and my
friends.

Some time elapsed, during which I never heard of him,

or of his work. At length, having occasion to go to Philadelphia, I, immediately after my arrival there, inquired for him, and paid him a visit. He was then drawing a White-headed Eagle. He received me with civility, and took me to the exhibition rooms of Rembrandt Peale, the artist, who had then portrayed Napoleon crossing the Alps. Mr. Wilson spoke not of birds nor drawings. Feeling, as I was forced to do, that my company was not agreeable, I parted from him; and after that I never saw him again. But judge of my astonishment sometime after, when, on reading the thirty-ninth page of the ninth volume of "American Ornithology," I found in it the following paragraph: —

"*March 23, 1810.* I bade adieu to Louisville, to which place I had four letters of recommendation, and was taught to expect much of everything there; but neither received one act of civility from those to whom I was recommended, one subscriber nor one new bird; though I delivered my letters, ransacked the woods repeatedly, and visited all the characters likely to subscribe. Science or literature has not one friend in this place."

THE OHIO

WHEN my wife, my eldest son (then an infant), and myself were returning from Pennsylvania to Kentucky, we found it expedient, the waters being unusually low, to provide ourselves with a *skiff*, to enable us to proceed to our abode at Henderson. I purchased a large, commodious, and light boat of that denomination. We procured a mattress, and our friends furnished us with ready prepared viands. We had two stout negro rowers, and in this trim we left the village of Shippingport, in expectation of reaching the place of our destination in a very few days.

It was in the month of October. The autumnal tints already decorated the shores of that queen of rivers, the Ohio. Every tree was hung with long and flowing festoons of different species of vines, many loaded with clustered fruits of varied brilliancy, their rich bronzed carmine mingling beautifully with the yellow foliage, which now predominated over the yet green leaves, reflecting more lively tints from the clear stream than ever landscape painter portrayed, or poet imagined.

The days were yet warm. The sun had assumed the rich and glowing hue which at that season produces the singular phenomenon called there the "Indian Summer." The moon had rather passed the meridian of her grandeur. We glided down the river, meeting no other ripple of the water than that formed by the propulsion of our boat. Leisurely we moved along, gazing all day on the grandeur and beauty of the wild scenery around us.

Now and then a large catfish rose to the surface of the water, in pursuit of a shoal of fry, which, starting simultaneously from the liquid element like so many silver arrows, produced a shower of light, while the pursuer with open jaws seized the stragglers, and, with a splash of his tail, disappeared from our view. Other fishes we heard, uttering beneath our bark a rumbling noise, the strange sound of which we discovered to proceed from the white perch, for on casting our net from the bow, we caught several of that species, when the noise ceased for a time.

Nature, in her varied arrangements, seems to have felt a partiality towards this portion of our country. As the traveller ascends or descends the Ohio, he cannot help remarking that alternately, nearly the whole length of the river, the margin, on one side, is bounded by lofty hills and a rolling surface, while on the other, extensive plains of the richest alluvial land are seen as far as the eye can command the view. Islands of varied size and form rise here and there from the bosom of the water, and the winding course of the stream frequently brings you to places where the idea of being on a river of great length changes to that of floating on a lake of moderate extent. Some of these islands are of considerable size and value; while others, small and insignificant, seem as if intended for contrast, and as serving to enhance the general interest of the scenery. These little islands are frequently overflowed during great freshets or floods, and receive at their heads prodigious heaps of drifted timber. We foresaw with great concern the alterations that cultivation would soon produce along those delightful banks.

As night came, sinking in darkness the broader portions of the river, our minds became affected by strong emotions, and wandered far beyond the present moments. The tinkling of bells told us that the cattle which bore them were gently roving from valley to valley in search of food, or returning to their distant homes. The hooting of the Great Owl, or the muffled noise of its wings, as it sailed smoothly over the stream, were matters of interest to us; so was the sound of the boatman's horn, as it came winding more and more softly from afar. When daylight returned, many songsters burst forth with echoing notes, more and more mellow to the listening ear. Here and there the lonely cabin of a squatter struck the eye, giving note of commencing civilization. The crossing of the stream by a Deer foretold how soon the hills would be covered with snow.

Many sluggish flatboats we overtook and passed; some laden with produce from the different head-waters of the small rivers that pour their tributary streams into the Ohio; others, of less dimensions, crowded with emigrants from distant parts, in search of a new home. Purer pleasures I never felt; nor have you, reader, I ween, unless indeed you have felt the like, and in such company.

The margins of the shores and of the river were, at this

season, amply supplied with game. A Wild Turkey, a Grouse, or a Blue-winged Teal, could be procured in a few moments; and we fared well, for, whenever we pleased we landed, struck up a fire, and provided as we were with the necessary utensils, procured a good repast.

Several of these happy days passed, and we neared our home, when, one evening, not far from Pigeon Creek (a small stream which runs into the Ohio from the State of Indiana), a loud and strange noise was heard, so like the yells of Indian warfare, that we pulled at our oars, and made for the opposite side as fast and as quietly as possible. The sounds increased, we imagined we heard cries of "murder;" and as we knew that some depredations had lately been committed in the country by dissatisfied parties of aborigines, we felt for a while extremely uncomfortable. Ere long, however, our minds became more calmed, and we plainly discovered that the singular uproar was produced by an enthusiastic set of Methodists, who had wandered thus far out of the common way for the purpose of holding one of their annual camp-meetings, under the shade of a beech forest. Without meeting with any other interruption, we reached Henderson, distant from Shippingport, by water, about two hundred miles.

When I think of these times,[1] and call back to my mind the grandeur and beauty of those almost uninhabited shores; when I picture to myself the dense and lofty summits of the forests, that everywhere spread along the hills and overhung the margins of the stream, unmolested by the axe of the settler; when I know how dearly purchased the safe navigation of that river has been, by the blood of many worthy Virginians; when I see that no longer any aborigines are to be found there, and that the vast herds of Elk, Deer, and Buffaloes which once pastured on these hills, and in these valleys, making for themselves great roads to the several salt-springs, have ceased

[1] This was in 1810 or 1811.

to exist; when I reflect that all this grand portion of ·our Union, instead of being in a state of nature, is now more or less covered with villages, farms, and towns, where the din of hammers and machinery is constantly heard; that the woods are fast disappearing under the axe by day, and the fire by night; that hundreds of steamboats are gliding to and fro, over the whole length of the majestic river, forcing commerce to take root and to prosper at every spot; when I see the surplus population of Europe coming to assist in the destruction of the forest, and transplanting civilization into its darkest recesses; when I remember that these extraordinary changes have all taken place in the short period of twenty years, I pause, wonder, and although I know all to be fact, can scarcely believe its reality.

Whether these changes are for the better or for the worse, I shall not pretend to say; but in whatever way my conclusions may incline, I feel with regret that there are on record no satisfactory accounts of the state of that portion of the country, from the time when our people first settled in it. This has not been because no one in America is able to accomplish such an undertaking. Our Irvings and our Coopers have proved themselves fully competent for the task. It has more probably been because the changes have succeeded each other with such rapidity as almost to rival the movements of their pens. However, it is not too late yet; and I sincerely hope that either or both of them will ere long furnish the generations to come with those delightful descriptions which they are so well qualified to give, of the original state of a country that has been so rapidly forced to change her form and attire under the influence of increasing population. Yes, I hope to read, ere I close my earthly career, accounts from those delightful writers of the progress of civilization in our Western Country. They will speak of the Clarks, the Croghans, the Boones, and many other men

of great and daring enterprise. They will analyze, as it
were, into each component part, the country as it once
existed, and will render the picture, as it ought to be,
immortal.

FISHING IN THE OHIO

IT is with mingled feelings of pleasure and regret that
I recall to my mind the many pleasant days I have
spent on the shores of the Ohio. The visions of former
years crowd on my view, as I picture to myself the fertile soil and genial atmosphere of our great western garden, Kentucky, and view the placid waters of the fair
stream that flows along its western boundary. Methinks
I am now on the banks of the noble river. Twenty years
of my life have returned to me; my sinews are strong,
and the "bowspring of my spirit is not slack;" bright
visions of the future float before me, as I sit on a grassy
bank, gazing on the glittering waters. Around me are
dense forests of lofty trees and thickly tangled undergrowth, amid which are heard the songs of feathered
choristers, and from whose boughs hang clusters of glowing fruits and beautiful flowers. Reader, I am very
happy. But now the dream has vanished, and here I am
in the British Athens, penning an episode for my Ornithological Biography, and having before me sundry well-
thumbed and weather-beaten folios, from which I expect to
be able to extract some interesting particulars respecting
the methods employed in those days in catching catfish.

But before entering on my subject I will present you
with a brief description of the place of my residence on
the banks of the Ohio. When I first landed at Henderson in Kentucky, my family, like the village, was quite
small. The latter consisted of six or eight houses, the
former of my wife, myself, and a young child. Few as

the houses were, we fortunately found one empty. It was a log *cabin*, not a log *house;* but as better could not be had, we were pleased. Well, then, we were located. The country around was thinly peopled, and all purchasable provisions rather scarce; but our neighbors were friendly, and we had brought with us flour and bacon-hams. Our pleasures were those of young people not long married, and full of life and merriment; a single smile from our infant was, I assure you, more valued by us than all the treasure of a modern Crœsus would have been. The woods were amply stocked with game, the river with fish; and now and then the hoarded sweets of the industrious bees were brought from some hollow tree to our little table. Our child's cradle was our richest piece of furniture, our guns and fishing-lines our most serviceable implements, for although we began to cultivate a garden, the rankness of the soil kept the seeds we planted far beneath the tall weeds that sprung up the first year. I had then a partner, a "man of business," and there was also with me a Kentucky youth, who much preferred the sports of the forest and river to either day-book or ledger. He was naturally, as I may say, a good woodsman, hunter, and angler, and, like me, thought chiefly of procuring supplies of fish and fowl. To the task accordingly we directed all our energies.

Quantity as well as quality was an object with us, and although we well knew that three species of catfish existed in the Ohio, and that all were sufficiently good, we were not sure as to the best method of securing them. We determined, however, to work on a large scale, and immediately commenced making a famous "trot-line." Now, reader, as you may probably know nothing about this engine, I shall describe it to you.

A trot-line is one of considerable length and thickness, both qualities, however, varying according to the extent of water, and the size of the fish you expect to catch. As the Ohio, at Henderson, is rather more than half a mile in breadth, and as catfishes weigh from one to an hundred pounds, we manufactured a line which measured about two hundred yards in length, as thick as the little finger of some fair one yet in her teens, and as white as the damsel's finger well could be, for it was wholly of Kentucky cotton, just, let me tell you, because that substance stands the water better than either hemp or flax. The main line finished, we made a hundred smaller ones, about five feet in length, to each of which we fastened a capital hook of Kirby and Co.'s manufacture. Now for the bait!

It was the month of May. Nature had brought abroad myriads of living beings; they covered the earth, glided through the water, and swarmed in the air. The catfish is a voracious creature, not at all nice in feeding, but one who, like the Vulture, contents himself with carrion when nothing better can be had. A few experiments proved to us that, of the dainties with which we tried to allure them to our hooks, they gave a decided preference, at that season, to *live toads*. These animals were very abundant about Henderson. They ramble or feed, whether by instinct or reason, during early or late twilight more than at any other time, especially after a shower, and are unable to bear the heat of the sun's rays for several hours before and after noon. We have a good number of these crawling things in America, particularly in the western and southern parts of the Union, and are very well supplied with frogs, snakes, lizards, and even crocodiles, which we call alligators; but there is enough of food for them all, and we generally suffer them to creep about, to leap or to flounder as they please, or in accordance with the habits which have been given them by the great Conductor of all.

During the month of May, and indeed until autumn, we found an abundant supply of toads. Many "fine ladies," no doubt, would have swooned, or at least screamed and gone into hysterics, had they seen one of our baskets filled with these animals, all alive and plump. Fortunately we had no tragedy queen or sentimental spinster at Henderson. Our Kentucky ladies mind their own affairs, and seldom meddle with those of others farther than to do all they can for their comfort. The toads, collected one by one, and brought home in baskets, were deposited in a barrel for use. And now that night is over, and as it is the first trial we are going to give our trot-line, just watch our movements from that high bank beside the stream. There sit down under the large cotton-wood tree. You are in no danger of catching cold at this season.

My assistant follows me with a gaff hook, while I carry the paddle of our canoe; a boy bears on his back a hundred toads as good as ever hopped. Our line — oh, I forgot to inform you that we had set it last night, but without the small ones you now see on my arm. Fastening one end to yon sycamore, we paddled our canoe, with the rest nicely coiled in the stern, and soon reached its extremity, when I threw over the side the heavy stone fastened to it as a sinker. All this was done that it might be thoroughly soaked, and without kinks or snarls in the morning. Now, you observe, we launch our light bark, the toads in the basket are placed next to my feet in the bow; I have the small lines across my knees already looped at the end. Nat, with the paddle, and assisted by the current, keeps the stern of our boat directly down stream; and David fixes by the skin of the back and hind parts, the living bait to the hook. I hold the main line all the while, and now, having fixed one linelet to it, over goes the latter. Can you see the poor toad kicking and flouncing in the water? "No?" — well, I do. You observe at length that all the lines, one after another, have been fixed, baited, and dropped. We now return swiftly to the shore.

"What a delightful thing is fishing!" have I more than
once heard some knowing angler exclaim, who, with "the
patience of Job," stands or slowly moves along some rivulet twenty feet wide, and three or four feet deep, with a
sham fly to allure a trout, which, when at length caught,
weighs half a pound.   Reader, I never had such patience.
Although I have waited ten years, and yet see only three-
fourths of the "Birds of America" engraved, although some
of the drawings of that work were patiently made so long
ago as 1805, and although I have to wait with patience
two years more before I see the end of it, I never could
hold a line or a rod for many minutes, unless I had — not
a "nibble" but a hearty bite, and could throw the fish at
once over my head on the ground.   No, no — if I fish for
trout, I must soon give up, or catch as I have done in
Pennsylvania's Lehigh, or the streams of Maine, fifty or
more in a couple of hours.   But the trot-line is in the
river, and there *it* may patiently wait, until I visit it
towards night.   Now I take up my gun and note-book,
and accompanied by my dog, intend to ramble through
the woods until breakfast.   Who knows but I may shoot
a turkey or a deer?   It is barely four o'clock, and see
what delightful mornings we have at this season in
Kentucky!

Evening has returned.   The heavens have already
opened their twinkling eyes, although the orb of day has
yet scarcely withdrawn itself from our view.   How calm
is the air!   The nocturnal insects and quadrupeds are
abroad; the Bear is moving through the dark cane-brake,
the land Crows are flying towards their roosts, their aquatic
brethren towards the interior of the forests, the Squirrel
is barking his adieu, and the Barred Owl glides silently
and swiftly from his retreat to seize upon the gay and
noisy animal.   The boat is pushed off from the shore;
the main line is in my hands; now it shakes, surely some
fish have been hooked.   Hand over hand I proceed to the

first hook. Nothing there! but now I feel several jerks, stronger and more frequent than before. Several hooks I pass; but see, what a fine catfish is twisting round and round the little line to which he is fast! Nat, look to your gaff — hook him close to the tail. Keep it up, my dear fellow! — there now, we have him. More are on, and we proceed. When we have reached the end many goodly fishes are lying in the bottom of our skiff. New bait has been put on, and, as we return, I congratulate myself and my companions on the success of our efforts; for there lies fish enough for ourselves and our neighbors.

A trot-line at this period was perfectly safe at Henderson, should I have allowed it to remain for weeks at a time. The navigation was mostly performed by flat-bottomed boats, which during calm nights floated in the middle current of the river, so that the people on board could not observe the fish that had been hooked. Not a single steamer had as yet ever gone down the Ohio; now and then, it is true, a barge or a keel-boat was propelled by poles and oars, but the nature of the river is such at that place, that these boats when ascending were obliged to keep near the Indiana shore, until above the landing of the village (below which I always fixed my lines), when they pulled across the stream.

Several species or varieties of catfish are found in the Ohio, namely, the Blue, the White, and the Mud Cats, which differ considerably in their form and color, as well as in their habits. The Mud Cat is the best, although it seldom attains so great a size as the rest. The Blue Cat is the coarsest, but when not exceeding from four to six pounds it affords tolerable eating. The White Cat is preferable to the last, but not so common; and the Yellow Mud Cat is the best and rarest. Of the Blue kind some have been caught that weighed a hundred pounds. Such fish, however, are looked upon as monsters.

The form in all the varieties inclines to the conical, the head being disproportionately large, while the body tapers away to the root of the tail. The eyes, which are small, are placed far apart, and situated as it were on the top of the forehead, but laterally. Their mouth is wide and armed with numerous small and very sharp teeth, while it is defended by single-sided spines, which, when the fish is in the agonies of death, stand out at right angles, and are so firmly fixed as sometimes to break before you can loosen them. The catfish has also feelers of proportionate length, apparently intended to guide its motions over the bottom, whilst its eyes are watching the objects passing above.

Trot-lines cannot be used with much success unless during the middle stages of the water. When very low, it is too clear, and the fish, although extremely voracious, will rarely risk its life for a toad. When the waters are rising rapidly, your trot-lines are likely to be carried away by one of the numerous trees that float in the stream. A "happy medium" is therefore best.

When the waters are rising fast and have become muddy, a single line is used for catching catfish. It is fastened to the elastic branch of some willow several feet above the water, and must be twenty or thirty feet in length. The entrails of a Wild Turkey, or a piece of fresh venison furnish good bait; and if, when you visit your line the next morning after you have set it, the water has not risen too much, the swinging of the willow indicates that a fish has been hooked, and you have only to haul the prize ashore.

One evening I saw that the river was rising at a great rate, although it was still within its banks. I knew that the white perch were running, that is, ascending the river from the sea, and, anxious to have a tasting of that fine fish, I baited a line with a crayfish, and fastened it to the bough of a tree. Next morning as I pulled in the line, it felt as if fast at the bottom, yet on drawing it slowly I found that it came. Presently I felt a strong pull, the line slipped through my fingers, and next instant a large catfish leaped out of the water. I played it for a while until it became exhausted, when I drew it ashore. It had swallowed the hook, and I cut off the line close to its head. Then passing a stick through one of the gills, I and a servant tugged the fish home. On cutting it open, we, to our surprise, found in its stomach a fine white perch, dead, but not in the least injured. The perch had been lightly hooked, and the catfish, after swallowing it, had been hooked in the stomach, so that, although the instrument was small, the torture caused by it no doubt tended to disable the catfish. The perch we ate, and the cat, which was fine, we divided into four parts, and distributed among our neighbors. My most worthy friend and relative, Nicholas Berthoud, Esq., who formerly resided at Shippingport in Kentucky, but now in New York, a better fisher than whom I never knew, once placed a trot-line in the basin below "Tarascon's Mills," at the foot of the Rapids of the Ohio. I cannot recollect the bait which was used; but on taking up the line we obtained a remarkably fine catfish, in which was found the greater part of a sucking pig.

I may here add that I have introduced a figure of the catfish in Plate XXXI. of the first volume of my illustrations, in which I have represented the White-headed Eagle.

A WILD HORSE

WHILE residing at Henderson in Kentucky, I became acquainted with a gentleman who had just returned from the country in the neighborhood of the head-waters of the Arkansas River, where he had purchased a newly caught "Wild Horse," a descendant of some of the horses originally brought from Spain, and set at liberty in the vast prairies of the Mexican lands. The animal was by no means handsome; he had a large head, with a considerable prominence in its frontal region, his thick and unkempt mane hung along his neck to the breast, and his tail, too scanty to be called flowing, almost reached the ground. But his chest was broad, his legs clean and sinewy, and his eyes and nostrils indicated spirit, vigor, and endurance. He had never been shod, and although he had been ridden hard, and had performed a long journey, his black hoofs had suffered no damage. His color inclined to bay, the legs of a deeper tint, and gradually darkening below until they became nearly black. I inquired what might be the value of such an animal among the Osage Indians, and was answered that, the horse being only four years old, he had given for him, with the tree and the buffalo-tug fastened to his head, articles equivalent to about thirty-five dollars. The gentleman added that he had never mounted a better horse, and had very little doubt that, if well fed, he could carry a man of ordinary weight from thirty-five to forty miles a day for a month, as he had travelled at that rate upon him, without giving him any other food than the grass of the prairies, or the canes of the bottom lands, until he had crossed the Mississippi at Natchez, when he fed him with corn. Having no farther use for him, now that he had ended his journey, he said he was anxious to sell him, and thought he might prove a good hunting-horse for me, as his gaits were easy, and he stood fire as well as any charger he had seen. Having some need of a horse possessed of qualities similar to those represented as belonging to the one in question, I asked if I might be allowed to try him. "Try him, sir, and welcome; nay, if you will agree to feed him and take care of him, you may keep him for a month if you choose." So I had the horse taken to the stable and fed.

About two hours afterwards, I took my gun, mounted the prairie nag, and went to the woods. I was not long in finding him very sensible to the spur, and as I observed that he moved with great ease, both to himself and his rider, I thought of leaping over a log several feet in diameter, to judge how far he might prove serviceable in deer-driving or bear-hunting. So I gave him the reins, and pressed my legs to his belly without using the spur, on which, as if aware that I wished to try his mettle, he bounded off, and cleared the log as lightly as an elk. I turned him, and made him leap the same log several times, which he did with equal ease, so that I was satisfied of his ability to clear any impediment in the woods. I next determined to try his strength, for which purpose I took him to a swamp, which I knew was muddy and tough. He entered it with his nose close to the water, as if to judge of its depth, at which I was well pleased, as he thus evinced due caution. I then rode through the swamp in different directions, and found him prompt, decided, and unflinching. Can he swim well? thought I, — for there are horses, which, although excellent, cannot swim at all, but will now and then lie on their side, as if contented to float with the current, when the rider must either swim and drag them to the shore, or abandon them. To the Ohio then I went, and rode into the water. He made off obliquely against the current, his head well raised above the surface, his nostrils expanded, his breathing free, and without any of the grunting noise emitted by many horses on such occasions. I turned him down the stream, then directly against it, and finding him quite to my mind, I returned to the shore, on reaching which he stopped of his own accord, spread his legs, and almost shook me off my seat. After this, I put him to a gallop, and returning home through the woods, shot from the saddle a Turkey-cock, which he afterwards approached as if he had been trained to the sport, and enabled me to take it up without dismounting.

As soon as I reached the house of Dr. Rankin, where I then resided, I sent word to the owner of the horse that I should be glad to see him. When he came, I asked him what price he would take; he said, fifty dollars in silver was the lowest. So I paid the money, took a bill of sale, and became master of the horse. The doctor, who was an excellent judge, said smiling to me, "Mr. Audubon, when you are tired of him, I will refund you the fifty dollars, for depend upon it he is a capital horse." The mane was trimmed, but the tail left untouched; the doctor had him shod "all round," and for several weeks he was ridden by my wife, who was highly pleased with him.

Business requiring that I should go to Philadelphia, Barro (he was so named after his former owner) was put up for ten days, and well tended. The time of my departure having arrived, I mounted him, and set off at the rate of four miles an hour — but here I must give you the line of my journey, that you may, if you please, follow my course on some such map as that of Tanner's. From Henderson through Russellville, Nashville, and Knoxville, Abingdon in Virginia, the Natural Bridge, Harrisonburg, Winchester, and Harper's Ferry, Frederick, and Lancaster, to Philadelphia. There I remained four days, after which I returned by way of Pittsburgh, Wheeling, Zanesville, Chillicothe, Lexington, and Louisville, to Henderson. But the nature of my business was such as to make me deviate considerably from the main roads, and I computed the whole distance at nearly two thousand miles, the post roads being rather more than sixteen hundred. I travelled not less than forty miles a day, and it was allowed by the doctor that my horse was in as good condition on my return as when I set out. Such a journey on a single horse may seem somewhat marvellous in the eyes of a European; but in these days almost every merchant had to perform the like, some from all parts of the western country, even from St. Louis on the Missouri, although the travellers not unfrequently, on their return, sold their horses at Baltimore, Philadelphia, or Pittsburg, at which latter place they took boat. My wife rode on a single horse from Henderson to Philadelphia, travelling at the same rate. The country was then comparatively new; few coaches travelled, and in fact the roads were scarcely fit for carriages. About twenty days were considered necessary for performing a journey on horseback from Louisville to Philadelphia, whereas now the same distance may be travelled in six or seven days,[1] or even sometimes less, this depending on the height of the water in the Ohio.

It may not be uninteresting to you to know the treatment which the horse received on those journeys. I rose every morning before day, cleaned my horse, pressed his back with my hand, to see if it had been galled, and placed on it a small blanket folded double, in such a manner that when the saddle was put on, half of the cloth was turned over it. The surcingle, beneath which the saddle-bags were placed, confined the blanket to the seat, and to the pad behind was fastened the great coat or cloak, tightly rolled up. The bridle had a snaffle bit; a breast-plate was buckled in front to each skirt, to render the seat secure during an ascent; but my horse required no crupper, his shoulders being high and well-formed. On starting he trotted off at the rate of four miles an hour, which he continued. I usually travelled from fifteen to twenty miles before breakfast, and after the first hour allowed my horse to drink as much as he would. When I halted for breakfast, I generally stopped two hours, cleaned the horse, and gave him as much corn-blades as he could eat. I then rode on until within half an hour of sunset, when I watered him well, poured a bucket of cold water over his back, had his skin well rubbed, his feet examined and

[1] This was written in 1835.

cleaned. The rack was filled with blades, the trough with corn, a good-sized pumpkin or some hen's-eggs, whenever they could be procured, were thrown in, and if oats were to be had, half a bushel of them was given in preference to corn, which is apt to heat some horses. In the morning, the nearly empty trough and rack afforded sufficient evidence of the state of his health.

I had not ridden him many days before he became so attached to me that on coming to some limpid stream in which I had a mind to bathe, I could leave him at liberty to graze, and he would not drink if told not to do so. He was ever sure-footed, and in such continual good spirits that now and then, when a Turkey happened to rise from a dusting-place before me, the mere inclination of my body forward was enough to bring him to a smart canter, which he would continue until the bird left the road for the woods, when he never failed to resume his usual trot. On my way homeward I met at the crossings of the Juniata River a gentleman from New Orleans, whose name is Vincent Nolte.[1] He was mounted on a superb horse, for which he had paid three hundred dollars, and a servant on horseback led another as a change. I was then

[1] Vincent Nolte, in "Fifty Years in Both Hemispheres," gives an account of his meeting on this occasion with Audubon, part of which is as follows: "About ten o'clock I arrived at a small inn, close by the falls of the Juniata River. The landlady showed me into a room and said I perhaps would not mind taking my meal with a strange gentleman, who was already there. This personage struck me as an odd fish. He was sitting at a table before the fire, with a Madras handkerchief wound around his head, exactly in the style of the French mariners of a seaport town. . . . He showed himself to be an original throughout, but admitted he was a Frenchman by birth, and a native of La Rochelle. However, he had come in his early youth to Louisiana, had grown up in the sea-service, and had gradually become a thorough American. This man, who afterwards won for himself so great a name in natural history, particularly in ornithology, was Audubon." It is needless to say that the personal history of Audubon as here given is entirely erroneous; but as the meeting was in 1811, and the book written *from memory* in 1854, Mr. Nolte must be pardoned for his misstatements, which were doubtless unintentional.

an utter stranger to him, and as I approached and praised his horse, he not very courteously observed that he wished I had as good a one. Finding that he was going to Bedford to spend the night, I asked him at what hour he would get there. "Just soon enough to have some trout ready for our supper, provided you will join when you get there." I almost imagined that Barro understood our conversation; he pricked up his ears, and lengthened his pace, on which Mr. Nolte caracoled his horse, and then put him to a quick trot; but all in vain, for I reached the hotel nearly a quarter of an hour before him, ordered the trout, saw to the putting away of my good horse, and stood at the door ready to welcome my companion. From that day Vincent Nolte has been a friend to me. It was from him I received letters of introduction to the Rathbones of Liverpool, for which I shall ever be grateful to him. We rode together as far as Shippingport, where my worthy friend Nicholas Berthoud, Esq., resided, and on parting with me he repeated what he had many times said before, that he never had seen so serviceable a creature as Barro.

If I recollect rightly, I gave a short verbal account of this journey, and of the good qualities of my horse, to my learned friend J. Skinner, Esq., of Baltimore, who, I believe, has noticed them in his excellent Sporting Magazine. We agreed that the importation of horses of this kind from the Western prairies might improve our breeds generally; and judging from those which I have seen, I am inclined to think that some of them may prove fit for the course. A few days after reaching Henderson, I parted with Barro, not without regret, for a hundred and twenty dollars.

BREAKING UP OF THE ICE

WHILE proceeding up the Mississippi above its junction
with the Ohio,[1] I found to my great mortification that
its navigation was obstructed by ice. The chief conductor of my bark, who was a French Canadian, was
therefore desired to take us to a place suitable for winter
quarters, which he accordingly did, bringing us into a great
bend of the river called Tawapatee Bottom. The waters
were unusually low, the thermometer indicated excessive
cold, the earth all around was covered with snow, dark
clouds were spread over the heavens, and as all appearances were unfavorable to the hope of a speedy prosecution
of our voyage, we quietly set to work. Our bark, which
was a large keel-boat, was moored close to the shore, the
cargo was conveyed to the woods, large trees were felled
over the water, and were so disposed as to keep off the
pressure of the floating masses of ice. In less than two
days, our stores, baggage, and ammunition were deposited
in a great heap under one of the magnificent trees of
which the forest was here composed, our sails were spread
over all, and a complete camp was formed in the wilderness. Everything around us seemed dreary and dismal,
and had we not been endowed with the faculty of deriving
pleasure from the examination of nature, we should have
made up our minds to pass the time in a state similar to
that of Bears during their time of hibernation. We soon
found employment, however, for the woods were full of
game; and Deer, Turkeys, Raccoons, and Opossums might
be seen even around our camp; while on the ice that now
covered the broad stream rested flocks of Swans, to sur-

[1] This was on the journey made by Audubon and his partner, Ferdinand
Rozier, from Louisville to St. Geneviève, then in Upper Louisiana. They
left Louisville in the autumn of 1810, and Audubon returned in the spring
of 1811.

prise which the hungry Wolves were at times seen to make energetic but unsuccessful efforts. It was curious to see the snow-white birds all lying flat on the ice, but keenly intent on watching the motions of their insidious enemies, until the latter advanced within the distance of a few hundred yards, when the Swans, sounding their trumpet-notes of alarm, would all rise, spread out their broad wings, and after running some yards and battering the ice until the noise was echoed like thunder through the woods, rose exultingly into the air, leaving their pursuers to devise other schemes for gratifying their craving appetites.

The nights being extremely cold, we constantly kept up a large fire, formed of the best wood. Fine trees of ash and hickory were felled, cut up into logs of convenient size, and rolled into a pile, on the top of which, with the aid of twigs, a fire was kindled. There were about fifteen of us, some hunters, others trappers, and all more or less accustomed to living in the woods. At night, when all had returned from their hunting grounds, some successful and others empty-handed, they presented a picture in the strong glare of the huge fire that illuminated the forest, which it might prove interesting to you to see, were it copied by a bold hand on canvas. Over a space of thirty yards or more, the snow was scraped away, and piled up into a circular wall, which protected us from the cold blast. Our cooking utensils formed no mean display, and before a week had elapsed, Venison, Turkeys, and Raccoons hung on the branches in profusion. Fish, too, and that of excellent quality, often graced our board, having been obtained by breaking holes in the ice of the lakes. It was observed that the Opossums issued at night from holes in the banks of the river, to which they returned about daybreak; and having thus discovered their retreat, we captured many of them by means of snares.

At the end of a fortnight our bread failed, and two of the

party were directed to proceed across the bend, towards a
village on the western bank of the Mississippi, in quest of
that commodity; for although we had a kind of substitute
for it in the dry white flesh of the breast of the wild Turkey,
bread is bread after all, and more indispensable to civilized
man than any other article of food.   The expedition left
the camp early one morning; one of the party boasted
much of his knowledge of woods, while the other said
nothing, but followed.   They walked on all day, and
returned next morning to the camp with empty wallets.
The next attempt, however, succeeded, and they brought
on a sledge a barrel of flour, and some potatoes.   After
a while we were joined by many Indians, the observation
of whose manners afforded us much amusement.

Six weeks were spent in Tawapatee Bottom.   The
waters had kept continually sinking, and our boat lay on
her side high and dry.   On both sides of the stream, the
ice had broken into heaps, forming huge walls.   Our pilot
visited the river daily, to see what prospect there might be
of a change.   One night, while, excepting himself, all were
sound asleep, he suddenly roused us with loud cries of
"The ice is breaking!   Get up, get up!   Down to the boat,
lads!   Bring out your axes!   Hurry on, or we may lose her!
Here, let us have a torch!"   Starting up as if we had been
attacked by a band of savages, we ran pell-mell to the bank.
The ice was indeed breaking up; it split with reports like
those of heavy artillery, and as the water had suddenly
risen from an overflow of the Ohio, the two streams seemed
to rush against each other with violence; in consequence
of which the congealed mass was broken into large fragments, some of which rose nearly erect here and there,
and again fell with thundering crash, as the wounded
whale, when in the agonies of death, springs up with
furious force and again plunges into the foaming waters.
To our surprise the weather, which in the evening had been
calm and frosty, had become wet and blowy.   The water

gushed from the fissures formed in the ice, and the prospect was extremely dismal. When day dawned, a spectacle strange and fearful presented itself: the whole mass of water was violently agitated, its covering was broken into small fragments, and although not a foot of space was without ice, not a step could the most daring have ventured to make upon it. Our boat was in imminent danger, for the trees which had been placed to guard it from the ice were cut or broken into pieces, and were thrust against her. It was impossible to move her; but our pilot ordered every man to bring down great bunches of cane, which were lashed along her sides; and before these were destroyed by the ice, she was afloat and riding above it. While we were gazing on the scene a tremendous crash was heard, which seemed to have taken place about a mile below, when suddenly the great dam of ice gave way. The current of the Mississippi had forced its way against that of the Ohio, and in less than four hours we witnessed the complete breaking up of the ice.

During that winter the ice was so thick on the Mississippi that, opposite St. Louis, horses and heavy wagons crossed the river. Many boats had been detained in the same manner as our own, so that provisions and other necessary articles had become very scarce, and sold at a high price. This was the winter of 1810–11.

THE PRAIRIE

On my return from the Upper Mississippi I found myself obliged to cross one of the wide prairies which, in that portion of the United States, vary the appearance of the country. The weather was fine; all around me was as fresh and blooming as if it had just issued from the bosom of Nature. My knapsack, my gun, and my dog were all I had for baggage and company. But, although well moccasined, I moved slowly along, attracted by the brilliancy of the flowers, and the gambols of the fawns around their dams, to all appearance as thoughtless of danger as I felt myself.

My march was of long duration; I saw the sun sinking below the horizon long before I could perceive any appearance of woodland, and nothing in the shape of man had I met with that day. The track which I followed was only an old Indian trace, and as darkness overshadowed the prairie I felt some desire to reach at least a copse, in which I might lie down to rest. The Night Hawks were skimming over and around me, attracted by the buzzing wings of the beetles which form their food, and the distant howling of wolves gave me some hope that I should soon arrive at the skirts of some woodlands.

I did so, and almost at the same instant, a firelight attracting my eye, I moved towards it, full of confidence that it proceeded from the camp of some wandering Indians. I was mistaken: I discovered by its glare that it was from the hearth of a small log cabin, and that a tall figure passed and repassed between it and me, as if busily engaged in household arrangements.

I reached the spot, and presenting myself at the door, asked the tall figure, which proved to be a woman, if I might take shelter under her roof for the night. Her voice was gruff, and her attire negligently thrown about her. She answered in the affirmative. I walked in, took a wooden stool, and quietly seated myself by the fire. The next object that attracted my notice was a finely formed young Indian, resting his head between his hands, with his elbows on his knees. A long bow rested against the log wall near him, while a quantity of arrows and two or three Raccoon skins lay at his feet. He moved not; he apparently breathed not. Accustomed to the habits of Indians, and knowing that they pay little attention to the

approach of civilized strangers (a circumstance which in
some countries is considered as evincing the apathy of
their character), I addressed him in French, a language
not infrequently partially known to the people in that
neighborhood. He raised his head, pointed to one of
his eyes with his finger, and gave me a significant glance
with the other. His face was covered with blood. The
fact was that an hour before this, as he was in the act of
discharging an arrow at a Raccoon in the top of a tree, the
arrow had split upon the cord, and sprung back with such
violence into his right eye as to destroy it forever.

Feeling hungry, I inquired what sort of fare I might
expect. Such a thing as a bed was not to be seen, but
many large untanned Bear and Buffalo hides lay piled in
a corner. I drew a fine time-piece from my breast, and
told the woman that it was late, and that I was fatigued.
She had espied my watch, the richness of which seemed
to operate upon her feelings with electric quickness. She
told me there was plenty of venison and jerked buffalo
meat, and that on removing the ashes I should find a
cake. But my watch had struck her fancy, and her curiosity had to be gratified by an immediate sight of it. I
took off the gold chain that secured it, from around my
neck, and presented it to her; she was all ecstasy, spoke
of its beauty, asked me its value, and put the chain round
her brawny neck, saying how happy the possession of
such a watch would make her. Thoughtless, and as I
fancied myself in so retired a spot secure, I paid little
attention to her talk or her movements. I helped my
dog to a good supper of venison, and was not long in
satisfying the demands of my own appetite.

The Indian rose from his seat, as if in extreme suffering. He passed and repassed me several times, and once
pinched me on the side so violently that the pain nearly
brought forth an exclamation of anger. I looked at him.
His eye met mine, but his look was so forbidding that it

struck a chill into the more nervous part of my system. He again seated himself, drew his butcher-knife from its greasy scabbard, examined its edge, as I would do that of a razor suspected dull, replaced it, and again taking his tomahawk from his back, filled the pipe of it with tobacco, and sent me expressive glances, whenever our hostess chanced to have her back towards us.

Never until that moment had my senses been awakened to the danger which I now suspected to be about me. I returned glance for glance to my companion, and rested well assured that, whatever enemies I might have, he was not of their number.

I asked the woman for my watch, wound it up, and under pretence of wishing to see how the weather might probably be on the morrow, took up my gun, and walked out of the cabin. I slipped a ball into each barrel, scraped the edges of my flints, renewed the primings, and returning to the hut gave a favorable report of my observations. I took a few Bear skins, made a pallet of them, and calling my faithful dog to my side, lay down, with my gun close to my body, and in a few minutes was, to all appearance, fast asleep.

A short time had elapsed when some voices were heard, and from the corner of my eye I saw two athletic youths making their entrance, bearing a dead stag on a pole. They disposed of their burden, and asking for whiskey, helped themselves freely to it. Observing me and the wounded Indian, they asked who I was, and why the devil that rascal (meaning the Indian, who, they knew, understood not a word of English) was in the house. The mother — for so she proved to be — bade them speak less loudly, made mention of my watch, and took them to a corner, where a conversation took place, the purport of which it required little shrewdness in me to guess. I tapped my dog gently. He moved his tail, and with indescribable pleasure I saw his fine eyes alternately fixed

on me, and raised towards the trio in the corner. I felt
that he perceived danger in my situation. The Indian
exchanged a last glance with me.

The lads had eaten and drunk themselves into such a
condition that I already looked upon them as *hors de combat;* and the frequent visits of the whiskey bottle to the
ugly mouth of their dam, I hoped would soon reduce her
to a like state. Judge of my astonishment, reader, when
I saw this incarnate fiend take a large carving-knife, and
go to the grindstone to whet its edge; I saw her pour the
water on the turning machine, and watched her working
away with the dangerous instrument, until the cold sweat
covered every part of my body, in despite of my determination to defend myself to the last. Her task finished,
she walked to her reeling sons, and said: " There, that'll
soon settle him! Boys, kill yon —— ——, and then for
the watch."

I turned, cocked my gun-locks silently, touched my
faithful companion, and lay ready to start up and shoot
the first who might attempt my life. The moment was
fast approaching, and that night might have been my last
in this world, had not Providence made preparations for
my rescue. All was ready. The infernal hag was advancing slowly, probably contemplating the best way of de-
spatching me, whilst her sons should be engaged with the
Indian. I was several times on the eve of rising and
shooting her on the spot; but she was not to be pun-
ished thus. The door was suddenly opened, and there
entered two stout travellers, each with a long rifle on his
shoulder. I bounced up on my feet, and making them
most heartily welcome, told them how well it was for me
that they should have arrived at that moment. The tale
was told in a minute. The drunken sons were secured,
and the woman, in spite of her defence and vociferations,
shared the same fate. The Indian fairly danced with
joy, and gave us to understand that, as he could not sleep

for pain, he would watch over us. You may suppose we slept much less than we talked. The two strangers gave me an account of their once having been themselves in a somewhat similar situation. Day came, fair and rosy, and with it the punishment of our captives.

They were now quite sobered. Their feet were unbound, but their arms were still securely tied. We marched them into the woods off the road, and having used them as Regulators were wont to use such delinquents, we set fire to the cabin, gave all the skins and implements to the young Indian warrior, and proceeded, well pleased, towards the settlements.

During upwards of twenty-five years, when my wanderings extended to all parts of our country, this was the only time at which my life was in danger from my fellow-creatures. Indeed, so little risk do travellers run in the United States that no one born there ever dreams of any to be encountered on the road; and I can only account for this occurrence by supposing that the inhabitants of the cabin were not Americans.

Will you believe, good-natured reader, that not many miles from the place where this adventure happened, and where fifteen years ago, no habitation belonging to civilized man was expected, and very few ever seen, large roads are now laid out, cultivation has converted the woods into fertile fields, taverns have been erected, and much of what we Americans call comfort is to be met with? So fast does improvement proceed in our abundant and free country.[1]

[1] This incident occurred during Audubon's return trip to St. Geneviève in the early spring of 1812.

THE REGULATORS

THE population of many parts of America is derived from the refuse of every other country. I hope I shall elsewhere prove to you, kind reader, that even in this we have reason to feel a certain degree of pride, as we often see our worst denizens becoming gradually freed from error, and at length changing to useful and respectable citizens. The most depraved of these emigrants are forced to retreat farther and farther from the society of the virtuous, the restraints imposed by whom they find incompatible with their habits and the gratification of their unbridled passions. On the extreme verge of civilization, however, their evil propensities find more free scope, and the dread of punishments for their deeds, or the infliction of that punishment, are the only means that prove effectual in reforming them.

In those remote parts, no sooner is it discovered that an individual has conducted himself in a notoriously vicious manner, or has committed some outrage upon society, than a conclave of the honest citizens takes place, for the purpose of investigating the case, with a rigor without which no good result could be expected. These honest citizens, selected from among the most respectable persons in the district, and vested with power suited to the necessity of preserving order on the frontiers, are named Regulators. The accused person is arrested, his conduct laid open, and if he is found guilty of a first crime, he is warned to leave the country, and go farther from society, within an appointed time. Should the individual prove so callous as to disregard the sentence, and remain in the same neighborhood, to commit new crimes, then woe be to him; for the Regulators, after proving him guilty a second time, pass and execute a sentence which, if not enough to make him perish under the infliction, is at least forever impressed upon his memory. The punishment inflicted is usually a severe castigation, and the destruction by fire of his cabin. Sometimes, in cases of reiterated theft or murder, death is considered necessary; and, in some instances, delinquents of the worst species have been shot, after which their heads have been stuck on poles, to deter others from following their example. I shall give you an account of one of these desperadoes, as I received it from a person who had been instrumental in bringing him to punishment.

The name of Mason is still familiar to many of the navigators of the Lower Ohio and Mississippi. By dint of industry in bad deeds, he became a notorious horse-stealer, formed a line of worthless associates from the eastern part of Virginia (a State greatly celebrated for its fine breed of horses) to New Orleans, and had a settlement on Wolf Island, not far from the confluence of the Ohio and Mississippi, from which he issued to stop the flatboats, and rifle them of such provisions and other articles as he and his party needed. His depredations became the talk of the whole Western country; and to pass Wolf Island was not less to be dreaded than to anchor under the walls of Algiers. The horses, the negroes, and the cargoes, his gang carried off and sold. At last, a body of Regulators undertook, at great peril, and for the sake of the country, to bring the villain to punishment.

Mason was as cunning and watchful as he was active and daring. Many of his haunts were successively found out and searched, but the numerous spies in his employ enabled him to escape in time. One day, however, as he was riding a beautiful horse in the woods he was met by one of the Regulators, who immediately recognized him, but passed him as if an utter stranger. Mason, not dreaming of danger, pursued his way leisurely, as if he had met no one. But he was dogged by the Regulator, and in such a manner as proved fatal to him. At dusk, Mason, having reached the lowest part of a ravine, no doubt well known to him, hoppled (tied together the fore-legs of) his stolen horse, to enable it to feed during the night without chance of straying far, and concealed himself in a hollow log to spend the night. The plan was good, but proved his ruin.

The Regulator, who knew every hill and hollow of the woods, marked the place and the log with the eye of an experienced hunter, and as he remarked that Mason was most efficiently armed, he galloped off to the nearest house where he knew he should find assistance. This was easily procured, and the party proceeded to the spot. Mason, on being attacked, defended himself with desperate valor; and as it proved impossible to secure him alive he was brought to the ground with a rifle ball. His head was cut off, and stuck on the end of a broken branch of a tree, by the nearest road to the place where the affray happened. The gang soon dispersed, in consequence of the loss of their leader, and this infliction of merited punishment proved beneficial in deterring others from following a similar predatory life.

The punishment by castigation is performed in the following manner. The individual convicted of an offence is led to some remote part of the woods, under the escort of some forty or fifty Regulators. When arrived at the chosen spot, the criminal is made fast to a tree, and a few of the Regulators remain with him, while the rest scour the forest to assure themselves that no strangers are within reach, after which they form an extensive ring, arranging themselves on their horses, well armed with rifles and pistols, at equal distances and in each other's sight. At a given signal that " all 's ready," those about the culprit, having provided themselves with young twigs of hickory, administer the number of lashes prescribed by the sentence, untie the sufferer, and order him to leave the country immediately.

One of these castigations, which took place more within my personal knowledge, was performed on a fellow who was neither a thief nor a murderer, but who had misbehaved otherwise sufficiently to bring himself under the sentence with mitigation. He was taken to a place where nettles were known to grow in great luxuriance, completely stripped and so lashed with them that, although not materially hurt, he took it as a hint not to be neglected, left the country, and was never again heard of by any of the party concerned.

Probably at the moment when I am copying these notes respecting the early laws of our frontier people, few or no Regulating Parties exist, the terrible examples that were made having impressed upon the new settlers a salutary dread, which restrains them from the commission of flagrant crimes.

THE EARTHQUAKE

TRAVELLING through the Barrens of Kentucky (of which I shall give you an account elsewhere) in the month of November, I was jogging on one afternoon, when I remarked a sudden and strange darkness rising from the western horizon. Accustomed to our heavy storms of thunder and rain I took no more notice of it, as I thought the speed of my horse might enable me to get under shelter of the roof of an acquaintance, who lived not far distant, before it should come up. I had proceeded about a mile, when I heard what I imagined to be the distant rumbling of a violent tornado, on which I spurred my steed, with a wish to gallop as fast as possible to a place of shelter; but it would not do, the animal knew better than I what was forthcoming, and instead of going faster, so nearly stopped that I remarked he placed one foot after another on the ground, with as much precaution

AUDUBON, 1839.

PAINTED IN EDINBURGH BY J. W. AUDUBON.

as if walking on a smooth sheet of ice. I thought he had suddenly foundered, and, speaking to him, was on the point of dismounting and leading him, when he all of a sudden fell a-groaning piteously, hung his head, spread out his four legs, as if to save himself from falling, and stood stock still, continuing to groan. I thought my horse was about to die, and would have sprung from his back had a minute more elapsed, but at that instant all the shrubs and trees began to move from their very roots, the ground rose and fell in successive furrows, like the ruffled waters of a lake, and I became bewildered in my ideas, as I too plainly discovered that all this awful commotion in nature was the result of an earthquake.

I had never witnessed anything of the kind before, although, like every other person, I knew of earthquakes by description. But what is description compared with the reality? Who can tell of the sensations which I experienced when I found myself rocking as it were on my horse, and with him moved to and fro like a child in a cradle, with the most imminent danger around, and expecting the ground every moment to open and present to my eye such an abyss as might engulf myself and all around me? The fearful convulsion, however, lasted only a few minutes, and the heavens again brightened as quickly as they had become obscured; my horse brought his feet to their natural position, raised his head, and galloped off as if loose and frolicking without a rider.

I was not, however, without great apprehension respecting my family, from which I was yet many miles distant, fearful that where they were the shock might have caused greater havoc than I had witnessed. I gave the bridle to my steed, and was glad to see him appear as anxious to get home as myself. The pace at which he galloped accomplished this sooner than I had expected, and I found with much pleasure that hardly any greater harm had taken place than the apprehension excited for my own safety.

Shock succeeded shock almost every day or night for several weeks, diminishing, however, so gradually as to dwindle away into mere vibrations of the earth. Strange to say, I for one became so accustomed to the feeling as rather to enjoy the fears manifested by others. I never can forget the effects of one of the slighter shocks which took place when I was at a friend's house, where I had gone to enjoy the merriment that, in our Western country, attends a wedding. The ceremony being performed, supper over, and the fiddles tuned, dancing became the order of the moment. This was merrily followed up to a late hour, when the party retired to rest. We were in what is called, with great propriety, a *log-house*, one of large dimensions, and solidly constructed. The owner was a physician, and in one corner were not only his lancets, tourniquets, amputating knives, and other sanguinary apparatus, but all the drugs which he employed for the relief of his patients, arranged in jars and phials of different sizes. These had some days before had a narrow escape from destruction, but had been fortunately preserved by closing the doors of the cases in which they were contained.

As I have said, we had all retired to rest, some to dream of sighs or smiles, some to sink into oblivion. Morning was fast approaching, when the rumbling noise that precedes the earthquake, began so loudly as to waken and alarm the whole party, and drive them out of bed in the greatest consternation. The scene which ensued it is impossible for me to describe, and it would require the humorous pencil of Cruikshank to do justice to it. Fear knows no restraint. Every person, young and old, filled with alarm at the creaking of the log-house, and apprehending instant destruction, rushed wildly out to the grass enclosure fronting the building. The full moon was slowly descending from her throne, covered at times by clouds that rolled heavily along, as if to conceal from her view the scenes of terror which prevailed on the earth below.

On the grass-plat we all met, in such condition as rendered it next to impossible to discriminate any of the party, all huddled together in a state of great dishabille. The earth waved like a field of corn before the breeze; the birds left their perches, and flew about, not knowing whither; and the doctor, recollecting the danger of his gallipots, ran to his shop room, to prevent their dancing off the shelves to the floor. Never for a moment did he think of closing the doors, but, spreading his arms, jumped about the front of the cases, pushing back here and there the falling jars; with so little success, however, that before the shock was over he had lost nearly all he possessed.

The shock at length ceased, and the frightened women now sensible of their undress, fled to their several apartments. The earthquake produced more serious consequences in other places. Near New Madrid and for some distance on the Mississippi, the earth was rent asunder in several places, one or two islands sunk forever, and the inhabitants fled in dismay towards the eastern shore.

THE HURRICANE

VARIOUS portions of our country have at different periods suffered severely from the influence of violent storms of wind, some of which have been known to traverse nearly the whole extent of the United States, and to leave such deep impressions in their wake as will not easily be forgotten. Having witnessed one of these awful phenomena, in all its grandeur, I shall attempt to describe it for your sake, kind reader, and for your sake only; the recollection of that astonishing revolution of the ethereal element even now bringing with it so disagreeable a sensation that I feel as if about to be affected by a sudden stoppage of the circulation of my blood.

I had left the village of Shawanee, situated on the banks of the Ohio, on my return from Henderson, which is also situated on the banks of the same beautiful stream. The weather was pleasant, and I thought not warmer than usual at that season. My horse was jogging quietly along, and my thoughts were, for once at least in the course of my life, entirely engaged in commercial speculations. I had forded Highland Creek, and was on the eve of entering a tract of bottom land or valley that lay between it and Canoe Creek, when on a sudden I remarked a great difference in the aspect of the heavens. A hazy thickness had overspread the country, and I for some time expected an earthquake; but my horse exhibited no propensity to stop and prepare for such an occurrence. I had nearly arrived at the verge of the valley, when I thought fit to stop near a brook, and dismounted to quench the thirst which had come upon me.

I was leaning on my knees, with my lips about to touch the water, when, from my proximity to the earth, I heard a distant murmuring sound of an extraordinary nature. I drank, however, and as I rose on my feet, looked towards the southwest, where I observed a yellowish oval spot, the appearance of which was quite new to me. Little time was left me for consideration, as the next moment a smart breeze began to agitate the taller trees. It increased to an unexpected height, and already the smaller branches and twigs were seen falling in a slanting direction towards the ground. Two minutes had scarcely elapsed, when the whole forest before me was in fearful motion. Here and there, where one tree pressed against another, a creaking noise was produced, similar to that occasioned by the violent gusts which sometimes sweep over the country. Turning instinctively towards the direction from which the wind blew, I saw to my great astonishment that the noblest trees of the forest bent their lofty heads for a while, and, unable to stand against the blast, were falling into pieces. First the branches were broken off with a crackling noise; then went the upper parts of the massy trunks; and in many places whole trees of gigantic size were falling entire to the ground. So rapid was the progress of the storm that before I could think of taking measures to insure my safety the hurricane was passing opposite the place where I stood. Never can I forget the scene which at that moment presented itself. The tops of the trees were seen moving in the strangest manner, in the central current of the tempest, which carried along with it a mingled mass of twigs and foliage that completely obscured the view. Some of the largest trees were seen bending and writhing under the gale; others suddenly snapped across; and many, after a momentary resistance, fell uprooted to the earth. The mass of branches, twigs, foliage, and dust that moved through the air was whirled onwards like a cloud of feathers, and on passing disclosed a wide space filled with fallen trees, naked stumps, and heaps of shapeless ruins which marked the path of the tempest. This space was about a fourth of a mile in breadth, and to my imagination resembled the dried up bed of the Mississippi, with its thousands of planters and sawyers strewed in the sand and inclined in various degrees. The horrible noise resembled that of the great cataracts of Niagara, and, as it howled along in the track of the desolating tempest, produced a feeling in my mind which it were impossible to describe.

The principal force of the hurricane was now over, although millions of twigs and small branches that had been brought from a great distance were seen following the blast, as if drawn onwards by some mysterious power. They even floated in the air for some hours after, as if supported by the thick mass of dust that rose high above the ground. The sky had now a greenish lurid hue, and an extremely disagreeable sulphurous odor was diffused in the atmosphere. I waited in amazement, having sustained no material injury, until nature at length resumed her wonted aspect. For some moments I felt undetermined whether I should return to Morgantown, or attempt to force my way through the wrecks of the tempest. My business, however, being of an urgent nature, I ventured into the path of the storm, and after encountering innumerable difficulties, succeeded in crossing it. I was obliged to lead my horse by the bridle, to enable him to leap over the fallen trees, whilst I scrambled over or under them in the best way I could, at times so hemmed in by the broken tops and tangled branches as almost to become desperate. On arriving at my house, I gave an account of what I had seen, when, to my astonishment, I was told there had been very little wind in the neighborhood, although in the streets and gardens many branches and twigs had fallen in a manner which excited great surprise.

Many wondrous accounts of the devastating effects of this hurricane were circulated in the country after its occurrence. Some log houses, we were told, had been overturned and their inmates destroyed. One person informed me that a wire sifter had been conveyed by the gust to a distance of many miles. Another had found a cow lodged in the fork of a large half-broken tree. But, as I am disposed to relate only what I have myself seen, I shall not lead you into the region of romance, but shall content myself with saying that much damage was done by this awful visitation. The valley is yet a desolate place, overgrown with briers and bushes, thickly entangled amidst the tops and trunks of the fallen trees, and is the resort of ravenous animals, to which they betake themselves when pursued by man, or after they have committed their depredations on the farms of the surrounding district. I have crossed the path of the storm at a distance of a hundred miles from the spot where I witnessed its fury, and again, four hundred miles farther off, in the State of

Ohio. Lastly, I observed traces of its ravages on the summits of the mountains connected with the Great Pine Forest of Pennsylvania, three hundred miles beyond the place last mentioned. In all these different parts it appeared to me not to have exceeded a quarter of a mile in breadth.

COLONEL BOONE

DANIEL BOONE, or, as he was usually called in the Western country, Colonel Boone, happened to spend a night with me under the same roof, more than twenty years ago. We had returned from a shooting excursion, in the course of which his extraordinary skill in the management of the rifle had been fully displayed. On retiring to the room appropriated to that remarkable individual and myself for the night, I felt anxious to know more of his exploits and adventures than I did, and accordingly took the liberty of proposing numerous questions to him. The stature and general appearance of this wanderer of the western forests approached the gigantic. His chest was broad and prominent; his muscular powers displayed themselves in every limb; his countenance gave indication of his great courage, enterprise, and perseverance; and when he spoke, the very motion of his lips brought the impression that whatever he uttered could not be otherwise than strictly true. I undressed, whilst he merely took off his hunting shirt, and arranged a few folds of blankets on the floor, choosing rather to lie there, as he observed, than on the softest bed. When we had both disposed of ourselves, each after his own fashion, he related to me the following account of his powers of memory, which I lay before you, kind reader, in his own words, hoping that the simplicity of his style may prove interesting to you.

" I was once," said he, " on a hunting expedition on the banks of the Green River, when the lower parts of this State (Kentucky) were still in the hands of nature, and none but the sons of the soil were looked upon as its lawful proprietors. We Virginians had for some time been waging a war of intrusion upon them, and I, amongst the rest, rambled through the woods in pursuit of their race as I now would follow the tracks of any ravenous animal. The Indians outwitted me one dark night, and I was as unexpectedly as suddenly made a prisoner by them. The trick had been managed with great skill; for no sooner had I extinguished the fire of my camp, and laid me down to rest, in full security as I thought, than I felt myself seized by an indistinguishable number of hands, and was immediately pinioned, as if about to be led to the scaffold for execution. To have attempted to be refractory would have proved useless and danger- ous to my life; and I suffered myself to be removed from my camp to theirs, a few miles distant, without uttering even a word of complaint. You are aware, I dare say, that to act in this manner was the best policy, as you understand that, by so doing, I proved to the Indians at once that I was born and bred as fearless of death as any of themselves.

" When we reached the camp, great rejoicings were exhibited. Two squaws and a few pappooses appeared particularly delighted at the sight of me, and I was assured, by very unequivocal gestures and words, that, on the morrow, the mortal enemy of the Red-skins would cease to live. I never opened my lips, but was busy con- triving some scheme which might enable me to give the rascals the slip before dawn. The women immediately fell a-searching about my hunting-shirt for whatever they might think valuable, and, fortunately for me, soon found my flask filled with *monongahela* (that is, reader, strong whiskey). A terrific grin was exhibited on their murderous countenances, while my heart throbbed with joy at the anticipation of their intoxication. The crew immediately began to beat their bellies and sing, as they passed the bottle from mouth to mouth. How often did I wish the flask ten times its size, and filled with aqua-fortis! I observed that the squaws drank more freely than the warriors, and again my spirits were about to be depressed, when the report of a gun was heard at a distance. The Indians all jumped on their feet. The singing and drinking were both brought to a stand, and I saw, with inexpressible joy, the men walk off to some distance and talk to the squaws. I knew that they were consulting about me, and I foresaw that in a few moments the warriors would go to discover the cause of the gun having been fired so near their camp. I expected that the squaws would be left to guard me. Well, sir, it was just so. They returned; the men took up their guns and walked away. The squaws sat down again, and in less than five minutes had my bottle up to their dirty mouths, gurgling down their throats the remains of the whiskey.

"With what pleasure did I see them becoming more and more drunk, until the liquor took such hold of them that it was quite impossible for these women to be of any service. They tumbled down, rolled about, and began to snore: when I, having no other chance of freeing myself from the cords that fastened me, rolled over and over towards the fire, and, after a short time, burned them asunder. I rose on my feet, stretched my stiffened sinews, snatched up my rifle, and, for once in my life, spared that of Indians. I now recollect how desirous I once or twice felt to lay open the skulls of the wretches with my tomahawk; but when I again thought upon killing beings unprepared and unable to defend themselves, it looked like murder without need, and I gave up the idea.

"But, sir, I felt determined to mark the spot, and walking to a thrifty ash sapling, I cut out of it three large chips, and ran off. I soon reached the river, soon crossed it, and threw myself deep into the cane-brakes, imitating the tracks of an Indian with my feet, so that no chance might be left for those from whom I had escaped to overtake me.

"It is now nearly twenty years since this happened, and more than five since I left the Whites' settlements, which I might probably never have visited again had I not been called on as a witness in a law-suit that was pending in Kentucky, and which I really believe would never have been settled had I not come forward and established the beginning of a certain boundary line. This is the story, sir.

"Mr. —— moved from Old Virginia into Kentucky, and having a large tract granted to him in the new State, laid claim to a certain parcel of land adjoining Green River, and, as chance would have it, took for one of his corners the very ash-tree on which I had made my mark, and finished his survey of some thousands of acres, beginning, as it is expressed in the deed, 'at an Ash marked by three distinct notches of the tomahawk of a white man.'

"The tree had grown much, and the bark had covered the marks; but, somehow or other, Mr. —— heard from some one all that I have already said to you, and thinking that I might remember the spot alluded to in the deed, but which was no longer discoverable, wrote for me to come and try at least to find the place or the tree. His letter mentioned that all my expenses should be paid, and not caring much about once more going back to Kentucky, I started and met Mr. ——. After some conversation, the affair with the Indians came to my recollection. I considered for a while, and began to think that after all I could find the very spot, as well as the tree, if it was yet standing.

"Mr. —— and I mounted our horses, and off we went to the Green River Bottoms. After some difficulties, for you must be aware, sir, that great changes have taken place in those woods, I found at last the spot where I had crossed the river, and, waiting for the moon to rise, made for the course in which I thought the ash-tree grew. On approaching the place, I felt as if the Indians were there still, and as if I was still a prisoner among them. Mr. —— and I camped near what I conceived the spot, and waited until the return of day.

"At the rising of the sun I was on foot, and, after a good deal of musing, thought that an ash-tree then in sight must be the very one on which I had made my mark. I felt as if there could be no doubt of it, and mentioned my thought to Mr. ——. 'Well, Colonel Boone,' said he, 'if you think so, I hope it may prove true, but we must have some witnesses; do you stay here about, and I will go and bring some of the settlers whom I know.' I agreed. Mr. —— trotted off, and I, to pass the time, rambled about to see if a Deer was still living in the land. But ah! sir, what a wonderful difference thirty years makes in the country! Why, at the time when I was caught by the Indians, you would not have walked out in any direction for more than a mile without shooting a buck or a Bear. There were then thousands of Buffaloes on the hills in Kentucky; the land looked as if it never would become poor; and to hunt in those days was a pleasure indeed. But when I was left to myself on the banks of Green River, I dare say for the last time in my life, a few *signs* only of Deer were to be seen. and as to a Deer itself, I saw none.

"Mr. —— returned, accompanied by three gentlemen. They looked upon me as if I had been Washington himself, and walked to the ash-tree, which I now called my own, as if in quest of a long-lost treasure. I took an axe from one of them, and cut a few chips off the bark. Still no signs were to be seen. So I cut again until I thought it was time to be cautious, and I scraped and worked away with my butcher knife until I *did* come to where my tomahawk had left an impression in the wood. We

now went regularly to work, and scraped at the tree with
care, until three hacks as plain as any three notches ever
were, could be seen. Mr. —— and the other gentlemen
were astonished, and, I must allow, I was as much surprised as pleased myself. I made affidavit of this remarkable occurrence in presence of these gentlemen. Mr. ——
gained his cause. I left Green River forever, and came to
where we now are; and, sir, I wish you a good night."

I trust, kind reader, that when I again make my appearance with another volume of Ornithological Biography, I
shall not have to search in vain for the impression which
I have made, but shall have the satisfaction of finding its
traces still unobliterated. I now withdraw, and, in the
words of the noted wanderer of the Western wilds, " wish
you a good night."

NATCHEZ IN 1820

ONE clear, frosty morning in December I approached in
my flatboat the city of Natchez. The shores were crowded
with boats of various kinds, laden with the produce of
the Western country; and there was a bustle about them
such as you might see at a general fair, each person
being intent on securing the advantage of a good market.
Yet the scene was far from being altogether pleasing,
for I was yet "under the hill;" but on removing from
the Lower Town I beheld the cliffs on which the city,
properly so called, has been built. Vultures unnumbered
flew close along the ground on expanded pinions, searching for food; large pines and superb magnolias here and
there raised their evergreen tops towards the skies; while
on the opposite shores of the Mississippi vast alluvial
beds stretched along, and the view terminated with the
dense forest. Steamers moved rapidly on the broad
waters of the great stream; the sunbeams fell with a

peculiarly pleasant effect on the distant objects; and as I watched the motions of the White-headed Eagle while pursuing the Fishing Hawk, I thought of the wonderful ways of that Power to whom I too owe my existence.

Before reaching the land I had observed that several saw-mills were placed on ditches or narrow canals, along which the water rushed from the inner swamps towards the river, and by which the timber is conveyed to the shore; and, on inquiring afterwards, I found that one of those temporary establishments had produced a net profit of upwards of six thousand dollars in a single season.

There is much romantic scenery about Natchez. The Lower Town forms a most remarkable contrast with the Upper; for in the former the houses were not regularly built, being generally dwellings formed of the abandoned flatboats, placed in rows, as if with the view of forming a long street. The inhabitants formed a medley which it is beyond my power to describe; hundreds of laden carts and other vehicles jogged along the declivity between the two towns; but when, by a very rude causeway, I gained the summit, I was relieved by the sight of an avenue of those beautiful trees called here the Pride of China. In the Upper Town I found the streets all laid off at right angles to each other, and tolerably well lined with buildings constructed with painted bricks or boards.

The agricultural richness of the surrounding country was shown by the heaps of cotton bales and other produce that encumbered the streets. The churches, however, did not please me; but as if to make up for this, I found myself unexpectedly accosted by my relative, Mr. Berthoud, who presented me with letters from my wife and sons. These circumstances put me in high spirits, and we proceeded towards the best hotel in the place, that of Mr. Garnier. The house, which was built on the Spanish plan, and of great size, was surrounded by large verandas overlooking a fine garden, and stood at a considerable distance from any other. At this period the city of Natchez had a population not exceeding three thousand individuals. I have not visited it often since, but I have no doubt that, like all the other towns in the western district of our country, it has greatly increased. It possessed a bank, and the mail arrived there thrice in the week from all parts of the Union.

The first circumstance that strikes a stranger is the mildness of the temperature. Several vegetables as pleasing to the eye as agreeable to the palate, and which are seldom seen in our Eastern markets before May, were here already in perfection. The Pewee Fly-catcher had chosen the neighborhood of the city for its winter quarters, and our deservedly famed Mocking-bird sang and danced gratis to every passer by. I was surprised to see the immense number of Vultures that strode along the streets or slumbered on the roofs. The country for many miles inland is gently undulated. Cotton is produced abundantly, and wealth and happiness have taken up their abode under most of the planters' roofs, beneath which the wearied traveller or the poor wanderer in search of a resting-place is sure to meet with comfort and relief. Game is abundant, and the free Indians were wont in those days to furnish the markets with ample supplies of vension and Wild Turkey. The Mississippi, which bathes the foot of the hill some hundred feet below the town, supplies the inhabitants with fish of various kinds. The greatest deficiency is that of water, which for common purposes is dragged on sledges or wheels from the river, while that used for drinking is collected in tanks from the roofs, and becomes very scarce during protracted droughts. Until of late years the orange-tree bore fruit in the open air; but, owing to the great change that has taken place in the temperature, severe though transient frosts occasionally occur, which now prevent this plant from coming to perfection in the open air.

The remains of an old Spanish fort are still to be seen at a short distance from the city. If I am correctly informed, about two years previous to this visit of mine a large portion of the hill near it gave way, sank about a hundred feet, and carried many of the houses of the Lower Town into the river. This, it would appear, was occasioned by the quicksand running springs that flow beneath the strata of mixed pebbles and clay of which the hill is composed. The part that has subsided presents the appearance of a basin or bowl, and is used as a depot for the refuse of the town, on which the Vultures feed when they can get nothing better. There it was that I saw a White-headed Eagle chase one of those filthy birds, knock it down, and feast on the entrails of a horse which the Carrion Crow had partly swallowed.

I did not meet at Natchez many individuals fond of ornithological pursuits, but the hospitality with which I was received was such as I am not likely to forget. Mr. Garnier subsequently proved an excellent friend to me, as you may find elsewhere recorded. Of another individual, whose kindness to me is indelibly impressed on my heart, I would say a few words, although he was such a man as Fénelon alone could describe. Charles Carré was of French origin, the son of a nobleman of the old régime. His acquirements and the benevolence of his disposition were such that when I first met him I could not help looking upon him as another Mentor. Although his few remaining locks were gray, his countenance still expressed the gayety and buoyant feelings of youth. He had the best religious principles; for his heart and his purse were ever open to the poor. Under his guidance it was that I visited the whole neighborhood of Natchez; for he was acquainted with all its history, from the period at which it had first come under the power of the Spaniards to that of their expulsion from the country, its possession by the French, and subsequently by ourselves. He was also well

versed in the Indian languages, spoke French with the
greatest purity, and was a religious poet. Many a pleasant hour have I spent in his company; but alas! he has
gone the way of all the earth!

THE LOST PORTFOLIO

WHILE I was at Natchez, on the 31st of December, 1820,
my kind friend, Nicholas Berthoud, Esq., proposed to me
to accompany him in his keel-boat to New Orleans.   At
one o'clock the steam-boat "Columbus" hauled off
from the landing and took our bark in tow.   The
steamer was soon ploughing along at full speed, and
little else engaged our minds than the thought of our soon
arriving at the emporium of the commerce of the Mississippi.   Towards evening, however, several inquiries were
made respecting particular portions of the luggage, among
which ought to have been one of my portfolios, containing
a number of drawings made by me while gliding down the
Ohio and Mississippi from Cincinnati to Natchez, and of
which some were to me peculiarly valuable, being of birds
previously unfigured, and perhaps undescribed.   The portfolio was nowhere to be found, and I recollected that I
had brought it under my arm to the margin of the stream,
and there left it to the care of one of my friend's servants, who, in the hurry of our departure, had neglected
to take it on board.   Besides the drawings of birds, there
was in this collection a sketch in black chalk to which I
always felt greatly attached while from home.   It is true
the features which it represented were indelibly engraved
in my heart; but the portrait of her to whom I owe so
much of the happiness that I have enjoyed was not the
less dear to me.   When I thought during the following
night of the loss I had sustained in consequence of my

own negligence, imagined the possible fate of the collection, and saw it in the hands of one of the numerous boatmen lounging along the shores, who might paste the drawings to the walls of his cabin, nail them to the steering-oars of his flatboat, or distribute them among his fellows, I felt little less vexed than I did some years before when the rats, as you know, devoured a much larger collection.

It was useless to fret myself, and so I began to devise a scheme for recovering the drawings. I wrote to Mr. Garnier and my venerable friend Charles Carré. Mr. Berthoud also wrote to a mercantile acquaintance. The letters were forwarded to Natchez from the first landing-place at which we stopped, and in the course of time we reached the great eddy running by the levee, or artificial embankment, at New Orleans. But before I present you with the answers to the letters sent to our acquaintances at Natchez, allow me to offer a statement of our adventures upon the Mississippi.

After leaving the eddy at Natchez, we passed a long file of exquisitely beautiful bluffs. At the end of twenty hours we reached Bayou Sara, where we found two brigs at anchor, several steamers, and a number of flatboats, the place being of considerable mercantile importance. Here the "Columbus" left us to shift for ourselves, her commander being anxious to get to Baton Rouge by a certain hour, in order to secure a good cargo of cotton. We now proceeded along the great stream, sometimes floating and sometimes rowing. The shores gradually became lower and flatter, orange-trees began to make their appearance around the dwellings of the wealthy planters, and the verdure along the banks assumed a brighter tint. The thermometer stood at 68° in the shade at noon; Butterflies fluttered among the flowers, of which many were in full blow; and we expected to have seen Alligators half awake floating on the numberless logs

that accompanied us in our slow progress.   The eddies
were covered with Ducks of various kinds, more especially
with the beautiful species that breeds by preference on
the great sycamores that every now and then present
themselves along our southern waters.   Baton Rouge is
a very handsome place, but at present I have no time to
describe it.   Levees now began to stretch along the river,
and wherever there was a sharp point on the shore, negroes
were there amusing themselves by raising shrimps, and
now and then a catfish, with scooping-nets.

The river increased in breadth and depth, and the sawyers and planters, logs so called, diminished in number
the nearer we drew towards the famed city.   At every
bend we found the plantations increased, and now the
whole country on both sides became so level and destitute of trees along the water's edge that we could see
over the points before us, and observe the great stream
stretching along for miles.   Within the levees the land is
much lower than the surface of the river when the water
is high; but at this time we could see over the levee
from the deck of our boat only the upper windows of the
planters' houses, or the tops of the trees about them, and
the melancholy-looking cypresses covered with Spanish
moss forming the background.   Persons rode along the
levees at full speed; Pelicans, Gulls, Vultures, and Carrion Crows sailed over the stream, and at times there
came from the shore a breeze laden with the delicious
perfume of the orange-trees, which were covered with
blossoms and golden fruits.

Having passed Bayou Lafourche, our boat was brought
to on account of the wind, which blew with violence.
We landed, and presently made our way to the swamps,
where we shot a number of those beautiful birds called
Boat-tailed Grakles.   The Mocking-birds on the fence
stakes saluted us with so much courtesy and with such
delightful strains that we could not think of injuring

them; but we thought it no harm to shoot a whole covey of Partridges. In the swamps we met with warblers of various kinds, lively and beautiful, waiting in these their winter retreats for the moment when Boreas should retire to his icy home, and the gentle gales of the South should waft them toward their breeding-places in the North. Thousands of Swallows flew about us, the Cat-birds mewed in answer to their chatterings, the Cardinal Grosbeak elevated his glowing crest as he stood perched on the magnolia branch, the soft notes of the Doves echoed among the woods, nature smiled upon us, and we were happy.

On the fourth of January we stopped at Bonnet Carré, where I entered a house to ask some questions about birds. I was received by a venerable French gentleman, whom I found in charge of about a dozen children of both sexes, and who was delighted to hear that I was a student of nature. He was well acquainted with my old friend Charles Carré, and must, I thought, be a good man, for he said he never suffered any of his pupils to rob a bird of her eggs or young, although, said he with a smile, "they are welcome to peep at them and love them." The boys at once surrounded me, and from them I received satisfactory answers to most of my queries respecting birds.

The 6th of January was so cold that the thermometer fell to 30°, and we had seen ice on the running-boards of our keel-boat. This was quite unlooked for, and we felt uncomfortable; but before the middle of the day, all nature was again in full play. Several beautiful steamers passed us. The vegetation seemed not to have suffered from the frost; green peas, artichokes, and other vegetables were in prime condition. This reminds me that on one of my late journeys I ate green peas in December in the Floridas, and had them once a week at least in my course over the whole of the Union, until I found myself and my family feeding on the same vegetable more than a hundred miles to the north of the St. John's River in New Brunswick.

Early on the 7th, thousands of tall spars, called masts by the mariners, came in sight; and as we drew nearer, we saw the port filled with ships of many nations, each bearing the flag of its country. At length we reached the levee, and found ourselves once more at New Orleans. In a short time my companions dispersed, and I commenced a search for something that might tend to compensate me for the loss of my drawings.

On the 16th of March following, I had the gratification of receiving a letter from Mr. A. P. Bodley, of Natchez, informing me that my portfolio had been found and deposited at the office of the "Mississippi Republican," whence an order from me would liberate it. Through the kindness of Mr. Garnier, I received it on the 5th of April. So very generous had been the finder of it, that when I carefully examined the drawings in succession, I found them all present and uninjured, save one, which had probably been kept by way of commission.

THE ORIGINAL PAINTER

As I was lounging one fair and very warm morning on the levee at New Orleans, I chanced to observe a gentleman whose dress and other accompaniments greatly attracted my attention. I wheeled about, and followed him for a short space, when, judging by everything about him that he was a true original, I accosted him.

But here, kind reader, let me give you some idea of his exterior. His head was covered by a straw hat, the brim of which might cope with those worn by the fair sex in 1830; his neck was exposed to the weather; the broad frill of a shirt, then fashionable, flapped about his breast, whilst an extraordinary collar, carefully arranged, fell over the top of his coat. The latter was of a light green color, harmonizing well with a pair of flowing yellow nankeen trousers, and a pink waistcoat, from the bosom of which, amidst a large bunch of the splendid flowers of the magnolia, protruded part of a young Alligator, which seemed more anxious to glide through the muddy waters of some retired swamp than to spend its life swinging to and fro among folds of the finest lawn. The gentleman held in one hand a cage full of richly-plumed Nonpareils, whilst in the other he sported a silk umbrella, on which I could plainly read, " Stolen from I," these words being painted in large white characters. He walked as if conscious of his own importance — that is, with a good deal of pomposity, singing, "My love is but a lassie yet," and that with such thorough imitation of the Scotch emphasis that had not his physiognomy brought to my mind a denial of his being from "within a mile of Edinburgh," I should have put him down in my journal for a true Scot. But no: his tournure, nay, the very shape of his visage, pronounced him an American from the farthest parts of our eastern Atlantic shores.

All this raised my curiosity to such a height that I accosted him with, "Pray, sir, will you allow me to examine the birds you have in that cage?" The gentleman stopped, straightened his body, almost closed his left eye, then spread his legs apart, and, with a look altogether quizzical, answered, "Birds, sir; did you say birds?" I nodded, and he continued, "What the devil do you know about birds, sir?"

Reader, this answer brought a blush into my face. I felt as if caught in a trap; for I was struck by the force of the gentleman's question — which, by the way, was not much in discordance with a not unusual mode of granting an answer in the United States. Sure enough, thought I, little or perhaps nothing do I know of the nature of those beautiful denizens of the air; but the next moment vanity gave me a pinch, and urged me to conceive that I knew at least as much about birds as the august personage in my presence. "Sir," replied I, "I am a student of Nature, and admire her works, from the noblest figure of man to the crawling reptile which you have in your bosom." — "Ah!" replied he, "a–a–a naturalist, I presume!" — "Just so, my good sir," was my answer. The gentleman gave me the cage; and I observed, from the corner of one of my eyes, that his were cunningly inspecting my face. I examined the pretty Finches as long as I wished, returned the cage, made a low bow, and was about to proceed on my walk, when this odd sort of being asked me a question quite accordant with my desire of knowing more of him: "Will you come with me, sir? If you will, you shall see some more curious birds, some of which are from different parts of the world. I keep quite a collection." I assured him I should feel gratified, and accompanied him to his lodgings.

We entered a long room, where, to my surprise, the first objects that attracted my attention were a large easel with a full-length unfinished portrait upon it, a table with palettes and pencils, and a number of pictures of various sizes placed along the walls. Several cages containing birds were hung near the windows, and two young gentlemen were busily engaged in copying some finished portraits. I was delighted with all I saw. Each picture spoke for itself: the drawing, the coloring, the handling, the composition, and the keeping — all proved, that, whoever was the artist, he certainly was possessed of superior talents.

I did not know if my companion was the painter of the picture, but, as we say in America, I strongly guessed, and, without waiting any longer, paid him the compliments which I thought he fairly deserved. "Ay," said he, "the world is pleased with my work. I wish I were so too; but time and industry are required, as well as talents, to make a good artist. If you will examine the birds, I'll to my labor." So saying, the artist took up his palette, and was searching for a rest-stick; but not finding the one with which he usually supported his hand, he drew the rod of a gun, and was about to sit, when he suddenly threw down his implements on the table, and, taking the gun, walked to me and asked if " I had ever seen a percussion-lock." I had not, for that improvement was not yet in vogue. He not only explained the superiority of the lock in question, but undertook to prove that it was capable of acting effectually under water. The bell was rung, a flat basin of water was produced, the gun was charged with powder, and the lock fairly immersed. The report terrified the birds, causing them to beat against the gilded walls of their prisons. I remarked this to the artist. He replied, "The devil take the birds! — more of them in the market; why, sir, I wish to show you that I am a marksman as well as a painter." The easel was cleared of the large picture, rolled to the further end of the room, and placed against the wall. The gun was loaded in a trice, and the painter, counting ten steps from the easel, and taking aim at the supporting-pin on the left, fired. The bullet struck the head of the wooden pin fairly, and sent the splinters in all directions. "A bad shot, sir," said this extraordinary person. "The ball ought to have driven the pin farther into the hole, but it struck on one side; I'll try at the hole itself." After reloading his piece, the artist took aim again, and fired. The bullet this time had accomplished its object, for it had passed through the aperture and hit the wall behind. "Mr. ——, ring the bell and close the windows," said the painter, and, turning to me, continued, "Sir, I will show you the *ne plus ultra* of shooting." I was quite amazed, and yet so delighted that I bowed my assent. A servant having appeared, a lighted candle was ordered. When it arrived, the artist placed it in a proper position, and retiring some yards, put out the light with a bullet, in the manner which I have elsewhere in this volume described. When light was restored, I observed the uneasiness of the poor little Alligator, as it strove to effect its escape from the artist's waistcoat. I mentioned this to him. "True, true," he replied. "I had quite forgot the reptile; he shall have a dram;" and unbuttoning his vest, unclasped a small chain, and placed the Alligator in the basin of water on the table.

Perfectly satisfied with the acquaintance which I had formed with this renowned artist, I wished to withdraw, fearing I might inconvenience him by my presence. But my time was not yet come. He bade me sit down, and paying no more attention to the young pupils in the room than if they had been a couple of cabbages, said, "If you have leisure and will stay awhile, I will show you how I paint, and will relate to you an incident of my life which will prove to you how sadly situated an artist is at times." In full expectation that more eccentricities were to be witnessed, or that the story would prove a valuable one, even to a naturalist, who is seldom a painter, I seated myself at his side, and observed with interest how adroitly he transferred the colors from his glistening palette to the canvas before him. I was about to compliment him on his facility of touch, when he spoke as follows: —

"This is, sir, or, I ought to say rather, this will be the portrait of one of our best navy officers — a man as brave as Cæsar, and as good a sailor as ever walked the deck of a seventy-four. Do you paint, sir?" I replied, "Not yet." — "Not yet! what do you mean?" — "I mean what I say: I intend to paint as soon as I can draw better than I do at present." — "Good," said he; "you are quite right. To draw is the first object; but, sir, if you should ever paint, and paint portraits, you will often meet with difficulties. For instance, the brave Commodore of whom this is the portrait, although an excellent man at everything else, is the worst sitter I ever saw; and the incident I promised to relate to you, as one curious enough, is connected with his bad mode of sitting. Sir, I forgot to ask if you would take any refreshment — a glass of wine, or — " I assured him I needed nothing more than his agreeable company, and he proceeded. "Well, sir, the first morning that the Commodore came to sit, he was in full uniform, and with his sword at his side. After a few moments of conversation, and when all was ready on my part, I bade him ascend this *throne*, place himself in the attitude which I contemplated, and assume an air becoming an officer of the navy. He mounted, placed himself as I had desired, but merely looked at me as if I had been a block of stone. I waited a few minutes, when, observing no change on his placid countenance, I ran the chalk over the canvas to form a rough outline. This done, I looked up to his face again, and opened a conversation which I thought would warm his warlike nature; but in vain. I waited and waited, talked and talked, until, my patience — sir, you must know I am not overburdened with phlegm — being almost run out, I rose, threw my palette and brushes on the floor, stamped, walking to and fro about the room, and vociferated such calumnies against our navy that I startled the good Commodore. He still looked at me with a placid countenance, and, as he has told me since, thought I had lost my senses. But I observed him all the while, and, fully as determined to carry my point as he would be to carry off an enemy's ship, I gave my oaths additional emphasis, addressed him as a representative of the navy, and, steering somewhat clear of personal insult, played off my batteries against the craft. The Commodore walked up to me, placed his hand on the hilt of his sword, and told me, in a resolute manner, that if I intended to insult the navy, he would instantly cut off my ears. His features exhibited all the spirit and animation of his noble nature, and as I had now succeeded in rousing the lion, I judged it time to retreat. So, changing my tone, I begged his pardon, and told him he now looked precisely as I wished to represent him. He laughed, and, returning to his seat, assumed a bold countenance. And now, sir, see the picture!"

At some future period I may present you with other instances of the odd ways in which this admired artist gave animation to his sitters. For the present, kind reader, we shall leave him finishing the Commodore, while we return to our proper studies.

THE COUGAR

THERE is an extensive swamp in the section of the State of Mississippi which lies partly in the Choctaw territory. It commences at the borders of the Mississippi, at no great distance from a Chickasaw village situated near the mouth of a creek known by the name of Vanconnah, and partly inundated by the swellings of several large bayous, the principal of which, crossing the swamp in its whole extent, discharges its waters not far from the mouth of the Yazoo River. This famous bayou is called False River. The swamp of which I am speaking follows the windings of the Yazoo, until the latter branches off to the northeast, and at this point forms the stream named Cold Water River, below which the Yazoo receives the draining of another bayou inclining towards the northwest and intersecting that known by the name of False River at a short distance from the place where the latter receives the waters of the Mississippi. This tedious account of the situation of the swamp is given with the view of pointing it out to all students of nature who may happen to go that way, and whom I would earnestly urge to visit its interior, as it abounds in rare and interesting productions, — birds, quadrupeds, and reptiles, as well as molluscous animals, many of which, I am persuaded, have never been described.

In the course of one of my rambles, I chanced to meet with a squatter's cabin on the banks of the Cold Water River. In the owner of this hut, like most of those adventurous settlers in the uncultivated tracts of our frontier districts, I found a person well versed in the chase, and acquainted with the habits of some of the larger species of quadrupeds and birds. As he who is desirous of instruction ought not to disdain listening to any one who has knowledge to communicate, however humble may be his lot, or however limited his talents, I entered the squatter's cabin, and immediately opened a conversation with him respecting the situation of the swamp, and its natural productions. He told me he thought it the very place I ought to visit, spoke of the game which it contained, and pointed to some Bear and Deer skins, adding that the individuals to which they had belonged formed but a small portion of the number of those animals which he had shot within it. My heart swelled with delight, and on asking if he would accompany me through the great morass, and allow me to become an inmate of his humble but hospitable mansion, I was gratified to find that he cordially assented to all my proposals. So I immediately unstrapped my drawing materials, laid up my gun, and sat down to partake of the homely but wholesome fare intended for the supper of the squatter, his wife, and his two sons.

The quietness of the evening seemed in perfect accordance with the gentle demeanor of the family. The wife and children, I more than once thought, seemed to look upon me as a strange sort of person, going about, as I told them I was, in search of birds and plants; and were I here to relate the many questions which they put to me in return for those I addressed to them, the catalogue would occupy several pages. The husband, a native of Connecticut, had heard of the existence of such men as myself, both in our own country and abroad, and seemed greatly pleased to have me under his roof. Supper over, I asked my kind host what had induced him to remove to this wild and solitary spot. "The people are growing too numerous now to thrive in New England," was his answer. I thought of the state of some parts of Europe, and calculating the denseness of their population compared with that of New England, exclaimed to myself, "How much more difficult must it be for men to thrive in those populous countries!" The conversation then changed, and the squatter, his sons and myself, spoke of hunting and fishing until at length, tired, we laid ourselves down on pallets of Bear skins, and reposed in peace on the floor of the only apartment of which the hut consisted.

Day dawned, and the squatter's call to his hogs, which, being almost in a wild state, were suffered to seek the greater portion of their food in the woods, awakened me. Being ready dressed I was not long in joining him. The hogs and their young came grunting at the well known call of their owner, who threw them a few ears of corn, and counted them, but told me that for some weeks their number had been greatly diminished by the ravages committed upon them by a large *Panther*, by which name the Cougar is designated in America, and that the ravenous animal did not content himself with the flesh of his pigs, but now and then carried off one of his calves, notwithstanding the many attempts he had made to shoot it. The *Painter*, as he sometimes called it, had on several occasions robbed him of a dead Deer; and to these exploits the squatter added several remarkable feats of audacity which it had performed, to give me an idea of the formidable character of the beast. Delighted by his description, I offered to assist him in destroying the enemy, at which he was highly pleased, but assured me that unless some of his neighbors should join us with their dogs and his own, the attempt would prove fruitless. Soon after, mounting a horse, he went off to his neighbors several of whom lived at a distance of some miles, and appointed a day of meeting.

The hunters, accordingly, made their appearance, one fine morning, at the door of the cabin, just as the sun was emerging from beneath the horizon. They were five in number, and fully equipped for the chase, being mounted on horses which in some parts of Europe might appear sorry nags, but which in strength, speed, and bottom, are better fitted for pursuing a Cougar or a Bear through woods and morasses than any in that country. A pack of large, ugly curs were already engaged in making acquaintance with those of the squatter. He and myself mounted his two best horses, whilst his sons were bestriding others of inferior quality.

Few words were uttered by the party until we had reached the edge of the swamp, where it was agreed that all should disperse and seek for the fresh track of the Painter, it being previously settled that the discoverer should blow his horn, and remain on the spot, until the rest should join him. In less than an hour, the sound of the horn was clearly heard, and, sticking close to the squatter, off we went through the thick woods, guided only by the now and then repeated call of the distant huntsmen. We soon reached the spot, and in a short time the rest of the party came up. The best dog was sent forward to track the Cougar, and in a few moments the whole pack were observed diligently trailing, and bearing in their course for the interior of the Swamp. The rifles were immediately put in trim, and the party followed the dogs, at separate distances, but in sight of each other, determined to shoot at no other game than the Panther.

The dogs soon began to mouth, and suddenly quickened their pace. My companion concluded that the beast was on the ground, and putting our horses to a gentle gallop, we followed the curs, guided by their voices. The noise of the dogs increased, when, all of a sudden their mode of barking became altered, and the squatter, urging me to push on, told me that the beast was *treed*, by which he meant that it had got upon some low branch of a large tree to rest for a few moments, and that should we not succeed in shooting him when thus situated, we might expect a long chase of it. As we approached the spot, we all by degrees united into a body, but on seeing the dogs at the foot of a large tree, separated again, and galloped off to surround it.

Each hunter now moved with caution, holding his gun ready, and allowing the bridle to dangle on the neck of his horse, as it advanced slowly towards the dogs. A shot from one of the party was heard, on which the Cougar was seen to leap to the ground, and bound off with such velocity as to show that he was very unwilling to stand our fire longer. The dogs set off in pursuit with great eagerness and a deafening cry. The hunter who had fired came up and said that his ball had hit the monster, and had probably broken one of his fore-legs near the shoulder, the only place at which he could aim. A slight trail of blood was discovered on the ground, but the curs proceeded at such a rate that we merely noticed this, and put spurs to our horses, which galloped on towards the centre of the Swamp. One bayou was crossed, then another still larger and more muddy; but the dogs were brushing forward, and as the horses began to pant at a furious rate, we judged it expedient to leave them and advance on foot. These determined hunters knew that the Cougar being wounded, would shortly ascend another tree, where in all probability he would remain for a considerable time, and that it would be easy to follow the track of the dogs. We dismounted, took off the saddles and bridles, set the bells attached to the horses' necks at liberty to jingle, hoppled the animals, and left them to shift for themselves.

Now, kind reader, follow the group marching through the swamp, crossing muddy pools, and making the best of their way over fallen trees and amongst the tangled rushes that now and then covered acres of ground. If you are a hunter yourself, all this will appear nothing to you; but if crowded assemblies of "beauty and fashion," or the quiet enjoyment of your "pleasure grounds" alone delight you, I must mend my pen before I attempt to give you an idea of the pleasure felt on such an expedition.

After marching for a couple of hours, we again heard the dogs. Each of us pressed forward, elated at the thought of terminating the career of the Cougar. Some of the dogs were heard whining, although the greater number barked vehemently. We felt assured that the Cougar was treed, and that he would rest for some time to recover from his fatigue. As we came up to the dogs, we discovered the ferocious animal lying across a large branch, close to the trunk of a cotton-wood tree. His broad breast lay towards us; his eyes were at one time bent on us and again on the dogs beneath and around him; one of his fore-legs hung loosely by his side, and he lay crouched, with his ears lowered close to his head, as if he thought he might remain undiscovered. Three balls were fired at him, at a given signal, on which he sprang a few feet from the branch, and tumbled headlong to the ground. Attacked on all sides by the enraged curs, the infuriated Cougar fought with desperate valor; but the squatter, advancing in front of the party, and almost in the midst of the dogs, shot him immediately behind and beneath the left shoulder. The Cougar writhed for a moment in agony, and in another lay dead.

The sun was now sinking in the west. Two of the hunters separated from the rest to procure venison, whilst the squatter's sons were ordered to make the best of their way home, to be ready to feed the hogs in the morning. The rest of the party agreed to camp on the spot. The Cougar was despoiled of its skin, and its carcass left to the hungry dogs. Whilst engaged in preparing our camp, we heard the report of a gun, and soon after one of our hunters returned with a small Deer. A fire was lighted, and each hunter displayed his *pone* of bread, along with a flask of whiskey. The deer was skinned in a trice, and slices placed on sticks before the fire. These materials afforded us an excellent meal, and as the night grew darker, stories and songs went round, until my companions, fatigued, laid themselves down, close under the smoke of the fire, and soon fell asleep.

I walked for some minutes round the camp, to contemplate the beauties of that nature from which I have certainly derived my greatest pleasures. I thought of the occurrences of the day, and glancing my eye around, remarked the singular effects produced by the phosphorescent qualities of the large decayed trunks which lay in all directions around me. How easy, I thought, would it be for the confused and agitated mind of a person bewildered in a swamp like this, to imagine in each of these luminous masses some wondrous and fearful being, the very sight of which might make the hair stand erect on his head. The thought of being myself placed in such a predicament burst over my mind, and I hastened to join my companions, beside whom I laid me down and slept, assured that no enemy could approach us without first rousing the dogs, which were growling in fierce dispute over the remains of the Cougar.

At daybreak we left our camp, the squatter bearing on his shoulder the skin of the late destroyer of his stock, and retraced our steps until we found our horses, which had not strayed far from the place where we had left them. These we soon saddled, and jogging along, in a direct course, guided by the sun, congratulating each other on the destruction of so formidable a neighbor as the Panther had been, we soon arrived at my host's cabin. The five neighbors partook of such refreshment as the house could afford, and dispersing, returned to their homes, leaving me to follow my favorite pursuits.

THE RUNAWAY

NEVER shall I forget the impression made on my mind by the *rencontre* which forms the subject of this article, and I even doubt if the relation of it will not excite in that of my reader emotions of varied character.

Late in the afternoon of one of those sultry days which render the atmosphere of the Louisiana swamps pregnant with baneful effluvia, I directed my course towards my distant home, laden with a pack, consisting of five or six Wood Ibises, and a heavy gun, the weight of which, even in those days, when my natural powers were unimpaired, prevented me from moving with much speed. Reaching the banks of a miry bayou, only a few yards in breadth, but of which I could not ascertain the depth, on account of the muddiness of its waters, I thought it might be dangerous to wade through it with my burden, for which reason, throwing to the opposite side each of my heavy birds in succession, together with my gun, powder-flask, and shot-bag, and drawing my hunting-knife from its scabbard, to defend myself, if need should be, against Alligators, I entered the water, followed by my faithful dog. As I advanced carefully, and slowly, " Plato " swam around me, enjoying the refreshing influence of the liquid element that cooled his fatigued and heated frame.

The water deepened, as did the mire of its bed; but with a stroke or two I gained the shore.

Scarcely had I stood erect on the opposite bank, when my dog ran to me, exhibiting marks of terror; his eyes seeming ready to burst from their sockets, and his mouth grinning with the expression of hatred, while his feelings found vent in a stifled growl. Thinking that all this was produced by the scent of a Wolf or Bear, I stooped to take up my gun, when a stentorian voice commanded me to "stand still, or die!" Such a *qui vive* in these woods was as unexpected as it was rare. I instantly raised and cocked my gun; and although I did not yet perceive the individual who had thus issued so peremptory a mandate, I felt determined to combat with him for the free passage of the grounds. Presently a tall, firmly built negro emerged from the bushy underwood, where until that moment he must have been crouched, and in a louder voice repeated his injunction. Had I pressed a trigger, his life would have instantly terminated; but observing that the gun which he aimed at my breast, was a wretched, rusty piece, from which fire could not readily be produced, I felt little fear, and therefore did not judge it necessary to proceed at once to extremities. I laid my gun at my side, tapped my dog quietly, and asked the man what he wanted.

My forbearance, and the stranger's long habit of submission, produced the most powerful effect on his mind. "Master," said he, "I am a runaway; I might perhaps shoot you down; but God forbids it, for I feel just now as if I saw him ready to pass his judgment against me for such a foul deed, and I ask mercy at your hands. For God's sake, do not kill me, master!" "And why," answered I, "have you left your quarters, where certainly you must have fared better than in these unwholesome swamps?" "Master, my story is a short, but a sorrowful one. My camp is close by, and, as I know you cannot reach home this night, if you will follow me there, depend upon *my honor* you shall be safe until the morning, when I will carry your birds, if you choose, to the great road."

The large, intelligent eyes of the negro, the complacency of his manners, and the tones of his voice, I thought invited me to venture; and as I felt that I was at least his equal, while moreover, I had my dog to second me, I answered that I would *follow him*. He observed the emphasis laid on the words, the meaning of which he seemed to understand so thoroughly that, turning to me, he said, " There, master, take my butcher's knife, while I throw away the flint and priming from my gun!" Reader, I felt confounded: this was too much for me: I refused the knife, and told him to keep his piece ready, in case we might accidentally meet a Cougar or a Bear.

Generosity exists everywhere. The greatest monarch acknowledges its impulse, and all around him, from the lowliest menial to the proud nobles that encircle his throne, at times experience that overpowering sentiment. I offered to shake hands with the runaway. " Master," said he, " I beg you thanks," and with this he gave me a squeeze that alike impressed me with the goodness of his heart and his great physical strength. From that moment we proceeded through the woods together. My dog smelt at him several times, but as he heard me speak in my usual tone of voice, he soon left us and rambled around as long as my whistle was unused. As we proceeded, I observed that he was guiding me towards the setting of the sun, and quite contrary to my homeward course. I remarked this to him, when he with the greatest simplicity replied, " Merely for our security."

After trudging along for some distance, and crossing several bayous, at all of which he threw his gun and knife to the opposite bank, and stood still until I had got over, we came to the borders of an immense cane-brake, from which I had, on former occasions, driven and killed several Deer. We entered, as I had frequently done before, now erect, then on " all fours." He regularly led the way, divided here and there the tangled stalks, and, whenever we reached a fallen tree, assisted me in getting over it, with all possible care. I saw that he was a perfect Indian in his knowledge of the woods, for he kept a direct course as precisely as any " Red-skin " I ever travelled with. All of a sudden he emitted a loud shriek, not unlike that of an Owl, which so surprised me, that I once more instantly levelled my gun. " No harm, master, I only give notice to my wife and children I am coming." A tremulous answer of the same nature gently echoed through the tree tops. The runaway's lips separated with an expression of gentleness and delight, when his beautiful set of ivory teeth seemed to smile through the dusk of evening that was thickening around us. " Master," said he, " my wife, though black, is as beautiful to me as the President's wife is to him ; she is my queen, and I look on our young ones as so many princes ; but you shall see them all, for here they are, thank God."

There, in the heart of the cane-brake, I found a regular camp. A small fire was lighted, and on its embers lay gridling some large slices of venison. A lad nine or ten years old was blowing the ashes from some fine sweet potatoes. Various articles of household furniture were carefully disposed around, and a large pallet of Bear and Deer skins, seemed to be the resting-place of the whole family. The wife raised not her eyes towards mine, and the little ones, three in number, retired into a corner, like so many discomfited Raccoons ; but the Runaway, bold, and apparently happy, spoke to them in such cheering words, that at once one and all seemed to regard me as one sent by Providence to relieve them from all their troubles. My clothes were hung up by them to dry, and the negro asked if he might clean and grease my gun, which I permitted him to do, while the wife threw a large piece of Deer's flesh to my dog, which the children were already caressing.

Only think of my situation, reader! Here I was, ten miles at least from home, and four or five from the nearest plantation, in the camp of runaway slaves, and quite at their mercy. My eyes involuntarily followed their motions, but as I thought I perceived in them a strong desire to make me their confidant and friend, I gradually relinquished all suspicions. The venison and potatoes looked quite tempting, and by this time I was in a condition to relish much less savory fare; so, on being humbly asked to divide the viands before us, I partook of as hearty a meal as I had ever done in my life.

Supper over, the fire was completely extinguished, and a small lighted pine-knot placed in a hollowed calabash. Seeing that both the husband and the wife were desirous of communicating something to me, I at once and fearlessly desired them to unburden their minds, when the Runaway told me a tale of which the following is the substance.

About eighteen months before, a planter, residing not very far off, having met with some losses, was obliged to expose his slaves at a public sale. The value of his negroes was well known, and on the appointed day the auctioneer laid them out in small lots, or offered them singly, in the manner which he judged most advantageous to their owner. The Runaway, who was well known as being the most valuable next to his wife, was put up by himself for sale, and brought an immoderate price. For his wife, who came next, and alone, eight hundred dollars were bidden and paid down. Then the children were exposed, and, on account of their breed, brought high prices. The rest of the slaves went off at rates corresponding to their qualifications.

The Runaway chanced to be bought by the overseer of the plantation; the wife was bought by an individual residing about a hundred miles off, and the children went to different places along the river. The heart of the husband

and father failed him under this dire calamity. For a while he pined in sorrow under his new master; but having marked down in his memory the names of the different persons who had purchased each dear portion of his family, he feigned illness, if indeed, he whose affections had been so grievously blasted could be said to feign it, refrained from food for several days, and was little regarded by the overseer, who felt himself disappointed in what he had considered a bargain.

On a stormy night, when the elements raged with all the fury of a hurricane, the poor negro made his escape, and being well acquainted with all the neighboring swamps, at once made directly for the cane-brake in the centre of which I found his camp. A few nights afterwards he gained the abode of his wife, and the very next after their meeting, he led her away. The children, one after another, he succeeded in stealing, until at last the whole of the objects of his love were under his care.

To provide for five individuals was no easy task in those wilds, which after the first notice was given of the wonderful disappearance of this extraordinary family, were daily ransacked by armed planters. Necessity, it is said, will bring the Wolf from the forest. The Runaway seems to have well understood the maxim, for under the cover of night he approached his first master's plantation, where he had ever been treated with the greatest kindness. The house-servants knew him too well not to aid him to the best of their power, and at the approach of each morning he returned to his camp with an ample supply of provisions. One day, while in search of wild fruits, he found a Bear dead before the muzzle of a gun that had been set for the purpose. Both articles he carried to his home. His friends at the plantation managed to supply him with some ammunition, and on damp and cloudy days he first ventured to hunt around his camp. Possessed of courage and activity, he gradually became more careless, and rambled farther in search of game. It was on one of his excursions that I met him, and he assured me the noise which I made in passing the bayou had caused him to lose the chance of killing a fine Deer, " although," said he, " my old musket misses fire sadly too often."

The Runaways, after disclosing their secret to me, both rose from their seat, with eyes full of tears. " Good master, for God's sake, do something for us and our children," they sobbed forth with one accord. Their little ones lay sound asleep in the fearlessness of their innocence. Who could have heard such a tale without emotion? I promised them my most cordial assistance. They both sat up that night to watch my repose, and I slept close to their urchins, as if on a bed of the softest down.

Day broke so fair, so pure, and so gladdening that I told them such heavenly appearances were ominous of good, and that I scarcely doubted of obtaining their full pardon. I desired them to take their children with them, and promised to accompany them to the plantation of their first master. They gladly obeyed. My Ibises were hung round their camp, and, as a memento of my having been there, I notched several trees; after which I bade adieu, perhaps for the last time, to that cane-brake. We soon reached the plantation, the owner of which, with whom I was well acquainted, received me with all the generous kindness of a Louisiana planter. Ere an hour had elapsed, the Runaway and his family were looked upon as his own. He afterwards repurchased them from their owners, and treated them with his former kindness; so that they were rendered as happy as slaves generally are in that country, and continued to cherish that attachment to each other which had led to their adventures. Since this event happened, it has, I have been informed, become illegal to separate slave families without their consent.

A TOUGH WALK FOR A YOUTH

ABOUT twelve years ago I was conveyed, along with my
son Victor, from Bayou Sara to the mouth of the Ohio,
on board the steamer " Magnet," commanded by Mr.
McKnight, to whom I here again offer my best thanks
for his attentions. The very sight of the waters of that
beautiful river filled me with joy as we approached the
little village of Trinity, where we were landed along with
several other passengers, the water being too low to enable
the vessel to proceed to Louisville. No horses could be
procured, and as I was anxious to continue my journey
without delay, I consigned my effects to the care of the
tavern-keeper, who engaged to have them forwarded by
the first opportunity. My son, who was not fourteen, with
all the ardor of youth, considered himself able to accomplish, on foot, the long journey which we contemplated.
Two of the passengers evinced a desire to accompany us,
" provided," said the tallest and stoutest of them, " the lad
can keep up. My business," he continued, " is urgent,
and I shall push for Frankfort pretty fast." Dinner, to
which we had contributed some fish from the river, being
over, my boy and I took a ramble along the shores of
Cash Creek, on which, some years before, I had been
detained several weeks by ice. We slept at the tavern,
and next morning prepared for our journey, and were
joined by our companions, although it was past twelve
before we crossed the creek.

One of our fellow-travellers, named Rose, who was a
delicate and gentlemanly person, acknowledged that he
was not a good walker, and said he was glad that my son
was with us, as he might be able to keep up with the lively
youth. The other, a burly personage, at once pushed
forwards. We walked in Indian file along the narrow
track cut through the canes, passed a wood-yard, and

VICTOR GIFFORD AUDUBON.

PAINTED BY AUDUBON ABOUT 1823.

entered the burnt forest, in which we met with so many
logs and briers that we judged it better to make for the
river, the course of which we followed over a bed of pebbles, my son sometimes ahead, and again falling back,
until we reached America, a village having a fine situation,
but with a shallow approach to the shore.   Here we halted
at the best house, as every traveller ought to do, whether
pedestrian or equestrian, for he is there sure of being well
treated, and will not have to pay more than in an inferior
place.   Now we constituted Mr. Rose purser.   We had
walked twelve miles over rugged paths and pebbly shores,
and soon proceeded along the edge of the river.   Seven
tough miles ended, we found a house near the bank, and
in it we determined to pass the night.   The first person we
met with was a woman picking cotton in a small field.   On
asking her if we might stay in her cabin for the night, she
answered we might, and hoped we could make shift with
the fare on which she and her husband lived.   While
she went to the house to prepare supper, I took my son
and Mr. Rose to the water, knowing how much we should
be refreshed by a bath.   Our fellow-traveller refused, and
stretched himself on a bench by the door.   The sun was
setting; thousands of Robins were flying southward in the
calm and clear air; the Ohio was spread before us smooth
as a mirror, and into its waters we leaped with pleasure.
In a short time the good man of the hut called us to supper, and in a trice we were at his heels.   He was a tall,
raw-boned fellow, with an honest, bronzed face.   After our
frugal meal we all four lay down on a large bed, spread
on the floor, while the good people went up to a loft.

The woodsman, having, agreeably to our instructions,
roused us at daybreak, told us that about seven miles
farther we should meet with a breakfast much better than
the last supper we had.   He refused any pecuniary compensation, but accepted from me a knife.   So we again
started.   My dear boy appeared very weak at first, but

soon recovered, and our stout companion, whom I shall call S., evidently showed symptoms of lassitude. On arriving at the cabin of a lazy man, blessed with an industrious wife and six healthy children, all of whom labored for his support, we were welcomed by the woman, whose motions and language indicated her right to belong to a much higher class. Better breakfast I never ate: the bread was made of new corn, ground on a tin grater by the beautiful hands of our blue-eyed hostess; the chickens had been prepared by one of her lovely daughters; some good coffee was added, and my son had fresh milk. The good woman, who now held a babe to her bosom, seemed pleased to see how heartily we all ate ; the children went to work, and the lazy husband went to the door to smoke a corn-cob pipe. A dollar was put into the ruddy hand of the chubby urchin, and we bade its mother farewell. Again we trudged along the beach, but after a while betook ourselves to the woods. My son became faint. Dear boy! never can I forget how he lay exhausted on a log, large tears rolling down his cheeks. I bathed his temples, spoke soothingly to him, and chancing to see a fine Turkey Cock run close by, directed his attention to it, when, as if suddenly refreshed, he got up and ran a few yards towards the bird. From that moment he seemed to acquire new vigor, and at length we reached Wilcox's, where we stopped for the night. We were reluctantly received at the house, and had little attention paid to us, but we had a meal and went to bed.

The sun rose in all its splendor, and the Ohio reflected its ruddy beams. A finer view of that river can scarcely be obtained than that from the house which we were leaving. Two miles through intricate woods brought us to Belgrade, and having passed Fort Massacre, we halted and took breakfast. S. gave us to understand that the want of roads made travelling very unpleasant; he was not, he added, in the habit of "skulking through the bushes, or tramping over stony bars in the full sunshine;" but how else he had travelled was not explained. Mr. Rose kept up about as well as Victor, and I now led the way. Towards sunset we reached the shores of the river, opposite the mouth of the Cumberland. On a hill, the property of a Major B., we found a house, and a solitary woman, wretchedly poor, but very kind. She assured us that if we could not cross the river, she would give us food and shelter for the night, but said that, as the moon was up, she could get us put over when her skiff came back. Hungry and fatigued, we laid us down on the brown grass, waiting either a scanty meal or the skiff that was to convey us across the river. I had already grated the corn for our supper, run down the chickens, and made a fire, when a cry of " Boat coming ! " roused us all. We crossed half of the Ohio, walked over Cumberland Isle, and after a short ferry found ourselves in Kentucky, the native land of my beloved sons. I was now within a few miles of the spot where, some years before, I had a horse killed under me by lightning.

It is unnecessary to detain you with a long narrative, and state every occurrence till we reached the banks of Green River. We had left Trinity at twelve o'clock of the 15th of October, and on the morning of the 18th four travellers, descending a hill, were admiring the reflection of the sun's rays on the forest-margined horizon. The frost, which lay thick on the ground and the fences, glittered in the sheen, and dissolved away; all nature seemed beautiful in its calm repose; but the pleasure which I felt in gazing on the scene was damped by the fatigue of my son, who now limped like a lamed Turkey, although, as the rest of the party were not much better off, he smiled, straightened himself, and strove to keep up with us. Poor S. was panting many yards behind, and was talking of purchasing a horse. We had now, however, a tolerably good road, and in the evening got to a house, where I inquired if we could have a supper and beds. When I came out, Victor was asleep on the grass, Mr. Rose looking at his sore toes, and S. just finishing a jug of monongahela. Here we resolved that, instead of going by Henderson, we should take a cut across to the right, and make direct for Smith's Ferry, by way of Highland Lick Creek.

Next day we trudged along, but nothing very remarkable occurred excepting that we saw a fine black Wolf, quite tame and gentle, the owner of which refused a hundred dollars for it. Mr. Rose, who was an engineer, and a man of taste, amused us with his flageolet, and frequently spoke of his wife, his children, and his fireside, which increased my good opinion of him. At an orchard we filled our pockets with October peaches, and when we came to Trade Water River we found it quite low. The acorns were already drifted on its shallows, and the Wood Ducks were running about picking them up. Passing a flat bottom, we saw a large Buffalo Lick. Where now are the bulls which erst scraped its earth away, bellowing forth their love or their anger?

Good Mr. Rose's feet became sorer and sorer each succeeding day; Mr. S. at length nearly gave up; my son had grown brisker. The 20th was cloudy, and we dreaded rain, as we knew the country to be flat and clayey. In Union County, we came to a large opening, and found the house of a justice, who led us kindly to the main road, and accompanied us for a mile, giving us excellent descriptions of brooks, woods, and barrens; notwithstanding which we should have been much puzzled, had not a neighbor on horseback engaged to show us the way. The rain now fell in torrents and rendered us very uncomfortable, but at length we reached Highland Lick, where we stumbled on a cabin, the door of which we thrust open, overturning a chair that had been placed behind it. On a dirty bed lay a man, a table with a journal or perhaps a ledger before him, a small cask in a corner near him, a brass pistol on a nail over his head, and a long Spanish dagger by his

side. He rose and asked what was wanted. " The way
to a better place, the road to Suggs's." " Follow the road,
and you 'll get to his house in about five miles ! " My
party were waiting for me, warming themselves by the
fires of the salt-kettles. The being I had seen was an overseer. By and by we crossed a creek; the country was
hilly, clayey, and slippery; Mr. S. was cursing, Rose
limped like a lame Duck, but Victor kept up like a
veteran.

Another day, kind reader, and I shall for a while shut
my journal. The morning of the 21st was beautiful; we
had slept comfortably at Suggs's, and we soon found ourselves on pleasant barrens, with an agreeable road. Rose
and S. were so nearly knocked up that they proposed to us
to go on without them. We halted and talked a few minutes
on the subject, when our companions stated their resolution to proceed at a slower pace. So we bade them
adieu. I asked my son how he felt; he laughed and
quickened his steps; and in a short time our former associates were left out of sight. In about two hours we
were seated in the Green River Ferry-boat, with our legs
hanging in the water. At Smith's Ferry this stream looks
like a deep lake; and the thick cane on its banks, the large
overhanging willows, and its dark, green waters, never fail
to form a fine picture, more especially in the calm of an
autumnal evening. Mr. Smith gave us a good supper,
sparkling cider, and a comfortable bed. It was arranged
that he should drive us to Louisville in his dearborn; and
so ended our walk of two hundred and fifty miles. Should
you wish to accompany us during the remainder of our
journey I have only to refer you to the article " Hospitality
in the Woods."

HOSPITALITY IN THE WOODS

HOSPITALITY is a virtue the exercise of which, although always agreeable to the stranger, is not always duly appreciated. The traveller who has acquired celebrity is not unfrequently received with a species of hospitality which is much alloyed by the obvious attention of the host to his own interest; and the favor conferred upon the stranger must have less weight when it comes mingled with almost interminable questions as to his perilous adventures. Another receives hospitality at the hands of persons who, possessed of all the comforts of life, receive the way-worn wanderer with pomposity, lead him from one part of their spacious mansion to another, and bidding him good-night, leave him to amuse himself in his solitary apartment, because he is thought unfit to be presented to a party of friends. A third stumbles on a congenial spirit, who receives him with open arms, offers him servants, horses, perhaps even his purse, to enable him to pursue his journey, and parts from him with regret. In all these cases the traveller feels more or less under obligation, and is accordingly grateful. But, kind reader, the hospitality received from the inhabitant of the forest, who can offer only the shelter of his humble roof and the refreshment of his homely fare, remains more deeply impressed on the memory of the bewildered traveller than any other. This kind of hospitality I have myself frequently experienced in our woods, and now proceed to relate an instance of it.

I had walked several hundred miles, accompanied by my son, then a stripling, and, coming upon a clear stream, observed a house on the opposite shore. We crossed in a canoe, and finding that we had arrived at a tavern, determined upon spending the night there. As we were both greatly fatigued, I made an arrangement with our host to be

conveyed in a light Jersey wagon a distance of a hundred
miles, the period of our departure to be determined by
the rising of the moon. Fair Cynthia, with her shorn
beams, peeped over the forest about two hours before
dawn, and our conductor, provided with a long twig of
hickory, took his station in the fore-part of the wagon.
Off we went at a round trot, dancing in the cart like peas
in a sieve. The road, which was just wide enough to allow
us to pass, was full of deep ruts, and covered here and
there with trunks and stumps, over all which we were
hurried. Our conductor, Mr. Flint, the landlord of the
tavern, boasting of his perfect knowledge of the country,
undertook to drive us by a short cut, and we willingly
confided ourselves to his management. So we jogged
along, now and then deviating to double the fallen timber.
Day commenced with promise of fine weather, but several
nights of white frost having occurred, a change was expected. To our sorrow, the change took place long
before we got to the road again. The rain fell in torrents;
the thunder bellowed; the lightning blazed. It was now
evening, but the storm had brought perfect night, black
and dismal. Our cart had no cover. Cold and wet, we
sat silent and melancholy, with no better expectation than
that of passing the night under the little shelter the cart
could afford us.

To stop was considered worse than to proceed. So we
gave the reins to the horses, with some faint hope that they
would drag us out of our forlorn state. Of a sudden the
steeds altered their course, and soon after we perceived
the glimmer of a faint light in the distance, and almost at
the same moment heard the barking of dogs. Our horses
stopped by a high fence and fell a-neighing, while I
hallooed at such a rate that an answer was speedily
obtained. The next moment a flaming pine torch crossed
the gloom, and advanced to the spot where we stood.
The negro boy who bore it, without waiting to question

us, enjoined us to follow the fence, and said that Master had sent him to show the strangers to the house. We proceeded, much relieved, and soon reached the gate of a little yard, in which a small cabin was perceived.

A tall, fine-looking young man stood in the open door, and desired us get out of the cart and walk in. We did so, when the following conversation took place. "A bad night this, strangers; how came you to be along the fence? You certainly must have lost your way, for there is no public road within twenty miles." "Ay," answered Mr. Flint, "sure enough we lost our way; but, thank God! we have got to a house; and thank *you* for your reception." "Reception!" replied the woodsman; "no very great thing after all; you are all here safe, and that's enough. Eliza," turning to his wife, "see about some victuals for the strangers, and you, Jupiter," addressing the negro lad, "bring some wood and mend the fire. Eliza, call the boys up, and treat the strangers the best way you can. Come, gentlemen, pull off your wet clothes, and draw to the fire. Eliza, bring some socks and a shirt or two."

For my part, kind reader, knowing my countrymen as I do, I was not much struck at all this; but my son, who had scarcely reached the age of thirteen, drew near to me, and observed how pleasant it was to have met with such good people. Mr. Flint bore a hand in getting his horses put under a shed. The young wife was already stirring with so much liveliness that to have doubted for a moment that all she did was a pleasure to her would have been impossible. Two negro lads made their appearance, looked at us for a moment, and going out, called the dogs. Soon after the cries of the poultry informed us that good cheer was at hand. Jupiter brought more wood, the blaze of which illumined the cottage. Mr. Flint and our host returned, and we already began to feel the comforts of hospitality. The woodsman remarked that it was a pity we had not chanced to come that day three weeks; " for," said he, " it was our wedding-day, and father gave us a good house-warming, and you might have fared better; but, however, if you can eat bacon and eggs, and a broiled chicken, you shall have that. I have no whiskey in the house, but father has some capital cider, and I'll go over and bring a keg of it." I asked how far off his father lived. " Only three miles, sir, and I'll be back before Eliza has cooked your supper." Off he went accordingly, and the next moment the galloping of his horse was heard. The rain fell in torrents, and now I also became struck with the kindness of our host.

To all appearance the united ages of the pair under whose roof we had found shelter did not exceed two score. Their means seemed barely sufficient to render them comfortable, but the generosity of their young hearts had no limits. The cabin was new. The logs of which it was formed were all of the tulip-tree, and were nicely pared. Every part was beautifully clean. Even the coarse slabs of wood that formed the floor looked as if newly washed and dried. Sundry gowns and petticoats of substantial homespun hung from the logs that formed one of the sides of the cabin, while the other was covered with articles of male attire. A large spinning-wheel, with rolls of wool and cotton, occupied one corner. In another was a small cupboard, containing the little stock of new dishes, cups, plates, and tin pans. The table was small also, but quite new, and as bright as polished walnut could be. The only bed that I saw was of domestic manufacture, and the counterpane proved how expert the young wife was at spinning and weaving. A fine rifle ornamented the chimney-piece. The fireplace was of such dimensions that it looked as if it had been purposely constructed for holding the numerous progeny expected to result from the happy union.

The black boy was engaged in grinding some coffee.
Bread was prepared by the fair hands of the bride, and
placed on a flat board in front of the fire. The bacon
and eggs already murmured and spluttered in the frying-
pan, and a pair of chickens puffed and swelled on a grid-
iron over the embers, in front of the hearth. The cloth
was laid, and everything arranged, when the clattering
of hoofs announced the return of the husband. In he
came, bearing a two-gallon keg of cider. His eyes
sparkled with pleasure as he said, "Only think, Eliza;
father wanted to rob us of the strangers, and was for
coming here to ask them to his own house, just as if we
could not give them enough ourselves; but here's the
drink. Come, gentlemen, sit down and help yourselves."
We did so, and I, to enjoy the repast, took a chair of the
husband's making, in preference to one of those called
Windsor, of which there were six in the cabin. This
chair was bottomed with a piece of Deer's skin tightly
stretched, and afforded a very comfortable seat.

The wife now resumed her spinning, and the husband
filled a jug with the sparkling cider, and, seated by the
blazing fire, was drying his clothes. The happiness he
enjoyed beamed from his eye, as at my request he
proceeded to give us an account of his affairs and
prospects, which he did in the following words: " I shall
be twenty-two next Christmas-day," said our host. "My
father came from Virginia when young, and settled on the
large tract of land where he yet lives, and where with
hard working he has done well. There were nine children of us. Most of them are married and settled in the
neighborhood. The old man has divided his lands among
some of us, and bought others for the rest. The land
where I am he gave me two years ago, and a finer piece
is not easily to be found. I have cleared a couple of
fields, and planted an orchard. Father gave me a stock
of cattle, some hogs, and four horses, with two negro

boys. I camped here for most of the time when clearing and planting; and when about to marry the young woman you see at the wheel, father helped me in raising this hut. My wife, as luck would have it, had a negro also, and we have begun the world as well off as most folks, and, the Lord willing, may — But, gentlemen, you don't eat; do help yourselves. Eliza, maybe the strangers would like some milk." The wife stopped her work, and kindly asked if we preferred sweet or sour milk; for you must know, reader, that sour milk is by some of our farmers considered a treat. Both sorts were produced, but, for my part, I chose to stick to the cider.

Supper over, we all neared the fire, and engaged in conversation. At length our kind host addressed his wife as follows: " Eliza, the gentlemen would like to lie down, I guess. What sort of bed can you fix for them? " Eliza looked up with a smile, and said: " Why, Willy, we will divide the bedding, and arrange half on the floor, on which we can sleep very well, and the gentlemen will have the best we can spare them." To this arrangement I immediately objected, and proposed lying on a blanket by the fire; but neither Willy nor Eliza would listen. So they arranged a part of their bedding on the floor, on which, after some debate, we at length settled. The negroes were sent to their own cabin, the young couple went to bed, and Mr. Flint lulled us all asleep with a long story intended to show us how passing strange it was that he should have lost his way.

" Tired nature's sweet restorer, balmy sleep," and so forth. But Aurora soon turned her off. Mr. Speed, our host, rose, went to the door, and returning assured us that the weather was too bad for us to attempt proceeding. I really believe he was heartily glad of it; but anxious to continue our journey, I desired Mr. Flint to see about his horses. Eliza by this time was up too, and I observed her whispering to her husband, when he immediately said

aloud, " To be sure, the gentlemen will eat breakfast before they go, and I will show them the way to the road."
Excuses were of no avail. Breakfast was prepared and
eaten. The weather brightened a little, and by nine we
were under way. Willy, on horseback, headed us. In a
few hours our cart arrived at a road, by following which we
at length got to the main one, and parted from our woodsman with the greater regret that he would accept nothing
from any of us. On the contrary, telling Mr. Flint, with
a smile, that he hoped he might some time again follow
the longest track for a short cut, he bade us adieu, and
trotted back to his fair Eliza and his happy home.

NIAGARA

AFTER wandering on some of our great lakes for many
months, I bent my course towards the celebrated Falls
of Niagara, being desirous of taking a sketch of them.
This was not my first visit to them, and I hoped it should
not be the last.

Artists (I know not if I can be called one) too often
imagine that what they produce must be excellent, and
with that foolish idea go on spoiling much paper and canvas, when their time might have been better employed in
a different manner. But, digressions aside, I directed
my steps towards the Falls of Niagara, with the view of
representing them on paper, for the amusement of my
family.

Returning as I then was from a tedious journey, and
possessing little more than some drawings of rare birds
and plants, I reached the tavern at Niagara Falls in such
plight as might have deterred many an individual from
obtruding himself upon a circle of well-clad and perhaps
well-bred society. Months had passed since the last of
my linen had been taken from my body, and used to clean

that useful companion, my gun. I was in fact covered just like one of the poorer class of Indians, and was rendered even more disagreeable to the eye of civilized man by not having, like them, plucked my beard, or trimmed my hair in any way. Had Hogarth been living, and there when I arrived, he could not have found a fitter subject for a Robinson Crusoe. My beard covered my neck in front, my hair fell much lower at my back, the leather dress which I wore had for months stood in need of repair, a large knife hung at my side, a rusty tin-box containing my drawings and colors, and wrapped up in a worn-out blanket that had served me for a bed, was buckled to my shoulders. To every one I must have seemed immersed in the depths of poverty, perhaps of despair. Nevertheless, as I cared little about my appearance during those happy rambles, I pushed into the sitting-room, unstrapped my little burden, and asked how soon breakfast would be ready.

In America, no person is ever refused entrance to the inns, at least far from cities. We know too well how many poor creatures are forced to make their way from other countries in search of employment or to seek uncultivated land, and we are ever ready to let them have what they may call for. No one knew who I was, and the landlord, looking at me with an eye of close scrutiny, answered that breakfast would be on the table as soon as the company should come down from their rooms. I approached this important personage, told him of my avocations, and convinced him that he might feel safe as to remuneration. From this moment I was, with him at least, on equal footing with every other person in his house. He talked a good deal of the many artists who had visited the Falls that season, from different parts, and offered to assist me by giving such accommodations as I might require to finish the drawings I had in contemplation. He left me, and as I looked about the room I saw several views of the Falls, by which I was so disgusted that I suddenly came to my better senses. " What! " thought I, " have I come here to mimic nature in her grandest enterprise, and add *my* caricature of one of the wonders of the world to those which I here see? No; I give up the vain attempt. I shall look on these mighty cataracts and imprint them, where alone they can be represented — on my mind! "

Had I taken a view, I might as well have given you what might be termed a regular account of the form, the height, the tremendous roar of these Falls; might have spoken of people perilling their lives by going between the rock and the sheet of water, calculated the density of the atmosphere in that strange position, related wondrous tales of Indians and their canoes having been precipitated the whole depth — might have told of the narrow, rapid, and rockbound river that leads the waters of the Erie into those of Ontario, remarking *en passant* the Devil's Hole and sundry other places or objects. But, supposing you had been there, my description would prove useless, and quite as puny as my intended view would have been for my family; and should you not have seen them, and are fond of contemplating the more magnificent of the Creator's works, go to Niagara, reader; for all the pictures you may see, all the descriptions you may read, of these mighty Falls, can only produce in your mind the faint glimmer of a glow-worm compared with the overpowering glory of the meridian sun.

I breakfasted amid a crowd of strangers, who gazed and laughed at me, paid my bill, rambled about and admired the Falls for a while, saw several young gentlemen *sketching on cards* the mighty mass of foaming waters, and walked to Buffalo, where I purchased new apparel and sheared my beard. I then enjoyed civilized life as much as, a month before, I had enjoyed the wildest solitudes and the darkest recesses of mountain and forest.

MEADVILLE

THE incidents that occur in the life of a student of nature are not all of the agreeable kind; in proof of which I shall present you, good reader, with an extract from one of my journals.

My money was one day stolen from me, by a person who perhaps imagined that to a naturalist it was of little importance. This happened on the shores of Upper Canada. The affair was as unexpected as it well could be, and as adroitly managed as if it had been planned and executed in Cheapside. To have repined when the thing could not be helped would certes not have been acting manfully. I therefore told my companion to keep a good heart, for I felt satisfied that Providence had some relief in store for us. The whole amount of cash left with two individuals fifteen hundred miles from home was just seven dollars and a half. Our passage across the lake had fortunately been paid for. We embarked and soon got to the entrance of Presque Isle Harbor, but could not pass the bar, on account of a violent gale which came on as we approached it. The anchor was dropped, and we remained on board during the night, feeling at times very disagreeable, under the idea of having taken so little care of our money. How long we might have remained at anchor I cannot tell, had not that Providence on whom I have never ceased to rely come to our aid. Through some means to me quite unknown, Captain Judd, of the U. S. Navy, then probably commandant at Presque Isle, sent a gig with six men to our relief. It was on the 29th of August, 1824, and never shall I forget that morning. My drawings were put into the boat with the greatest care. We shifted into it, and seated ourselves according to directions politely given us. Our brave fellows pulled hard, and every moment brought us nearer to the American shore. I leaped upon it with elated heart. My drawings were safely landed, and for anything else I cared little at the moment. I searched in vain for the officer of our navy, to whom I still feel grateful, and gave one of our dollars to the sailors to drink the " freedom of the waters; " after which we betook ourselves to a humble inn to procure bread and milk, and consider how we were to proceed.

Our plans were soon settled, for to proceed was decidedly the best. Our luggage was rather heavy, so we hired a cart to take it to Meadville, for which we offered five dollars. This sum was accepted, and we set off. The country through which we passed might have proved favorable to our pursuits, had it not rained nearly the whole day. At night we alighted and put up at a house belonging to our conductor's father. It was Sunday night. The good folks had not yet returned from a distant meeting-house, the grandmother of our driver being the only individual about the premises. We found her a cheerful dame, who bestirred herself as actively as age would permit, got up a blazing fire to dry our wet clothes, and put as much bread and milk on the table as might have sufficed for several besides ourselves.

Being fatigued by the jolting of the cart, we asked for a place in which to rest, and were shown into a room in which were several beds. We told the good woman that I should paint her portrait next morning for the sake of her children. My companion and myself were quickly in bed, and soon asleep, in which state we should probably have remained till morning, had we not been awakened by a light, which we found to be carried by three young damsels, who, having observed where we lay, blew it out, and got into a bed opposite to ours. As we had not spoken, it is probable the girls supposed us sound asleep, and we heard them say how delighted they would be to have their portraits taken, as well as that of their grandmother. My heart silently met their desire, and we fell asleep without further disturbance. In our backwoods it is frequently the case that one room suffices for all the members of a family.

Day dawned, and as we were dressing we discovered that we were alone in the apartment, the good country girls having dressed in silence, and left us before we had awakened. We joined the family and were kindly greeted. No sooner had I made known my intentions as to the portraits than the young folks disappeared, and soon after returned attired in their Sunday clothes. The black chalk was at work in a few minutes, to their great delight, and as the fumes of the breakfast that was meantime preparing reached my sensitive nose, I worked with redoubled ardor. The sketches were soon finished, and soon too was the breakfast over. I played a few airs on my flageolet, while our guide was putting the horses to the cart, and by ten o'clock we were once more under way towards Meadville. Never shall I forget Maxon Randell and his hospitable family. My companion was as pleased as myself, and as the weather was now beautiful we enjoyed our journey with all that happy thoughtlessness best suited to our character. The country now became covered with heavy timber, principally evergreens, the pines and the cucumber trees loaded with brilliant fruits, and the spruces throwing a shade over the land in good keeping for a mellow picture. The lateness of the crops was the only disagreeable circumstance that struck us; hay was yet standing, probably, however, a second crop; the peaches were quite small and green, and a few persons here and there, as we passed the different farms, were reaping oats. At length we came in sight of French Creek, and soon after reached Meadville. Here we paid the five dollars promised to our conductor, who instantly faced about, and applying the whip to his nags, bade us adieu, and set off.

We had now only one hundred and fifty cents. No time was to be lost. We put our baggage and ourselves under the roof of a tavern keeper known by the name of J. E. Smith, at the sign of the Traveller's Rest, and soon after took a walk to survey the little village that was to be laid under contribution for our further support. Its appearance was rather dull, but, thanks to God, I have never despaired while rambling thus for the sole purpose of admiring his grand and beautiful works. I had opened the case that contained my drawings, and putting my portfolio under my arm, and a few good credentials in my pocket, walked up Main Street, looking to the right and left, examining the different *heads* which occurred, until I fixed my eyes on a gentleman in a store who looked as if he might want a sketch. I begged him to allow me to sit down. This granted, I remained purposely silent until he very soon asked me what was "*in that portfolio.*" These three words sounded well, and without waiting another instant, I opened it to his view. This was a Hollander, who complimented me much on the execution of the drawings of birds and flowers in my portfolio. Showing him a sketch of the best friend I have in the world at present, I asked him if he would like one in the same style of himself. He not only answered in the affirmative, but assured me that he would exert himself in procuring as many more customers as he could. I thanked him, be assured, kind reader; and having fixed upon the next morning for drawing the sketch, I returned to the Traveller's Rest, with a hope that tomorrow might prove propitious. Supper was ready, and as in America we generally have but one sort of *table d'hôte*, we sat down, when, every individual looking upon me as a missionary priest, on account of my hair, which in those days flowed loosely on my shoulders, I was asked to say grace, which I did with a fervent spirit.

Daylight returned. I visited the groves and woods around with my companion, returned, breakfasted, and went to the store, where, notwithstanding my ardent desire to begin my task, it was ten o'clock before the sitter was ready. But, reader, allow me to describe the *artist's room.*

See me ascending a crazy flight of steps, from the back part of a store room into a large garret extending over the store and counting room, and mark me looking round to see how the light could be stopped from obtruding on me through no less than four windows facing each other at right angles. Then follow me scrutinizing the corners, and finding in one a cat nursing her young among a heap of rags intended for the paper mill. Two hogsheads filled with oats, a parcel of Dutch toys carelessly thrown on the floor, a large drum and a bassoon in another part, fur caps hanging along the wall, and the portable bed of the merchant's clerk swinging like a hammock near the centre, together with some rolls of sole leather, made up the picture. I saw all this at a glance, and closing the extra windows with blankets, I soon procured a *painter's light*.

A young gentleman sat to try my skill. I finished his phiz, which was approved of. The merchant then took the chair, and I had the good fortune to please him also. The room became crowded with the gentry of the village. Some laughed, while others expressed their wonder; but my work went on, notwithstanding the observations which were made. My sitter invited me to spend the evening with him, which I did, and joined him in some music on the flute and violin. I returned to my companion with great pleasure, and you may judge how much that pleasure was increased when I found that he also had made two sketches. Having written a page or two of our journals, we retired to rest.

The following day was spent much in the same manner. I felt highly gratified that from under my gray coat my talents had made their way, and I was pleased to discover that industry and moderate abilities prove at least as valuable as first-rate talents without the former of these qualities. We left Meadville on foot, having forwarded our baggage by wagon. Our hearts were light, our pockets replenished, and we walked in two days to Pittsburgh, as happy as circumstances permitted us to be.

THE BURNING OF THE FORESTS.

WITH what pleasure have I seated myself by the blazing fire of some lonely cabin, when, faint with fatigue, and chilled with the piercing blast, I had forced my way to it through the drifted snows that covered the face of the country as with a mantle. The affectionate mother is hushing her dear babe to repose, while a group of sturdy children surround their father, who has just returned from the chase, and deposited on the rough flooring of his hut the varied game which he has procured. The great back-log, that with some difficulty has been rolled into the ample chimney, urged, as it were, by lighted pieces of pine, sends forth a blaze of light over the happy family. The dogs of the hunter are already licking away the trickling waters of the thawing icicles that sparkle over their shaggy coats, and the comfort-loving cat is busied in passing her furry paws over each ear, or with her rough tongue smoothing her glossy coat.

How delightful to me has it been when, kindly received and hospitably treated under such a roof, by persons whose means were as scanty as their generosity was great, I have entered into conversation with them respecting subjects of interest to me, and received gratifying information. When the humble but plentiful repast was ended, the mother would take from the shelf the Book of books, and mildly request the attention of her family, while the father read aloud a chapter. Then to Heaven would ascend their humble prayers, and a good-night would be bidden to all friends far and near. How comfortably have I laid my wearied frame on the Buffalo hide, and covered me with the furry skin of some huge Bear! How pleasing have been my dreams of home and happiness, as I there lay, secure from danger and sheltered from the inclemency of the weather.

I recollect that once while in the State of Maine, I passed such a night as I have described. Next morning the face of nature was obscured by the heavy rains that fell in torrents, and my generous host begged me to remain, in such pressing terms that I was well content to accept his offer. Breakfast over, the business of the day commenced; the spinning-wheels went round, and the boys employed themselves, one in searching for knowledge, another in attempting to solve some ticklish arithmetical problem. In a corner lay the dogs, dreaming of plunder, while close to the ashes stood grimalkin, seriously purring in concert with the wheels. The hunter and I seated ourselves each on a stool, while the matron looked after her domestic arrangements.

" Puss," quoth the dame, " get away; you told me last night of this day's rain, and I fear you may now give us worse news with tricky paws." Puss accordingly went off, leaped on a bed, and rolling herself in a ball, composed herself for a comfortable nap. I asked the husband what his wife meant by what she had just said. " The good woman," said he, " has some curious notions at times, and she believes, I think, in the ways of animals of all kinds. Now, her talk to the cat refers to the fires of the woods around us, and although they have happened long ago, she fears them quite as much as ever, and, indeed, she and I and all of us have good reason to dread them, as they have brought us many calamities." Having read of the great fires to which my host alluded, and frequently observed with sorrow the mournful state of the forests, I felt anxious to know something of the causes by which these direful effects had been produced. I therefore requested him to give me an account of the events resulting from those fires which he had witnessed. Willingly he at once went on, nearly as follows: —

" About twenty-five years ago the larch, or hackmatack, trees were nearly all killed by insects. This took place in

what hereabouts is called the 'black soft growth' land,
that is, the spruce, pine, and all other firs. The destruction
of the trees was effected by the insects cutting the leaves,
and you must know that, although other trees are not
killed by the loss of their leaves, the evergreens always
are. Some few years after this destruction of the larch,
the same insects attacked the spruces, pines, and other
firs, in such a manner that, before half a dozen years were
over, they began to fall, and, tumbling in all directions,
they covered the whole country with matted masses.
You may suppose that when partially dried or seasoned,
they would prove capital fuel, as well as supplies for
the devouring flames, which accidentally, or perhaps by
intention, afterwards raged over the country, and continued burning at intervals for years, in many places stopping all communication by the roads; the resinous nature
of the firs being of course best fitted to insure and keep
up the burning of the deep beds of dry leaves or of the
other trees." Here I begged him to give me some idea
of the form of the insects which had caused such havoc.

"The insects," said he, "were, in their caterpillar form,
about three quarters of an inch in length, and as green as
the leaves of the trees they fed on, when they committed
their ravages. I must tell you also that, in most of the
places over which the fire passed, a new growth of wood
has already sprung up, of what we lumberers call hard
wood, which consists of all other sorts but pine or fir; and
I have always remarked that wherever the first natural
growth of a forest is destroyed, either by the axe, the
hurricane, or the fire, there springs up spontaneously another of quite a different kind." I again stopped my host
to inquire if he knew the method or nature of the first
kindling of the fires.

"Why, sir," said he, "there are different opinions
about this. Many believe that the Indians did it, either to
be the better able to kill the game, or to punish their

enemies the Pale-faces. My opinion, however, is different; and I derive it from my experience in the woods as a
lumberer. I have always thought that the fires began by
the accidental fall of a dry trunk against another, when
their rubbing together, especially as many of them are
covered with resin, would produce fire. The dry leaves
on the ground are at once kindled, next the twigs
and branches, when nothing but the intervention of the
Almighty could stop the progress of the fire.

"In some instances, owing to the wind, the destructive
element approached the dwellings of the inhabitants of
the woods so rapidly that it was difficult for them to escape. In some parts, indeed, hundreds of families were
obliged to flee from their homes, leaving all they had
behind them, and here and there some of the affrighted
fugitives were burnt alive."

At this moment a rush of wind came down the chimney,
blowing the blaze of the fire towards the room. The wife
and daughter, imagining for a moment that the woods were
again on fire, made for the door, but the husband explain-
ing the cause of their terror, they resumed their work.

"Poor things," said the lumberer, "I dare say that
what I have told you brings sad recollections to the minds
of my wife and eldest daughter, who, with myself, had to
fly from our home, at the time of the great fires." I felt
so interested in his relation of the causes of the burnings
that I asked him to describe to me the particulars of his
misfortunes at the time. "If Prudence and Polly," said
he, looking towards his wife and daughter, "will promise
to sit still should another puff of smoke come down the
chimney, I will do so." The good-natured smile with
which he made this remark elicited a return from the
women and he proceeded: —

"It is a difficult thing, sir, to describe, but I will do my
best to make your time pass pleasantly. We were sound
asleep one night in a cabin about a hundred miles from

this, when, about two hours before day, the snorting of the horses and lowing of the cattle which I had ranging in the woods suddenly awakened us. I took yon rifle and went to the door, to see what beast had caused the hubbub, when I was struck by the glare of light reflected on all the trees before me, as far as I could see through the woods. My horses were leaping about, snorting loudly, and the cattle ran among them with their tails raised straight over their backs. On going to the back of the house, I plainly heard the crackling made by the burning brushwood, and saw the flames coming towards us in a far extended line. I ran to the house, told my wife to dress herself and the child as quick as possible, and take the little money we had, while I managed to catch and saddle the two best horses. All this was done in a very short time, for I guessed that every moment was precious to us.

"We then mounted, and made off from the fire. My wife, who is an excellent rider, stuck close to me; my daughter, who was then a small child, I took in one arm. When making off as I said, I looked back and saw that the frightful blaze was close upon us, and had already laid hold of the house. By good luck, there was a horn attached to my hunting-clothes, and I blew it, to bring after us, if possible, the remainder of my live stock, as well as the dogs. The cattle followed for a while; but, before an hour had elapsed, they all ran as if mad through the woods, and that, sir, was the last of them. My dogs, too, although at other times extremely tractable, ran after the Deer that in bodies sprung before us, as if fully aware of the death that was so rapidly approaching.

"We heard blasts from the horns of our neighbors as we proceeded, and knew that they were in the same predicament. Intent on striving to the utmost to preserve our lives, I thought of a large lake some miles off, which might possibly check the flames; and, urging my wife to whip up her horse, we set off at full speed, making the best way we could over the fallen trees and brush-heaps, which lay like so many articles placed on purpose to keep up the terrific fires that advanced with a broad front upon us.

"By this time we could feel the heat; and we were afraid that our horses would drop every instant. A singular kind of breeze was passing over our heads, and the glare of the atmosphere shone over the daylight. I was sensible of a slight faintness, and my wife looked pale. The heat had produced such a flush in the child's face that when she turned towards either of us, our grief and perplexity were greatly increased. Ten miles, you know, are soon gone over on swift horses; but, notwithstanding this, when we reached the borders of the lake, covered with sweat and quite exhausted, our hearts failed us. The heat of the smoke was insufferable, and sheets of blazing fire flew over us in a manner beyond belief. We reached the shores, however, coasted the lake for a while, and got round to the lee side. There we gave up our horses, which we never saw again. Down among the rushes we plunged by the edge of the water, and laid ourselves flat, to wait the chance of escaping from being burnt or devoured. The water refreshed us, and we enjoyed the coolness.

"On went the fire, rushing and crashing through the woods. Such a sight may we never see! The heavens, themselves, I thought were frightened, for all above us was a red glare mixed with clouds of smoke, rolling and sweeping away. Our bodies were cool enough, but our heads were scorching, and the child, who now seemed to understand the matter, cried so as nearly to break our hearts.

"The day passed on, and we became hungry. Many wild beasts came plunging into the water beside us, and others swam across to our side and stood still. Although faint and weary, I managed to shoot a Porcupine, and we all tasted its flesh. The night passed, I cannot tell you how. Smouldering fires covered the ground, and trees stood like pillars of fire, or fell across each other. The stifling and sickening smoke still rushed over us, and the burnt cinders and ashes fell thick about us. How we got through that night I really cannot tell, for about some of it I remember nothing." Here the hunter paused, and took breath. The recital of his adventure seemed to have exhausted him. His wife proposed that we should have a bowl of milk, and the daughter having handed it to us, we each took a draught.

"Now," said he, "I will proceed. Towards morning, although the heat did not abate, the smoke became less, and blasts of fresh air sometimes made their way to us. When morning came, all was calm, but a dismal smoke still filled the air, and the smell seemed worse than ever. We were now cooled enough, and shivered as if in an ague fit; so we removed from the water, and went up to a burning log, where we warmed ourselves. What was to become of us, I did not know. My wife hugged the child to her breast, and wept bitterly; but God had preserved us through the worst of the danger, and the flames had gone past, so I thought it would be both ungrateful to him and unmanly to despair now. Hunger once more pressed upon us, but this was easily remedied. Several Deer were still standing in the water, up to the head, and I shot one of them. Some of its flesh was soon roasted; and after eating it we felt wonderfully strengthened.

"By this time the blaze of the fire was beyond our sight, although the ground was still burning in many places, and it was dangerous to go among the burnt trees. After resting awhile, and trimming ourselves, we prepared to commence our march. Taking up the child, I led the way over the hot ground and rocks; and, after two weary days and nights, during which we shifted in the best manner we could, we at last reached the 'hard woods' which had been free of the fire. Soon after we came to a house, where we were kindly treated for a while. Since then, sir, I have worked hard and constantly as a lumberer; but, thanks be to God, here we are safe, sound. and happy!"

A LONG CALM AT SEA

On the 17th of May, 1826, I left New Orleans on board the ship "Delos," commanded by Joseph Hatch, Esq., of Kennebunk, bound for Liverpool. The steamer "Hercules," which towed the ship, left us several miles outside of the Balize, about ten hours after our departure; but there was not a breath of wind, the waters were smoother than the prairies of the Opelousas, and notwithstanding our great display of canvas, we lay like a dead whale, floating at the mercy of the currents. The weather was uncommonly fair, and the heat excessive; and in this helpless state we continued for many days. About the end of a week we had lost sight of the Balize, although I was assured by the commander that all this while the ship had rarely answered the helm. The sailors whistled for wind, and raised their hands in all directions, anxious as they were to feel some motion in the air; but all to no purpose; it was a dead calm, and we concluded that "Æolus" had agreed with "Neptune" to detain us, until our patience should be fairly tried, or our sport exhausted; for sport we certainly had, both on board and around the ship. I doubt if I can better contribute to your amusement at present than by giving you a short account of the occurrences that took place during this sleepy fit of the being on whom we depended for our progress toward merry England.

Vast numbers of beautiful Dolphins glided by the side of the vessel, glancing like burnished gold through the day, and gleaming like meteors by night. The captain and his mates were expert at alluring them with baited hooks, and not less so at piercing them with five-pronged instruments, which they called grains; and I was delighted with the sport, because it afforded me an opportunity of observing and noting some of the habits of this beautiful fish, as well as several other kinds.

On being hooked, the Dolphin flounces vigorously, shoots off with great impetuosity to the very end of the line, when, being suddenly checked, it often rises perpendicularly several feet out of the water, shakes itself violently in the air, gets disentangled, and thus escapes. But when well secured, it is held in play for a while by the experienced fisher, soon becomes exhausted, and is hauled on board. Some persons prefer pulling them in at once, but they seldom succeed, as the force with which the fish shakes itself on being raised out of the water is generally sufficient to enable it to extricate itself. Dolphins move in shoals, varying from four or five to twenty or more, hunting in packs in the waters, as Wolves pursue their prey on land. The object of their pursuit is generally the Flying-fish, now and then the Bonita; and when nothing better can be had, they will follow the little Rudder-fish, and seize it immediately under the stern of the ship. The Flying-fishes after having escaped for a while by dint of their great velocity, on being again approached by the Dolphin, emerge from the waters, and spreading their broad wing-like fins, sail through the air and disperse in all directions, like a covey of timid Partridges before the rapacious Falcon. Some pursue a direct course, others diverge on either side; but in a short time they all drop into their natural element. While they are travelling in the air, their keen and hungry pursuer, like a greyhound, follows in their wake, and performing a succession of leaps, many feet in extent, rapidly gains upon the quarry, which is often seized just as it falls into the sea.

Dolphins manifest a very remarkable sympathy with each other. The moment one of them is hooked or grained, those in company make up to it, and remain around until the unfortunate fish is pulled on board, when they generally move off together, seldom biting at anything thrown out to them. This, however, is the case only with the larger individuals, which keep apart from the young, in the same manner as is observed in several species of birds; for when the smaller Dolphins are in large shoals, they all remain under the bows of a ship, and bite in succession at any sort of line, as if determined to see what has become of their lost companions, in consequence of which they are often all caught.

You must not suppose that the Dolphin is without its enemies. Who, in this world, man or fish, has not enough of them? Often it conceives itself on the very eve of swallowing a fish, which, after all, is nothing but a piece of lead, with a few feathers fastened to it, to make it look like a Flying-fish, when it is seized and severed in two by the insidious Balacouda, which I have once seen to carry off by means of its sharp teeth, the better part of a Dolphin that was hooked, and already hoisted to the surface of the water.

The Dolphins caught in the Gulf of Mexico during this calm were suspected to be poisonous; and to ascertain whether this was really the case, our cook, who was an African negro, never boiled or fried one without placing beside it a dollar. If the silver was not tarnished by the time the Dolphin was ready for the table, the fish was presented to the passengers, with an assurance that it was perfectly good. But as not a single individual of the hundred that we caught had the property of converting silver into copper, I suspect that our African sage was no magician.

One morning, that of the 22d of June, the weather sultry, I was surprised on getting out of my hammock, which was slung on deck, to find the water all around swarming with Dolphins, which were sporting in great glee. The sailors assured me that this was a certain "token of wind," and, as they watched the movements of the fishes, added, "ay, and of a fair breeze too." I caught several Dolphins in the course of an hour, after which scarcely any remained about the ship. Not a breath of air came to our relief all that day, no, nor even the next. The sailors were in despair, and I should probably have become despondent also, had not my spirits been excited by finding a very large Dolphin on my hook. When I had hauled it on board, I found it to be the largest I had ever caught. It was a magnificent creature. See how it quivers in the agonies of death! its tail flaps the hard deck, producing a sound like the rapid roll of a drum. How beautiful the changes of its colors! Now it is blue, now green, silvery, golden, and burnished copper! Now it presents a blaze of all the hues of the rainbow intermingled; but, alack! it is dead, and the play of its colors is no longer seen. It has settled into the deep calm that has paralyzed the energies of the blustering winds, and smoothed down the proud waves of the ocean.

The best bait for the Dolphin is a long strip of Shark's flesh. I think it generally prefers this to the semblance of the Flying-fish, which indeed it does not often seize unless when the ship is under way, and it is made to rise to the surface. There are times, however, when hunger and the absence of their usual food will induce the Dolphins to dash at any sort of bait; and I have seen some caught by means of a piece of white linen fastened to a hook. Their appetite is as keen as that of the Vulture, and whenever a good opportunity occurs, they gorge themselves to such a degree that they become an easy prey to their enemies the Balacouda and the Bottle-nosed Porpoise. One that had been grained while lazily swimming immediately under the stern of our ship, was found to have its stomach completely crammed with Flying-fish, all regularly disposed side by side, with their tails downwards — by which I mean to say that the Dolphin always *swallows its prey tail-foremost.* They looked in fact like so many salted Herrings packed in a box, and were to the number of twenty-two, each six or seven inches in length.

The usual length of the Dolphins caught in the Gulf of Mexico is about three feet, and I saw none that exceeded four feet two inches. The weight of one of the latter size was only eighteen pounds; for this fish is extremely narrow in proportion to its length, although rather deep in its form. When just caught, the upper fin, which reaches from the forehead to within a short distance of the tail, is of a fine dark blue. The upper part of the body in its whole length is azure, and the lower parts are of a golden hue, mottled irregularly with deep-blue spots. It seems that they at times enter very shallow water, as in the course of my last voyage along the Florida coast, some were caught in a seine, along with their kinsman the "Cavalier," of which I shall speak elsewhere.

The flesh of the Dolphin is rather firm, very white, and lies in flakes when cooked. The first caught are generally eaten with great pleasure, but when served many days in succession, they become insipid. It is not, as an article of food, equal to the Balacouda, which is perhaps as good as any fish caught in the waters of the Gulf of Mexico.

STILL BECALMED

On the 4th of June, we were still in the same plight, although the currents of the Gulf had borne us to a great distance from the place where, as I have informed you, we had amused ourselves with catching Dolphins. These currents are certainly very singular, for they carried us hither and thither, at one time rendering us apprehensive of drifting on the coast of Florida, at another threatening to send us to Cuba. Sometimes a slight motion in the air revived our hopes, swelled our sails a little, and carried us through the smooth waters like a skater gliding on ice; but in a few hours it was again a dead calm.

One day several small birds, after alighting on the spars, betook themselves to the deck. One of them, a female Rice Bunting, drew our attention more particularly, for, a few moments after her arrival, there came down, as if in her wake, a beautiful Peregrine Falcon. The plunderer hovered about for a while, then stationed himself on the end of one of the yard-arms, and suddenly pouncing on the little gleaner of the meadows, clutched her and carried her off in exultation. But, reader, mark the date, and judge besides of my astonishment when I saw the Falcon feeding on the Finch while on wing, precisely with the same ease and composure as the Mississippi Kite might show while devouring high in air a Red-throated Lizard, swept from one of the magnificent trees of the Louisiana woods.

There was a favorite pet on board belonging to our captain, and which was nothing more nor less than the female companion of a cock — in other words, a common hen. Some liked her because she now and then dropped a fresh egg — a rare article at sea, even on board the "Delos;" others, because she exhibited a pleasing simplicity of character; others again, because, when they had pushed her overboard, it gave them pleasure to see the poor thing in terror strike with her feet, and strive to reach her floating home, which she would never have accomplished, however, had it not been for the humane interference of our captain, Mr. Joseph Hatch, of Kennebunk. Kind, good-hearted man! when, several weeks after, the same pet hen accidentally flew overboard, as we were scudding along at a furious rate, I thought I saw a tear stand in his eye, as she floated panting in our wake. But as yet we are becalmed, and heartily displeased at old "Æolus" for overlooking us.

One afternoon we caught two Sharks. In one of them, a female, about seven feet long, we found ten young ones, all alive, and quite capable of swimming, as we proved by experiment; for, on casting one of them into the sea, it immediately made off, as if it had been accustomed to shift for itself. Of another, that had been cut in two, the head half swam off out of our sight. The rest were cut in pieces, as was the old shark, as bait for the Dolphins, which I have already said are fond of such food.

Our captain, who was much intent on amusing me, informed me that the Rudder-fishes were plentiful astern, and immediately set to dressing hooks for the purpose of catching them. There was now some air above us, the cotton sheets aloft bulged out, the ship moved through the water, and the captain and I repaired to the cabin window. I was furnished with a fine hook, a thread line, and some small bits of bacon, as was the captain, and we dropped our bait among the myriads of delicate little fishes below. Up they came, one after another, so fast in succession that, according to my journal, we caught three hundred and seventy in about two hours. What a mess! and how delicious when roasted! If ever I am again becalmed in the Gulf of Mexico, I shall not forget the Rudder-fish. The little things scarcely measured three inches in length; they were thin and deep in form, and afforded excellent eating. It was curious to see them keep to the lee of the rudder in a compact body; and so voracious were they that they actually leaped out of the water at the sight of the bait, as "sunnies" are occasionally wont to do in our rivers. But the very instant that the ship became still, they dispersed around her sides, and would no longer bite. I made a figure of one of them, as indeed I tried to do of every other species that occurred during this deathlike calm. Not one of these fishes did I ever see when crossing the Atlantic, although many kinds at times come close to the stern of any vessel in the great sea, and are called by the same name.

Another time we caught a fine Porpoise, which measured about two yards in length. This took place at night, when the light of the moon afforded me a clear view of the spot. The fish, contrary to custom, was grained, instead of being harpooned; but in such a way and so effectually, through the forehead, that it was thus held fast, and allowed to flounce and beat about the bows of the ship, until the person who had struck it gave the line holding the grains to the captain, slid down upon the bobstays with a rope, and after a while managed to secure it by the tail. Some of the crew then hoisted it on board. When it arrived on deck, it gave a deep groan, flapped with great force, and soon expired. On opening it next morning, eight hours after death, we found its intestines still warm. They were arranged in the same manner as those of a pig; the paunch contained several cuttle-fishes partially digested. The lower jaw extended beyond the upper about three-fourths of an inch, and both were furnished with a single row of conical teeth, about half an inch long, and just so far separated as to admit those of one jaw between the corresponding ones of the other. The animal might weigh about four hundred pounds; its eyes were extremely small, its flesh was considered delicate by some on board; but in my opinion, if it be good, that of a large Alligator is equally so; and on neither do I intend to feast for some time. The captain told me that he had seen these Porpoises leap at times perpendicularly out of the water to the height of several feet, and that small boats have now and then been sunk by their falling into them when engaged with their sports.

During all this time flocks of Pigeons were crossing the Gulf, between Cuba and the Floridas; many a Rose-breasted Gull played around by day; Noddies alighted on the rigging by night; and now and then the Frigate bird was observed ranging high over head in the azure of the cloudless sky.

The directions of the currents were tried, and our captain, who had an extraordinary genius for mechanics, was frequently employed in turning powder-horns and other articles. So calm and sultry was the weather that we had a large awning spread, under which we took our meals and spent the night. At length we got so wearied of it that the very sailors, I thought, seemed disposed to leap overboard and swim to land. But at length, on the thirty-seventh day after our departure, a smart breeze overtook us. Presently there was an extraordinary bustle on board; about twelve the Tortugas light-house bore north of us, and in a few hours more we gained the Atlantic. Æolus had indeed awakened from his long sleep; and on the nineteenth day after leaving the Capes of Florida, I was landed at Liverpool.

GREAT EGG HARBOR

SOME years ago, after having spent the spring in observing the habits of the migratory Warblers and other land birds, which arrived in vast numbers in the vicinity of Camden in New Jersey, I prepared to visit the sea shores of that State, for the purpose of making myself acquainted with their feathered inhabitants. June had commenced, the weather was pleasant, and the country seemed to smile in the prospect of bright days and gentle gales. Fishermen-gunners passed daily between Philadelphia and the various small seaports, with Jersey wagons, laden with fish, fowls, and other provisions, or with such articles as were required by the families of those hardy boatmen; and I bargained with one of them to take myself and my baggage to Great Egg Harbor.

One afternoon, about sunset, the vehicle halted at my lodgings, and the conductor intimated that he was anxious to proceed as quickly as possible. A trunk, a couple of guns, and such other articles as are found necessary by persons whose pursuits are similar to mine, were immediately thrust into the wagon, and were followed by their owner. The conductor whistled to his steeds, and off we went at a round pace over the loose and deep sand that in almost every part of this State forms the basis of the roads. After a while we overtook a whole caravan of similar vehicles, moving in the same direction, and when we got near them our horses slackened their pace to a regular walk, the driver leaped from his seat, I followed his example, and we presently found ourselves in the midst of a group of merry wagoners, relating their adventures of the week, it being now Saturday night. One gave intimation of the number of "Sheep-heads" he had taken to town, another spoke of the Curlews which yet remained on the sands, and a third boasted of having

JOHN WOODHOUSE AUDUBON.

PAINTED BY AUDUBON ABOUT 1823.

gathered so many dozens of Marsh Hens' eggs. I inquired if the Fish Hawks were plentiful near Great Egg Harbor, and was answered by an elderly man, who with a laugh asked if I had ever seen the "Weak fish" along the coast without the bird in question. Not knowing the animal he had named, I confessed my ignorance, when the whole party burst into a loud laugh, in which, there being nothing better for it, I joined.

About midnight the caravan reached a half-way house, where we rested a while. Several roads diverged from this spot, and the wagons separated, one only keeping us company. The night was dark and gloomy, but the sand of the road indicated our course very distinctly. Suddenly the galloping of horses struck my ear, and on looking back we perceived that our wagon must in an instant be in imminent danger. The driver leaped off, and drew his steeds aside, barely in time to allow the runaways to pass without injuring us. Off they went at full speed, and not long after their owner came up panting, and informed us that they had suddenly taken fright at some noise proceeding from the woods, but hoped they would soon stop. Immediately after we heard a crack; then for a few moments all was silent; but the neighing of horses presently assured us that they had broken loose. On reaching the spot we found the wagon upset, and a few yards farther on were the horses, quietly browsing by the roadside.

The first dawn of morn in the Jerseys in the month of June is worthy of a better description than I can furnish, and therefore I shall only say that the moment the sunbeams blazed over the horizon, the loud and mellow notes of the Meadow Lark saluted our ears. On each side of the road were open woods, on the tallest trees of which I observed at intervals the nest of a Fish Hawk, far above which the white-breasted bird slowly winged its way, as it commenced its early journey to the sea, the odor of which filled me with delight.   In half an hour more we were in the centre of Great Egg Harbor.

There I had the good fortune to be received into the house of a thoroughbred fisherman-gunner, who, besides owning a comfortable cot only a few hundred yards from the shore, had an excellent woman for a wife, and a little daughter as playful as a kitten, though as wild as a Sea-Gull.   In less than half an hour I was quite at home, and the rest of the day was spent in devotion.

Oysters, though reckoned out of season at this period, are as good as ever when fresh from their beds, and my first meal was of some as large and white as any I have eaten.   The sight of them placed before me on a clean table, with an honest and industrious family in my company, never failed to afford more pleasure than the most sumptuous fare under different circumstances; and our conversation being simple and harmless, gayety shone in every face.   As we became better acquainted, I had to answer several questions relative to the object of my visit. The good man rubbed his hands with joy, as I spoke of shooting and fishing, and of long excursions through the swamps and marshes around.

My host was then, and I hope still is, a tall, strong-boned, muscular man, of dark complexion, with eyes as keen as those of the Sea-Eagle.   He was a tough walker, laughed at difficulties, and could pull an oar with any man.   As to shooting, I have often doubted whether he or Mr. Egan, the worthy pilot of Indian Isle, was best; and rarely indeed have I seen either of them miss a shot.

At daybreak on Monday, I shouldered my double-barrelled gun, and my host carried with him a long fowling-piece, a pair of oars, and a pair of oyster-tongs, while the wife and daughter brought along a seine.   The boat was good, the breeze gentle, and along the inlets we sailed for parts well known to my companions.   To such naturalists as are qualified to observe many different objects at the same time, Great Egg Harbor would probably afford as ample a field as any part of our coast, excepting the Florida Keys. Birds of many kinds are abundant, as are fishes and testaceous animals. The forests shelter many beautiful plants, and even on the driest sand-bar you may see insects of the most brilliant tints. Our principal object, however, was to procure certain birds known there by the name of Lawyers, and to accomplish this we entered and followed for several miles a winding inlet or bayou, which led us to the interior of a vast marsh, where after some search we found the birds and their nests. Our seine had been placed across the channel, and when we returned to it the tide had run out, and left in it a number of fine fish, some of which we cooked and ate on the spot. One, which I considered as a curiosity, was saved, and transmitted to Baron Cuvier. Our repast ended, the seine was spread out to dry, and we again betook ourselves to the marshes to pursue our researches until the return of the tide. Having collected enough to satisfy us, we took up our oars, and returned to the shore in front of the fisherman's house, where we dragged the seine several times with success.

In this manner I passed several weeks along those delightful and healthy shores, one day going to the woods, to search the swamps in which the Herons bred, passing another amid the joyous cries of the Marsh Hens, and on a third carrying slaughter among the White-breasted Sea-Gulls; by way of amusement sometimes hauling the fish called the Sheep's-head from an eddy along the shore, or watching the gay Terns as they danced in the air, or plunged into the waters to seize the tiny fry. Many a drawing I made at Great Egg Harbor, many a pleasant day I spent along its shores; and much pleasure would it give me once more to visit the good and happy family in whose house I resided there.

THE GREAT PINE SWAMP

I LEFT Philadelphia, at four of the morning, by the coach, with no other accoutrements than I knew to be absolutely necessary for the jaunt which I intended to make. These consisted of a wooden box, containing a small stock of linen, drawing-paper, my journal, colors, and pencils, together with twenty-five pounds of shot, some flints, the due quantum of cash, my gun *Tear-jacket*, and a heart as true to Nature as ever.

Our coaches are none of the best, nor do they move with the velocity of those of some other countries. It was eight, and a dark night, when I reached Mauch Chunk, now so celebrated in the Union for its rich coal-mines, and eighty-eight miles distant from Philadelphia. I had passed through a very diversified country, part of which was highly cultivated, while the rest was yet in a state of nature, and consequently much more agreeable to me. On alighting, I was shown to the traveller's room, and on asking for the landlord, saw coming towards me a fine-looking young man, to whom I made known my wishes. He spoke kindly, and offered to lodge and board me at a much lower rate than travellers who go there for the very simple pleasure of being dragged on the railway. In a word, I was fixed in four minutes, and that most comfortably.

No sooner had the approach of day been announced by the cocks of the little village, than I marched out with my gun and note-book, to judge for myself of the wealth of the country. After traversing much ground, and crossing many steep hills, I returned, if not wearied, at least much disappointed at the extraordinary scarcity of birds. So I bargained to be carried in a cart to the central parts of the Great Pine Swamp, and, although a heavy storm was rising, ordered my conductor to proceed. We winded round many a mountain and at last crossed the highest. The storm had become tremendous, and we were thoroughly drenched, but, my resolution being fixed, the boy was obliged to continue his driving. Having already travelled about fifteen miles or so, we left the turnpike, and struck up a narrow and bad road, that seemed merely cut out to enable the people of the Swamp to receive the necessary supplies from the village which I had left. Some mistakes were made, and it was almost dark when a post directed us to the habitation of a Mr. Jediah Irish, to whom I had been recommended. We now rattled down a steep declivity, edged on one side by almost perpendicular rocks, and on the other by a noisy stream, which seemed grumbling at the approach of strangers. The ground was so overgrown by laurels and tall pines of different kinds that the whole presented only a mass of darkness.

At length we reached the house, the door of which was already opened, the sight of strangers being nothing uncommon in our woods, even in the most remote parts. On entering, I was presented with a chair, while my conductor was shown the way to the stable, and on expressing a wish that I should be permitted to remain in the house for some weeks, I was gratified by receiving the sanction of the good woman to my proposal, although her husband was then from home. As I immediately began to talk about the nature of the country, and inquired if birds were numerous in the neighborhood, Mrs. Irish, more *au fait* in household affairs than ornithology, sent for a nephew of her husband's, who soon made his appearance, and in whose favor I became at once prepossessed. He conversed like an educated person, saw that I was comfortably disposed of, and finally bade me good-night in such a tone as made me quite happy.

The storm had rolled away before the first beams of the morning sun shone brightly on the wet foliage, displaying all its richness and beauty. My ears were greeted by the notes, always sweet and mellow, of the Wood Thrush and other songsters. Before I had gone many steps, the woods echoed to the report of my gun, and I picked from among the leaves a lovely Sylvia,[1] long sought for, but until then sought for in vain. I needed no more, and standing still for a while, I was soon convinced that the Great Pine Swamp harbored many other objects as valuable to me.

The young man joined me, bearing his rifle, and offered to accompany me through the woods, all of which he well knew. But I was anxious to transfer to paper the form and beauty of the little bird I had in my hand; and requesting him to break a twig of blooming laurel, we returned to the house, speaking of nothing else than the picturesque beauty of the country around.

A few days passed, during which I became acquainted with my hostess and her sweet children, and made occasional rambles, but spent the greater portion of my time in drawing. One morning, as I stood near the window of my room, I remarked a tall and powerful man alight from his horse, loose the girth of the saddle, raise the latter with one hand, pass the bridle over the head of the animal with the other, and move towards the house, while the horse betook himself to the little brook to drink. I heard some movements in the room below, and again the same tall person walked towards the mill and stores, a few hundred yards from the house. In America business is the first object in view at all times, and right it is that it should be so. Soon after my hostess entered my room, accompanied by the fine-looking woodsman, to whom, as Mr. Jediah Irish, I was introduced. Reader, to describe to you the qualities of that excellent man were vain; you should know him, as I do, to estimate the value of such men in our sequestered forests. He not only made me welcome, but promised all his assistance in forwarding my views.

[1] *Sylvia parus*, Hemlock Warbler; Ornith. Biog. vol. ii. page 205.

The long walks and long talks we have had together I can never forget, nor the many beautiful birds which we pursued, shot, and admired. The juicy venison, excellent Bear flesh, and delightful trout that daily formed my food, methinks I can still enjoy. And then, what pleasure I had in listening to him as he read his favorite poems of Burns, while my pencil was occupied in smoothing and softening the drawing of the bird before me! Was not this enough to recall to my mind the early impressions that had been made upon it by the description of the golden age, which I here found realized?

The Lehigh about this place forms numerous short turns between the mountains, and affords frequent falls, as well as below the falls deep pools, which render this stream a most valuable one for mills of any kind. Not many years before this date, my host was chosen by the agent of the Lehigh Coal Company, as their mill-wright, and manager for cutting down the fine trees which covered the mountains around. He was young, robust, active, industrious, and persevering. He marched to the spot where his abode now is, with some workmen, and by dint of hard labor first cleared the road mentioned above, and reached the river at the centre of a bend, where he fixed on erecting various mills. The pass here is so narrow that it looks as if formed by the bursting asunder of the mountain, both sides ascending abruptly, so that the place where the settlement was made is in many parts difficult of access, and the road then newly cut was only sufficient to permit men and horses to come to the spot where Jediah and his men were at work. So great, in fact, were the difficulties of access that, as he told me, pointing to a spot about one hundred and fifty feet above us, they for many months slipped from it their barrelled provisions, assisted by ropes, to their camp below. But no sooner was the first saw-mill erected than the axe-men began their devastations. Trees, one after another, were, and are yet, constantly heard falling during the days; and in calm nights, the greedy mills told the sad tale that in a century the noble forests around should exist no more. Many mills were erected, many dams raised, in defiance of the impetuous Lehigh. One full third of the trees have already been culled, turned into boards, and floated as far as Philadelphia.

In such an undertaking the cutting of the trees is not all. They have afterwards to be hauled to the edge of the mountains bordering the river, launched into the stream, and led to the mills over many shallows and difficult places. Whilst I was in the Great Pine Swamp, I frequently visited one of the principal places for the launching of logs. To see them tumbling from such a height, touching here and there the rough angle of a projecting rock, bouncing from it with the elasticity of a foot-ball, and at last falling with an awful crash into the river, forms a sight interesting in the highest degree, but impossible for me to describe. Shall I tell you that I have seen masses of these logs heaped above each other to the number of five thousand? I may so tell you, for such I have seen. My friend Irish assured me that at some seasons, these piles consisted of a much greater number, the river becoming in those places completely choked up.

When *freshets* (or floods) take place, then is the time chosen for forwarding the logs to the different mills. This is called a *Frolic*. Jediah Irish, who is generally the leader, proceeds to the upper leap with his men, each provided with a strong wooden handspike, and a short-handled axe. They all take to the water, be it summer or winter, like so many Newfoundland spaniels. The logs are gradually detached, and, after a time, are seen floating down the dancing stream, here striking against a rock and whirling many times round, there suddenly checked in dozens by a shallow, over which they have to be forced with the handspikes. Now they arrive at the edge of a dam, and are again pushed over. Certain numbers are left in each dam, and when the party has arrived at the last, which lies just where my friend Irish's camp was first formed, the drenched leader and his men, about sixty in number, make their way home, find there a healthful repast, and spend the evening and a portion of the night in dancing and frolicking, in their own simple manner, in the most perfect amity, seldom troubling themselves with the idea of the labor prepared for them on the morrow.

That morrow now come, one sounds a horn from the door of the store-house, at the call of which each returns to his work. The sawyers, the millers, the rafters, and raftsmen are all immediately busy. The mills are all going, and the logs, which a few months before were the supporters of broad and leafy tops, are now in the act of being split asunder. The boards are then launched into the stream, and rafts are formed of them for market.

During the months of summer and autumn, the Lehigh, a small river of itself, soon becomes extremely shallow, and to float the rafts would prove impossible, had not art managed to provide a supply of water for this express purpose. At the breast of the lower dam is a curiously constructed lock, which is opened at the approach of the rafts. They pass through this lock with the rapidity of lightning, propelled by the water that had been accumulated in the dam, and which is of itself generally sufficient to float them to Mauch Chunk, after which, entering regular canals, they find no other impediments, but are conveyed to their ultimate destination.

Before population had greatly advanced in this part of Pennsylvania, game of all description found within that range was extremely abundant. The Elk itself did not disdain to browse on the shoulders of the mountains near the Lehigh. Bears and the common Deer must have been plentiful, as, at the moment when I write, many of both are seen and killed by the resident hunters. The Wild

Turkey, the Pheasant, and the Grouse, are also tolerably abundant, and as to trout in the streams — ah, reader, if you are an angler, do go there and try for yourself. For my part, I can only say that I have been made weary with pulling up from the rivulets the sparkling fish, allured by the struggles of the common grasshopper.

A comical affair happened with the Bears, which I shall relate to you, good reader. A party of my friend Irish's raftsmen, returning from Mauch Chunk one afternoon, through sundry short-cuts over the mountains, at the season when the huckleberries are ripe and plentiful, were suddenly apprised of the proximity of some of these animals by their snuffing the air. No sooner was this perceived than, to the astonishment of the party, not fewer than eight Bears, I was told, made their appearance. Each man, being provided with his short-handled axe, faced about, and willingly came to the scratch; but the assailed soon proved the assailants, and with claw and tooth drove the men off in a twinkling. Down they all rushed from the mountain; the noise spread quickly; rifles were soon procured and shouldered; but when the spot was reached, no Bears were to be found; night forced the hunters back to their homes, and a laugh concluded the affair.

I spent six weeks in the Great Pine Forest — Swamp it cannot be called — where I made many a drawing. Wishing to leave Pennsylvania, and to follow the migratory flocks of our birds to the South, I bade adieu to the excellent wife and rosy children of my friend, and to his kind nephew. Jediah Irish, shouldering his heavy rifle, accompanied me, and trudging directly across the mountains, we arrived at Mauch Chunk in good time for dinner. Shall I ever have the pleasure of seeing that good, that generous man again? [1]

---

[1] Audubon and Mr. Irish met many times afterwards, the last being, I believe, in Philadelphia, on the eve of Audubon's departure for his Missouri River trip.

At Mauch Chunk, where we both spent the night, Mr. White, the civil engineer, visited me, and looked at the drawings which I had made in the Great Pine Forest. The news he gave me of my sons, then in Kentucky, made me still more anxious to move in their direction; and long before daybreak, I shook hands with the good man of the forest, and found myself moving towards the capital of Pennsylvania,[1] having as my sole companion a sharp, frosty breeze. Left to my thoughts, I felt amazed that such a place as the Great Pine Forest should be so little known to the Philadelphians, scarcely any of whom could direct me towards it. How much it is to be regretted, thought I, that the many young gentlemen who are there, so much at a loss how to employ their leisure days, should not visit these wild retreats, valuable as they are to the student of nature. How differently would they feel, if, instead of spending weeks in smoothing a useless bow, and walking out in full dress, intent on displaying the make of their legs, to some rendezvous where they may enjoy their wines, they were to occupy themselves in contemplating the rich profusion which nature has poured around them, or even in procuring some desiderated specimen for their Peale's Museum, once so valuable, and so finely arranged! But, alas, no! they are none of them aware of the richness of the Great Pine Swamp, nor are they likely to share the hospitality to be found there.

THE LOST ONE

A "LIVE-OAKER" employed on the St. John's River, in East Florida, left his cabin, situated on the banks of that stream, and, with his axe on his shoulder, proceeded towards the swamp in which he had several times before plied his trade of felling and squaring the giant trees

[1] Then Philadelphia.

that afford the most valuable timber for naval architecture and other purposes.

At the season which is the best for this kind of labor, heavy fogs not unfrequently cover the country, so as to render it difficult for one to see farther than thirty or forty yards in any direction. The woods, too, present so little variety that every tree seems the mere counterpart of every other; and the grass, when it has not been burnt, is so tall that a man of ordinary stature cannot see over it, whence it is necessary for him to proceed with great caution, lest he should unwittingly deviate from the ill-defined trail which he follows. To increase the difficulty, several trails often meet, in which case, unless the explorer be perfectly acquainted with the neighborhood, it would be well for him to lie down, and wait until the fog should disperse. Under such circumstances, the best woodsmen are not unfrequently bewildered for a while; and I well remember that such an occurrence happened to myself, at a time when I had imprudently ventured to pursue a wounded quadruped, which led me some distance from the track.

The live-oaker had been jogging onwards for several hours, and became aware that he must have travelled considerably more than the distance between his cabin and the "hummock" which he desired to reach. To his alarm, at the moment when the fog dispersed, he saw the sun at its meridian height, and could not recognize a single object around him.

Young, healthy, and active, he imagined he had walked with more than usual speed, and had passed the place to which he was bound. He accordingly turned his back upon the sun, and pursued a different route, guided by a small trail. Time passed, and the sun headed his course; he saw it gradually descend in the west; but all around him continued as if enveloped with mystery. The huge gray trees spread their giant boughs over him, the rank

grass extended on all sides, not a living being crossed his
path; all was silent and still, and the scene was like a
dull and dreary dream of the land of oblivion. He wandered like a forgotten ghost that had passed into the land
of spirits, without yet meeting one of his kind with whom
to hold converse.

The condition of a man lost in the woods is one of the
most perplexing that could be imagined by a person who
has not himself been in a like predicament. Every object he sees, he at first thinks he recognizes, and while
his whole mind is bent on searching for more that may
gradually lead to his extrication, he goes on committing
greater errors the farther he proceeds. This was the case
with the live-oaker. The sun was now setting with a fiery
aspect, and by degrees it sunk in its full circular form, as
if giving warning of a sultry morrow. Myriads of insects,
delighted at its departure, now filled the air on buzzing
wings. Each piping frog arose from the muddy pool in
which it had concealed itself; the Squirrel retired to its
hole, the Crow to its roost, and, far above, the harsh,
croaking voice of the Heron announced that, full of anxiety, it was wending its way towards the miry interior of
some distant swamp. Now the woods began to resound
to the shrill cries of the Owl; and the breeze, as it swept
among the columnar stems of the forest trees, came laden
with heavy and chilling dews. Alas! no moon with her
silvery light shone on the dreary scene, and the Lost
One, wearied and vexed, laid himself down on the damp
ground. Prayer is always consolatory to man in every
difficulty or danger, and the woodsman fervently prayed to
his Maker, wished his family a happier night than it was
his lot to experience, and with a feverish anxiety waited
the return of day.

You may imagine the length of that dull, cold, moon-
less night. With the dawn of day came the usual fogs of
those latitudes. The poor man started on his feet, and

with a sorrowful heart, pursued a course which he thought might lead him to some familiar object, although, indeed, he scarcely knew what he was doing. No longer had he the trace of a track to guide him, and yet, as the sun rose, he calculated the many hours of daylight he had before him, and the farther he went, the faster he walked. But vain were all his hopes; that day was spent in fruitless endeavors to regain the path that led to his home, and when night again approached, the terror that had been gradually spreading over his mind, together with the nervous debility produced by fatigue, anxiety, and hunger, rendered him almost frantic. He told me that at this moment he beat his breast, tore his hair, and, had it not been for the piety with which his parents had in early life imbued his mind, and which had become habitual, would have cursed his existence. Famished as he now was, he laid himself on the ground, and fed on the weeds and grasses that grew around him. That night was spent in the greatest agony and terror. "I knew my situation," he said to me. "I was fully aware that unless Almighty God came to my assistance, I must perish in those uninhabited woods. I knew that I had walked more than fifty miles, although I had not met with a brook, from which I could quench my thirst, or even allay the burning heat of my parched lips and bloodshot eyes. I knew that if I should not meet with some stream I must die, for my axe was my only weapon, and although Deer and Bears now and then started within a few yards, or even feet of me, not one of them could I kill; and although I was in the midst of abundance, not a mouthful did I expect to procure, to satisfy the cravings of my empty stomach. Sir, may God preserve you from ever feeling as I did the whole of that day."

For several days after, no one can imagine the condition in which he was, for when he related to me this painful adventure, he assured me that he had lost all recollection of what had happened. "God," he continued, "must have taken pity on me one day, for, as I ran wildly through those dreadful pine barrens, I met with a tortoise. I gazed upon it with amazement and delight, and, although I knew that were I to follow it undisturbed, it would lead me to some water, my hunger and thirst would not allow me to refrain from satisfying both, by eating its flesh, and drinking its blood. With one stroke of my axe the beast was cut in two, and in a few moments I had despatched all but the shell. Oh, sir, how much I thanked God, whose kindness had put the Tortoise in my way! I felt greatly renewed. I sat down at the foot of a pine, gazed on the heavens, thought of my poor wife and children, and again and again thanked my God for my life; for now I felt less distracted in mind, and more assured that before long I must recover my way, and get back to my home."

The Lost One remained and passed the night, at the foot of the same tree under which his repast had been made. Refreshed by a sound sleep, he started at dawn to resume his weary march. The sun rose bright, and he followed the direction of the shadows. Still the dreariness of the woods was the same, and he was on the point of giving up in despair, when he observed a Raccoon lying squatted in the grass. Raising his axe, he drove it with such violence through the helpless animal that it expired without a struggle. What he had done with the tortoise, he now did with the Raccoon, the greater part of which he actually devoured at one meal. With more comfortable feelings he then resumed his wanderings — his journey, I cannot say — for although in the possession of all his faculties, and in broad daylight, he was worse off than a lame man groping his way in the dark out of a dungeon, of which he knew not where the doors stood.

Days, one after another, passed — nay, weeks in succession. He fed now on cabbage-trees, then on frogs

and snakes.   All that fell in his way was welcome and
savory.   Yet he became daily more emaciated, until at
length he could scarcely crawl.   Forty days had elapsed,
by his own reckoning, when he at last reached the banks
of the river.   His clothes in tatters, his once bright axe
dimmed with rust, his face begrimed with beard, his
hair matted, and his feeble frame little better than a
skeleton covered with parchment, there he laid himself
down to die.   Amid the perturbed dreams of his fevered
fancy, he thought he heard the noise of oars far away on
the silent river.   He listened, but the sounds died away
on his ear.   It was, indeed, a dream, the last glimmer of
expiring hope, and now the light of life was about to be
quenched forever.   But again the sound of oars woke him
from his lethargy.   He listened so eagerly that the hum
of a fly could not have escaped his ear.   They were, indeed, the measured beats of oars.   And now, joy to the
forlorn soul! the sound of human voices thrilled to his
heart, and awoke the tumultuous pulses of returning hope.
On his knees did the eye of God see that poor man by the
broad, still stream that glittered in the sunbeams, and
human eyes soon saw him too, for round that headland
covered with tangled brushwood, boldly advances the little boat, propelled by its lusty rowers.   The Lost One
raises his feeble voice on high; it was a loud, shrill
scream of joy and fear.   The rowers pause, and look
around.   Another, but feebler scream, and they observe
him.   It comes, his heart flutters, his sight is dimmed,
his brain reels, he gasps for breath.   It comes — it has
run upon the beach, and the Lost One is found.

   This is no tale of fiction, but the relation of an actual
occurrence, which might be embellished, no doubt, but
which is better in the plain garb of truth.   The notes by
which I recorded it were written in the cabin of the once
lost live-oaker, about four years after the painful incident
occurred.   His amiable wife, and loving children, were

present at the recital, and never shall I forget the tears that flowed from their eyes as they listened to it, albeit it had long been more familiar to them than a tale thrice told. Sincerely do I wish, good reader, that neither you nor I may ever elicit such sympathy by having undergone such sufferings, although no doubt, such sympathy would be a rich recompense for them.

It only remains for me to say that the distance between the cabin and the live-oak hummock to which the woodsman was bound, scarcely exceeded eight miles, while the part of the river where he was found was thirty-eight miles from his house. Calculating his daily wanderings at ten miles, we may believe they amounted in all to four hundred. He must therefore have rambled in a circuitous direction, which people generally do in such circumstances. Nothing but the great strength of his constitution, and the merciful aid of his Maker, could have supported him for so long a time.

THE LIVE-OAKERS

THE greater part of the forests of East Florida consist principally of what in that country are called "pine barrens." In these districts, the woods are rather thin, and the only trees that are seen in them are tall pines of indifferent quality, beneath which is a growth of rank grass, here and there mixed with low bushes, and sword-palmettoes. The soil is of a sandy nature, mostly flat, and consequently either covered with water during the rainy season, or parched in the summer or autumn, although you meet at times with ponds of stagnant water, where the cattle, which are abundant, allay their thirst, and around which resort the various kinds of game found in these wilds.

The traveller, who has pursued his course for many miles over the barrens, is suddenly delighted to see in the distance the appearance of a dark "hummock" of live-oaks and other trees, seeming as if they had been planted in the wilderness.   As he approaches, the air feels cooler and more salubrious, the song of numerous birds delights his ear, the herbage assumes a more luxuriant appearance, the flowers become larger and brighter, and a grateful fragrance is diffused around.   These objects contribute to refresh his mind, as much as the sight of the waters of some clear spring gliding among the undergrowth seems already to allay his thirst.   Overhead festoons of innumerable vines, jessamines, and bignonias, link each tree with those around it, their slender stems being interlaced as if in mutual affection.   No sooner, in the shade of these beautiful woods, has the traveller finished his mid-day repast than he perceives small parties of men lightly accoutred, and each bearing an axe, approaching towards his resting-place.   They exchange the usual civilities, and immediately commence their labors, for they too have just finished their meal.

I think I see them proceeding to their work.   Here two have stationed themselves on the opposite sides of the trunk of a noble and venerable live-oak.   Their keen-edged and well-tempered axes seem to make no impression on it, so small are the chips that drop at each blow around the mossy and wide-spreading roots.   There, one is ascending the stem of another, of which, in its fall, the arms have stuck among the tangled tops of the neighboring trees.   See how cautiously he proceeds, barefooted, and with a handkerchief around his head.   Now he has climbed to the height of about forty feet from the ground; he stops, and squaring himself with the trunk on which he so boldly stands, he wields with sinewy arms his trusty blade, the repeated blows of which, although the tree be as tough as it is large, will soon sever it in two.   He has changed sides, and his back is turned to you. The trunk now remains connected only by a thin strip of wood. He places his feet on the part which is lodged, and shakes it with all his might. Now swings the huge log under his leaps, now it suddenly gives way, and as it strikes upon the ground its echoes are repeated through the hummock, and every Wild Turkey within hearing utters his gobble of recognition. The wood-cutter however, remains collected and composed; but the next moment, he throws his axe to the ground, and, assisted by the nearest grape-vine, slides down and reaches the earth in an instant.

Several men approach and examine the prostrate trunk. They cut at both its extremities, and sound the whole of its bark, to enable them to judge if the tree has been attacked by the white rot. If such has unfortunately been the case, there, for a century or more, this huge log will remain until it gradually crumbles; but if not, and if it is free of injury or "wind-shakes," while there is no appearance of the sap having already ascended, and its pores are altogether sound, they proceed to take its measurement. Its shape ascertained, and the timber that is fit for use laid out by the aid of models, which, like fragments of the skeleton of a ship, show the forms and sizes required, the "hewers" commence their labors. Thus, reader, perhaps every known hummock in the Floridas is annually attacked, and so often does it happen that the white rot or some other disease has deteriorated the quality of the timber, that the woods may be seen strewn with trunks that have been found worthless, so that every year these valuable oaks are becoming scarcer. The destruction of the young trees of this species caused by the fall of the great trunks is of course immense, and as there are no artificial plantations of these trees in our country, before long a good-sized live-oak will be so valuable that its owner will exact an enormous price for it, even while it yet stands in the wood. In my opinion, formed on personal observation, live-oak hummocks are *not quite* so plentiful as they are represented to be, and of this I will give you *one* illustration.

On the 25th of February, 1832, I happened to be far up the St. John's River in East Florida, in the company of a person employed by our government in protecting the live-oaks of that section of the country, and who received a good salary for his trouble. While we were proceeding along one of the banks of that most singular stream, my companion pointed out some large hummocks of dark-leaved trees on the opposite side, which he said were entirely formed of live-oaks. I thought differently, and as our controversy on the subject became a little warm, I proposed that our men should row us to the place, where we might examine the leaves and timber, and so decide the point. We soon landed, but after inspecting the woods, not a single tree of the species did we find, although there were thousands of large "swamp-oaks." My companion acknowledged his mistake, and I continued to search for birds.

One dark evening as I was seated on the banks of this same river, considering what arrangements I should make for the night, as it began to rain in torrents, a man who happened to see me, came up and invited me to go to his cabin, which he said was not far off. I accepted his kind offer, and followed him to his humble dwelling. There I found his wife, several children, and a number of men, who, as my host told me, were, like himself, live-oakers. Supper was placed on a large table, and on being desired to join the party, I willingly assented, doing my best to diminish the contents of the tin pans and dishes set before the company by the active and agreeable housewife. We then talked of the country, its climate and productions, until a late hour, when we laid ourselves down on Bears' skins, and reposed till daybreak.

I longed to accompany these hardy woodcutters to the

hummock where they were engaged in preparing live-oak timber for a man-of-war. Provided with axes and guns, we left the house to the care of the wife and children, and proceeded for several miles through a pine-barren, such as I have attempted to describe. One fine Wild Turkey was shot, and when we arrived at the *shanty* put up near the hummock, we found another party of wood-cutters waiting our arrival, before eating their breakfast, already prepared by a negro man, to whom the Turkey was consigned to be roasted for part of that day's dinner.

Our repast was an excellent one, and vied with a Kentucky breakfast; beef, fish, potatoes, and other vegetables, were served up, with coffee in tin cups, and plenty of biscuit. Every man seemed hungry and happy, and the conversation assumed the most humorous character. The sun now rose above the trees, and all, excepting the cook, proceeded to the hummock, on which I had been gazing with great delight, as it promised rare sport. My host, I found, was the chief of the party; and although he also had an axe, he made no other use of it than for stripping here and there pieces of bark from certain trees which he considered of doubtful soundness. He was not only well versed in his profession, but generally intelligent, and from him I received the following account, which I noted at the time.

The men who are employed in cutting the live-oak, after having discovered a good hummock, build shanties of small logs, to retire to at night, and feed in by day. Their provisions consist of beef, pork, potatoes, biscuit, flour, rice and fish, together with excellent whiskey. They are mostly hale, strong, and active men, from the eastern parts of the Union, and receive excellent wages, according to their different abilities. Their labors are only of a few months' duration. Such hummocks as are found near navigable streams are first chosen, and when it is absolutely necessary, the timber is sometimes hauled

five or six miles to the nearest water-course, where, although it sinks, it can with comparative ease, be shipped
to its destination.   The best time for cutting the live-oak
is considered to be from the first of December to the beginning of March, or while the sap is completely down.
When the sap is flowing, the tree is "bloom," and more
apt to be "shaken."   The white-rot, which occurs so frequently in the live-oak, and is perceptible only by the
best judges, consists of round spots, about an inch and a
half in diameter, on the outside of the bark, through
which, at that spot, a hard stick may be driven several
inches, and generally follows the heart up or down the
trunk of the tree.   So deceiving are these spots and trees
to persons unacquainted with this defect, that thousands
of trees are cut, and afterwards abandoned.   The great
number of trees of this sort strewn in the woods would
tend to make a stranger believe that there is much more
good oak in the country than there really is; and perhaps, in reality, not more than one-fourth of the quantity
usually reported, is to be procured.

The live-oakers generally revisit their distant homes
in the Middle and Eastern Districts, where they spend
the summer, returning to the Floridas at the approach of
winter.   Some, however, who have gone there with their
families, remain for years in succession; although they
suffer much from the climate, by which their once good
constitutions are often greatly impaired.   This was the
case with the individual above mentioned, from whom I
subsequently received much friendly assistance in my
pursuits.

SPRING GARDEN

HAVING heard many wonderful accounts of a certain
spring near the sources of the St. John's River in
East Florida, I resolved to visit it, in order to judge for
myself. On the 6th of January, 1832, I left the plantation of my friend John Bulow, accompanied by an amiable and accomplished Scotch gentleman, an engineer
employed by the planters of those districts in erecting
their sugar-house establishments. We were mounted on
horses of the Indian breed, remarkable for their activity
and strength, and were provided with guns and some provisions. The weather was pleasant, but not so our way,
for no sooner had we left the "King's Road," which had
been cut by the Spanish government for a goodly distance, than we entered a thicket of scrubby oaks, succeeded by a still denser mass of low palmettoes, which
extended about three miles, and among the roots of which
our nags had great difficulty in making good their footing.
After this we entered the pine barrens, so extensively
distributed in this portion of the Floridas. The sand
seemed to be all sand and nothing but sand, and the palmettoes at times so covered the narrow Indian trail which
we followed, that it required all the instinct or sagacity
of ourselves and our horses to keep it. It seemed to us
as if we were approaching the end of the world. The
country was perfectly flat, and, so far as we could survey
it, presented the same wild and scraggy aspect. My companion, who had travelled there before, assured me that,
at particular seasons of the year, he had crossed the barrens when they were covered with water fully knee-deep,
when, according to his expression, they "looked most
awful;" and I readily believed him, as we now and then
passed through muddy pools, which reached the saddle-
girths of our horses. Here and there large tracts covered

with tall grasses, and resembling the prairies of the western wilds, opened to our view. Wherever the country happened to be sunk a little beneath the general level, it was covered with cypress trees, whose spreading arms were hung with a profusion of Spanish moss. The soil in such cases consisted of black mud, and was densely covered with bushes, chiefly of the Magnolia family.

We crossed in succession the heads of three branches of Haw Creek, of which the waters spread from a quarter to half a mile in breadth, and through which we made our way with extreme difficulty. While in the middle of one, my companion told me that once, when in the very spot where we then stood, his horse chanced to place his fore-feet on the back of a large alligator, which, not well pleased at being disturbed in his repose, suddenly raised his head, opened his monstrous jaws, and snapped off part of the lips of the affrighted pony. You may imagine the terror of the poor beast, which, however, after a few plunges, resumed its course, and succeeded in carrying its rider through in safety. As a reward for this achievement, it was ever after honored with the appellation of " Alligator."

We had now travelled about twenty miles, and, the sun having reached the zenith, we dismounted to partake of some refreshment. From a muddy pool we contrived to obtain enough of tolerably clear water to mix with the contents of a bottle, the like of which I would strongly recommend to every traveller in these swampy regions; our horses, too, found something to grind among the herbage that surrounded the little pool; but as little time was to be lost, we quickly remounted, and resumed our disagreeable journey, during which we had at no time proceeded at a rate exceeding two miles and a half in the hour.

All at once, however, a wonderful change took place: — the country became more elevated and undulating; the timber was of a different nature, and consisted of red and live-oaks, magnolias, and several kinds of pine. Thousands of "Mole-hills," or the habitations of an animal here called "the Salamander," and "Gopher's burrows" presented themselves to the eye, and greatly annoyed our horses, which now and then sank to the depth of a foot, and stumbled at the risk of breaking their legs, and what we considered fully as valuable, our necks. We now saw beautiful lakes of the purest water, and passed along a green space, having a series of them on each side of us. These sheets of water became larger and more numerous the farther we advanced — some of them extending to a length of several miles, and having a depth of from two to twenty feet of clear water; but their shores being destitute of vegetation, we observed no birds near them. Many tortoises, however, were seen basking in the sun, and all, as we approached, plunged into the water. Not a trace of man did we observe during our journey, scarcely a bird, and not a single quadruped, not even a Rat; nor can one imagine a poorer and more desolate country than that which lies between the Halifax River, which we had left in the morning, and the undulating grounds at which we had now arrived.

But at length we perceived the tracks of living beings, and soon after saw the huts of Colonel Rees's negroes. Scarcely could ever African traveller have approached the city of Timbuctoo with more excited curiosity than we felt in approaching this plantation. Our Indian horses seemed to participate in our joy, and trotted at a smart rate towards the principal building, at the door of which we leaped from our saddles, just as the sun was withdrawing his ruddy light. Colonel Rees was at home, and received us with great kindness. Refreshments were immediately placed before us, and we spent the evening in agreeable conversation.

The next day I walked over the plantation, and examining the country around, found the soil of good quality, it having been reclaimed from swampy ground of a black color, rich, and very productive. The greater part of the cultivated land was on the borders of a lake, which communicates with others, leading to the St. John's River, distant about seven miles, and navigable so far by vessels not exceeding fifty or sixty tons. After breakfast, our amiable host showed us the way to the celebrated spring, the sight of which afforded me pleasure sufficient to counterbalance the tediousness of my journey.

This spring presents a circular basin, having a diameter of about sixty feet, from the centre of which the water is thrown up with great force, although it does not rise to a height of more than a few inches above the general level. A kind of whirlpool is formed, on the edges of which are deposited vast quantities of shells, with pieces of wood, gravel, and other substances, which have coalesced into solid masses, having a very curious appearance. The water is quite transparent, although of a dark color, but so impregnated with sulphur that it emits an odor which to me was highly nauseous. Its surface lies fifteen or twenty feet below the level of the woodland lakes in the neighborhood, and its depth, in the autumnal months, is about seventeen feet, when the water is lowest. In all the lakes, the same species of shell as those thrown up by the spring, occur in abundance, and it seems more than probable that it is formed of the water collected from them by infiltration, or forms the subterranean outlet of some of them. The lakes themselves are merely reservoirs, containing the residue of the waters which fall during the rainy seasons, and contributing to supply the waters of the St. John's River, with which they all seem to communicate by similar means. This spring pours its waters into "Rees's Lake," through a deep and broad channel called Spring Garden Creek. This channel is said to be in some places fully sixty feet deep, but it becomes more shallow as you advance towards the entrance of the lake, at which you are surprised to find yourself on a mud-flat covered only by about fifteen inches of water, under which the depositions from the spring lie to a depth of four or five feet in the form of the softest mud, while under this again is a bed of fine white sand. When this mud is stirred up by the oars of your boat or otherwise, it appears of a dark-green color, and smells strongly of sulphur. At all times it sends up numerous bubbles of air, which probably consist of suphuretted hydrogen gas.

The mouth of this curious spring is calculated to be two and a half feet square; and the velocity of its water, during the rainy season, is three feet per second. This would render the discharge per hour about 499,500 gallons. Colonel Rees showed us the remains of another spring of the same kind, which had dried up from some natural cause.

My companion, the engineer, having occupation for another day, I requested Colonel Rees to accompany me in his boat towards the river St. John's, which I was desirous of seeing, as well as the curious country in its neighborhood. He readily agreed, and after an early breakfast next morning, we set out, accompanied by two servants to manage the boat. As we crossed Rees's Lake, I observed that its northeastern shores were bounded by a deep swamp, covered by a rich growth of tall cypresses, while the opposite side presented large marshes and islands ornamented by pines, live-oaks, and orange-trees. With the exception of a very narrow channel, the creek was covered with nympheæ, and in its waters swam numerous Alligators, while Ibises, Gallinules, Anhingas, Coots, and Cormorants were seen pursuing their avocations on its surface or along its margins. Over our heads the Fish Hawks were sailing, and on the broken trees around we saw many of their nests.

We followed Spring Garden Creek for about two miles and a half, and passed a mud bar, before we entered "Dexter's Lake." The bar was stuck full of unios, in such profusion that each time the negroes thrust their hands into the mud they took up several. According to their report these shell-fish are quite unfit for food. In this lake the water had changed its hue, and assumed a dark chestnut color, although it was still transparent. The depth was very uniformly five feet, and the extent of the lake was about eight miles by three. Having crossed it we followed the creek, and soon saw the entrance of Woodruff's Lake, which empties its still darker waters into the St. John's River.

I here shot a pair of curious Ibises, which you will find described in my fourth volume, and landed on a small island covered with wild orange trees, the luxuriance and freshness of which were not less pleasing to the sight than the perfume of their flowers was to the smell. The group seemed to me like a rich bouquet formed by nature to afford consolation to the weary traveller, cast down by the dismal scenery of swamps and pools and rank grass around him. Under the shade of these beautiful evergreens, and amidst the golden fruits that covered the ground, while the Humming-birds fluttered over our heads, we spread our cloth on the grass, and with a happy and thankful heart, I refreshed myself with the bountiful gifts of an ever-careful Providence. Colonel Rees informed me that this charming retreat was one of the numerous *terræ incognitæ* of this region of lakes, and that it should henceforth bear the name of "Audubon's Isle."

In conclusion, let me inform you that the spring has been turned to good account by my generous host, Colonel Rees, who, aided by my amiable companion, the engineer, has directed its current so as to turn a mill, which suffices to grind the whole of his sugar-cane.

DEATH OF A PIRATE

IN the calm of a fine moonlight night, as I was admiring the beauty of the clear heavens, and the broad glare of light that glanced from the trembling surface of the waters around, the officer on watch came up and entered into conversation with me. He had been a turtler in other years, and a great hunter to boot, and although of humble birth and pretensions, energy and talent, aided by education, had raised him to a higher station. Such a man could not fail to be an agreeable companion, and we talked on various subjects, principally, you may be sure, birds and other natural productions. He told me he once had a disagreeable adventure, when looking out for game, in a certain cove on the shores of the Gulf of Mexico; and, on my expressing a desire to hear it, he willingly related to me the following particulars, which I give you, not, perhaps, precisely in his own words, but as nearly so as I can remember.

"Towards evening, one quiet summer day, I chanced to be paddling along a sandy shore, which I thought well fitted for my repose, being covered with tall grass, and as the sun was not many degrees above the horizon, I felt anxious to pitch my mosquito bar or net, and spend the night in this wilderness. The bellowing notes of thousands of bull-frogs in a neighboring swamp might lull me to rest, and I looked upon the flocks of Blackbirds that were assembling as sure companions in this secluded retreat.

"I proceeded up a little stream, to insure the safety of my canoe from any sudden storm, when, as I gladly advanced, a beautiful yawl came unexpectedly in view. Surprised at such a sight in a part of the country then scarcely known, I felt a sudden check in the circulation of my blood. My paddle dropped from my hands, and fearfully indeed, as I picked it up, did I look towards the unknown boat. On reaching it, I saw its sides marked with stains of blood, and looking with anxiety over the gunwale, I perceived, to my horror, two human bodies covered with gore. Pirates or hostile Indians, I was persuaded, had perpetrated the foul deed, and my alarm naturally increased; my heart fluttered, stopped, and heaved with unusual tremors, and I looked towards the setting sun in consternation and despair. How long my reveries lasted I cannot tell; I can only recollect that I was roused from them by the distant groans of one apparently in mortal agony. I felt as if refreshed by the cold perspiration that oozed from every pore, and I reflected that though alone, I was well armed, and might hope for the protection of the Almighty.

"Humanity whispered to me that, if not surprised and disabled, I might render assistance to some sufferer, or even be the means of saving a useful life. Buoyed up by this thought, I urged my canoe on shore, and seizing it by the bow, pulled it at one spring high among the grass.

"The groans of the unfortunate person fell heavy on my ear as I cocked and reprimed my gun, and I felt determined to shoot the first that should rise from the grass. As I cautiously proceeded, a hand was raised over the weeds, and waved in the air in the most supplicating manner. I levelled my gun about a foot below it, when the next moment the head and breast of a man covered with blood were convulsively raised, and a faint hoarse voice asked me for mercy and help! A deathlike silence followed his fall to the ground. I surveyed every object around with eyes intent, and ears impressible by the slightest sound, for my situation that moment I thought as critical as any I had ever been in. The croaking of the frogs, and the last Blackbirds alighting on their roosts, were the only sounds or sights; and I now proceeded towards the object of my mingled alarm and commiseration.

"Alas! the poor being who lay prostrate at my feet was so weakened by loss of blood that I had nothing to fear from him. My first impulse was to run back to the water, and having done so, I returned with my cap filled to the brim. I felt at his heart, washed his face and breast, and rubbed his temples with the contents of a phial which I kept about me as an antidote for the bites of snakes. His features, seamed by the ravages of time, looked frightful and disgusting; but he had been a powerful man, as the breadth of his chest plainly showed. He groaned in the most appalling manner, as his breath struggled through the mass of blood that seemed to fill his throat. His dress plainly disclosed his occupation. A large pistol he had thrust into his bosom, a naked cutlass lay near him on the ground, a red silk handkerchief was bound over his projecting brows, and over a pair of loose trousers he wore fisherman's boots. He was, in short, a pirate.

"My exertions were not in vain, for as I continued to bathe his temples he revived, his pulse resumed some strength, and I began to hope that he might perhaps survive the deep wounds he had received. Darkness, deep darkness, now enveloped us. I spoke of making a fire. 'Oh! for mercy's sake,' he exclaimed, 'don't.' Knowing, however, that under existing circumstances it was expedient for me to do so, I left him, went to his boat, and brought the rudder, the benches, and the oars, which with my hatchet I soon splintered. I then struck a light, and presently stood in the glare of a blazing fire. The pirate seemed struggling between terror and gratitude for my assistance; he desired me several times in half English and Spanish to put out the flames; but after I had given him a draught of strong spirits, he at length became more composed. I tried to stanch the blood that flowed from the deep gashes in his shoulders and side. I expressed my regret that I had no food about me, but when I spoke of eating he sullenly waved his head.

"My situation was one of the most extraordinary that I have ever been placed in. I naturally turned my talk towards religious subjects, but, alas, the dying man hardly believed in the existence of a God. 'Friend,' said he, 'for friend you seem to be, I have never studied the ways of Him of whom you talk. I am an outlaw, perhaps you will say a wretch — I have been for many years a pirate. The instructions of my parents were of no avail to me, for I have always believed that I was born to be a most cruel man. I now lie here, about to die in the weeds, because I long ago refused to listen to their many admonitions. Do not shudder when I tell you — these now useless hands murdered the mother whom they had embraced. I feel that I have deserved the pangs of the wretched death that hovers over me; and I am thankful that one of my kind will alone witness my last gaspings.'

"A fond but feeble hope that I might save his life, and perhaps assist in procuring his pardon, induced me to speak to him on the subject. 'It is all in vain, friend — I have no objection to die — I am glad that the villains who wounded me were not my conquerors — I want no pardon from *any one*. Give me some water, and let me die alone.' With the hope that I might learn from his conversation something that might lead to the capture of his guilty associates, I returned from the creek with another capful of water, nearly the whole of which I managed to introduce into his parched mouth, and begged him, for the sake of his future peace, to disclose his history to me. 'It is impossible,' said he; 'there will not be time, the beatings of my heart tell me so. Long before day these sinewy limbs will be motionless. Nay, there will hardly be a drop of blood in my body; and that blood will only serve to make the grass grow. My wounds are mortal, and I must and will die without what you call confession.'

"The moon rose in the east. The majesty of her placid beauty impressed me with reverence. I pointed towards her, and asked the pirate if he could not recognize God's features there. 'Friend, I see what you are driving at,' was his answer; 'you, like the rest of our enemies, feel the desire of murdering us all. Well — be it so. To die is, after all, nothing more than a jest; and were it not for the pain, no one, in my opinion, need care a jot about it. But, as you really have befriended me, I will tell you all that is proper.'

"Hoping his mind might take a useful turn, I again bathed his temples, and washed his lips with spirits. His sunk eyes seemed to dart fire at mine; a heavy and deep sigh swelled his chest, and struggled through his blood-choked throat, and he asked me to raise him for a little. I did so, when he addressed me somewhat as follows; for, as I have told you, his speech was a mixture of Spanish, French, and English, forming a jargon the like of which I had never heard before, and which I am utterly unable to imitate. However, I shall give you the substance of his declaration.

"'First, tell me how many bodies you found in the boat, and what sort of dresses they had on.' I mentioned their number and described their apparel. 'That's right,' said he; 'they are the bodies of the scoundrels who followed me in that infernal Yankee barge. Bold rascals they were, for when they found the water too shallow for their craft, they took to it, and waded after me. All my companions had been shot, and to lighten my own boat I flung them overboard; but as I lost time in this, the two ruffians caught hold of my gunwale, and struck on my head and body in such a manner that after I had disabled and killed them both in the boat, I was scarce able to move. The other villains carried off our schooner and one of our boats, and perhaps ere now have hung all my companions whom they did not kill at the time. I have commanded my beautiful vessel many years, captured many ships, and sent many rascals to the devil. I always hated the Yankees, and only regret that I have not killed more of them. — I sailed from Matanzas. — I have often been in concert with others. I have money without counting, but it is buried where it will never be found, and it would be useless to tell you of it.' His throat filled with blood, his voice failed, the cold hand of death was laid on his brow; feebly and hurriedly he muttered, 'I am a dying man. Farewell!'

"Alas! it is painful to see death in any shape; in this it was horrible, for there was no hope. The rattling of his throat announced the moment of dissolution, and already did the body fall on my arms with a weight that was insupportable. I laid him on the ground. A mass of dark blood poured from his mouth; then came a frightful groan, the last breathing of that foul spirit; and what now lay at my feet in the wild desert? — a mangled mass of clay!

"The remainder of that night was passed in no enviable mood; but my feelings cannot be described. At dawn I dug a hole with the paddle of my canoe, rolled the body into it, and covered it. On reaching the boat I found several buzzards feeding on the bodies, which I in vain attempted to drag to the shore. I therefore covered them with mud and weeds, and launching my canoe, paddled from the cove with a secret joy for my escape, overshadowed with the gloom of mingled dread and abhorrence."

THE WRECKERS OF FLORIDA

LONG before I reached the lovely islets that border the southeastern shores of the Floridas, the accounts I had heard of " The Wreckers" had deeply prejudiced me against them. Often had I been informed of the cruel and' cowardly methods which it was alleged they employed to allure vessels of all nations to the dreaded reefs, that they might plunder their cargoes, and rob their crews and passengers of their effects. I therefore could have little desire to meet with such men under any circumstances, much less to become liable to receive their aid; and with the name of Wreckers there were associated in my mind ideas of piratical depredations, barbarous usage, and even murder.

One fair afternoon, while I was standing on the polished deck of the United States revenue cutter, the " Marion," a sail hove in sight, bearing in an opposite course, and close-hauled to the wind. The gentle rake of her masts, as she rocked to and fro in the breeze, brought to my mind the wavings of the reeds on the fertile banks of the Mississippi. By and by the vessel, altering her course, approached us. The " Marion," like a sea-bird with extended wings, swept through the waters, gently inclining to either side, while the unknown vessel leaped as it were, from wave to wave, like the dolphin in eager pursuit of his prey. In a short time we were gliding side by side, and the commander of the strange schooner saluted our captain, who promptly returned the compliment. What a beautiful vessel! we all thought; how trim, how clean rigged, and how well manned! She swims like a duck; and now with a broad sheer, off she makes for the reefs a few miles under our lee. There, in that narrow passage, well known to her commander, she rolls, tumbles, and dances, like a giddy thing, her copper sheathing now gleaming and again disappearing under the waves. But the passage is thridded, and now, hauling on the wind, she resumes her former course, and gradually recedes from the view. Reader, it was a Florida Wrecker.

When at the Tortugas, I paid a visit to several vessels of this kind, in company with my excellent friend Robert Day, Esq. We had observed the regularity and quickness of the men then employed at their arduous tasks, and as we approached the largest schooner, I admired her form, so well adapted to her occupation, her great breadth of beam, her light draught, the correctness of her water-line, the neatness of her painted sides, the smoothness of her well-greased masts, and the beauty of her rigging. We were welcomed on board with all the frankness of our native tars. Silence and order prevailed on her decks. The commander and the second officer led us into a spacious cabin, well-lighted, and furnished with every convenience for fifteen or more passengers. The former brought me his collection of marine shells, and whenever I pointed to one that I had not seen before, offered it with so much kindness that I found it necessary to be careful in expressing my admiration of any particular shell. He had also many eggs of rare birds, which were all handed over to me, with an assurance that before the month should expire, a new set could easily be procured; " for," said he, " we have much idle time on the reefs at this season." Dinner was served, and we partook of their fare, which consisted of fish, fowl, and other materials. These rovers, who were both from " down east," were stout, active men, cleanly and smart in their attire. In a short time we were all extremely social and merry. They thought my visit to the Tortugas, in quest of birds, was rather a " curious fancy; " but, notwithstanding, they expressed their pleasure while looking at some of my drawings, and offered their services in procuring specimens. Expeditions far and near were proposed, and on settling that one of them was to take place on the morrow, we parted friends.

Early next morning, several of these kind men accompanied me to a small Key called Booby Island, about ten miles distant from the lighthouse. Their boats were well-manned, and rowed with long and steady strokes, such as whalers and men-of-war's men are wont to draw. The captain sang, and at times, by way of frolic, ran a race with our own beautiful bark. The Booby Isle was soon reached, and our sport there was equal to any we had elsewhere. They were capital shots, had excellent guns, and knew more about Boobies and Noddies than nine-tenths of the best naturalists in the world. But what will you say when I tell you the Florida Wreckers are excellent at a Deer hunt, and that at certain seasons, " when business is slack," they are wont to land on some extensive Key, and in a few hours procure a supply of delicious venison.

Some days afterwards, the same party took me on an expedition in quest of sea shells. There we were all in water, at times to the waist, and now and then much deeper. Now they would dip, like ducks, and on emerging would hold up a beautiful shell. This occupation they seemed to enjoy above all others.

The duties of the " Marion," having been performed, intimation of our intended departure reached the Wreckers. An invitation was sent to me to go and see them on board their vessels, which I accepted. Their object on this occasion was to present me with some superb corals, shells, live Turtles of the Hawk-bill species, and a great quantity of eggs. Not a " picayune " would they receive in return, but putting some letters in my hands, requested me "to be so good as to put them in the mail at Charleston," adding that they were for their wives " down east." So anxious did they appear to be to do all they could for me, that they proposed to sail before the " Marion," and meet her under way, to give me some birds that were rare on the coast, and of which they knew the haunts. Circumstances connected with " the service " prevented this, however, and with sincere regret, and a good portion of friendship, I bade these excellent fellows adieu. How different, thought I, is often the knowledge of things acquired by personal observation from that obtained by report!

I had never before seen Florida Wreckers, nor has it since been my fortune to fall in with any; but my good friend Dr. Benjamin Strobel, having furnished me with a graphic account of a few days which he spent with them, I shall present you with it in his own words: —

"On the 12th day of September, while lying in harbor at Indian Key, we were joined by five wrecking vessels. Their licenses having expired, it was necessary to go to Key West to renew them. We determined to accompany them the next morning; and here it will not be amiss for me to say a few words respecting these far-famed Wreckers, their captains and crews. From all that I had heard, I expected to see a parcel of dirty, pirate-looking vessels, officered and manned by a set of black-whiskered fellows, who carried murder in their very looks. I was agreeably surprised on discovering the vessels were fine large sloops and schooners, regular clippers, kept in first-rate order. The captains generally were jovial, good-natured sons of Neptune who manifested a disposition to be polite and hospitable, and to afford every facility to persons passing up and down the Reef. The crews were hearty, well-dressed and honest-looking men.

"On the 13th, at the appointed hour, we all set sail together; that is, the five Wreckers and the schooner 'Jane.' As our vessel was not noted for fast sailing, we accepted an invitation to go on board of a Wrecker. The fleet got under way about eight o'clock in the morning, the wind light but fair, the water smooth, the day fine. I can scarcely find words to express the pleasure and gratification which I this day experienced. The sea was of a beautiful, soft, pea-green color, smooth as a sheet of glass, and as transparent, its surface agitated only by our vessels as they parted its bosom, or by the Pelican in pursuit of his prey, which rising for a considerable distance in the air, would suddenly plunge down with distended mandibles, and secure his food. The vessels of our little fleet with every sail set that could catch a breeze, and the white foam curling round the prows, glided silently along, like islands of flitting shadows, on an immovable sea of light. Several fathoms below the surface of the water, and under us, we saw great quantities of fish diving and sporting among the sea-grass, sponges, sea-feathers, and corals, with which the bottom was covered. On our right hand were the Florida Keys, which, as we made them in the distance, looked like specks upon the surface of the water, but as we neared them, rose to view as if by enchantment, clad in the richest livery of spring, each variety of color and hue rendered soft and delicate by a clear sky and a brilliant sun overhead. All was like a fairy scene; my heart leaped up in delighted admiration, and I could not but exclaim, in the language of Scott, —

> ' Those seas behold
> Round thrice an hundred islands rolled.

The trade wind played round us with balmy and refreshing sweetness; and, to give life and animation to the scene, we had a contest for the mastery between all the vessels of the fleet, while a deep interest was excited in favor of this or that vessel, as she shot ahead, or fell astern.

" About three o'clock in the afternoon, we arrived off the Bay of Honda. The wind being light and no prospect of reaching Key West that night, it was agreed that we should make a harbor here. We entered a beautiful basin, and came to anchor about four o'clock. Boats were got out, and several hunting parties formed. We landed, and were soon on the scent, some going in search of shells, others of birds. An Indian, who had been picked up somewhere along the coast by a Wrecker, and who was employed as a hunter, was sent ashore in search of venison. Previous to his leaving the vessel, a rifle was loaded with a single ball and put into his hands. After an absence of several hours, he returned with two Deer, which he had killed at a single shot. He watched until they were both in range of his gun, side by side, when he fired and brought them down.

"All hands having returned, and the fruits of our excursion being collected, we had wherewithal to make an abundant supper. Most of the game was sent on board the largest vessel, where we proposed supping. Our vessels were all lying within hail of each other, and as soon as the moon arose, boats were seen passing from vessel to vessel, and all were busily and happily engaged in exchanging civilities. One could never have supposed that these men were professional rivals, so apparent was the good feeling that prevailed among them. About nine o'clock we started for supper; a number of persons had already collected, and as soon as we arrived on board the vessel, a German sailor, who played remarkably well on the violin, was summoned on the quarter-deck, when all hands, with a good will, cheerily danced to lively airs until supper was ready. The table was laid in the cabin, and groaned under its load of venison, Wild Ducks, Pigeons, Curlews, and fish. Toasting and singing succeeded the supper, and among other curious matters introduced, the following song was sung by the German fiddler, who accompanied his voice with his instrument. He is said to be the author of the song. I say nothing of the poetry, but merely give it as it came on my ear. It is certainly very characteristic : —

THE WRECKERS' SONG.

Come, ye good people, one and all,
Come listen to my song;
A few remarks I have to make,
Which won't be very long.

'T is of our vessel, stout and good
As ever yet was built of wood,
Along the reef where the breakers roar,
The Wreckers on the Florida shore !

Key Tavernier 's our rendezvous ;
At anchor there we lie,
And see the vessels in the Gulf,
Carelessly passing by.
When night comes on we dance and sing,
Whilst the current some vessel is floating in ;
When daylight comes, a ship 's on shore,
Among the rocks where the breakers roar.

When daylight dawns we 're under way,
And every sail is set,
And if the wind it should prove light,
Why, then our sails we wet.
To gain her first each eager strives,
To save the cargo and the people's lives,
Amongst the rocks where the breakers roar,
The Wreckers on the Florida shore.

When we get 'longside we find she 's bilged;
We know well what to do,
Save the cargo that we can,
The sails and rigging too ;
Then down to Key West we soon will go,
When quickly our salvage we shall know ;
When everything it is fairly sold,
Our money down to us it is told.

Then one week's *cruise* we 'll have on shore,
Before we do sail again,
And drink success to the sailor lads
That are ploughing of the main.
And when you are passing by this way,
On the Florida reef should you chance to stray,
Why we will come to you on the shore,
Amongst the rocks where the breakers roar.

Great emphasis was laid upon particular words by the
singer, who had a broad German accent. Between the

verses he played an interlude, remarking, ' Gentlemen, I
makes dat myself.'   The chorus was trolled by twenty
or thirty voices, which, in the stillness of the night,
produced no unpleasant effect."

ST. JOHN'S RIVER IN FLORIDA

SOON after landing at St. Augustine, in East Florida, I
formed acquaintance with Dr. Simmons, Dr. Porcher,
Judge Smith, the Misses Johnson, and other individuals,
my intercourse with whom was as agreeable as beneficial to me.   Lieutenant Constantine Smith, of the United
States army, I found of a congenial spirit, as was the
case with my amiable but since deceased friend, Dr.
Bell of Dublin.   Among the planters who extended their
hospitality to me, I must particularly mention General
Hernandez, and my esteemed friend John Bulow, Esq.
To all these estimable individuals I offer my sincere
thanks.

While in this part of the peninsula I followed my usual
avocation, although with little success, it then being winter.
I had letters from the Secretaries of the Navy and Treas-
ury of the United States, to the commanding officers of
vessels of war of the revenue service, directing them to
afford me any assistance in their power; and the schooner
" Spark " having come to St. Augustine, on her way to the
St. John's River, I presented my credentials to her commander Lieutenant Piercy, who readily and with politeness received me and my assistants on board.   We soon
after set sail with a fair breeze.   The strict attention to duty
on board even this small vessel of war, afforded matter of
surprise to me.   Everything went on with the regularity
of a chronometer: orders were given, answered to, and
accomplished, before they had ceased to vibrate on the

TRINGA ALPINA, RED-BACKED SANDPIPER.

(Now Pelidna alpina pacifica.)

FROM THE UNPUBLISHED DRAWING BY J. J. AUDUBON, NOVEMBER 24, 1831.

ear. The neatness of the crew equalled the cleanliness of
the white planks of the deck; the sails were in perfect
condition; and, built as the " Spark " was, for swift sailing,
on she went, gambolling from wave to wave.

I thought that, while thus sailing, no feeling but that of
pleasure could exist in our breasts; but, alas! how fleeting are our enjoyments. When we were almost at the
entrance of the river, the wind changed, the sky became
clouded, and, before many minutes had elapsed, the little
bark was lying to "like a Duck," as her commander expressed himself. It blew a hurricane — let it blow,
reader. At break of day we were again at anchor within
the bar of St. Augustine.

Our next attempt was successful. Not many hours
after we had crossed the bar, we perceived the star-like
glimmer of the light in the great lantern at the entrance
of the St. John's River. This was before daylight; and,
as the crossing of the sand-banks or bars, which occur at
the mouths of all the streams of this peninsula is difficult,
and can be accomplished only when the tide is up, one of
the guns was fired as a signal for the government pilot.
The good man, it seemed, was unwilling to leave his
couch, but a second gun brought him in his canoe alongside. The depth of the channel was barely sufficient.
My eyes, however, were not directed towards the waters,
but on high, where flew some thousands of snowy Pelicans, which had fled affrighted from their resting-grounds.
How beautifully they performed their broad gyrations, and
how matchless, after a while, was the marshalling of their
files, as they flew past us.

On the tide we proceeded apace. Myriads of Cormorants covered the face of the waters, and over it Fish-
Crows innumerable were already arriving from their distant roosts. We landed at one place to search for the
birds whose charming melodies had engaged our attention, and here and there some young Eagles we shot, to

add to our store of fresh provisions. The river did not seem to me equal in beauty to the fair Ohio; the shores were in many places low and swampy, to the great delight of the numberless Herons that moved along in gracefulness, and the grim Alligators that swam in sluggish sullenness. In going up a bayou, we caught a great number of the young of the latter for the purpose of making experiments upon them.

After sailing a considerable way, during which our commander and officers took the soundings, as well as the angles and bearings of every nook and crook of the sinuous stream, we anchored one evening at a distance of fully one hundred miles from the mouth of the river. The weather, although it was the 12th of February, was quite warm, the thermometer on board standing at 75°, and on shore at 90°. The fog was so thick that neither of the shores could be seen, and yet the river was not a mile in breadth. The "blind mosquitoes" covered every object, even in the cabin, and so wonderfully abundant were these tormentors that they more than once fairly extinguished the candles whilst I was writing my journal, which I closed in despair, crushing between the leaves more than a hundred of the little wretches. Bad as they are, however, these blind mosquitoes do not bite. As if purposely to render our situation doubly uncomfortable, there was an establishment for jerking beef on the nearer shores, to the windward of our vessel, from which the breeze came laden with no sweet odors.

In the morning when I arose, the country was still covered with thick fogs, so that although I could plainly hear the notes of the birds on shore, not an object could I see beyond the bowsprit, and the air was as close and sultry as on the previous evening. Guided by the scent of the jerkers' works we went on shore, where we found the vegetation already far advanced. The blossoms of the jessamine, ever pleasing, lay steeped in dew, the

humming bee was collecting her winter's store from the
snowy flowers of the native orange; and the little warblers
frisked along the twigs of the smilax. Now, amid the
tall pines of the forest, the sun's rays began to force their
way, and as the dense mists dissolved in the atmosphere,
the bright luminary at length shone forth. We explored
the woods around, guided by some friendly live-oakers
who had pitched their camp in the vicinity. After a while
the "Spark" again displayed her sails, and as she silently
glided along, we spied a Seminole Indian approaching
us in his canoe. The poor, dejected son of the woods,
endowed with talents of the highest order, although rarely
acknowledged by the proud usurpers of his native soil,
has spent the night in fishing, and the morning in procuring the superb feathered game of the swampy thickets;
and with both he comes to offer them for our acceptance.
Alas! thou fallen one, descendant of an ancient line of
freeborn hunters, would that I could restore to thee thy
birthright, thy natural independence, the generous feelings that were once fostered in thy brave bosom. But
the irrevocable deed is done, and I can merely admire
the perfect symmetry of his frame, as he dexterously
throws on our deck the Trout and Turkeys which he has
captured. He receives a recompense, and without smile
or bow, or acknowledgment of any kind, off he starts
with the speed of an arrow from his own bow.

Alligators were extremely abundant, and the heads of
the fishes which they had snapped off, lay floating around
on the dark waters. A rifle bullet was now and then sent
through the eye of one of the largest, which, with a tremendous splash of its tail, expired. One morning we
saw a monstrous fellow lying on the shore. I was desirous of obtaining him to make an accurate drawing of his
head, and accompanied by my assistant and two of the
sailors, proceeded cautiously towards him. When within
a few yards, one of us fired, and sent through his side an

ounce ball which tore open a hole large enough to receive a man's hand. He slowly raised his head, bent himself upwards, opened his huge jaws, swung his tail to and fro, rose on his legs, blew in a frightful manner, and fell to the earth. My assistant leaped on shore, and, contrary to my injunctions, caught hold of the animal's tail, when the alligator, awakening from its trance, with a last effort crawled slowly towards the water, and plunged heavily into it. Had he thought of once flourishing his tremendous weapon, there might have been an end of his assailant's life, but he fortunately went in peace to his grave, where we left him, as the water was too deep. The same morning, another of equal size was observed swimming directly for the bows of our vessel, attracted by the gentle rippling of the water there. One of the officers, who had watched him, fired, and scattered his brain through the air, when he tumbled and rolled at a fearful rate, blowing all the while most furiously. The river was bloody for yards around, but although the monster passed close by the vessel, we could not secure him, and after a while he sunk to the bottom.

Early one morning, I hired a boat and two men, with the view of returning to St. Augustine by a short-cut. Our baggage being placed on board, I bade adieu to the officers, and off we started. About four in the afternoon we arrived at the short-cut, forty miles distant from our point of departure, and where we had expected to procure a wagon, but were disappointed. So we laid our things on the bank, and leaving one of my assistants to look after them, I set out accompanied by the other and my Newfoundland dog. We had eighteen miles to go; and as the sun was only two hours high, we struck off at a good rate. Presently we entered a pine-barren. The country was as level as a floor; our path, although narrow, was well-beaten, having been used by the Seminole Indians for ages, and the weather was calm and beautiful. Now and then a rivulet occurred, from which we quenched our thirst, while the magnolias and other flowering plants on its banks relieved the dull uniformity of the woods. When the path separated into two branches, both seemingly leading the same way, I would follow one, while my companion took the other, and unless we met again in a short time, one of us would go across the intervening forest.

The sun went down behind a cloud, and the southeast breeze that sprung up at this moment, sounded dolefully among the tall pines. Along the eastern horizon lay a bed of black vapor, which gradually rose, and soon covered the heavens. The air felt hot and oppressive, and we knew that a tempest was approaching. Plato was now our guide, the white spots on his coat being the only objects that we could discern amid the darkness, and as if aware of his utility in this respect, he kept a short way before us on the trail. Had we imagined ourselves more than a few miles from the town, we should have made a camp, and remained under its shelter for the night; but conceiving that the distance could not be great, we resolved to trudge along.

Large drops began to fall from the murky mass overhead; thick impenetrable darkness surrounded us, and to my dismay, the dog refused to proceed. Groping with my hands on the ground, I discovered that several trails branched out at the spot where he lay down; and when I had selected one, he went on. Vivid flashes of lightning streamed across the heavens, the wind increased to a gale, and the rain poured down upon us like a torrent. The water soon rose on the level ground so as almost to cover our feet, and we slowly advanced, fronting the tempest. Here and there a tall pine on fire presented a magnificent spectacle, illumining the trees around it, and surrounding them with a halo of dim light, abruptly bordered with the deep black of the night. At one time we passed through a tangled thicket of low trees, at another crossed a stream flushed by the heavy rain, and again proceeded over the open barrens.

How long we thus, half lost, groped our way is more than I can tell you; but at length the tempest passed over, and suddenly the clear sky became spangled with stars. Soon after, we smelt the salt marshes, and walking directly towards them, like pointers advancing on a covey of partridges, we at last to our great joy descried the light of the beacon near St. Augustine. My dog began to run briskly around, having met with ground on which he had hunted before, and taking a direct course, led us to the great causeway that crosses the marshes at the back of the town. We refreshed ourselves with the produce of the first orange-tree that we met with, and in half an hour more arrived at our hotel. Drenched with rain, steaming with perspiration, and covered to the knees with mud, you may imagine what figures we cut in the eyes of the good people whom we found snugly enjoying themselves in the sitting-room. Next morning, Major Gates, who had received me with much kindness, sent a wagon with mules and two trusty soldiers for my companion and luggage.

THE FLORIDA KEYS

I

As the " Marion " neared the Inlet called " Indian Key," which is situated on the eastern coast of the peninsula of Florida, my heart swelled with uncontrollable delight. Our vessel once over the coral reef that everywhere stretches along the shore like a great wall reared by an army of giants, we found ourselves in safe anchoring grounds, within a few furlongs of the land. The next moment saw the oars of a boat propelling us towards the shore, and in brief time we stood on the desired beach. With what delightful feelings did we gaze on the objects around us! — the gorgeous flowers, the singular and beautiful plants, the luxuriant trees. The balmy air which we breathed filled us with animation, so pure and salubrious did it seem to be. The birds which we saw were almost all new to us; their lovely forms appeared to be arrayed in more brilliant apparel than I had ever seen before, and as they fluttered in happy playfulness among the bushes, or glided over the light green waters, we longed to form a more intimate acquaintance with them.

Students of nature spend little time in introductions, especially when they present themselves to persons who feel an interest in their pursuits. This was the case with Mr. Thruston, the deputy collector of the island, who shook us all heartily by the hand, and in a trice had a boat manned, and at our service. Accompanied by him, his pilot and fishermen, off we went, and after a short pull landed on a large key. Few minutes had elapsed when shot after shot might be heard, and down came whirling through the air the objects of our desire. One thrust himself into the tangled groves that covered all but the beautiful coral beach that in a continued line bordered the island, while others gazed on the glowing and diversified hues of the curious inhabitants of the deep. I saw one of my party rush into the limpid element to seize on a crab, that, with claws extended upward, awaited his approach, as if determined not to give way. A loud voice called him back to the land, for sharks are as abundant along these shores as pebbles, and the hungry prowlers could not have found a more savory dinner.

The pilot, besides being a first-rate shot, possessed a most intimate acquaintance with the country. He had been a "conch diver," and no matter what number of fathoms measured the distance between the surface of the water and its craggy bottom, to seek for curious shells in their retreat seemed to him more pastime than toil. Not a Cormorant or Pelican, a Flamingo, an Ibis, or Heron had ever in his days formed its nest without his having marked the spot; and as to the Keys to which the Doves are wont to resort, he was better acquainted with them than many fops are with the contents of their pockets. In a word, he positively knew every channel that led to these islands, and every cranny along their shores. For years his employment had been to hunt those singular animals called Sea-cows or Manatees, and he had conquered hundreds of them, " merely," as he said, because the flesh and hide bring " a fair price " at Havana. He never went anywhere to land without " Long Tom," which proved indeed to be a wonderful gun, and which made smart havoc when charged with " groceries " a term by which he designated the large shot he used. In like manner, he never paddled his light canoe without having by his side the trusty javelin with which he unerringly transfixed such fishes as he thought fit either for market or for his own use. In attacking Turtles, netting, or overturning them, I doubt if his equal ever lived on the Florida coast. No sooner was he made acquainted with my errand, than he freely offered his best services, and from that moment until I left Key West he was seldom out of my hearing.

While the young gentlemen who accompanied us were engaged in procuring plants, shells, and small birds, he tapped me on the shoulder, and with a smile said to me, " Come along, I'll show you something better worth your while." To the boat we betook ourselves, with the captain and only a pair of tars, for more he said would not answer. The yawl for a while was urged at a great rate, but as we approached a point, the oars were taken in, and the pilot alone sculling desired us to make ready, for in a few minutes we should have " rare sport." As we advanced, the more slowly did we move, and the most profound silence was maintained, until suddenly coming

almost in contact with a thick shrubbery of mangroves,
we beheld, right before us, a multitude of Pelicans. A
discharge of artillery seldom produced more effect; the
dead, the dying, and the wounded, fell from the trees upon
the water, while those unscathed flew screaming through
the air in terror and dismay. " There," said he, " did not
I tell you so; is it not rare sport? " The birds, one after
another, were lodged under the gunwales, when the pilot
desired the captain to order the lads to pull away. Within
about half a mile we reached the extremity of the Key.
" Pull away," cried the pilot, " never mind them on the
wing, for those black rascals don't mind a little firing —
now, boys, lay her close under the nests." And there we
were with four hundred Cormorant's nests over our heads.
The birds were sitting, and when we fired, the number that
dropped as if dead, and plunged into the water was such,
that I thought by some unaccountable means or other we
had killed the whole colony. You would have smiled at
the loud laugh and curious gestures of the pilot. " Gentlemen," said he, " almost a blank shot! " And so it was,
for, on following the birds as one after another peeped up
from the water, we found only a few unable to take to
wing. " Now," said the pilot, " had you waited until *I had
spoken* to the black villains, you might have killed a score
or more of them." On inspection, we found that our
shots had lodged in the tough dry twigs of which these
birds form their nests, and that we had lost the more favorable opportunity of hitting them, by not waiting until they
rose. " Never mind," said the pilot, " if you wish it, you
may load *The Lady of the Green Mantle* [1] with them in less
than a week. Stand still, my lads; and now, gentlemen, in
ten minutes you and I will bring down a score of them."
And so we did. As we rounded the island, a beautiful
bird of the species called Peale's Egret came up, and was
shot. We now landed, took in the rest of our party, and

[1] The name given by the wreckers and smugglers to the " Marion."

returned to Indian Key, where we arrived three hours
before sunset.

The sailors and other individuals to whom my name and
pursuits had become known, carried our birds to the pilot's
house. His good wife had a room ready for me to draw
in, and my assistant might have been seen busily engaged
in skinning, while George Lehman was making a sketch
of the lovely isle.

Time is ever precious to the student of nature. I placed
several birds in their natural attitudes, and began to outline them. A dance had been prepared also, and no sooner
was the sun lost to our eye, than males and females, including our captain and others from the vessel, were seen
advancing gayly towards the house in full apparel. The
birds were skinned, the sketch was on paper, and I told
my young men to amuse themselves. As to myself, I could
not join in the merriment, for, full of the remembrance of
you, reader, and of the patrons of my work both in
America and in Europe, I went on "grinding" — not on
an organ, like the Lady of Bras d'Or, but on paper, to the
finishing not merely of my outlines, but of my notes respecting the objects seen this day.

The room adjoining that in which I worked was soon
filled. Two miserable fiddlers screwed their screeching,
silken strings, — not an inch of catgut graced their instruments, — and the bouncing of brave lads and fair lasses
shook the premises to the foundation. One with a slip
came down heavily on the floor, and the burst of laughter
that followed echoed over the isle. Diluted claret was
handed round to cool the ladies, while a beverage of more
potent energies warmed their partners. After supper our
captain returned to the "Marion," and I, with my young
men, slept in light swinging hammocks under the eaves of
the piazza.

It was the end of April, when the nights were short, and
the days therefore long. Anxious to turn every moment

to account, we were on board Mr. Thruston's boat at three next morning. Pursuing our way through the deep and tortuous channels that everywhere traverse the immense muddy soap-like flats that stretch from the outward Keys to the Main, we proceeded on our voyage of discovery. Here and there we met with great beds of floating sea-weeds, which showed us that Turtles were abundant there, these masses being the refuse of their feeding. On talking to Mr. Thruston of the nature of these muddy flats, he mentioned that he had once been lost amongst their narrow channels for several days and nights, when in pursuit of some smugglers' boat, the owners of which were better acquainted with the place than the men who were along with him. Although in full sight of several of the Keys, as well as of the main land, he was unable to reach either until a heavy gale raised the water, when he sailed directly over the flats, and returned home almost exhausted with fatigue and hunger. His present pilot often alluded to the circumstance afterwards, ending with a great laugh, and asserting that had he " been there, the rascals would not have escaped."

Coming under a Key on which multitudes of Frigate Pelicans had begun to form their nests, we shot a good number of them, and observed their habits. The boastings of our pilot were here confirmed by the exploits which he performed with his long gun, and on several occasions he brought down a bird from a height of fully a hundred yards. The poor bird, unaware of the range of our artillery, sailed calmly along, so that it was not difficult for " Long Tom," or rather for his owner, to furnish us with as many as we required. The day was spent in this manner, and towards night we returned, laden with booty, to the hospitable home of the pilot.

The next morning was delightful. The gentle sea-breeze glided over the flowery isle, the horizon was clear, and all was silent, save the long breakers that rushed over

the distant reefs. As we were proceeding towards some
Keys seldom visited by men, the sun rose from the bosom
of the waters with a burst of glory that flashed on my soul
the idea of that power which called into existence so magnificent an object. The moon, thin and pale, as if ashamed
to show her feeble light, concealed herself in the dim west.
The surface of the waters shone in its tremulous smoothness, and the deep blue of the clear heavens was pure as the
world that lies beyond them. The Heron heavily flew
towards the land, like a glutton retiring at daybreak, with
well lined paunch, from the house of some wealthy patron
of good cheer. The Night Heron and the Owl, fearful of
day, with hurried flight sought safety in the recesses of
the deepest swamps; while the Gulls and Terns, ever
cheerful, gambolled over the water, exulting in the prospect of abundance. I also exulted in hope, my whole
frame seemed to expand; and our sturdy crew showed by
their merry faces that nature had charms for them too.
How much of beauty and joy is lost to them who never
view the rising sun, and of whose waking existence, the
best half is nocturnal.

Twenty miles our men had to row before we reached
"Sandy Island," and as on its level shores we all leaped,
we plainly saw the southernmost cape of the Foridas. The
flocks of birds that covered the shelly beaches, and those
hovering overhead, so astonished us that we could for a
while scarcely believe our eyes. The first volley procured
a supply of food sufficient for two days' consumption.
Such tales, you have already been told, are well enough
at a distance from the place to which they refer; but you
will doubtless be still more surprised when I tell you that
our first fire among a crowd of the Great Godwits laid
prostrate sixty-five of these birds. Rose-colored Curlews
stalked gracefully beneath the mangroves. Purple Herons
rose at almost every step we took, and each cactus supported the nest of a White Ibis. The air was darkened by

whistling wings, while, on the waters, floated Gallinules and other interesting birds. We formed a kind of shed with sticks and grass, the sailor cook commenced his labors, and ere long we supplied the deficiencies of our fatigued frames. The business of the day over, we secured ourselves from insects by means of mosquito-nets, and were lulled to rest by the cacklings of the beautiful Purple Gallinules!

In the morning we rose from our sandy beds, and —

THE FLORIDA KEYS '

II

I LEFT you abruptly, perhaps uncivilly, reader, at the dawn of day, on Sandy Island, which lies just six miles from the extreme point of South Florida. I did so because I was amazed at the appearance of things around me, which in fact looked so different then from what they seemed at night, that it took some minutes' reflection to account for the change. When we laid ourselves down in the sand to sleep, the waters almost bathed our feet; when we opened our eyes in the morning, they were at an immense distance. Our boat lay on her side, looking not unlike a whale reposing on a mud bank. The birds in myriads were probing their exposed pasture-ground. There great flocks of Ibises fed apart from equally large collections of Godwits, and thousands of Herons gracefully paced along, ever and anon thrusting their javelin bills into the body of some unfortunate fish confined in a small pool of water. Of Fish-Crows, I could not estimate the number, but from the havoc they made among the crabs, I conjecture that these animals must have been scarce by the time of next ebb. Frigate Pelicans chased the Jager, which himself had just robbed a poor Gull of its prize, and all the Gallinules, ran with spread wings from the mud-banks to the thickets of the island, so timorous had they become when they perceived us.

Surrounded as we were by so many objects that allured us, not one could we yet attain, so dangerous would it have been to venture on the mud; and our pilot, having assured us that nothing could be lost by waiting, spoke of our eating, and on this hint told us that he would take us to a part of the island where " our breakfast would be abundant although uncooked." Off we went, some of the sailors carrying baskets, others large tin pans and wooden vessels, such as they use for eating their meals in. Entering a thicket of about an acre in extent, we found on every bush several nests of the Ibis, each containing three large and beautiful eggs, and all hands fell to gathering. The birds gave way to us, and ere long we had a heap of eggs that promised delicious food. Nor did we stand long in expectation, for, kindling a fire, we soon prepared in one way or other enough to satisfy the cravings of our hungry maws. Breakfast ended, the pilot, looking at the gorgeous sunrise, said : " Gentlemen, prepare yourselves for fun; the tide is coming."

Over these enormous mud-flats, a foot or two of water is quite sufficient to drive all the birds ashore, even the tallest Heron or Flamingo, and the tide seems to flow at once over the whole expanse. Each of us, provided with a gun, posted himself behind a bush, and no sooner had the water forced the winged creatures to approach the shore than the work of destruction commenced. When it at length ceased, the collected mass of birds of different kinds looked not unlike a small haycock. Who could not with a little industry have helped himself to a few of their skins? Why, reader, surely no one as fond of these things as I am. Every one assisted in this, and even the sailors themselves tried their hand at the work.

Our pilot, good man, told us he was no hand at such occupations and would go after something else. So taking

"Long Tom" and his fishing-tackle, he marched off quietly along the shores. About an hour afterwards we saw him returning, when he looked quite exhausted, and on our inquiring the cause said, "There is a dewfish yonder, and a few balacoudas, but I am not able to bring them, or even to haul them here; please send the sailors after them." The fishes were accordingly brought, and as I had never seen a dewfish, I examined it closely, and took an outline of its form, which some days hence you may perhaps see. It exceeded a hundred pounds in weight, and afforded excellent eating. The balacouda is also a good fish, but at times a dangerous one, for, according to the pilot, on more than one occasion "some of these gentry" had followed him when waist-deep in the water, in pursuit of a more valuable prize, until in self-defence, he had to spear them, fearing that "the gentlemen" might at one dart cut off his legs, or some other nice bit, with which he was unwilling to part.

Having filled our cask from a fine well, long since dug in the sand of Cape Sable, either by Seminole Indians or pirates, no matter which, we left Sandy Isle about full tide, and proceeded homeward, giving a call here and there at different Keys, with the view of procuring rare birds, and also their nests and eggs. We had twenty miles to go, "as the birds fly," but the tortuosity of the channels rendered our course fully a third longer. The sun was descending fast, when a black cloud suddenly obscured the majestic orb. Our sails swelled by a breeze that was scarcely felt by us; and the pilot, requesting us to sit on the weather gunwale, told us that we were "going to get it." One sail was hauled in and secured, and the other was reefed, although the wind had not increased. A low murmuring noise was heard, and across the cloud that now rolled along in tumultuous masses shot vivid flashes of lightning. Our experienced guide steered directly across a flat towards the nearest land. The sailors passed their

quids from one cheek to the other, and our pilot having
covered himself with his oil jacket, we followed his example. " Blow, sweet breeze," cried he at the tiller, and
" we 'll reach the land before the blast overtakes us, for,
gentlemen, it is a furious cloud yon."

A furious cloud indeed was the one which now, like an
eagle on outstretched wings, approached so swiftly that
one might have deemed it in haste to destroy us. We
were not more than a cable's length from the shore, when,
with an imperative voice, the pilot calmly said to us, " Sit
quite still, gentlemen, for I should not like to lose you
overboard just now ; the boat can't upset, my word for that,
if you will but sit still — Here we have it !"

Reader, persons who have never witnessed a hurricane,
such as not unfrequently desolates the sultry climates of
the South, can scarcely form an idea of their terrific grandeur. One would think that, not content with laying
waste all on land, it must needs sweep the waters of the
shallows quite dry, to quench its thirst. No respite for an
instant does it afford to the objects within the reach of its
furious current. Like the scythe of the destroying angel,
it cuts everything by the roots, as it were, with the careless
ease of the experienced mower. Each of its revolving
sweeps collects a heap that might be likened to the full-
sheaf which the husbandman flings by his side. On it
goes with a wildness and fury that are indescribable, and
when at last its frightful blasts have ceased, Nature, weeping and disconsolate, is left bereaved of her beauteous off-
spring. In some instances, even a full century is required
before, with all her powerful energies, she can repair her
loss. The planter has not only lost his mansion, his crops,
and his flocks, but he has to clear his lands anew, covered
and entangled as they are with the trunks and branches
of trees that are everywhere strewn. The bark, overtaken
by the storm, is cast on the lee-shore, and if any are left to
witness the fatal results, they are the " wreckers " alone,

who, with inward delight, gaze upon the melancholy spectacle.

Our light bark shivered like a leaf the instant the blast reached her sides. We thought she had gone over; but the next instant she was on the shore. And now in contemplation of the sublime and awful storm, I gazed around me. The waters drifted like snow; the tough mangroves hid their tops amid their roots, and the loud roaring of the waves driven among them blended with the howl of the tempest. It was not rain that fell; the masses of water flew in a horizontal direction, and where a part of my body was exposed I felt as if a smart blow had been given me on it. But enough — in half an hour it was over. The pure blue sky once more embellished the heavens, and although it was now quite night, we considered our situation a good one.

The crew and some of the party spent the night in the boat. The pilot, myself, and one of my assistants took to the heart of the mangroves, and having found high land, we made a fire as well as we could, spread a tarpauling, and fixing our insect bars over us, soon forgot in sleep the horrors that had surrounded us.

Next day the " Marion " proceeded on her cruise, and in a few more days, having anchored in another safe harbor, we visited other Keys, of which I will, with your leave, give you a short account.

The deputy-collector of Indian Isle gave me the use of his pilot for a few weeks, and I was the more gratified by this, that besides knowing him to be a good man, and a perfect sailor, I was now convinced that he possessed a great knowledge of the habits of birds, and could without loss of time lead me to their haunts. We were a hundred miles or so farther to the south. Gay May; like a playful babe, gambolled on the bosom of his mother Nature, and everything was replete with life and joy. The pilot had spoken to me of some birds which I was very desirous of obtaining. One morning, therefore, we went in two boats to some distant isle, where they were said to breed. Our difficulties in reaching that Key might to some seem more imaginary than real, were I faithfully to describe them. Suffice it for me to tell you that after hauling our boats and pushing them with our hands, for upwards of nine miles, over the flats, we at last reached the deep channel that usually surrounds each of the mangrove islands. We were much exhausted by the labor and excessive heat, but we were now floating on deep water, and by resting a short while under the shade of some mangroves, we were soon refreshed by the breeze that gently blew from the Gulf. We further repaired our strength by taking some food; and I may as well tell you here that, during all the time I spent in that part of the Floridas, my party restricted themselves to fish and soaked biscuit, while our only and constant beverage was molasses and water. I found that in these warm latitudes, exposed as we constantly were to alternate heat and moisture, ardent spirits and more substantial food would prove dangerous to us. The officers, and those persons who from time to time kindly accompanied us, adopted the same regimen, and not an individual of us had ever to complain of so much as a headache.

But we were under the mangroves ; at a great distance on one of the flats, the Heron which I have named *Ardea occidentalis* [1] was seen moving majestically in great numbers. The tide rose and drove them away, and as they came towards us, to alight and rest for a time on the tallest trees, we shot as many as I wished. I also took under my charge several of their young alive.

At another time we visited the " Mule Keys." There the prospect was in many respects dismal in the extreme. As I followed their shores, I saw bales of cotton floating in all the coves, while spars of every description lay on

[1] Plate cclxxxi., ed. 1827–1839 ; plate ccclxviii., ed. 1843.

the beach, and far off on the reefs I could see the last remains of a lost ship, her dismantled hulk. Several schooners were around her ; they were wreckers. I turned me from the sight with a heavy heart. Indeed, as I slowly proceeded, I dreaded to meet the floating or cast-ashore bodies of some of the unfortunate crew. Our visit to the Mule Keys was in no way profitable, for besides meeting with but a few birds, in two or three instances I was, whilst swimming in the deep channel of a mangrove isle, much nearer a large shark than I wish ever to be again.

"The service" requiring all the attention, prudence, and activity of Captain Day and his gallant officers, another cruise took place, of which you will find some account in the sequel; and while I rest a little on the deck of the "Lady of the Green Mantle," let me offer my humble thanks to the Being who has allowed me the pleasure of thus relating to you, kind reader, a small part of my adventures.

THE TURTLERS

THE Tortugas are a group of islands lying about eighty miles from Key West, and the last of those that seem to defend the peninsula of the Floridas. They consist of five or six extremely low, uninhabitable banks, formed of shelly sand, and are resorted to principally by that class of men called wreckers and turtlers. Between these islands are deep channels, which, although extremely intricate, are well known to those adventurers, as well as to the commanders of the revenue cutters, whose duties call them to that dangerous coast. The great coral reef, or wall, lies about eight miles from these inhospitable isles, in the direction of the Gulf, and on it many an ignorant or careless navigator has suffered shipwreck. The whole ground around them is densely covered with corals, seafans, and other productions of the deep, amid which crawl innumerable testaceous animals, while shoals of curious and beautiful fishes fill the limpid waters above them. Turtles of different species resort to these banks, to deposit their eggs in the burning sand, and clouds of sea-fowl arrive every spring for the same purpose. These are followed by persons called " eggers," who, when their cargoes are completed, sail to distant markets, to exchange their ill-gotten ware for a portion of that gold on the acquisition of which all men seem bent.

The " Marion " having occasion to visit the Tortugas, I gladly embraced the opportunity of seeing those celebrated islets. A few hours before sunset the joyful cry of " Land ! " announced our approach to them ; but as the breeze was fresh, and the pilot was well acquainted with all the windings of the channels, we held on, and dropped anchor before twilight. If you have never seen the sun setting in those latitudes, I would recommend to you to make a voyage for the purpose, for I much doubt if, in any other portion of the world, the departure of the orb of day is accompanied with such gorgeous appearances. Look at the great red disk, increased to triple its ordinary dimensions ! Now it has partially sunk beneath the distant line of waters, and with its still remaining half irradiates the whole heavens with a flood of golden light, purpling the far-off clouds that hover over the western horizon. A blaze of refulgent glory streams through the portals of the west, and the masses of vapor assume the semblance of mountains of molten gold. But the sun has now disappeared, and from the east slowly advances the gray curtain which night draws over the world.

The Night-hawk is flapping its noiseless wings in the gentle sea-breeze ; the Terns, safely landed, have settled on their nests ; the Frigate Pelicans are seen wending their way to distant mangroves ; and the Brown Gannet, in search of a resting-place, has perched on the yard of the vessel. Slowly advancing landward, their heads alone above the water, are observed the heavily laden Turtles, anxious to deposit their eggs in the well-known sands. On the surface of the gently rippling stream, I dimly see their broad forms, as they toil along, while at intervals may be heard their hurried breathings, indicative of suspicion and fear. The moon with her silvery light now illumines the scene, and the Turtle, having landed, slowly and laboriously drags her heavy body over the sand, her "flippers" being better adapted for motion in the water than on shore. Up the slope, however, she works her way; and see how industriously she removes the sand beneath her, casting it out on either side. Layer after layer she deposits her eggs, arranging them in the most careful manner, and with her hind paddles brings the sand over them. The business is accomplished, the spot is covered over, and with a joyful heart the Turtle swiftly retires towards the shore, and launches into the deep.

But the Tortugas are not the only breeding places of the Turtles; these animals, on the contrary, frequent many other Keys, as well as various parts of the coast of the mainland. There are four different species, which are known by the names of the *Green* Turtle, the *Hawk-billed* Turtle, the *Logger-head* Turtle, and the *Trunk* Turtle. The first is considered the best as an article of food, in which capacity it is well known to most epicures. It approaches the shores, and enters the bays, inlets, and rivers, early in the month of April, after having spent the winter in the deep waters. It deposits its eggs in convenient places, at two different times in May, and once again in June. The first deposit is the largest, and the last the least, the total quantity being, at an average, about two hundred and forty. The Hawk-billed Turtle, whose shell is so valuable as an article of commerce, being used for various purposes in the arts, is the next with respect to the quality of its flesh. It resorts to the outer Keys only, where it deposits its eggs in two sets, first in July, and again in August, although it "crawls" the beaches of these Keys much earlier in the season, as if to look for a safe place. The average number of its eggs is about three hundred. The Logger-head visits the Tortugas in April, and lays from that period until late in June three sets of eggs, each set averaging one hundred and seventy. The Trunk Turtle, which is sometimes of an enormous size, and which has a pouch like a Pelican, reaches the shores latest. The shell and flesh are so soft that one may push his finger into them, almost as into a lump of butter. This species is therefore considered as the least valuable, and, indeed, is seldom eaten, unless by the Indians, who, ever alert when the Turtle season commences, first carry off the eggs, and afterwards catch the Turtles themselves. The average number of eggs which it lays in the season, in two sets, may be three hundred and fifty.

The Logger-head and the Trunk Turtles are the least cautious in choosing the places in which to deposit their eggs, whereas the two other species select the wildest and most secluded spots. The Green Turtle resorts either to the shores of the Main, between Cape Sable and Cape Florida, or enters Indian, Halifax, and other large rivers or inlets, from which it makes its retreat as speedily as possible, and betakes itself to the open sea. Great numbers, however, are killed by the turtlers and Indians, as well as by various species of carnivorous animals, as Cougars, Lynxes, Bears, and Wolves. The Hawk-bill, which is still more wary, and is always the most difficult to surprise, keeps to the sea-islands. All the species employ nearly the same method in depositing their eggs in the sand, and as I have several times observed them in the act, I am enabled to present you with a circumstantial account of it.

On first nearing the shores, and mostly on fine, calm, moonlight nights, the Turtle raises her head above the water, being still distant thirty or forty yards from the beach, looks around her, and attentively examines the objects on the shore. Should she observe nothing likely to disturb her intended operations, she emits a loud hissing sound, by which such of her many enemies as are unaccustomed to it are startled, and so are apt to remove to another place, although unseen by her. Should she hear any noise, or perceive indications of danger, she instantly sinks, and goes off to a considerable distance; but should everything be quiet, she advances slowly towards the beach, crawls over it, her head raised to the full stretch of her neck, and when she has reached a place fitted for her purpose, she gazes all round in silence. Finding " all well " she proceeds to form a hole in the sand, which she effects by removing it from *under* her body with her *hind* flippers, scooping it out with so much dexterity that the sides seldom if ever fall in. The sand is raised alternately with each flipper, as with a large ladle, until it has accumulated behind her, when, supporting herself with her head and fore part on the ground fronting her body, she, with a spring from each flipper, sends the sand around her, scattering it to the distance of several feet. In this manner the hole is dug to the depth of eighteen inches, or sometimes more than two feet. This labor I have seen performed in the short period of nine minutes. The eggs are then dropped one by one, and disposed in regular layers, to the number of a hundred and fifty, or sometimes nearly two hundred. The whole time spent in this part of the operation may be about twenty minutes. She now scrapes the loose sand back over the eggs, and so levels and smooths the surface that few persons on seeing the spot could imagine anything had been done to it. This accomplished to her mind, she retreats to the water with all possible despatch, leaving the hatching of the eggs to the heat of the sand. When a Turtle, a Logger-head for example, is in the act of dropping her eggs, she will not move, although one should go up to her, or even seat himself on her back, for it seems that at this moment she finds it necessary to proceed at all events, and is unable to intermit her labor. The moment it is finished, however, off she starts; nor would it then be possible for one, unless he were as strong as a Hercules, to turn her over and secure her.

To upset a Turtle on the shore, one is obliged to fall on his knees, and placing his shoulder behind her fore-arm, gradually raise her up by pushing with great force, and then with a jerk throw her over. Sometimes it requires the united strength of several men to accomplish this; and, if the Turtle should be of very great size, as often happens on that coast, even handspikes are employed. Some turtlers are so daring as to swim up to them while lying asleep on the surface of the water, and turn them over in their own element, when, however, a boat must be at hand, to enable them to secure their prize. Few Turtles can bite beyond the reach of their fore-legs, and few, when once turned over, can, without assistance, regain their natural position; but, notwithstanding this, their flippers are generally secured by ropes so as to render their escape impossible.

Persons who search for Turtles' eggs, are provided with a light stiff cane or a gun-rod, with which they go along the shores probing the sand near the tracks of the animals, which, however, cannot always be seen, on account of the winds and heavy rains that often obliterate them. The nests are discovered not only by men, but also by beasts of prey, and the eggs are collected, or destroyed on the spot, in great numbers, as on certain parts of the shores hundreds of Turtles are known to deposit their eggs within the space of a mile. They form a new hole each time they lay, and the second is generally dug near the first, as if the animal were quite unconscious of what had befallen it. It will readily be understood that the numerous eggs seen in a Turtle on cutting it up, could not be all laid the same season. The whole number deposited by an individual in one summer may amount to four hundred, whereas, if the animal is caught on or near her nest, as I have witnessed, the remaining eggs, all small, without shells, and as it were threaded like so many large beads, exceed three thousand. In an instance where I found that number, the Turtle weighed nearly four hundred pounds. The young, soon after being hatched, and when yet scarcely larger than a dollar, scratch their way through their sandy covering, and immediately betake themselves to the water.

The food of the Green Turtle consists chiefly of marine plants, more especially the Grasswrack (*Zostera marina*) which they cut near the roots to procure the most tender and succulent parts. Their feeding-grounds, as I have elsewhere said, are easily discovered by floating masses of these plants on the flats, or along the shores to which they resort. The Hawk-billed species feeds on sea-weeds, crabs, various kinds of shell-fish and fishes; the Logger-head mostly on the fish of conch-shells of large size, which they are enabled, by means of their powerful beak, to crush to pieces with apparently as much ease as a man cracks a walnut. One which was brought on board the "Marion," and placed near the fluke of one of her anchors, made a deep indentation in that hammered piece of iron, which quite surprised me. The Trunk Turtle feeds on mollusca, fish, crustacea, sea urchins, and various marine plants.

All the species move through the water with surprising speed; but the Green and Hawk-billed, in particular, remind you, by their celerity and the ease of their motions, of the progress of a bird in the air. It is, therefore, no easy matter to strike one with a spear, and yet this is often done by an accomplished turtler.

While at Key West, and other islands on the coast, where I made the observations here presented to you, I chanced to have need to purchase some Turtles, to feed my friends on board " The Lady of the Green Mantle "— not my friends her gallant officers, or the brave tars who formed her crew, for all of them had already been satiated with Turtle soup, but my friends the Herons, of which I had a goodly number alive in coops, intending to carry them to John Bachman of Charleston, and other persons for whom I ever feel a sincere regard. So I went to a " crawl " accompanied by Dr. Benjamin Strobel, to inquire about prices, when, to my surprise, I found that the smaller the Turtles above ten-pounds weight, the dearer they were, and that I could have purchased one of the Logger-head kind that weighed more than seven hundred pounds, for little more money than another of only thirty pounds. While I gazed on the large one, I thought of the soups the contents of its shell would have furnished for a " Lord Mayor's dinner," of the numerous eggs which its swollen body contained, and of the curious carriage which might be made of its shell — a car in which Venus herself might sail over the Caribbean Sea, provided her tender Doves lent their aid in drawing the divinity, and provided no shark or hurricane came to upset it. The turtler assured me that although the " great monster " was, in fact, better meat than any other of a less size, there was no disposing of it, unless, indeed, it had been in his power to have sent it to some very distant market. I would willingly have purchased it, but I knew that if killed, its flesh could not keep much longer than a day, and on that account I bought eight or ten small ones, which " my friends " really relished exceedingly, and which served to support them for a long time.

Turtles, such as I have spoken of, are caught in various ways on the coasts of the Floridas, or in estuaries and rivers. Some turtlers are in the habit of setting great nets across the entrance of streams, so as to answer the purpose either at the flow or at the ebb of the waters.

These nets are formed of very large meshes, into which the Turtles partially enter, when, the more they attempt to extricate themselves, the more they get entangled. Others harpoon them in the usual manner; but in my estimation no method is equal to that employed by Mr. Egan, the pilot of Indian Isle.

That extraordinary turtler had an iron instrument which he called a *peg*, and which at each end had a point not unlike what nail-makers call a brad, it being four-cornered but flattish, and of a shape somewhat resembling the beak of an Ivory-billed Woodpecker, together with a neck and shoulder. Between the two shoulders of this instrument a fine tough-line, fifty or more fathoms in length, was fastened by one end being passed through a hole in the centre of the peg and the line itself was carefully coiled up, and placed in a convenient part of the canoe. One extremity of this peg enters a sheath of iron that loosely attaches it to a long wooden spear, until a Turtle has been pierced through the shell by the other extremity. He of the canoe paddles away as silently as possible whenever he spies a Turtle basking on the water, until he gets within a distance of ten or twelve yards, when he throws the spear so as to hit the animal about the place which an entomologist would choose, were it a large insect, for pinning it to a piece of cork. As soon as the Turtle is struck, the wooden handle separates from the peg, in consequence of the looseness of its attachment. The smart of the wound urges on the animal as if distracted, and it appears that the longer the peg remains in its shell, the more firmly fastened it is, so great a pressure is exercised upon it by the shell of the Turtle, which, being suffered to run like a whale, soon becomes fatigued, and is secured by hauling in the line with great care. In this manner, as the pilot informed me, eight hundred Green Turtles were caught by one man in twelve months.

Each turtler has his *crawl*, which is a square wooden building or pen formed of logs, which are so far separated as to allow the tide to pass freely through, and stand erect in the mud. The Turtles are placed in this enclosure, fed and kept there until sold. If the animals thus confined have not laid their eggs previous to their seizure, they drop them in the water, so that they are lost. The price of Green Turtles, when I was at Key West, was from four to six cents per pound.

The loves of the Turtles are conducted in the most extraordinary manner; but as the recital of them must prove out of place here, I shall pass them over. There is, however, a circumstance relating to their habits which I cannot omit, although I have it not from my own ocular evidence, but from report. When I was in the Floridas several of the turtlers assured me that any Turtle taken from the depositing ground, and carried on the deck of a vessel several hundred miles, would, if then let loose, certainly be met with at the same spot, either immediately after, or in the following breeding season. Should this prove true, and it certainly may, how much will be enhanced the belief of the student in the uniformity and solidity of Nature's arrangements, when he finds that the Turtle, like a migratory bird, returns to the same locality, with perhaps a delight similar to that experienced by the traveller, who, after visiting distant countries, once more returns to the bosom of his cherished family.

THE FORCE OF THE WATERS

THE men who are employed in cutting down the trees, and conveying the logs to the saw-mills or the places for shipping, are, in the State of Maine, called "lumberers." Their labors may be said to be continual. Before winter has commenced, and while the ground is yet uncovered

with a great depth of snow, they leave their homes to proceed to the interior of the pine forests, which in that part
of the country are truly magnificent, and betake themselves
to certain places already well known to them. Their provisions, axes, saws, and other necessary articles, together
with provender for their cattle, are conveyed by oxen in
heavy sledges. Almost at the commencement of their
march, they are obliged to enter the woods, and they have
frequently to cut a way for themselves for considerable
spaces, as the ground is often covered with the decaying
trunks of immense trees, which have fallen either from age,
or in consequence of accidental burnings. These trunks, and
the undergrowth which lies entangled in their tops render
many places almost impassable even to men on foot. Over
miry ponds they are sometimes forced to form causeways,
this being, under all circumstances, the easiest mode of
reaching the opposite side. Then, reader, is the time for
witnessing the exertions of their fine large cattle. No
rods do their drivers use to pain their flanks; no oaths or
imprecations are ever heard to fall from the lips of these
most industrious and temperate men, for in them, as in
most of the inhabitants of our Eastern States, education
and habit have tempered the passions, and reduced the
moral constitution to a state of harmony. Nay, the sobriety
that exists in many of the villages of Maine, I acknowledge,
I have often considered as carried to excess, for on asking
for brandy, rum, or whiskey, not a drop could I obtain, and
it is probable there was an equal lack of spirituous liquors
of every other kind. Now and then I saw some good old
wines, but they were always drunk in careful moderation.
But to return to the management of the oxen. Why,
reader, the lumbermen speak to them as if they were
rational beings. Few words seem to suffice, and their
whole strength is applied to the labor, as if in gratitude
to those who treat them with so much gentleness and
humanity.

While present on more than one occasion at what Americans call "ploughing matches," which they have annually in many of the States, I have been highly gratified, and in particular at one, of which I have still a strong recollection, and which took place a few miles from the fair and hospitable city of Boston. There I saw fifty or more ploughs drawn by as many pairs of oxen, which performed their work with so much accuracy and regularity — without the infliction of whip or rod, but merely guided by the verbal mandates of the ploughmen — that I was perfectly astonished.

After surmounting all obstacles, the lumberers with their stock arrive at the spot which they have had in view, and immediately commence building a camp. The trees around soon fall under the blows of their axes, and before many days have elapsed a low habitation is reared and fitted within for the accommodation of their cattle, while their provender is secured on a kind of loft covered with broad shingles or boards. Then their own cabin is put up; rough bedsteads, manufactured on the spot, are fixed in the corners; a chimney composed of a frame of sticks plastered with mud leads away the smoke; the skins of Bears or Deer, with some blankets, form their bedding, and around the walls are hung their changes of homespun clothing, guns, and various necessaries of life. Many prefer spending the night on the sweet-scented hay and corn blades of their cattle, which are laid on the ground. All arranged within, the lumberers set their "dead falls," large "steel traps," and "spring guns," in suitable places round their camps, to procure some of the Bears that ever prowl around such establishments.

Now the heavy clouds of November, driven by the northern blasts, pour down the snow in feathery flakes. The winter has fairly set in, and seldom do the sun's gladdening rays fall on the wood-cutter's hut. In warm flannels his body is enveloped, the skin of a Raccoon covers his head and brows, his Moose-skin leggings reach the girdle that secures them around his waist, while on broad moccasins, or snow-shoes, he stands from the earliest dawn until night, hacking away at majestic pines, that for a century past have embellished the forest. The fall of these valuable trees no longer resounds on the ground; and, as they tumble here and there nothing is heard but the rustling and cracking of their branches, their heavy trunks sinking into the deep snows. Thousands of large pines thus cut down every winter afford room for younger trees, which spring up profusely to supply the wants of man.

Weeks and weeks have elapsed; the earth's pure white covering has become thickly and firmly crusted by the increasing intensity of the cold, the fallen trees have all been sawn into measured logs, and the long repose of the oxen has fitted them for hauling them to the nearest frozen streams. The ice gradually becomes covered with the accumulating mass of timber, and, their task completed, the lumberers wait impatiently for the breaking up of the winter.

At this period they pass the time in hunting the Moose, the Deer, and the Bear, for the benefit of their wives and children; and as these men are most excellent woodsmen great havoc is made among the game. Many skins of Sables, Martens, and Musk-Rats they have procured during the intervals of their labor, or under night. The snows are now giving way, as the rains descend in torrents, and the lumberers collect their utensils, harness their cattle, and prepare for their return. This they accomplish in safety.

From being lumberers they now become millers, and with pleasure each applies the grating file to his saws. Many logs have already reached the dams on the swollen waters of the rushing streams, and the task commences, which is carried on through the summer, of cutting them up into boards.

The great heats of the dog-days have parched the ground ; every creek has become a shallow, except here and there where in a deep hole the salmon and the trout have found a retreat; the sharp, slimy angles of multitudes of rocks project, as if to afford resting-places to the Wood-ducks and Herons that breed on the borders of these streams. Thousands of " saw-logs " remain in every pool, beneath and above each rapid or fall. The miller's dam has been emptied of its timber, and he must now resort to some expedient to procure a fresh supply.

It was my good fortune to witness the method employed for the purpose of collecting the logs that had not reached their destination, and I had the more pleasure that it was seen in company with my little family. I wish, for your sake, reader, that I could describe in an adequate manner the scene which I viewed; but, although not so well qualified as I could wish, rely upon it that the desire which I feel to gratify you will induce me to use all my endeavors to give you an *idea* of it.

It was the month of September. At the upper extremity of Dennysville, which is itself a pretty village, are the saw-mills and ponds of the hospitable Judge Lincoln and other persons. The creek that conveys the logs to these ponds, and which bears the name of the village, is interrupted in its course by many rapids and narrow embanked gorges. One of the latter is situated about half a mile above the mill-dams, and is so rocky and rugged in its bottom and sides as to preclude the possibility of the trees passing along it at low water, while, as I conceived, it would have given no slight labor to an army of woodsmen or millers to move the thousands of large logs that had accumulated in it. They lay piled in confused heaps to a great height along an extent of several hundred yards, and were in some places so close as to have formed a kind of dam. Above the gorge there is a large natural reservoir, in which the head-waters of the creek settle, while only a small portion of them ripples through the gorge below, during the later weeks of summer and in early autumn, when the streams are at their lowest.

At the *neck* of this basin the lumberers raised a temporary barrier with the refuse of their sawn logs. The boards were planted nearly upright, and supported at their tops by a strong tree extending from side to side of the creek, which might there be about forty feet in breadth. It was prevented from giving way under pressure of the rising waters by having strong abutments of wood laid against its centre, while the ends of these abutments were secured by wedges, which could be knocked off when necessary.

The temporary dam was now finished. Little or no water escaped through the barrier, and that in the creek above it rose in the course of three weeks to its top, which was about ten feet high, forming a sheet that extended upwards fully a mile from the dam. My family was invited early one morning to go and witness the extraordinary effect which would be produced by the breaking down of the barrier, and we all accompanied the lumberers to the place. Two of the men, on reaching it, threw off their jackets, tied handkerchiefs round their heads, and fastened to their bodies a long rope, the end of which was held by three or four others, who stood ready to drag their companions ashore, in case of danger or accident. The two operators, each bearing an axe, walked along the abutments, and at a given signal knocked out the wedges. A second blow from each sent off the abutments themselves, and the men, leaping with extreme dexterity from one cross log to another, sprung to the shore with almost the quickness of thought.

Scarcely had they effected their escape from the frightful peril which threatened them, when the mass of waters burst forth with a horrible uproar. All eyes were bent towards the huge heaps of logs in the gorge below. The tumultuous burst of the waters instantly swept away every object that opposed their progress, and rushed in foaming waves among the timbers that everywhere blocked up the passage. Presently a slow, heavy motion was perceived in the mass of logs; one might have imagined that some mighty monster lay convulsively writhing beneath them, struggling with a fearful energy to extricate himself from the crushing weight. As the waters rose, this movement increased; the mass of timber extended in all directions, appearing to become more and more entangled each moment; the logs bounced against each other, thrusting aside, demersing, or raising into the air those with which they came in contact; it seemed as if they were waging a war of destruction, such as ancient authors describe the efforts of the Titans, the foamings of whose wrath might to the eye of the painter have been represented by the angry curlings of the waters, while the tremulous and rapid motions of the logs, which at times reared themselves almost perpendicularly, might by the poet have been taken for the shakings of the confounded and discomfited giants.

Now the rushing element filled up the gorge to its brim. The logs, once under way, rolled, reared, tossed, and tumbled amid the foam, as they were carried along. Many of the smaller trees broke across, from others great splinters were sent up, and all were in some degree seamed and scarred. Then in tumultuous majesty swept along the mingled wreck, the current being now increased to such a pitch that the logs, as they were dashed against the rocky shores, resounded like the report of distant artillery, or the angry rumblings of the thunder. Onward it rolls, the emblem of wreck and ruin, destruction and chaotic strife. It seemed to me as if I witnessed the rout of a vast army, surprised, overwhelmed, and overthrown. The roar of the cannon, the groans of the dying, and the shouts of the avengers were thundering through my brain, and amid the frightful confusion of the scene, there came over my spirit a melancholy feeling, which had not entirely vanished at the end of many days.

In a few hours almost all the timber that had lain heaped in the rocky gorge, was floating in the great pond of the millers; and as we walked homeward we talked of the *Force of the Waters.*

JOURNEY IN NEW BRUNSWICK AND MAINE

THE morning after that which we had spent with Sir Archibald Campbell and his delightful family, saw us proceeding along the shores of the St. John River, in the British Province of New Brunswick. As we passed the Government House, our hearts bade its generous inmates adieu; and as we left Fredericton behind, the recollection of the many acts of kindness which we had received from its inhabitants came powerfully on our minds. Slowly advancing over the surface of the translucent stream, we still fancied our ears saluted by the melodies of the unrivalled band of the 43d Regiment. In short, with the remembrance of kindness experienced, the feeling of expectations gratified, the hope of adding to our knowledge, and the possession of health and vigor, we were luxuriating in happiness.

The "Favorite," the bark in which we were, contained not only my whole family, but nearly a score and a half of individuals of all descriptions, so that the crowded state of the cabin soon began to prove rather disagreeable. The boat itself was a mere scow, commanded by a person of rather uncouth aspect and rude manners. Two sorry nags he had fastened to the end of a long tow-line, on the nearer of which rode a negro youth, less than half clad, with a long switch in one hand, and the joined bridles in the other, striving with all his might to urge them on at the rate of something more than two miles an hour. How fortunate it is for one to possess a little of the knowledge of a true traveller! Following the advice of a good and somewhat aged one, we had provided ourselves with a large basket, which was not altogether empty when we reached the end of our aquatic excursion. Here and there the shores of the river were delightful, the space between them and the undulating hills that bounded the prospect being highly cultivated, while now and then the abrupt and rocky banks assumed a most picturesque appearance. Although it was late in September, the mowers were still engaged in cutting the grass, and the gardens of the farmers showed patches of green peas. The apples were still green, and the vegetation in general reminded us that we were in a northern latitude.

Gradually and slowly we proceeded, until in the afternoon we landed to exchange our jaded horses. We saw a house on an eminence, with groups of people assembled round it, but there no dinner could be obtained, because, as the landlord told us, an election was going on. So the basket was had recourse to, and on the greensward we refreshed ourselves with its contents. This done, we returned to the scow, and resumed our stations. As usual in such cases, in every part of the world that I have visited, our second set of horses was worse than the first. However, on we went; to tell you how often the tow-line gave way would not be more amusing to you than it was annoying to us. Once our commander was in consequence plunged into the stream, but after some exertion he succeeded in regaining his gallant bark, when he consoled himself by giving utterance to a volley of blasphemies, which it would as ill become me to repeat, as it would be disagreeable to you to hear. We slept somewhere that night; it does not suit my views of travelling to tell you where.

Before day returned to smile on the "Favorite" we

proceeded. Some rapids we came to, when every one, glad to assist her, leaped on shore, and tugged *à la cordelle.* Some miles farther we passed a curious cataract, formed by the waters of the Pokioke. There Sambo led his steeds up the sides of a high bank, when, lo! the whole party came tumbling down, like so many hogsheads of tobacco rolled from a store-house to the banks of the Ohio. He at the steering oar hoped "the black rascal" had broken his neck, and congratulated himself in the same breath for the safety of the horses, which presently got on their feet. Sambo, however, alert as an Indian chief, leaped on the naked back of one, and showing his teeth, laughed at his master's curses. Shortly after this we found our boat very snugly secured on the top of a rock, midway in the stream, just opposite the mouth of Eel River.

Next day at noon, none injured, but all chop-fallen, we were landed at Woodstock village, yet in its infancy. After dining there we procured a cart, and an excellent driver, and proceeded along an execrable road to Houlton in Maine, glad enough, after all our mishaps, at finding ourselves in our own country. But before I bid farewell to the beautiful river of St. John, I must tell you that its navigation seldom exceeds eight months each year, the passage during the rest being performed on the ice, of which we were told that last season there was an unusual quantity, so much, indeed, as to accumulate, by being jammed at particular spots, to the height of nearly fifty feet above the ordinary level of the river, and that when it broke loose in spring, the crash was awful. All the low grounds along the river were suddenly flooded, and even the elevated plain on which Fredericton stands was covered to the depth of four feet. Fortunately, however, as on the greater streams of the Western and Southern Districts, such an occurrence seldom takes place.

Major Clarke, commander of the United States garrison, received us with remarkable kindness. The next day was spent in a long though fruitless ornithological excursion, for although we were accompanied by officers and men from the garrison, not a bird did any of our party procure that was of any use to us. We remained a few days, however, after which, hiring a cart, two horses, and a driver, we proceeded in the direction of Bangor.

Houlton is a neat village, consisting of some fifty houses. The fort is well situated, and commands a fine view of Mars' Hill, which is about thirteen miles distant. A custom-house has been erected here, the place being on the boundary line of the United States and the British Provinces. The road which was cut by the soldiers of this garrison, from Bangor to Houlton, through the forests, is at this moment a fine turnpike, of great breadth, almost straight in its whole length, and perhaps the best now in the Union. It was incomplete, however, for some miles, so that our travelling over that portion was slow and disagreeable. The rain, which fell in torrents, reduced the newly raised earth to a complete bed of mud, and at one time our horses became so completely mired that, had we not been extricated by two oxen, we must have spent the night near the spot. Jogging along at a very slow pace, we were overtaken by a gay wagoner, who had excellent horses, two of which a little "siller" induced him to join to ours, and we were taken to a tavern, at the "Cross Roads," where we spent the night in comfort. While supper was preparing, I made inquiries respecting birds, quadrupeds, and fishes, and was pleased to hear that many of these animals abounded in the neighborhood. Deer, Bears, Trout, and Grouse were quite plentiful, as was the Great Gray Owl.

When we resumed our journey next morning Nature displayed all her loveliness, and Autumn with her mellow tints, her glowing fruits, and her rich fields of corn, smiled in placid beauty. Many of the fields had not yet been reaped, the fruits of the forests and orchards hung clustering around us, and as we came in view of the Penobscot River, our hearts thrilled with joy. Its broad transparent waters here spread out their unruffled surface, there danced along the rapids, while canoes filled with Indians glided swiftly in every direction, raising before them the timorous waterfowl that had already flocked in from the north. Mountains, which you well know are indispensable in a beautiful landscape, reared their majestic crests in the distance. The Canada Jay leaped gaily from branch to twig; the Kingfisher, as if vexed at being suddenly surprised, rattled loudly as it swiftly flew off; and the Fish Hawk and Eagle spread their broad wings over the waters. All around was beautiful, and we gazed on the scene with delight, as seated on a verdant bank, we refreshed our frames from our replenished stores. A few rare birds were procured here, and the rest of the road being level and firm, we trotted on at a good pace for several hours, the Penobscot keeping company with us.

Now we came to a deep creek, of which the bridge was undergoing repairs, and the people saw our vehicle approach with much surprise. They, however, assisted us with pleasure, by placing a few logs across, along which our horses one after the other were carefully led, and the cart afterwards carried. These good fellows were so averse to our recompensing them for their labor that after some altercation we were obliged absolutely to force what we deemed a suitable reward upon them.

Next day we continued our journey along the Penobscot, the country changing its aspect at every mile, and when we first descried Old Town, that village of sawmills looked like an island covered with manufactories. The people here are noted for their industry and perseverance, and any one possessing a mill, and attending to his saws, and the floating of the timber into his dams, is sure to obtain a competency in a few years. Speculations in land covered with pine, lying to the north of this place, are carried on to a great extent, and to discover a good tract of such ground many a miller of Old Town undertakes long journeys. Reader, with your leave, I will here introduce one of them.

Good luck brought us into acquaintance with Mr. Gillies, whom we happened to meet in the course of our travels, as he was returning from an exploring tour. About the first of August he formed a party of sixteen persons, each carrying a knapsack and an axe. Their provisions consisted of two hundred and fifty pounds of pilot bread, one hundred and fifty of salt pork, four of tea, two large loaves of sugar, and some salt. They embarked in light canoes twelve miles north of Bangor, and followed the Penobscot as far as Wassataquoik River, a branch leading to the northwest, until they reached the Seboois Lakes, the principal of which lie in a line, with short portages between them. Still proceeding northwest they navigated these lakes, and then turning west, carried their canoes to the great lake Baamchenunsgamook; thence north to Wallaghasquegantook Lake, then along a small stream to the upper Umsaskiss Pond, when they reached the Albagash River which leads into the St. John in about latitude 47°. Many portions of that country had not been visited before even by the Indians, who assured Mr. Gillies of this fact. They continued their travels down the St. John to the Grand Falls, where they met with a portage of half a mile, and having reached Meduxmekeag Creek, a little above Woodstock, the party walked to Houlton, having travelled twelve hundred miles, and described almost an oval over the country by the time they returned to Old Town, on the Penobscot.

While anxiously looking for "lumber-lands," they ascended the eminences around, then climbed the tallest trees, and by means of a good telescope, inspected the

pine woods in the distance. And such excellent judges
are these persons of the value of the timber which they
thus observe, when it is situated at a convenient distance
from water, that they never afterwards forget the different spots at all worthy of their attention. They had
observed only a few birds and quadrupeds, the latter
principally Porcupines. The borders of the lakes and
rivers afforded them fruits of various sorts, and abundance
of cranberries, while the uplands yielded plenty of wild
white onions, and a species of black plum. Some of the
party continued their journey in canoes down the St.
John, ascended Eel River, and the lake of the same
name to Matanemheag River, due southwest of the St.
John, and after a few portages fell into the Penobscot.

I had made arrangements to accompany Mr. Gillies on
a journey of this kind, when I judged it would be more
interesting as well as useful to me to visit the distant
country of Labrador.

The road which we followed from Old Town to Bangor
was literally covered with Penobscot Indians returning
from market. On reaching the latter beautiful town, we
found very comfortable lodging in an excellent hotel, and
next day we proceeded by the mail to Boston.

A MOOSE HUNT

In the spring of 1833 the Moose were remarkably abundant in the neighborhood of the Schoodiac Lakes; and,
as the snow was so deep in the woods as to render it
almost impossible for them to escape, many of them were
caught. About the 1st of March, 1833, three of us set
off on a hunt, provided with snow-shoes, guns, hatchets,
and provisions for a fortnight. On the first day we went
fifty miles, in a sledge drawn by one horse, to the nearest

lake, where we stopped for the night, in the hut of an Indian named Lewis, of the Passamaquoddy tribe, who had abandoned the wandering life of his race, and turned his attention to farming and lumbering. Here we saw the operation of making snow-shoes, which requires more skill than one might imagine. The men generally make the bows to suit themselves, and the women weave in the threads, which are usually made of the skin of the Caribou Deer.

The next day we went on foot sixty-two miles farther, when a heavy rain-storm coming on, we were detained a whole day. The next morning we put on snow-shoes, and proceeded about thirteen miles, to the head of the Musquash Lake, where we found a camp, which had been erected by some lumberers in the winter; and here we established our headquarters. In the afternoon an Indian had driven a female Moose-deer, and two young ones of the preceding year, within a quarter of a mile of our camp, when he was obliged to shoot the old one. We undertook to procure the young alive, and after much exertion succeeded in getting one of them, and shut it up in the shed made for the oxen; but as the night was falling, we were compelled to leave the other in the woods. The dogs having killed two fine Deer that day, we feasted upon some of their flesh, and upon Moose, which certainly seemed to us the most savory meat we had ever eaten, although a keen appetite is very apt to warp one's judgment in such a case. After supper we laid ourselves down before the huge fire we had built up, and were soon satisfied that we had at last discovered the most comfortable mode of sleeping.

In the morning we started off on the track of a Moose, which had been driven from its haunt, or yard, by the Indians the day before; and although the snow was in general five feet deep, and in some places much deeper, we travelled three miles before we came to the spot where the Moose had rested for the night. He had not left this place more than an hour, when we came to it. So we pushed on faster than before, trusting that ere long we should overtake him. We had proceeded about a mile and a half farther, when he took a sudden turn, which threw us off his track, and when we again found it, we saw that an Indian had taken it up, and gone in pursuit of the harassed animal. In a short time we heard the report of a gun, and immediately running up, we saw the Moose, standing in a thicket, wounded, when we brought him down. The animal finding himself too closely pursued, had turned upon the Indian, who fired, and instantly ran into the bushes to conceal himself. It was three years old, and consequently not nearly grown, although already about six feet and a half in height.

It is difficult to conceive how an animal could have gone at such a rate when the snow was so deep, with a thick crust at top. In one place, he had followed the course of a brook, over which the snow had sunk considerably on account of the higher temperature of the water, and we had an opportunity of seeing evidence of the great power which the species possess in leaping over objects that obstruct his way. There were places in which the snow had drifted to so great a height that you would have imagined it impossible for any animal to leap over it, and yet we found that he had done so at a single bound, without leaving the least trace. As I did not measure these snow-heaps, I cannot positively say how high they were, but I am well persuaded that some of them were ten feet.

We proceeded to skin and dress the Moose, and buried the flesh under the snow, where it will keep for weeks. On opening the animal we were surprised to see the great size of the heart and lungs, compared with the contents of the abdomen. The heart was certainly larger than that of any animal which I had seen. The head bears a great resemblance to that of a horse, but the "muffle" is more than twice as large, and when the animal is irritated or frightened, it projects that part much farther than usual. It is stated in some descriptions of the Moose that he is short-winded and tender-footed, but he certainly is capable of long continued and very great exertion, and his feet, for anything that I have seen to the contrary, are as hard as those of any other quadruped. The young Moose was so exhausted and fretted that it offered no opposition to us as we led it to the camp; but in the middle of the night we were awakened by a great noise in the hovel, and found that as it had in some measure recovered from its terror and state of exhaustion, it began to think of getting home, and was now much enraged at finding itself so securely imprisoned. We were unable to do anything with it, for if we merely approached our hands to the openings of the hut, it would spring at us with the greatest fury, roaring and erecting its mane, in a manner that convinced us of the futility of all attempts to save it alive. We threw to it the skin of a Deer, which it tore to pieces in a moment. This individual was a yearling, and about six feet high. When we went to look for the other, which we had left in the woods, we found that he had "taken his back-track" or retraced his steps, and gone to the "beat," about a mile and a half distant, and which it may be interesting to describe.

At the approach of winter, parties of Moose-deer, from two to fifty in number, begin to lessen their range, and proceed slowly to the south side of some hill, where they feed within still narrower limits, as the snow begins to fall. When it accumulates on the ground, the snow, for a considerable space, is divided into well trodden, irregular paths, in which they keep, and browse upon the bushes at the sides, occasionally striking out a new path, so that, by the spring, many of those made at the beginning of winter are obliterated. A "yard" for half a dozen Moose, would probably contain about twenty acres.

A good hunter, although still a great way off, will not only perceive that there is a yard in the vicinity, but can tell the direction in which it lies, and even be pretty sure of the distance. It is by the marks on the trees that he discovers this circumstance; he finds the young maple, and especially the moose-wood and birch, with the bark gnawed off to the height of five or six feet on one side, and the twigs bitten, with the impression of the teeth left in such a manner, that the position of the animal when browsing on them, may be ascertained. Following the course indicated by these marks, the hunter gradually finds them more distinct and frequent, until at length he arrives at the yard; but there he finds no Moose, for long before he reaches the place, their extremely acute smell and hearing warn them of his approach, when they leave the yard, generally altogether, the strongest leading in one track, or in two or three parties. When pursued they usually separate, except the females, which keep with their young, and go before to break the track for them; nor will they leave them under any circumstances until brought down by their ruthless pursuers. The males, especially the old ones, being quite lean at this season, go off at great speed, and unless the snow is extremely deep, soon outstrip the hunters. They usually go in the direction of the wind, making many short turns to keep the scent, or to avoid some bad passage; and although they may sink to the bottom at every step, they cannot be overtaken in less than three or four days. The females, on the contrary, are remarkably fat, and it is not at all unfrequent to find in one of them a hundred pounds of raw tallow. But let us return to the young buck, which had regained the yard.

We found him still more untractable than the female we had left in the hovel; he had trodden down the snow for a small space around him, which he refused to leave, and would spring with great fury at any one who approached the spot too near; and as turning on snow-shoes is not an easy operation, we were content to let him alone, and try to find one in a better situation for capture, knowing that if we did eventually secure him, he would probably, in the struggle injure himself too much to live. I have good reason to believe that the only practicable mode of taking them uninjured, except when they are very young, is, when they are exhausted and completely defenceless, to bind them securely, and keep them so till they have become pacified, and convinced of the uselessness of any attempt at resistance. If allowed to exert themselves as they please, they almost always kill themselves, as we found by experience.

On the following day we again set out, and coming across the tracks of two young bucks, which had been started by the Indians, we pursued them, and in two or three miles, overtook them. As it was desirable to obtain them as near the camp as possible, we attempted to steer them that way. For a while we succeeded very well in our scheme, but at last one of them, after making many ineffectual attempts to get another way, turned upon his pursuer, who, finding himself not very safe, felt obliged to shoot him. His companion, who was a little more tractable, we drove on a short way, but as he had contrived to take many turnings, he could approach us on his back-track too swiftly, so that we were compelled to shoot him also. We "dressed" them, taking with us the tongues and muffles, which are considered the most delicate parts.

We had not walked more than a quarter of a mile, when we perceived some of the indications before mentioned, which we followed for half a mile, when we came across a yard, and going round it, we found where the Moose had left it, though we afterwards learned that we had missed a fine buck, which the dogs, however, discovered later. We soon overtook a female with a young one, and were not long in sight of them when they stood at bay. It is really wonderful how soon they beat down a hard space in the snow to stand upon, when it is impossible for a dog to touch them, as they stamp so violently with their fore-feet that it is certain death to approach them. This Moose had only one calf with her, though the usual number is two, almost invariably a male and a female. We shot them with a ball through the brain.

The Moose bears a considerable resemblance to the horse in his conformation, and in his disposition a still greater, having much of the sagacity as well as viciousness of that animal. We had an opportunity of observing the wonderful acuteness of its hearing and smelling. As we were standing by one, he suddenly erected his ears, and put himself on the alert, evidently aware of the approach of some person. About ten minutes after, one of our party came up, who must have been at the time at least half a mile off, and the wind was from the Moose towards him.

This species of Deer feeds on the hemlock, cedar, fir, or pine, but will not touch the spruce. It also eats the twigs of the maple, birch, and soft shoots of other trees. In the autumn they may be enticed by imitating their peculiar cry, which is described as truly frightful. The hunter gets up into a tree, or conceals himself in some other secure place, and imitates this cry by means of a piece of birch-bark rolled up to give the proper tone. Presently he hears the Moose come dashing along, and when he gets near enough, takes a good aim, and soon despatches him. It is very unsafe to stand within reach of the animal, for he would certainly endeavor to demolish you.

A full-grown male Moose is said to measure nine feet in height, and with his immense branching antlers presents a truly formidable appearance. Like the Virginia Deer, and the male Caribou, they shed their horns every year about the beginning of December. The first year their horns are not dropped in spring. When irritated the Moose makes a great grinding with his teeth, erects his mane, lays back his ears, and stamps with violence. When disturbed he makes a hideous whining noise, much in the manner of the Camel.

In that wild and secluded part of the country, seldom visited but by the Indians, the common Deer were without number, and it was with great difficulty that we kept the dogs with us, as they were continually meeting with "beats." In its habits that species greatly resembles the Moose. The Caribou has a very broad, flat foot, and can spread it on the snow to the fetlock, so as to be able to run on a crust scarcely hard enough to bear a dog. When the snow is soft, they keep in immense droves around the margins of the large lakes to which they betake themselves when pursued, the crust being much harder there than elsewhere. When it becomes more firm, they strike into the woods. As they possess such facility of running on snow, they do not require to make any yards, and consequently have no fixed place in the winter. The speed of this animal is not well known, but I am inclined to believe it much greater than that of the fleetest horse.

In our camp we saw great numbers of Crossbills, Grosbeaks, and various other small birds. Of the first of these were two species which were very tame, and alighted on our hut with the greatest familiarity. We caught five or six at once, under a snow-shoe. The Pine-Martin and Wild Cat were also very abundant.[1]

---

[1] The "Moose Hunt" was communicated to me by my young friend, Thomas Lincoln, of Dennysville in Maine.

LABRADOR

WHEN I look back upon the many pleasant hours that I spent with the young gentlemen who composed my party, during our excursions along the coast of sterile and stormy Labrador, I think that a brief account of our employments may prove not altogether uninteresting to my readers.

We had purchased our stores at Boston, with the aid of my generous friend, Dr. Parkman of that city; but unfortunately many things necessary on an expedition like ours were omitted. At Eastport in Maine we therefore laid in these requisites. No traveller, let me say, ought to neglect anything that is calculated to insure the success of his undertaking, or to contribute to his personal comfort, when about to set out on a long and perhaps hazardous voyage. Very few opportunities of replenishing stores of provisions, clothing, or ammunition, occur in such a country as Labrador; and yet, we all placed too much confidence in the zeal and foresight of our purveyors at Eastport. We had abundance of ammunition, excellent bread, meat, and potatoes; but the butter was quite rancid, the oil only fit to grease our guns, the vinegar too liberally diluted with cider, the mustard and pepper deficient in due pungency. All this, however, was not discovered until it was too late to be remedied. Several of the young men were not clothed as hunters should be, and some of the guns were not so good as we could have wished. We were, however, fortunate with respect to our vessel, which was a notable sailer, did not leak, had a good crew, and was directed by a capital seaman.

The hold of the schooner was floored, and an entrance made to it from the cabin, so that in it we had a very good parlor, dining-room, drawing-room, library, etc., all those apartments, however, being comprised in one. An extravagantly elongated deal table ranged along the centre; one of the party had slung his hammock at one end, and in its vicinity slept the cook and a lad who acted as armorer. The cabin was small; but being fitted in the usual manner with side berths, was used for a dormitory. It contained a small table and a stove, the latter of diminutive size, but smoky enough to discomfit a host. We had adopted in a great measure the clothing worn by the American fishermen on that coast, namely, thick blue cloth trousers, a comfortable waistcoat, and a pea-jacket of blanket. Our boots were large, round-toed, strong, and well studded with large nails to prevent sliding on the rocks. Worsted comforters, thick mittens, and round broad-brimmed hats, completed our dress, which was more picturesque than fashionable. As soon as we had an opportunity, the boots were exchanged for Esquimaux mounted moccasins of Seal-skin, impermeable to water, light, easy, and fastening at top about the middle of the thigh to straps, which when buckled over the hips secured them well. To complete our equipment, we had several good boats, one of which was extremely light and adapted for shallow water.

No sooner had we reached the coast and got into harbor, than we agreed to follow certain regulations intended for the general benefit. Every morning the cook was called before three o'clock. At half-past three, breakfast was on the table, and everybody equipped. The guns, ammunition, botanical boxes, and baskets for eggs or minerals were all in readiness. Our breakfast consisted of coffee, bread, and various other materials. At four, all except the cook, and one seaman, went off in different directions, not forgetting to carry with them a store of cooked provisions. Some betook themselves to the islands, others to the deep bays; the latter on landing wandered over the country till noon, when laying themselves down on the rich moss, or sitting on the granite rock, they would rest for an hour, eat their dinner, and talk of their successes or disappointments. I often regret that I did not take sketches of the curious groups formed by my young friends on such occasions, and when, after returning at night, all were engaged in measuring, weighing, comparing, and dissecting the birds we had procured; operations which were carried on with the aid of a number of candles thrust into the necks of bottles. Here one examined the flowers and leaves of a plant, there another explored the recesses of a Diver's gullet, while a third skinned a Gull or a Grouse. Nor was one journal forgotten. Arrangements were made for the morrow, and at twelve we left matters to the management of the cook, and retired to our roosts.

If the wind blew hard, all went on shore, and, excepting on a few remarkably rainy days, we continued our pursuits, much in the same manner during our stay in the country. The physical powers of the young men were considered in making our arrangements. Shattuck and Ingalls went together; the captain and Coolidge were fond of each other, the latter having also been an officer; Lincoln and my son being the strongest and most determined hunters, generally marched by themselves; and I went with one or other of the parties, according to circumstances, although it was by no means my custom to do so regularly, as I had abundance of work on hand in the vessel.

The return of my young companions and the sailors was always looked for with anxiety. On getting on board, they opened their budgets, and laid their contents on the deck, amid much merriment, those who had procured most specimens being laughed at by those who had obtained the rarest, and the former joking the latter in return. A substantial meal always awaited them, and fortunate we were in having a capital cook, although he was a little too fond of the bottle.

Our "Fourth of July" was kept sacred, and every Saturday night the toast of "wives and sweethearts" was the first given, "parents and friends" the last. Never was there a more merry set. Some with the violin and flute accompanied the voices of the rest, and few moments were spent in idleness. Before a month had elapsed, the spoils of many a fine bird hung around the hold; shrubs and flowers were in the press, and I had several drawings finished, some of which you have seen, and of which I hope you will ere long see the remainder. Large jars were filling apace with the bodies of rare birds, fishes, quadrupeds and reptiles, as well as molluscous animals. We had several pets too, Gulls, Cormorants, Guillemots, Puffins, Hawks, and a Raven. In some of the harbors, curious fishes were hooked in our sight, so clear was the water.

We found that camping out at night was extremely uncomfortable, on account of the annoyance caused by flies and mosquitoes, which attacked the hunters in swarms at all times, but more especially when they lay down, unless they enveloped themselves in thick smoke, which is not much more pleasant. Once when camping the weather became very bad, and the party was twenty miles distant from Whapatigan as night threw her mantle over the earth. The rain fell in torrents, the northeast wind blew furiously, and the air was extremely cold. The oars of the boats were fixed so as to support some blankets, and a small fire was with difficulty kindled, on the embers of which a scanty meal was cooked. How different from a camp on the shores of the Mississippi, where wood is abundant, and the air generally not lacking heat, where mosquitoes, although plentiful enough, are not accompanied by Caribou flies, and where the barkings of a joyful Squirrel, or the notes of the Barred Owl, that grave buffoon of our western woods, never fail to gladden the camper as he cuts to the right and left such branches and

canes as most easily supply materials for forming a lodging for the night. On the coast of Labrador there are no
such things; granite and green moss are spread around,
silence like that of the grave envelops all, and when
night has closed the dreary scene from your sight, the
Wolves, attracted by the scent of the remains of your
scanty repast, gather around you. Cowards as they are
they dare not venture on a charge; but their howlings
effectually banish sleep. You must almost roast your
feet to keep them warm, while your head and shoulders
are chilled by the blast. When morning comes, she
smiles not on you with rosy cheeks, but appears muffled
in a gray mantle of cold mist, which shows you that there
is no prospect of a fine day. The object of the expedition, which was to procure some Owls that had been
observed there by day, was entirely frustrated. At early
dawn the party rose stiffened and dispirited, and glad
were they to betake themselves to their boats, and return
to their floating home.

Before we left Labrador, several of my young friends
began to feel the want of suitable clothing. The sailor's
ever-tailoring system, was, believe me, fairly put to the
test. Patches of various colors ornamented knees and
elbows; our boots were worn out; our greasy garments
and battered hats were in harmony with our tanned and
weather-beaten faces; and, had you met with us, you
might have taken us for a squad of wretched vagrants;
but we were joyous in the expectation of a speedy return, and exulted at the thoughts of our success.

As the chill blast that precedes the winter's tempest
thickened the fogs on the hills and ruffled the dark waters,
each successive day saw us more anxious to leave the
dreary wilderness of grim rocks and desolate moss-clad
valleys. Unfavorable winds prevented us for a while
from spreading our white sails; but at last one fair morning smiled on the wintry world, the "Ripley" was towed

from the harbor, her tackle trimmed, and as we bounded over the billows, we turned our eyes towards the wilds of Labrador, and heartily bade them farewell forever!

THE EGGERS OF LABRADOR

The distinctive appellation of "eggers" is given to certain persons who follow, principally or exclusively, the avocation of procuring the eggs of wild birds, with the view of disposing of them at some distant port. Their great object is to plunder every nest, wherever they can find it, no matter where, and at whatever risk. They are the pest of the feathered tribes, and their brutal propensity to destroy the poor creatures after they have robbed them, is abundantly gratified whenever an opportunity presents itself.

Much had been said to me respecting these destructive pirates before I visited the coast of Labrador, but I could not entirely credit all their cruelties until I had actually witnessed their proceedings, which were such as to inspire no small degree of horror. But you shall judge for yourself.

See yon shallop, shyly sailing along; she sneaks like a thief wishing, as it were, to shun the very light of heaven. Under the lee of every rocky isle some one at the tiller steers her course. Were his trade an honest one, he would not think of hiding his back behind the terrific rocks that seem to have been placed there as a resort to the myriads of birds that annually visit this desolate region of the earth, for the purpose of rearing their young at a distance from all disturbers of their peace. How unlike the open, the bold, the honest mariner, whose face needs no mask, who scorns to skulk under any circumstances. The vessel herself is a shabby

AUDUBON, 1850.

FROM A DAGUERREOTYPE. OWNED BY MRS. ELIZABETH BERTHOUD GRIMSHAW.

thing; her sails are patched with stolen pieces of better canvas, the owners of which have probably been stranded on some inhospitable coast, and have been plundered, perhaps murdered, by the wretches before us. Look at her again! Her sides are neither painted, nor even pitched; no, they are daubed over, plastered and patched with strips of Seal-skins laid along the seams. Her deck has never been washed or sanded; her hold — for no cabin has she — though at present empty, sends forth an odor pestilential as that of a charnel house. The crew, eight in number, lie sleeping at the foot of their tottering mast, regardless of the repairs needed in every part of her rigging. But see! she scuds along, and as I suspect her crew to be bent on the commission of some evil deed, let us follow her to the first harbor.

There rides the filthy thing! The afternoon is half over. Her crew have thrown their boat overboard, they enter and seat themselves, each with a rusty gun. One of them sculls the skiff towards an island for a century past the breeding-place of myriads of Guillemots, which are now to be laid under contribution. At the approach of the vile thieves, clouds of birds rise from the rock and fill the air around, wheeling and screaming over their enemies. Yet thousands remain in an erect posture, each covering its single egg, the hope of both parents. The reports of several muskets loaded with heavy shot are now heard, while several dead and wounded birds fall heavily on the rock, or into the water. Instantly all the sitting birds rise and fly off affrighted to their companions above, and hover in dismay over their assassins, who walk forward exultingly, and with their shouts mingling oaths and execrations. Look at them! See how they crush the chick within its shell, how they trample on every egg in their way with their huge and clumsy boots. Onward they go, and when they leave the isle, not an egg that they can find is left entire. The dead birds they

collect and carry to their boat. Now they have regained
their filthy shallop; they strip the birds by a single jerk,
of their feathery apparel while the flesh is yet warm, and
throw them on some coals, where in a short time they are
broiled. The rum is produced when the Guillemots are
fit for eating, and after stuffing themselves with this oily
fare, and enjoying the pleasure of beastly intoxication,
over they tumble on the deck of their crazed craft, where
they pass the short hours of night in turbid slumber.

The sun now rises above the snow-clad summit of the
eastern mount. "Sweet is the breath of morn," even in
this desolate land. The gay Bunting erects his white
crest, and gives utterance to the joy he feels in the presence of his brooding mate. The Willow Grouse on the
rock crows his challenge aloud. Each floweret chilled by
the night air expands its pure petals. The gentle breeze
shakes from the blades of grass the heavy dew-drops. On
the Guillemot isle the birds have again settled, and now
renew their loves. Startled by the light of day, one of
the eggers springs to his feet and rouses his companions,
who stare around them for a while, endeavoring to collect
their senses. Mark them, as with clumsy fingers they
clear their drowsy eyes! Slowly they rise on their feet.
See how the filthy lubbers stretch out their arms, and
yawn; you shrink back, for verily "that throat might
frighten a shark."

But the master soon recollecting that so many eggs are
worth a dollar or a crown, casts his eye towards the rock,
marks the day in his memory and gives orders to depart.
The light breeze enables them to reach another harbor a
few miles distant, one which, like the last, lies concealed
from the ocean by some other rocky isle. Arrived there,
they re-act the scene of yesterday, crushing every egg
they can find. For a week each night is passed in drunk-
enness and brawls, until, having reached the last breeding-place on the coast, they return, touch at every isle in

succession, shoot as many birds as they need, collect the fresh eggs, and lay in a cargo. At every step each ruffian picks up an egg so beautiful that any man with a feeling heart would pause to consider the motive which could induce him to carry it off. But nothing of this sort occurs to the egger, who gathers and gathers until he has swept the rock bare. The dollars alone chink in his sordid mind, and he assiduously plies the trade which no man would ply who had the talents and industry to procure subsistence by honorable means.

With a bark nearly half filled with fresh eggs they proceed to the principal rock, that on which they first landed. But what is their surprise when they find others there helping themselves as industriously as they can! In boiling rage they charge their guns and ply their oars. Landing on the rock they run up to the eggers, who, like themselves, are desperadoes. The first question is a discharge of musketry, the answer another. Now, man to man, they fight like tigers. One is carried to his boat with a fractured skull, another limps with a shot in his leg, and a third feels how many of his teeth have been driven through the hole in his cheek. At last, however, the quarrel is settled; the booty is to be equally divided; and now see them all drinking together. Oaths and curses and filthy jokes are all that you hear; but see, stuffed with food, and reeling with drink, down they drop one by one; groans and execrations from the wounded mingle with the snoring of the heavy sleepers. There let the brutes lie.

Again it is dawn, but no one stirs. The sun is high; one by one they open their heavy eyes, stretch their limbs, yawn, and raise themselves from the deck. But see, here comes a goodly company. A hundred honest fishermen, who for months past have fed on salt meat, have felt a desire to procure some eggs. Gallantly their boats advance, impelled by the regular pull of their long oars. Each buoyant bark displays the flag of its nation. No weapons do they bring, nor anything that can be used as such save their oars and their fists. Cleanly clad in Sunday attire, they arrive at the desired spot, and at once prepare to ascend the rock. The eggers, now numbering a dozen, all armed with guns and bludgeons, bid defiance to the fishermen. A few angry words pass between the parties. One of the eggers, still under the influence of drink, pulls his trigger, and an unfortunate sailor is seen to reel in agony. Three loud cheers fill the air. All at once rush on the malefactors; a horrid fight ensues, the result of which is that every egger is left on the rock beaten and bruised. Too frequently the fishermen man their boats, row to the shallops, and break every egg in the hold.

The eggers of Labrador not only rob the birds in this cruel manner, but also the fishermen, whenever they can find an opportunity; and the quarrels they excite are numberless. While we were on the coast, none of our party ever ventured on any of the islands which these wretches call their own, without being well provided with means of defence. On one occasion, when I was present, we found two eggers at their work of destruction. I spoke to them respecting my visit, and offered them premiums for rare birds and some of their eggs; but although they made fair promises, not one of the gang ever came near the "Ripley."

These people gather all the eider-down they can find; yet so inconsiderate are they, that they kill every bird which comes in their way. The eggs of Gulls, Guillemots, and Ducks are searched for with care; and the Puffins and some other birds they massacre in vast numbers for the sake of their feathers. So constant and persevering are their depredations that these species, which, according to the accounts of the few settlers I saw in the country, were exceedingly abundant twenty years ago, have abandoned their ancient breeding places, and removed much farther north in search of peaceful security. Scarcely, in fact, could I procure a young Guillemot before the eggers left the coast, nor was it until late in July that I succeeded, after the birds had laid three or four eggs each, instead of one, and when, nature having been exhausted, and the season nearly spent, thousands of these birds left the country without having accomplished the purpose for which they had visited it. This war of extermination cannot last many years more. The eggers themselves will be the first to repent the entire disappearance of the myriads of birds that made the coast of Labrador their summer residence, and unless they follow the persecuted tribes to the northward, they must renounce their trade.

THE SQUATTERS OF LABRADOR

Go where you will, if a shilling can there be procured, you may expect to meet with individuals in search of it.

In the course of last summer, I met with several persons, as well as families, whom I could not compare to anything else than what in America we understand by the appellation of "squatters." The methods they employed to accumulate property form the subject of the observations which I now lay before you.

Our schooner lay at anchor in a beautiful basin on the coast of Labrador, surrounded by uncouth granitic rocks, partially covered with stunted vegetation. While searching for birds and other objects I chanced one morning to direct my eye towards the pinnacle of a small island, separated from the mainland by a very narrow channel, and presently commenced inspecting it with my telescope. There I saw a man on his knees with clasped hands, and face inclined heavenwards. Before him was a small monument of unhewn stones, supporting a wooden cross. In a word, reader, the person whom I thus unexpectedly discovered was engaged in prayer. Such an incident in that desolate land was affecting, for there one seldom finds traces of human beings; and the aid of the Almighty, although necessary everywhere, seems there peculiarly required to enable them to procure the means of subsistence. My curiosity having been raised, I betook myself to my boat, landed on the rock, and scrambled to the place, where I found the man still on his knees. When his devotions were concluded, he bowed to me, and addressed me in very indifferent French. I asked him why he had chosen so dreary a spot for his prayers. "Because," answered he, "the sea lies before me, and from it I receive my spring and summer sustenance. When winter approaches, I pray fronting the mountains on the main, as at that period the Caribous come towards the shore, and I kill them, feed on their flesh, and form my bedding of their skins." I thought the answer reasonable, and as I longed to know more of him, followed him to his hut. It was low, and very small, formed of stones plastered with mud to a considerable thickness. The roof was composed of a sort of thatching made of weeds and moss. A large Dutch stove filled nearly one half the place; a small port-hole then stuffed with old rags, served at times instead of a window; the bed was a pile of Deerskins; a bowl, a jug, and an iron pot were placed on a rude shelf; three old and rusty muskets, their locks fastened by thongs, stood in a corner; and his buckshot, powder, and flints, were tied up in bags of skin. Eight Esquimaux dogs yelled and leaped about us. The strong smell that emanated from them, together with the smoke and filth of the apartment, rendered my stay in it extremely disagreeable.

Being a native of France, the good man showed much politeness, and invited me to take some refreshment, when, without waiting for my assent, he took up his bowl, and went off I knew not whither. No sooner had he and his strange dogs disappeared than I went out also, to breathe the pure air, and gaze on the wild and majestic scenery around. I was struck with the extraordinary luxuriance of the plants and grasses that had sprung up on the scanty soil in the little valley which the squatter had chosen for his home. Their stalks and broad blades reached my waist. June had come, and the flies, mosquitoes, and other insects filled the air, and were as troublesome to me as if I had been in a Florida swamp.

The squatter returned, but he was chop-fallen; nay, I thought his visage had assumed a cadaverous hue. Tears ran down his cheeks, and he told me that his barrel of *rum* had been stolen by the "eggers" or some fishermen. He said that he had been in the habit of hiding it in the bushes, to prevent its being carried away by those merciless thieves, who must have watched him in some of his frequent walks to the spot. "Now," said he, "I can expect none till next spring, and God knows what will become of me in the winter."

Pierre Jean Baptiste Michaux had resided in that part of the world for upwards of ten years. He had run away from the fishing-smack that had brought him from his fair native land, and expected to become rich some day by the sale of the furs, Seal-skins, eider-down, and other articles, which he collected yearly, and sold to the traders who regularly visited his dreary abode. He was of moderate stature, firmly framed, and as active as a Wild Cat. He told me that excepting the loss of his rum, he had never experienced any other cause of sorrow, and that he felt as "happy as a lord."

Before parting with this fortunate mortal, I inquired how his dogs managed to find sufficient food. "Why, sir, during spring and summer they ramble along the shores, where they meet with abundance of dead fish, and in winter they eat the flesh of the Seals which I kill late in autumn, when these animals return from the north. As to myself, everything eatable is good, and when hard pushed, I relish the fare of my dogs, I assure you, as much as they do themselves."

Proceeding along the rugged indentations of the bay with my companions, I reached the settlement of another person, who, like the first, had come to Labrador with the view of making his fortune. We found him after many difficulties; but as our boats turned a long point jutting out into the bay, we were pleased to see several small schooners at anchor, and one lying near a sort of wharf. Several neat-looking houses enlivened the view, and on landing, we were kindly greeted with a polite welcome from a man who proved to be the owner of the establishment. For the rude simplicity of him of the rum-cask, we found here the manners and dress of a man of the world. A handsome fur cap covered his dark brow, his clothes were similar to our own, and his demeanor was that of a gentleman. On my giving my name to him, he shook me heartily by the hand, and on introducing each of my companions to him, he extended the like courtesy to them also. Then, to my astonishment, he addressed me as follows: "My dear sir, I have been expecting you these three weeks, having read *in the papers* your intention to visit Labrador; and some fishermen told me of your arrival at Little Natasquam. Gentlemen, walk in."

Having followed him to his neat and comfortable mansion, he introduced us to his wife and children. Of the latter there were six, all robust and rosy. The lady, although a native of the country, was of French extraction, handsome, and sufficiently accomplished to make an excellent companion to a gentleman. A smart girl brought us a luncheon, consisting of bread, cheese, and good port wine, to which, having rowed fourteen or fif-

teen miles that morning, we helped ourselves in a manner
that seemed satisfactory to all parties. Our host gave us
newspapers from different parts of the world, and showed
us his small, but choice collection of books. He inquired
after the health of the amiable Captain Bayfield of the
Royal Navy, and the officers under him, and hoped they
would give him a call.

Having refreshed ourselves, we walked out with him,
when he pointed to a very small garden, where a few vegetables sprouted out, anxious to see the sun. Gazing on
the desolate country around, I asked him how *he* had thus
secluded himself from the world. For it he had no relish,
and although he had received a liberal education, and had
mixed with society, he never intended to return to it.
"The country around," said he, "is all my own, much
farther than you can see. No fees, no lawyers, no taxes
are *here*. I do pretty much as I choose. My means are
ample through my own industry. These vessels come
here for Seal-skins, Seal-oil, and salmon, and give me in
return all the necessaries, and indeed comforts, of the life
I love to follow; and what else could *the world* afford
me?" I spoke of the education of his children. "My
wife and I teach them all that is *useful* for them to know,
and is not that enough? My girls will marry their countrymen, my sons the daughters of my neighbors, and I
hope all of them will live and die in the country!" I
said no more, but by way of compensation for the trouble
I had given him, purchased from his eldest child a beautiful Fox's skin.

Few birds, he said, came round him in summer, but in
winter thousands of Ptarmigans were killed, as well as
great numbers of Gulls. He had a great dislike to all
fishermen and eggers, and I really believe was always
glad to see the departure even of the hardy navigators
who annually visited him for the sake of his salmon, Seal-
skins, and oil. He had more than forty Esquimaux

dogs; and as I was caressing one of them he said, "Tell my brother-in-law at Bras d'Or, that we are all well here, and that, after visiting my wife's father, I will give him a call."

Now, reader, his wife's father resided at the distance of seventy miles down the coast, and, like himself, was a recluse. He of Bras d'Or, was at double that distance; but, when the snows of winter have thickly covered the country, the whole family, in sledges drawn by dogs, travel with ease, and pay their visits, or leave their cards. This good gentleman had already resided there more than twenty years. Should he ever read this article, I desire him to believe that I shall always be grateful to him and his wife for their hospitable welcome.

When our schooner, the "Ripley," arrived at Bras d'Or, I paid a visit to Mr. ——, the brother-in-law, who lived in a house imported from Quebec, which fronted the strait of Belle Isle, and overlooked a small island, over which the eye reached the coast of Newfoundland, whenever it was the wind's pleasure to drive away the fogs that usually lay over both coasts. The gentleman and his wife, we were told, were both out on a walk, but would return in a very short time, which they in fact did, when we followed them into the house, which was yet unfinished. The usual immense Dutch stove formed a principal feature of the interior. The lady had once visited the metropolis of Canada, and seemed desirous of acting the part of a blue-stocking. Understanding that I knew something of the fine arts, she pointed to several of the vile prints hung on the bare walls, which she said were *elegant* Italian pictures, and continued her encomiums upon them, assuring me that she had purchased them from an Italian, who had come there with a trunk full of them. She had paid a shilling sterling for each, frame included. I could give no answer to the good lady on this subject, but I felt glad to find that she possessed a feeling heart, for one of her children had caught a Siskin, and was tormenting the poor bird, when she rose from her seat, took the little fluttering thing from the boy, kissed it, and gently launched it into the air. This made me quite forget the tattle about the fine arts.

Some excellent milk was poured out for us in clean glasses. It was a pleasing sight, for not a cow had we yet seen in the country. The lady turned the conversation on music, and asked me if I played on any instrument. I answered that I did, but very indifferently. Her forte, she said, was music, of which she was indeed immoderately fond. Her instrument had been sent to Europe to be repaired, but would return that season, when the whole of her children would again perform many beautiful airs; for in fact anybody could use it with ease, as when she or the children felt fatigued, the servant played on it for them. Rather surprised at the extraordinary powers of this family of musicians, I asked what sort of an instrument it was, when she described it as follows: "Gentlemen, my instrument is large, longer than broad, and stands on four legs, like a table. At one end is a crooked handle, by turning which round, either fast or slow, I do assure you we make most excellent music." The lips of my young friends and companions instantly curled, but a glance from me as instantly recomposed their features. Telling the fair one that it must be a hand-organ she used, she laughingly said, "Ah, that is it; it is a hand-organ, but I had forgot the name, and for the life of me could not recollect it."

The husband had gone out to work, and was in the harbor calking an old schooner. He dined with me on board the "Ripley," and proved to be also an excellent fellow. Like his brother-in-law, he had seen much of the world, having sailed nearly round it; and, although no scholar like him, too, he was disgusted with it. He held his land on the same footing as his neighbors, caught

Seals without number, lived comfortably and happily, visited his father-in-law and the scholar, by the aid of his dogs, of which he kept a great pack, bartered or sold his commodities, as his relations did, and cared about nothing else in the world. Whenever the weather was fair, he walked with his dame over the moss-covered rocks of the neighborhood; and during winter killed Ptarmigans and Caribous, while his eldest son attended to the traps, and skinned the animals caught in them. He had the only horse that was to be found in that part of the country, as well as several cows; but, above all, he was kind to every one, and every one spoke well of him. The only disagreeable thing about his plantation or settlement, was a heap of fifteen hundred carcasses of skinned Seals, which, at the time when we visited the place, in the month of August, notwithstanding the coolness of the atmosphere, sent forth a stench that, according to the ideas of some naturalists, might have sufficed to attract all the Vultures in the United States.

During our stay at Bras d'Or, the kind-hearted and good Mrs. —— daily sent us fresh milk and butter, for which we were denied the pleasure of making any return.

COD FISHING

ALTHOUGH I had seen, as I thought, abundance of fish along the coasts of the Floridas, the numbers which I found in Labrador quite astonished me. Should your surprise while reading the following statements be as great as mine was while observing the facts related, you will conclude, as I have often done, that Nature's means of providing small animals for the use of larger ones, and *vice versa*, are as ample as is the grandeur of that world which she has so curiously constructed.

The coast of Labrador is visited by European as well as American fishermen, all of whom are, I believe, entitled to claim portions of fishing-ground assigned to each nation by mutual understanding. For the present, however, I shall confine my observations to those of our own country, who, after all, are probably the most numerous. The citizens of Boston, and many others of our eastern seaports, are those who chiefly engage in this department of our commerce. Eastport in Maine sends out every year a goodly fleet of schooners and " pickaxes " to Labrador, to procure Cod, Mackerel, Halibut, and sometimes Herring, the latter being caught in the intermediate space. The vessels from that port, and others in Maine and Massachusetts, sail as soon as the warmth of spring has freed the gulf of ice, that is, from the beginning of May to that of June.

A vessel of one hundred tons or so is provided with a crew of twelve men, who are equally expert as sailors and fishers, and for every couple of these hardy tars, a Hampton boat is provided, which is lashed on the deck, or hung in stays. Their provision is simple, but of good quality, and it is very seldom that any spirits are allowed, beef, pork and biscuit with water being all they take with them. The men are supplied with warm clothing, waterproof oiled jackets and trousers, large boots, broad-brimmed hats with a round crown, and stout mittens, with a few shirts. The owner or captain furnishes them with lines, hooks, and nets, and also provides the bait best adapted to insure success. The hold of the vessel is filled with casks, of various dimensions, some containing salt, and others for the oil that may be procured.

The bait generally used at the beginning of the season consists of mussels salted for the purpose; but as soon as the capelings reach the coast they are substituted to save expense, and in many instances the flesh of Gannets and other sea-fowl is employed. The wages of fishermen vary from sixteen to thirty dollars per month, according to the qualifications of the individual.

The labor of these men is excessively hard, for, unless on Sunday, their allowance of rest in the twenty-four hours seldom exceeds three. The cook is the only person who fares better in this respect, but he must also assist in curing the fish. He has breakfast, consisting of coffee, bread, and meat, ready for the captain and the whole crew, by three o'clock every morning, excepting Sunday. Each person carries with him his dinner ready cooked, which is commonly eaten on the fishing-grounds.

Thus, at three in the morning, the crew are prepared for their day's labor, and ready to betake themselves to their boats, each of which has two oars and lugsails. They all depart at once, and either by rowing or sailing, reach the banks to which the fishes are known to resort. The little squadron drop their anchors at short distances from each other, in a depth of from ten to twenty feet, and the business is immediately commenced. Each man has two lines, and each stands in one end of the boat, the middle of which is boarded off, to hold the fish. The baited lines have been dropped into the water, one on each side of the boat; their leads have reached the bottom, a fish has taken the hook, and after giving the line a slight jerk, the fisherman hauls up his prize with a continued pull, throws the fish athwart a small round bar of iron placed near his back, which forces open the mouth, while the weight of the body, however small the fish may be, tears out the hook. The bait is still good, and over the side the line again goes, to catch another fish, while that on the left is now drawn up, and the same course pursued. In this manner, a fisher busily plying at each end, the operation is continued until the boat is so laden that her gunwale is brought within a few inches of the surface, when they return to the vessel in harbor, seldom distant more than eight miles from the banks.

During the greater part of the day the fishermen have kept up a constant conversation, of which the topics are the pleasure of finding a good supply of cod, their domestic affairs, the political prospects of the nation, and other matters similarly connected. Now the repartee of one elicits a laugh from the other; this passes from man to man, and the whole flotilla enjoy the joke. The men of one boat strive to outdo those of the others in hauling up the greatest quantity of fish in a given time, and this forms another source of merriment. The boats are generally filled about the same time, and all return together.

Arrived at the vessel, each man employs a pole armed with a bent iron, resembling the prong of a hay-fork, with which he pierces the fish, and throws it with a jerk on deck, counting the number thus discharged with a loud voice. Each cargo is thus safely deposited, and the boats instantly return to the fishing-ground, when, after anchoring, the men eat their dinner, and begin anew. There, good reader, with your leave, I will let them pursue their avocations for a while, as I am anxious that you should witness what is doing on board the vessel.

The captain, four men, and the cook have, in the course of the morning, erected long tables fore and aft the main hatchway ; they have taken to the shore most of the salt barrels, and have placed in a row their large empty casks, to receive the livers. The hold of the vessel is quite clear, except a corner where is a large heap of salt. And now the men, having dined precisely at twelve, are ready with their large knives. One begins with breaking off the head of the fish, a slight pull of the hand and a gash with the knife, effecting this in a moment. He slits up its belly, with one hand pushes it aside to his neighbor, then throws overboard the head, and begins to doctor another. The next man tears out the entrails, separates the liver, which he throws into a cask, and casts the rest overboard. A third person dexterously passes his knife beneath the vertebræ of the fish, separates them from the flesh, heaves the latter through the hatchway, and the former into the water.

Now, if you will peep into the hold, you will see the last stage of the process, the salting and packing. Six experienced men generally manage to head, clean, bone, salt, and pack all the fish caught in the morning by the return of the boats with fresh cargoes, when all hands set to work, and clear the deck of the fish. Thus their labors continue till midnight, when they wash their faces and hands, put on clean clothes, hang their fishing apparel on the shrouds, and, betaking themselves to the forecastle, are soon in a sound sleep.

At three the next morning, comes the captain from his berth, rubbing his eyes, and in a loud voice calling, " All hands, ho ! " Stiffened in limb, and but half awake, the crew quickly appear on the deck. Their fingers and hands are so cramped and swollen by pulling the lines that it is difficult for them to straighten even a thumb; but this matters little at present, for the cook, who had a good nap yesterday, has risen an hour before them, and prepared their coffee and eatables. Breakfast despatched, they exchange their clean clothes for the fishing apparel, and leap into their boats, which had been washed the previous night, and again the flotilla bounds to the fishing-grounds.

As there may not be less than one hundred schooners or pickaxes in the harbor, three hundred boats resort to the banks each day, and, as each boat may procure two thousand Cods per diem, when Saturday night comes about six hundred thousand fishes have been brought to the harbor. This having caused some scarcity on the fishing-grounds, and Sunday being somewhat of an idle day, the captain collects the salt ashore, and sets sail for some other convenient harbor, which he expects to reach long before sunset. If the weather be favorable, the men get a good deal of rest during the voyage, and on Monday things go on as before.

I must not omit to tell you, reader, that, while proceeding from one harbor to another, the vessel has passed near a rock which is the breeding-place of myriads of Puffins. She has laid to for an hour or so, while part of the crew have landed, and collected a store of eggs, excellent as a substitute for cream, and not less so when hard boiled as food for the fishing-grounds. I may as well inform you also how these adventurous fellows distinguish the fresh eggs from the others. They fill up some large tubs with water, throw in a quantity of eggs, and allow them to remain a minute or so, when those which come to the surface are tossed overboard, and even those that manifest any upward tendency share the same treatment. All that remain at bottom, you may depend upon it, good reader, are perfectly sound, and not less palatable than any that you have ever eaten, or that your best guinea fowl has just dropped in your barn-yard. But let us return to the Codfish.

The fish already procured and salted is taken ashore at the new harbor by part of the crew, whom the captain has marked as the worst hands at fishing. There, on the bare rocks, or on elevated scaffolds of considerable extent, the salted Cod are laid side by side to dry in the sun. They are turned several times a day, and in the intervals the men bear a hand on board at clearing and stowing away the daily produce of the fishing-banks. Towards evening they return to the drying-grounds, and put up the fish in piles resembling so many hay-stacks, disposing those towards the top in such a manner that the rain cannot injure them, and placing a heavy stone on the summit to prevent their being thrown down should it blow hard during the night. You see, reader, that the life of a Labrador fisherman is not one of idleness.

The capelings have approached the shores, and in

myriads enter every basin and stream, to deposit their spawn, for now July is arrived. The Cods follow them as the bloodhound follows his prey, and their compact masses literally line the shores. The fishermen now adopt another method; they have brought with them long and deep seines, one end of which is by means of a line fastened to the shore, while the other is, in the usual manner, drawn out in a broad sweep, to inclose as great a space as possible, and hauled on shore by means of a capstan. Some of the men, in boats, support the corked part of the net, and beat the water to frighten the fishes within towards the land, while others, armed with poles, enter the water, hook the fishes, and fling them on the beach, the net being gradually drawn closer as the number of fish diminishes. What do you think, reader, as to the number of Cod secured in this manner in a single haul? Thirty, or thirty thousand? You may form some notion of the matter when I tell you that the young gentlemen of my party, while going along the shores, caught Codfish alive with their hands, and trout of many pounds' weight with a piece of twine and a mackerel-hook hung to their gun-rods; and that, if two of them walked knee-deep along the rocks, holding a handkerchief by the corners, they swept it full of capelings. Should you not trust me in this, I refer you to the fishermen themselves, or recommend you to go to Labrador, where you will give credit to the testimony of your eyes.

The seining of the Codfish, I believe, is not *quite* lawful, for a great proportion of the codlings which are dragged ashore at last are so small as to be considered useless; and, instead of being returned to the water, as they ought to be, are left on the shore, where they are ultimately eaten by Bears, Wolves, and Ravens. The fish taken along the coast, or on fishing stations only a few miles off, are of small dimensions; and I believe I am correct in saying that few of them weigh more than two pounds when perfectly cured, or exceed six when taken out of the water. The fish are liable to several diseases, and at times are annoyed by parasitic animals, which in a short time render them lean and unfit for use.

Some individuals, from laziness or other causes, fish with naked hooks, and thus frequently wound the Cod, without securing them ; in consequence of which the shoals are driven away, to the detriment of the other fishers. Some carry their cargoes to other parts before drying them, while others dispose of them to agents from distant shores. Some have only a pickaxe of fifty tons, while others are owners of seven or eight vessels of equal or larger burden; but whatever be their means, should the season prove favorable, they are generally well repaid for their labor. I have known instances of men who, on their first voyage, ranked as " boys," and in ten years after were in independent circumstances, although they still continue to resort to the fishing; for, said they to me, "How could we be content to spend our time in idleness at home?" I know a person of this class who has carried on the trade for many years, and who has quite a little fleet of schooners, one of which, the largest and most beautifully built, has a cabin as neat and comfortable as any that I have ever seen in a vessel of the same size. This vessel took fish on board only when perfectly cured, or acted as pilot to the rest, and now and then would return home with an ample supply of halibut, or a cargo of prime mackerel. On another occasion, I will offer some remarks on the improvements which I think might be made in the Cod-fisheries of the coast of Labrador.

A BALL IN NEWFOUNDLAND

ON our return from the singularly wild and interesting country of Labrador, the "Ripley" sailed close along the northern coast of Newfoundland. The weather was mild and clear, and, while my young companions amused themselves on the deck with the music of various instruments, I gazed on the romantic scenery spread along the bold and often magnificent shores. Portions of the wilds appeared covered with a luxuriance of vegetable growth, far surpassing that of the regions which we had just left, and in some of the valleys I thought I saw trees of moderate size. The number of habitations increased apace, and many small vessels and boats danced on the waves of the coves which we passed. Here a precipitous shore looked like the section of a great mountain, of which the lost half had sunk into the depths of the sea, and the dashing of the waters along its base was such as to alarm the most daring seaman. The huge masses of broken rock impressed my mind with awe and reverence, as I thought of the power that still gave support to the gigantic fragments which everywhere hung, as if by magic, over the sea, awaiting, as it were, the proper moment to fall upon and crush the impious crew of some piratical vessel. There, again, gently swelling hills reared their heads towards the sky, as if desirous of existing within the influence of its azure purity; and I thought the bleatings of Reindeer came on my ear. Dark clouds of Curlews were seen winging their way towards the south, and thousands of Larks and Warblers were flitting through the air. The sight of these birds excited in me a wish that I also had wings to fly back to my country and friends.

Early one morning our vessel doubled the northern cape of the Bay of St. George, and, as the wind was light, the sight of that magnificent expanse of water, which extends inward to the length of eighteen leagues, with a breadth of thirteen, gladdened the hearts of all on board. A long range of bold shores bordered it on one side, throwing a deep shadow over the water, which added greatly to the beauty of the scene. On the other side, the mild beams of the autumnal sun glittered on the water, and whitened the sails of the little barks that were sailing to and fro, like so many silvery Gulls. The welcome sight of cattle feeding in cultivated meadows, and of people at their avocations, consoled us for the labors which we had undergone, and the privations which we had suffered; and, as the " Ripley " steered her course into a snug harbor that suddenly opened to our view, the number of vessels that were anchored there, and a pretty village that presented itself increased our delight.

Although the sun was fast approaching the western horizon when our anchor was dropped, no sooner were the sails furled than we all went ashore. There appeared a kind of curious bustle among the people, as if they were anxious to know who we were; for our appearance, and that of our warlike looking schooner showed that we were not fishermen. As we bore our usual arms and hunting accoutrements, which were half Indian and half civilized, the individuals we met on shore manifested considerable suspicion, which our captain observing, he instantly made a signal, when the star-spangled banner glided to the mast-head, and saluted the flags of France and Britain in kindly greeting. We were welcomed and supplied with abundance of fresh provisions. Glad at once more standing on something like soil, we passed through the village, and walked round it, but as night was falling were quickly obliged to return to our floating home, where, after a hearty supper, we serenaded with repeated glees the peaceful inhabitants of the village.

At early dawn I was on deck admiring the scene of industry that presented itself. The harbor was already covered with fishing-boats employed in procuring mackerel, some of which we appropriated to ourselves. Signs of cultivation were observed on the slopes of the hills, the trees seemed of goodly size, a river made its way between two ranges of steep rocks, and here and there a group of Micmac Indians were searching along the shores for lobsters, crabs, and eels, all of which we found abundant and delicious. A canoe laden with Reindeer meat came alongside, paddled by a pair of athletic Indians, who exchanged their cargo for some of our stores. You would have been amused to see the manner in which these men, and their families on shore cooked the lobsters; they threw them alive into a great wood fire, and as soon as they were broiled devoured them, while yet so hot that none of us could have touched them. When properly cooled, I tasted these roasted lobsters, and found them infinitely better flavored than boiled ones. The country was represented as abounding in game. The temperature was higher by twenty degrees than that of Labrador, and yet I was told that the ice in the bay seldom broke up before the middle of May, and that few vessels attempted to go to Labrador before the 10th of June, when the cod-fishery at once commences.

One afternoon we were visited by a deputation from the inhabitants of the village, inviting our whole party to a ball which was to take place that night, and requesting us to take with us our musical instruments. We unanimously accepted the invitation, which had been made from friendly feelings; and finding that the deputies had a relish for "old Jamaica" we helped them pretty freely to some, which soon showed that it had lost nothing of its energies by having visited Labrador. At ten o'clock, the appointed hour, we landed, and were lighted to the dancing-hall by paper lanterns, one of us carrying a flute, another a violin, and I with a flageolet stuck into my waistcoat pocket.

The hall proved nothing else than the ground-floor of

a fisherman's house. We were presented to his wife, who, like her neighbors, was an adept in the piscatory art. She courtesied, not *à la* Taglioni, it is true, but with a modest assurance, which to me was quite as pleasing as the airiness with which the admired performer just mentioned might have paid her respects. The good woman was rather unprepared, and quite *en negligée*, as was the apartment, but full of activity, and anxious to arrange things in becoming style. In one hand she held a bunch of candles, in the other a lighted torch, and distributing the former at proper intervals along the walls, she applied the latter to them in succession. This done, she emptied the contents of a large tin vessel into a number of glasses, which were placed on a tea-tray on the only table in the room. The chimney, black and capacious, was embellished with coffee-pots, milk-jugs, cups and saucers, knives and forks, and all the paraphernalia necessary on so important an occasion. A set of primitive wooden stools and benches was placed around, for the reception of the belles of the village, some of whom now dropped in, flourishing in all the rosy fatness produced by an invigorating northern climate, and in decoration vying with the noblest Indian queen of the West. Their stays seemed ready to burst open, and their shoes were equally pressed. Around their necks, brilliant beads mingled with ebony tresses, and their naked arms might have inspired apprehension had they not been constantly employed in arranging flowing ribbons, gaudy flowers, and muslin flounces.

Now arrived one of the beaux, just returned from the fishing, who, knowing all, and being equally known, leaped without ceremony on the loose boards that formed a kind of loft overhead, where he soon exchanged his dripping apparel for a dress suited to the occasion, when he dropped upon the floor, and strutting up and down, bowed and scraped to the ladies, with as much ease, if not elegance, as a Bond Street highly scented exquisite. Others came in by degrees, ready dressed, and music was called for. My son, by way of overture, played " Hail Columbia, happy land," then went on with " La Marseillaise," and ended with " God save the King." Being merely a spectator, I ensconced myself in a corner, by the side of an old European gentleman, whom I found an agreeable and well informed companion, to admire the decorum of the motley assemblage.

The dancers stood in array, little time having been spent in choosing partners, and a Canadian accompanying my son on his Cremona, mirth and joy soon abounded. Dancing is certainly one of the most healthful and innocent amusements; I have loved it a vast deal more than watching for the nibble of a trout, and I have sometimes thought the enjoyment of it softened my nature as much as the pale, pure light of the moon softens and beautifies a winter night. A maiden lady who sat at my side, and who was the only daughter of my talkative companion, relished my remarks on the subject so much that the next set saw her gracing the floor with her tutored feet.

At each pause of the musicians refreshments were handed round by the hostess and her son, and I was not a little surprised to see all the ladies, maids and matrons, swallow, like their sweethearts and husbands, a full glass of pure rum, with evident pleasure. I should perhaps have recollected that, in cold climates, a glass of ardent spirits is not productive of the same effects as in burning latitudes, and that refinement had not yet induced these healthy and robust dames to affect a delicacy foreign to their nature.

It was now late, and knowing how much I had to accomplish next day, I left the party and proceeded to the shore. My men were sound asleep in the boat, but in a few moments I was on board the "Ripley." My young friends arrived towards daylight, but many of the fishermen's sons and daughters kept up the dance, to the music of the Canadian, until after our breakfast was over.

THE BAY OF FUNDY

It was in the month of May that I sailed in the United States revenue cutter, the "Swiftsure," engaged in a cruise in the Bay of Fundy. Our sails were quickly unfurled and spread out to the breeze. The vessel seemed to fly over the surface of the liquid element, as the sun rose in full splendor, while the clouds that floated here and there formed, with their glowing hues, a rich contrast with the pure azure of the heavens above us. We approached apace the island of Grand Menan, of which the stupendous cliffs gradually emerged from the deep with the majestic boldness of her noblest native chief. Soon our bark passed beneath its craggy head, covered with trees, which, on account of the height, seemed scarcely larger than shrubs. The prudent Raven spread her pinions, launched from the cliff, and flew away before us; the Golden Eagle, soaring aloft, moved majestically along in wide circles; the Guillemots sat on their eggs upon the shelving precipices, or plunging into the water, dived, and rose again at a great distance; the broad-breasted Eider Duck covered her eggs among the grassy tufts; on a naked rock the Seal lazily basked, its sleek sides glistening in the sunshine; while shoals of porpoises were swiftly gliding through the waters around us, showing by their gambols that, although doomed to the deep, their life was not devoid of pleasure. Far away stood the bold shores of Nova Scotia, gradually fading in the distance, of which the gray tints beautifully relieved the wing-like sails of many a fishing bark.

Cape after cape, forming eddies and counter currents far too terrific to be described by a landsman, we passed in succession, until we reached a deep cove, near the shores of White Head Island, which is divided from Grand Menan by a narrow strait, where we anchored secure from every blast that could blow. In a short time we found ourselves under the roof of Captain Frankland, the sole owner of the isle, of which the surface contains about fifteen hundred acres. He received us all with politeness and gave us permission to seek out its treasures, which we immediately set about doing, for I was anxious to study the habits of certain Gulls that breed there in great numbers. As Captain Coolidge, our worthy commander, had assured me, we found them on their nests on almost every *tree* of a wood that covered several acres. What a treat, reader, was it to find birds of this kind lodged on fir-trees, and sitting comfortably on their eggs! Their loud cackling notes led us to their place of resort, and ere long we had satisfactorily observed their habits, and collected as many of themselves and their eggs as we considered sufficient. In our walks we noticed a Rat, the only quadruped found on the island, and observed abundance of gooseberries, currants, raspberries, strawberries, and huckleberries. Seating ourselves on the summit of the rocks, in view of the vast Atlantic, we spread out our stores, and refreshed ourselves with our simple fare.

Now we followed the objects of our pursuit through the tangled woods, now carefully picked our steps over the spongy grounds. The air was filled with the melodious concerts of birds, and all Nature seemed to smile in quiet enjoyment. We wandered about until the setting sun warned us to depart, when, returning to the house of the proprietor, we sat down to an excellent repast, and amused ourselves with relating anecdotes and forming arrangements for the morrow. Our captain complimented us on our success, when we reached the "Swiftsure," and in due time we betook ourselves to our hammocks.

The next morning, a strange sail appearing in the distance, preparations were instantly made to pay her commander a visit. The signal staff of White Head Island displayed the British flag, while Captain Frankland and his men stood on the shore, and as we gave our sails to the wind, three hearty cheers filled the air, and were instantly responded to by us. The vessel was soon approached, but all was found right with her, and squaring our yards, onward we sped, cheerily bounding over the gay billows, until our captain sent us ashore at Eastport.

At another time my party was received on board the revenue cutter's tender, the "Fancy," — a charming name for so beautiful a craft. We set sail towards evening. The cackling of the "old wives" that covered the bay filled me with delight, and thousands of Gulls and Cormorants seemed as if anxious to pilot us into Head Harbor Bay, where we anchored for the night. Leaping on the rugged shore, we made our way to the lighthouse, where we found Mr. Snelling, a good and honest Englishman from Devonshire. His family consisted of three wild-looking lasses, beautiful, like the most finished productions of nature. In his lighthouse snugly ensconced, he spent his days in peaceful forgetfulness of the world, subsisting principally on the fish of the bay.

When day broke, how delightful it was to see fair Nature open her graceful eyelids, and present herself arrayed in all that was richest and purest before her Creator. Ah, reader, how indelibly are such moments engraved on my soul! With what ardor have I at such times gazed around me, full of the desire of being enabled to comprehend all that I saw! How often have I longed to converse with the feathered inhabitants of the forest, all of which seemed then intent on offering up their thanks to the object of my own adoration! But the wish could not be gratified, although I now feel satisfied that I have enjoyed as much of the wonders and beauties of nature as it was proper for me to enjoy. The delightful trills of the Winter Wren rolled through the underwood, the Red Squirrel smacked time with his chops, the loud notes of

the Robin sounded clearly from the tops of the trees, the
rosy Grosbeak nipped the tender blossoms of the maples,
and high overhead the Loons passed in pairs, rapidly
wending their way towards far distant shores. Would
that I could have followed in their wake! The hour of
our departure had come; and, as we sailed up the bay,
our pilot, who had been fishing for cod, was taken on
board. A few of his fish were roasted on a plank before
the embers, and formed the principal part of our breakfast. The breeze was light, and it was not until afternoon that we arrived at Point Lepreaux Harbor, where
every one, making choice of his course, went in search of
curiosities and provender.

Now, reader, the little harbor in which, if you wish it,
we shall suppose we still are, is renowned for a circumstance which I feel much inclined to endeavor to explain
to you. Several species of Ducks, that in myriads cover
the waters of the Bay of Fundy, are at times destroyed in
this particular spot in a very singular manner. When
July has come, all the water birds that are no longer capable of reproducing, remain like so many forlorn bach-
elors and old maids, to renew their plumage along the
shores. At the period when these poor birds are unfit
for flight, troops of Indians make their appearance in
light bark canoes, paddled by their squaws and papooses.
They form their flotilla into an extended curve, and drive
before them the birds, not in silence, but with simultan-
eous horrific yells, at the same time beating the surface
of the water with long poles and paddles. Terrified by
the noise, the birds swim a long way before them, endeavoring to escape with all their might. The tide is
high, every cove is filled, and into the one where we now
are, thousands of Ducks are seen entering. The Indians
have ceased to shout, and the canoes advance side by side.
Time passes on, the tide swiftly recedes as it rose, and
there are the birds left on the beach. See with what

pleasure each wild inhabitant of the forest seizes his
stick, the squaws and younglings following with similar
weapons! Look at them rushing on their prey, falling
on the disabled birds, and smashing them with their cud-
gels, until all are destroyed! In this manner upwards of
five hundred wild fowls have often been procured in a
few hours.

Three pleasant days were spent at Point Lepreaux,
when the "Fancy" spread her wings to the breeze. In
one harbor we fished for shells with a capital dredge, and
in another searched along the shore for eggs. The Passamaquoddy chief is seen gliding swiftly over the deep
in his fragile bark. He has observed a porpoise breathing. Watch him, for now he is close upon the unsuspect-
ing dolphin. He rises erect, aims his musket; smoke
rises curling from the pan, and rushes from the iron tube,
when soon after the report comes on the ear. Meantime
the porpoise has suddenly turned back downwards, — it is
dead. The body weighs a hundred pounds or more, but
this to the tough-fibred son of the woods is nothing; he
reaches it with his muscular arms, and at a single jerk,
while with his legs he dexterously steadies the canoe, he
throws it lengthwise at his feet. Amidst the highest
waves of the Bay of Fundy, these feats are performed by
the Indians during the whole of the season when the porpoises resort thither.

You have often, no doubt, heard of the extraordinary
tides of this bay; so had I, but, like others, I was loath
to believe the reports were strictly true. So I went to
the pretty town of Windsor in Nova Scotia, to judge for
myself. But let us leave the "Fancy" for a while, and
imagine ourselves at Windsor. Late one day in August
my companions and I were seated on the grassy and elevated bank of the river, about eighty feet or so above its
bed, which was almost dry, and extended for nine miles
below like a sandy wilderness. Many vessels lay on

the high banks taking in their lading of gypsum. We thought the appearance very singular, but we were too late to watch the tide that evening. Next morning we resumed our station, and soon perceived the water flowing towards us, and rising with a rapidity of which we had previously seen no example. We planted along the steep declivity of the bank a number of sticks, each three feet long, the base of one being placed on a level with the top of that below it, and when about half flow the tide reached their tops, one after another, rising three feet in ten minutes, or eighteen in the hour; and, at high water the surface was sixty-five feet above the bed of the river! On looking for the vessels which we had seen the preceding evening, we were told most of them were gone with the night tide.

But now we are again on board the "Fancy;" Mr. Claredge stands near the pilot, who sits next to the man at the helm. On we move swiftly for the breeze has freshened; many islands we pass in succession; the wind increases to a gale; with reefed sails we dash along, and now rapidly pass a heavily laden sloop gallantly running across our course with undiminished sail; when suddenly we see her upset. Staves and spars are floating around, and presently we observe three men scrambling up her sides, and seating themselves on the keel, where they make signals of distress to us. By this time we have run to a great distance; but Claredge, cool and prudent, as every seaman ought to be, has already issued his orders to the helmsman and crew, and now near the wind we gradually approach the sufferers. A line is thrown to them, and the next moment we are alongside the vessel. A fisher's boat, too, has noticed the disaster; and, with long strokes of her oars, advances, now rising on the curling wave, and now sinking out of sight. By our mutual efforts the men are brought on board, and the sloop is slowly towed into a safe harbor. An hour later my party

was safely landed at Eastport, where, on looking over the
waters, and observing the dense masses of vapor that
veiled the shores, we congratulated ourselves at having
escaped from the Bay of Fundy.

A FLOOD

MANY of our larger streams, such as the Mississippi, the
Ohio, the Illinois, the Arkansas, and the Red River, exhibit at certain seasons the most extensive overflowings
of their waters, to which the name of *floods* is more appropriate than the term *freshets*, usually applied to the sudden risings of smaller streams. If we consider the vast
extent of country through which an inland navigation is
afforded by the never-failing supply of water furnished by
these wonderful rivers, we cannot suppose them exceeded
in magnitude by any other in the known world. It will
easily be imagined what a wonderful spectacle must present itself to the eye of the traveller who for the first
time views the enormous mass of waters, collected from
the vast central regions of our continent, booming along,
turbid and swollen to overflowing, in the broad channels
of the Mississippi and Ohio, the latter of which has a
course of more than a thousand miles, and the former of
several thousands.

To give you some idea of a *Booming Flood* of these
gigantic streams, it is necessary to state the causes which
give rise to it. These are, the sudden melting of the
snows on the mountains, and heavy rains continued for
several weeks. When it happens that, during a severe
winter, the Alleghany Mountains have been covered with
snow to the depth of several feet, and the accumulated
mass has remained unmelted for a length of time, the
materials of a flood are thus prepared. It now and then

happens that the winter is hurried off by a sudden increase of temperature, when the accumulated snows melt away simultaneously over the whole country, and the southeasterly wind, which then usually blows, brings along with it a continued fall of heavy rain, which, mingling with the dissolving snow, deluges the alluvial portions of the western country, filling up the rivulets, ravines, creeks, and small rivers. These delivering their waters to the great streams, cause the latter not merely to rise to a surprising height, but to overflow their banks, wherever the land is low. On such occasions the Ohio itself presents a splendid, and at the same time, an appalling spectacle; but when its waters mingle with those of the Mississippi, then, kind reader, is the time to view an American flood in all its astonishing magnificence.

At the foot of the Falls of the Ohio, the water has been known to rise upwards of sixty feet above its lowest level. The river, at this point, has already run a course of nearly seven hundred miles from its origin at Pittsburgh in Pennsylvania, during which it has received the waters of its numberless tributaries, and overflowing all the bottom lands or valleys, has swept along the fences and dwellings which have been unable to resist its violence. I could relate hundreds of incidents which might prove to you the dreadful effects of such an inundation, and which have been witnessed by thousands besides myself. I have known, for example, of a cow swimming through a window, elevated at least seven feet from the ground, and sixty-two feet above low-water mark. The house was then surrounded by water from the Ohio, which runs in front of it, while the neighboring country was overflowed; yet, the family did not remove from it, but remained in its upper portion, having previously taken off the sashes of the lower windows, and opened the doors. But let us return to the Mississippi.

There the overflow is astonishing, for no sooner has the

water reached the upper part of the banks than it rushes out and overspreads the whole of the neighboring swamps, presenting an ocean overgrown with stupendous forest-trees. So sudden is the calamity that every individual, whether man or beast, has to exert his utmost ingenuity to enable him to escape from the dreaded element. The Indian quickly removes to the hills of the interior, the cattle and game swim to the different strips of land that remain uncovered in the midst of the flood, or attempt to force their way through the waters until they perish from fatigue. Along the banks of the river, the inhabitants have rafts ready made, on which they remove themselves, their cattle, and their provisions, and which they then fasten with ropes or grape-vines to the larger trees, while they contemplate the melancholy spectacle presented by the current, as it carries off their houses and wood-yards piece by piece. Some who have nothing to lose, and are usually known by the name of *squatters*, take this opportunity of traversing the woods in canoes, for the purpose of procuring game, and particularly the skins of animals, such as the Deer and Bear, which may be converted into money. They resort to the low ridges surrounded by the waters, and destroy thousands of Deer, merely for their skins, leaving the flesh to putrefy.

The river itself, rolling its swollen waters along, presents a spectacle of the most imposing nature. Although no large vessel, unless propelled by steam, can now make its way against the current, it is seen covered by boats, laden with produce, which, running out from all the smaller streams, float silently towards the city of New Orleans, their owners meanwhile not very well assured of finding a landing-place even there. The water is covered with yellow foam and pumice, the latter having floated from the Rocky Mountains of the Northwest. The eddies are larger and more powerful than ever. Here and there tracts of forest are observed undermined, the trees gradually giving way, and falling into the stream. Cattle, horses, Bears, and Deer are seen at times attempting to swim across the impetuous mass of foaming and boiling water; whilst here and there a Vulture or an Eagle is observed perched on a bloated carcass, tearing it up in pieces, as regardless of the flood as on former occasions it would have been of the numerous sawyers and planters with which the surface of the river is covered when the water is low. Even the steamer is frequently distressed. The numberless trees and logs that float along break its paddles, and retard its progress. Besides, it is on such occasions difficult to procure fuel to maintain its fires; and it is only at very distant intervals that a wood-yard can be found which the water has not carried off.

Following the river in your canoe, you reach those parts of the shores that are protected against the overflowings of the waters, and are called *levees*. There you find the whole population of the district at work repairing and augmenting those artificial barriers, which are several feet above the level of the fields. Every person appears to dread the opening of a *crevasse*, by which the waters may rush into his fields. In spite of all exertions, however, the crevasse opens, the water bursts impetuously over the plantations, and lays waste the crops which so lately were blooming in all the luxuriance of spring. It opens up a new channel, which, for aught I know to the contrary, may carry its waters even to the Mexican Gulf.

I have floated on the Mississippi and Ohio when thus swollen, and have in different places visited the submersed lands of the interior, propelling a light canoe by the aid of a paddle. In this manner I have traversed immense portions of the country overflowed by the waters of these rivers, and particularly when floating over the Mississippi bottom-lands I have been struck with awe at the sight. Little or no current is met with, unless when the canoe passes over the bed of a bayou. All is silent and melancholy, unless when the mournful bleating of the hemmed-in Deer reaches your ear, or the dismal scream of an Eagle or a Raven is heard, as the foul bird rises, disturbed by your approach, from the carcass on which it was allaying its craving appetite. Bears, Cougars, Lynxes, and all other quadrupeds that can ascend the trees are observed crouched among their top branches. Hungry in the midst of abundance, although they see floating around them the animals on which they usually prey, they dare not venture to swim to them. Fatigued by the exertions which they have made to reach the dry land, they will there stand the hunter's fire, as if to die by a ball were better than to perish amid the waste of waters. On occasions like this, all these animals are shot by hundreds.

Opposite the city of Natchez, which stands on a bluff bank of considerable elevation, the extent of inundated land is immense, the greater portion of the tract lying between the Mississippi and the Red River, which is more than thirty miles in breadth, being under water. The mail-bag has often been carried through the immersed forests, in a canoe, for even a greater distance, in order to be forwarded to Natchitochez.

But now, kind reader, observe this great flood gradually subsiding, and again see the mighty changes which it has effected. The waters have now been carried into the distant ocean. The earth is everywhere covered by a deep deposit of muddy loam, which in drying splits into deep and narrow chasms, presenting a reticulated appearance, and from which, as the weather becomes warmer, disagreeable, and at times noxious, exhalations arise, and fill the lower stratum of the atmosphere as with a dense fog. The banks of the river have almost everywhere been broken down in a greater or less degree. Large streams are now found to exist, where none were formerly to be seen, having forced their way in direct lines from the

upper parts of the bends. These are by the navigator
called *short-cuts*. Some of them have proved large enough
to produce a change in the navigation of the Mississippi.
If I mistake not, one of these, known by the name of the
Grand Cut-off, and only a few miles in length, has di-
verted the river from its natural course, and has shortened
it by fifty miles. The upper parts of the islands present
a bulwark consisting of an enormous mass of floated trees
of all kinds, which have lodged there. Large sand-banks
have been completely removed by the impetuous whirls
of the waters, and have been deposited in other places.
Some appear quite new to the eye of the navigator, who
has to mark their situation and bearings in his log-book.
The trees on the margins of the banks have in many parts
given way. They are seen bending over the stream, like
the grounded arms of an overwhelmed army of giants.
Everywhere are heard the lamentations of the farmer and
planter, whilst their servants and themselves are busily
employed in repairing the damages occasioned by the
floods. At one crevasse an old ship or two, dismantled
for the purpose, are sunk, to obstruct the passage opened
by the still rushing waters, while new earth is brought
to fill up the chasms. The squatter is seen shouldering
his rifle, and making his way through the morass, in
search of his lost stock, to drive the survivors home, and
save the skins of the drowned. New fences have everywhere to be formed; even new houses must be erected, to
save which from a like disaster, the settler places them
on an elevated platform supported by pillars made by the
trunks of trees. The land must be ploughed anew, and
if the season is not too far advanced, a crop of corn and
potatoes may yet be raised. But the rich prospects of
the planter are blasted. The traveller is impeded in his
journey, the creeks and smaller streams having broken up
their banks in a degree proportionate to their size. A
bank of sand, which seems firm and secure, suddenly

gives way beneath the traveller's horse, and the next moment the animal has sunk in the quicksand, either to the chest in front, or over the crupper behind, leaving its master in a situation not to be envied.

Unlike the mountain torrents and small rivers of other parts of the world, the Mississippi rises but slowly during these floods, continuing for several weeks to increase at the rate of about an inch a day. When at its height, it undergoes little fluctuation for some days, and after this, subsides as slowly as it rose. The usual duration of a flood is from four to six weeks, although, on some occasions, it is protracted to two months.

Every one knows how largely the idea of floods and cataclysms enters into the speculations of the geologist. If the streamlets of the European continent afford illustrations of the formation of strata, how much more must the Mississippi, with its ever-shifting sand-banks, its crumbling shores, its enormous masses of drift timber, the source of future beds of coal, its extensive and varied alluvial deposits, and its mighty mass of waters rolling sullenly along, like the flood of eternity.

THE SQUATTERS OF THE MISSISSIPPI

ALTHOUGH every European traveller who has glided down the Mississippi, at the rate of ten miles an hour, has told his tale of the squatters, yet none has given any other account of them, than that they are "a sallow, sickly looking sort of miserable beings," living in swamps, and subsisting on pig-nuts, Indian-corn, and Bear's-flesh. It is obvious, however, that none but a person acquainted with their history, manners, and condition, can give any real information respecting them.

The individuals who become squatters, choose that sort

of life of their own free will. They mostly remove from
other parts of the United States, after finding that land
has become too high in price, and they are persons who,
having a family of strong and hardy children, are anxious
to enable them to provide for themselves. They have
heard from good authorities that the country extending
along the great streams of the West, is of all parts of the
Union, the richest in its soil, the growth of its timber,
and the abundance of its game; that, besides, the Mississippi is the great road to and from all the markets in the
world; and that every vessel borne by its waters affords
to settlers some chance of selling their commodities, or
of exchanging them for others. To these recommenda-
tions is added another, of even greater weight with persons of the above denomination, namely, the prospect of
being able to settle on land, and perhaps to hold it for
a number of years, without purchase, rent or tax of any
kind. How many thousands of individuals in all parts of
the globe would gladly try their fortune with such prospects, I leave to you, reader, to determine.

As I am not disposed too highly to color the picture
which I am about to submit to your inspection, instead
of pitching on individuals who have removed from our
eastern boundaries, and of whom certainly there are a
good number, I shall introduce to you the members of a
family from Virginia, first giving you an idea of their
condition in that country, previous to their migration to
the west. The land which they and their ancestors have
possessed for a hundred years, having been constantly
forced to produce crops of one kind or another, is now
completely worn out. It exhibits only a superficial layer
of red clay, cut up by deep ravines, through which much
of the soil has been conveyed to some more fortunate
neighbor, residing in a yet rich and beautiful valley.
Their strenuous efforts to render it productive have
failed. They dispose of everything too cumbrous or ex-

pensive for them to remove, retaining only a few horses, a servant or two, and such implements of husbandry and other articles as may be necessary on their journey, or useful when they arrive at the spot of their choice.

I think I see them at this moment harnessing their horses, and attaching them to their wagons, which are already filled with bedding, provisions, and the younger children, while on their outside are fastened spinning-wheels and looms, and a bucket filled with tar and tallow swings between the hind wheels. Several axes are secured to the bolster, and the feeding-trough of the horses contains pots, kettles, and pans. The servant, now become a driver, rides the near saddled horse, the wife is mounted on another, the worthy husband shoulders his gun, and his sons, clad in plain substantial homespun, drive the cattle ahead, and lead the procession, followed by the hounds and other dogs. Their day's journey is short, and not agreeable; the cattle, stubborn or wild, frequently leave the road for the woods, giving the travellers much trouble; the harness of the horses here and there gives way, and needs immediate repair; a basket, which has accidentally dropped, must be gone after, for nothing that they have can be spared; the roads are bad, and now and then all hands are called to push on the wagon, or prevent it from upsetting. Yet by sunset they have proceeded perhaps twenty miles. Rather fatigued, all assemble round the fire, which has been lighted, supper is prepared, and a camp being erected, there they pass the night.

Days and weeks, nay months, of unremitting toil, pass before they gain the end of their journey. They have crossed both the Carolinas, Georgia, and Alabama. They have been travelling from the beginning of May to that of September, and with heavy hearts they traverse the State of Mississippi. But now, arrived on the banks of the broad stream, they gaze in amazement on the dark deep woods around them. Boats of various kinds they see gliding downwards with the current, while others slowly ascend against it. A few inquiries are made at the nearest dwelling, and assisted by the inhabitants with their boats, and canoes, they at once cross the Mississippi, and select their place of habitation.

The exhalations arising from the swamps and morasses around them have a powerful effect on these new settlers, but all are intent on preparing for the winter. A small patch of ground is cleared by the axe and the fire, a temporary cabin is erected, to each of the cattle is attached a jingling bell before it is let loose into the neighboring cane-brake, and the horses remain about the house, where they find sufficient food at that season. The first trading-boat that stops at their landing, enables them to provide themselves with some flour, fish-hooks, and ammunition, as well as other commodities. The looms are mounted, the spinning-wheels soon furnish some yarn, and in a few weeks the family throw off their ragged clothes, and array themselves in suits adapted to the climate. The father and sons meanwhile have sown turnips and other vegetables; and from some Kentucky flatboat, a supply of live poultry has been procured.

October tinges the leaves of the forest, the morning dews are heavy, the days hot, the nights chill, and the unacclimated family in a few days are attacked with ague. The lingering disease almost prostrates their whole faculties, and one seeing them at such a period might well call them sallow and sickly. Fortunately the unhealthy season soon passes over, and the hoar-frosts make their appearance. Gradually each individual recovers strength. The largest ash-trees are felled; their trunks are cut, split, and corded in front of the building; a large fire is lighted at night on the edge of the water, and soon a steamer calls to purchase the wood, and thus add to their comforts during the winter.

The first fruit of their industry imparts new courage to them; their exertions multiply, and when spring returns, the place has a cheerful look. Venison, Bear's-flesh, Wild Turkeys, Ducks and Geese, with now and then some fish, have served to keep up their strength, and now their enlarged field is planted with corn, potatoes, and pumpkins. Their stock of cattle, too, has augmented; the steamer, which now stops there as if by preference, buys a calf or a pig, together with the whole of their wood. Their store of provisions is renewed, and brighter rays of hope enliven their spirits.

Who is he of the settlers on the Mississippi that cannot realize some profit? Truly none who is industrious. When the autumnal months return, all are better prepared to encounter the ague which then prevails. Substantial food, suitable clothing, and abundant firing, repel its attacks; and before another twelvemonth has elapsed the family is naturalized. The sons have by this time discovered a swamp covered with excellent timber, and as they have seen many great rafts of saw logs, bound for the mills of New Orleans, floating past their dwelling, they resolve to try the success of a little enterprise. Their industry and prudence have already enhanced their credit. A few cross-saws are purchased, and some broad-wheeled "carry-logs" are made by themselves. Log after log, is hauled to the bank of the river, and in a short time their first raft is made on the shore, and loaded with cord-wood. When the next freshet sets it afloat, it is secured by long grape-vines or cables, until the proper time being arrived, the husband and sons embark on it, and float down the mighty stream.

After encountering many difficulties, they arrive in safety at New Orleans, where they dispose of their stock, the money obtained for which may be said to be all profit, supply themselves with such articles as may add to their convenience or comfort, and with light hearts procure a passage on the upper deck of a steamer, at a very cheap rate, on account of the benefit of their labor in taking in wood or otherwise.

And now the vessel approaches their home. See the joyous mother and daughters as they stand on the bank! A store of vegetables lies around them, a large tub of fresh milk is at their feet, and in their hands are plates, filled with rolls of butter. As the steamer stops, three broad straw hats are waved from the upper deck, and soon husband and wife, brothers and sisters, are in each other's embrace. The boat carries off the provisions for which value has been left, and as the captain issues his orders for putting on the steam, the happy family enter their humble dwelling. The husband gives his bag of dollars to the wife, while the sons present some token of affection to the sisters. Surely, at such a moment, the squatters are richly repaid for all their labors.

Every successive year has increased their savings. They now possess a large stock of horses, cows, and hogs, with abundance of provisions, and domestic comfort of every kind. The daughters have been married to the sons of neighboring squatters, and have gained sisters to themselves by the marriage of their brothers. The government secures to the family the lands on which, twenty years before, they settled in poverty and sickness. Larger buildings are erected on piles, secure from the inundations; where a single cabin once stood, a neat village is now to be seen; warehouses, stores, and workshops increase the importance of the place. The squatters live respected, and in due time die regretted by all who knew them.

Thus are the vast frontiers of our country peopled, and thus does cultivation, year after year, extend over the western wilds. Time will no doubt be, when the great valley of the Mississippi, still covered with primeval forests interspersed with swamps, will smile with corn-fields

and orchards, while crowded cities will rise at intervals
along its banks, and enlightened nations will rejoice in
the bounties of Providence.

IMPROVEMENTS IN THE NAVIGATION OF THE MISSISSIPPI

I HAVE so frequently spoken of the Mississippi that an
account of the progress of navigation on that extraordinary
stream may be interesting even to the student of nature.
I shall commence with the year 1808, at which time a
great portion of the western country, and the banks of
the Mississippi River, from above the city of Natchez
particularly, were little more than a waste, or to use words
better suited to my feelings, remained in their natural
state. To ascend the great stream against a powerful
current, rendered still stronger wherever islands occurred,
together with the thousands of sand-banks, as liable to
changes and shiftings as the alluvial shores themselves,
which at every deep curve or *bend* were seen giving way,
as if crushed down by the weight of the great forests that
everywhere reached to the very edge of the water, and
falling and sinking in the muddy stream by acres at a
time, was an adventure of no small difficulty and risk, and
which was rendered more so by the innumerable logs,
called *sawyers* and *planters*, that everywhere raised their
heads above the water, as if bidding defiance to all intruders. Few white inhabitants had yet marched towards
its shores, and these few were of a class little able to
assist the navigator. Here and there a solitary encampment of native Indians might be seen, but its inmates were
as likely to prove foes as friends, having from their birth
been made keenly sensible of the encroachments of the
white men upon their lands.

Such was then the nature of the Mississippi and its shores. That river was navigated, principally in the direction of the current, in small canoes, pirogues, keel-boats, some flatboats, and a few barges. The canoes and pirogues, being generally laden with furs from the different heads of streams that feed the great river, were of little worth after reaching the market of New Orleans, and seldom reascended, the owners making their way home through the woods, amidst innumerable difficulties. The flatboats were demolished and used as fire-wood. The keel-boats and barges were employed in conveying produce of different kinds besides furs, such as lead, flour, pork, and other articles. These returned laden with sugar, coffee, and dry goods suited for the markets of St. Geneviève and St. Louis on the upper Mississippi, or branched off and ascended the Ohio to the foot of the Falls near Louisville in Kentucky. But, reader, follow their movements, and judge for yourself of the fatigues, troubles, and risks of the men employed in that navigation. A keel-boat was generally manned by ten hands, principally Canadian French, and a patroon or master. These boats seldom carried more than from twenty to thirty tons. The barges frequently had forty or fifty men, with a patroon, and carried fifty or sixty tons. Both these kinds of vessels were provided with a mast, a square sail, and coils of cordage known by the name of *cordelles*. Each boat or barge carried its own provisions. We shall suppose one of these boats under way, and, having passed Natchez, entering upon what were the difficulties of their ascent. Wherever a point projected, so as to render the course or bend below it of some magnitude, there was an eddy, the returning current of which was sometimes as strong as that of the middle of the great stream. The bargemen therefore rowed up pretty close under the bank, and had merely to keep watch in the bow, lest the boat should run against a planter or sawyer. But the boat has reached the

point, and there the current is to all appearance of double
strength, and right against it. The men, who have all
rested a few minutes, are ordered to take their stations,
and lay hold of their oars, for the river must be crossed,
it being seldom possible to double such a point, and proceed along the same shore. The boat is crossing, its
head slanting to the current, which is, however, too strong
for the rowers, and when the other side of the river has
been reached, it has drifted perhaps a quarter of a mile.
The men are by this time exhausted, and, as we shall
suppose it to be twelve o'clock, fasten the boat to the
shore or to a tree. A small glass of whiskey is given to
each, when they cook and eat their dinner, and after repairing their fatigue by an hour's repose, recommence
their labors. The boat is again seen slowly advancing
against the stream. It has reached the lower end of a
large sand-bar, along the edge of which it is propelled by
means of long poles, if the bottom be hard. Two men
called bowsmen remain at the prow, to assist, in concert
with the steersman, in managing the boat, and keeping its
head right against the current. The rest place themselves
on the land side of the footway of the vessel, put one end
of their poles on the ground, the other against their
shoulders, and push with all their might. As each of the
men reaches the stern, he crosses to the other side, runs
along it, and comes again to the landward side of the
bow, when he recommences operations. The barge in
the meantime is ascending at a rate not exceeding one
mile in the hour.

The bar is at length passed, and as the shore in sight
is straight on both sides of the river, and the current
uniformly strong, the poles are laid aside, and the men
being equally divided, those on the river side take to
their oars, whilst those on the land side lay hold of the
branches of willows, or other trees, and thus slowly propel
the boat. Here and there however, the trunk of a fallen

tree, partly lying on the bank, and partly projecting beyond it, impedes their progress, and requires to be doubled.
This is performed by striking it with the iron points of the
poles and gaff-hooks. The sun is now quite low, and the
barge is again secured in the best harbor within reach.
The navigators cook their supper, and betake themselves
to their blankets or Bear skins to rest, or perhaps light a
large fire on the shore, under the smoke of which they
repose, in order to avoid the persecutions of the myriads
of mosquitoes which are found along the river during
the whole summer. Perhaps, from dawn to sunset, the
boat may have advanced fifteen miles. If so, it has done
well. The next day, the wind proves favorable, the sail
is set, the boat takes all advantages, and meeting with
no accident, has ascended thirty miles, perhaps double
that distance. The next day comes with a very different
aspect. The wind is right ahead, the shores are without trees of any kind, and the canes on the bank are so
thick and stout that not even the cordelles can be used.
This occasions a halt. The time is not altogether lost, as
most of the men, being provided with rifles, betake themselves to the woods, and search for the Deer, the Bears, or
the Turkeys that are generally abundant there. Three
days may pass before the wind changes, and the advantages gained on the previous fine day are forgotten.
Again the boat proceeds, but in passing over a shallow
place, runs on a log, swings with the current, but hangs
fast, with her lee side almost under water. Now for the
poles! All hands are on deck, bustling and pushing. At
length, towards sunset, the boat is once more afloat, and is
again taken to the shore, where the wearied crew pass
another night.

I shall not continue this account of difficulties, it having
already become painful in the extreme. I could tell you
of the crew abandoning the boat and cargo, and of numberless accidents and perils; but be it enough to say that

advancing in this tardy manner, the boat that left New Orleans on the first of March often did not reach the Falls of the Ohio until the month of July, — nay, sometimes not until October; and after all this immense trouble, it brought only a few bags of coffee, and at most one hundred hogsheads of sugar. Such was the state of things in 1808. The number of barges at that period did not amount to more than twenty-five or thirty, and the largest probably did not exceed one hundred tons burden. To make the best of this fatiguing navigation, I may conclude by saying that a barge which came up in three months had done wonders, for, I believe, few voyages were performed in that time.

If I am not mistaken, the first steamboat that went down out of the Ohio to New Orleans was named the "Orleans," and, if I remember right, was commanded by Captain Ogden. This voyage, I believe, was performed in the spring of 1810. It was, as you may suppose, looked upon as the *ne plus ultra* of enterprise. Soon after, another vessel came from Pittsburgh, and before many years elapsed, to see a vessel so propelled had become a common occurrence. In 1826, after a lapse of time that proved sufficient to double the population of the United States of America, the navigation of the Mississippi had so improved, both in respect to facility and quickness, that I know no better way of giving you an idea of it than by presenting you with an extract from a letter written by my eldest son, which was taken from the books of N. Berthoud, Esq., with whom he at that time resided.

"You ask me in your last letter for a list of the arrivals and departures here. I give you an abstract from our list of 1826, showing the number of boats which plied each year, their tonnage, the trips they performed, and the quantity of goods landed here from New Orleans and intermediate places: —

	Boats.	Tons.	Trips.	Tons.
1823, from Jan. 1 to Dec. 31,	42	7860	98	19,453
1824, " " " Nov. 25,	36	6393	118	20,291
1825, " " " Aug. 15,	42	7484	140	24,102
1826, " " " Dec. 31,	51	9386	182	28,914

The amount for the present year will be much greater than any of the above. The number of flatboats and keel-boats is beyond calculation. The number of steamboats above the Falls I cannot say much about, except that one or two arrive at and leave Louisville every day. Their passage from Cincinnati is commonly fourteen or sixteen hours. The " Tecumseh," a boat which runs between this place and New Orleans, which is of 210 tons, arrived here on the 10th inst. in nine days, seven hours, from port to port; and the " Philadelphia," of 300 tons, made the passage in nine days, nine and a half hours, the computed distance being 1650 miles. These are the quickest trips made. There are now in operation on the waters west of the Alleghany Mountains 140 or 150 boats. We had last spring (1826) a very high freshet, which came four and a half feet deep in the counting-room. The rise was 57 feet 3 inches perpendicular."

All the steamboats of which this· is an account did not perform voyages to New Orleans only, but to all points on the Mississippi, and other rivers which fall into it. I am certain that since the above date the number has increased, but to what extent I cannot at present say.

When steamboats first plied between Shippingport and New Orleans, the cabin passage was a hundred dollars, and a hundred and fifty dollars on the upward voyage. In 1829, I went down to Natchez from Shippingport for twenty-five dollars, and ascended from New Orleans on board the "Philadelphia," in the beginning of January, 1830, for sixty dollars, having taken two state-rooms for my wife and myself. On that voyage we met with a tri-fling accident, which protracted it to fourteen days, the computed distance being, as mentioned above, 1650 miles, although the real distance is probably less. I do not remember to have spent a day without meeting with a steamboat, and some days we met several. I might here be tempted to give you a description of one of these steamers of the western waters, but the picture having been often drawn by abler hands, I shall desist.

KENTUCKY SPORTS

It may not be amiss, kind reader, before I attempt to give you some idea of the pleasures experienced by the sportsmen of Kentucky, to introduce the subject with a slight description of that State.

Kentucky was formerly attached to Virginia, but in those days the Indians looked upon that portion of the western wilds as their own, and abandoned the district only when forced to do so, moving with disconsolate hearts farther into the recesses of the unexplored forests. Doubtless the richness of its soil, and the beauty of its borders, situated as they are along one of the most beautiful rivers in the world, contributed as much to attract the Old Virginians as the desire, so generally experienced in America, of spreading over the uncultivated tracts, and bringing into cultivation lands that have for unknown ages teemed with the wild luxuriance of untamed nature. The conquest of Kentucky was not performed without many difficulties. The warfare that long existed between the intruders and the Redskins was sanguinary and protracted; but the former at length made good their footing, and the latter drew off their shattered bands, dismayed by the mental superiority and indomitable courage of the white men.

This region was probably discovered by a daring hunter, the renowned Daniel Boone. The richness of its soil, its magnificent forests, its numberless navigable streams, its salt springs and licks, its saltpetre caves, its coal strata, and the vast herds of Buffaloes and Deer that browsed on its hills and amidst its charming valleys, afforded ample inducements to the new settler, who pushed forward with a spirit far above that of the most undaunted tribes which for ages had been the sole possessors of the soil.

The Virginians thronged towards the Ohio. An axe, a couple of horses, and a heavy rifle, with store of ammunition, were all that were considered necessary for the equipments of the man, who, with his family, removed to the new State, assured that, in that land of exuberant fertility, he could not fail to provide amply for all his wants. To have witnessed the industry and perseverance of these emigrants must at once have proved the vigor of their minds. Regardless of the fatigue attending every movement which they made, they pushed through an unexplored region of dark and tangled forests, guiding themselves by the sun alone, and reposing at night on the bare ground. Numberless streams they had to cross on rafts, with their wives and children, their cattle and their luggage, often drifting to considerable distances before they could effect a landing on the opposite shores. Their cattle would often stray amid the rice pasturage of these shores, and occasion a delay of several days. To these troubles add the constantly impending danger of being murdered, while asleep in their encampments, by the prowling and ruthless Indians; while they had before them a distance of hundreds of miles to be traversed, before they could reach certain places of rendezvous called *Stations*. To encounter difficulties like these must have required energies of no ordinary kind; and the reward which these veteran settlers enjoy was doubtless well merited.

Some removed from the Atlantic shores to those of the Ohio in more comfort and security. They had their wagons, their negroes, and their families. Their way was

VICTOR GIFFORD AUDUBON, 1853.

cut through the woods by their own axemen, the day before their advance, and when night overtook them, the
hunters attached to the party came to the place pitched
upon for encamping, loaded with the dainties of which the
forest yielded an abundant supply, the blazing light of a
huge fire guiding their steps as they approached, and the
sounds of merriment that saluted their ears assuring them
that all was well. The flesh of the Buffalo, the Bear, and
the Deer soon hung, in large and delicious steaks, in front
of the embers; the cakes already prepared were deposited
in their proper places, and under the rich drippings of the
juicy roasts were quickly baked. The wagons contained
the bedding, and whilst the horses which had drawn them
were turned loose to feed on the luxuriant undergrowth of
the woods — some perhaps hoppled, but the greater number merely with a light bell hung to their neck, to guide
their owners in the morning to the spot where they might
have rambled — the party were enjoying themselves after
the fatigues of the day.

In anticipation all is pleasure; and these migrating
bands feasted in joyous sociality, unapprehensive of any
greater difficulties than those to be encountered in forcing
their way through the pathless woods to the land of abundance; and although it took months to accomplish the
journey, and a skirmish now and then took place between
them and the Indians, who sometimes crept unperceived
into their very camp, still did the Virginians cheerfully
proceed towards the western horizon, until the various
groups all reached the Ohio, when, struck with the beauty
of that magnificent stream, they at once commenced the
task of clearing land, for the purpose of establishing a
permanent residence.

Others, perhaps encumbered with too much luggage,
preferred descending the stream. They prepared *arks*
pierced with port-holes, and glided on the gentle current,
more annoyed, however, than those who marched by land

by the attacks of the Indians who watched their motions. Many travellers have described these boats, formerly called *arks*, but now named *flatboats*. But have they told you, kind reader, that in those times a boat thirty or forty feet in length, by ten or twelve in breadth, was considered a stupendous fabric; that this boat contained men, women and children, huddled together, with horses, cattle, hogs and poultry for their companions, while the remaining portion was crammed with vegetables and packages of seeds? The roof or deck of the boat was not unlike a farm-yard, being covered with hay, ploughs, carts, wagons, and various agricultural implements, together with numerous others, among which the spinning-wheels of the matrons were conspicuous. Even the sides of the floating-mass were loaded with the wheels of the different vehicles, which themselves lay on the roof. Have they told you that these boats contained the little all of each family of venturous emigrants, who, fearful of being discovered by the Indians under night moved in darkness, groping their way from one part to another of these floating habitations, denying themselves the comfort of fire or light, lest the foe that watched them from the shore should rush upon them and destroy them? Have they told you that this boat was used, after the tedious voyage was ended, as the first dwelling of these new settlers? No, kind reader, such things have not been related to you before. The travellers who have visited our country have had other objects in view.

I shall not describe the many massacres which took place among the different parties of white and red men, as the former moved down the Ohio; because I have never been very fond of battles, and indeed have always wished that the world were more peaceably inclined than it is; and shall merely add that, in one way or other, Kentucky was wrested from the original owners of the soil. Let us, therefore, turn our attention to the sports still enjoyed in that now happy portion of the United States.

We have individuals in Kentucky, kind reader, that even there are considered wonderful adepts in the management of the rifle. To *drive a nail* is a common feat, not more thought off by the Kentuckians than to cut off a Wild Turkey's head, at a distance of a hundred yards. Others will *bark* off Squirrels one after another, until satisfied with the number procured. Some, less intent on destroying game, may be seen under night *snuffing a candle* at the distance of fifty yards, off-hand, without extinguishing it. I have been told that some have proved so expert and cool as to make choice of the eye of a foe at a wonderful distance, boasting beforehand of the sureness of their piece, which has afterwards been fully proved when the enemy's head has been examined!

Having resided some years in Kentucky, and having more than once been witness of rifle sport, I shall present you with the results of my observation, leaving you to judge how far rifle-shooting is understood in that State.

Several individuals who conceive themselves expert in the management of the gun are often seen to meet for the purpose of displaying their skill, and betting a trifling sum, put up a target, in the centre of which a common-sized nail is hammered for about two-thirds of its length. The marksmen make choice of what they consider a proper distance, which may be forty paces. Each man cleans the interior of his tube, which is called *wiping* it, places a ball in the palm of his hand, pouring as much powder from his horn upon it as will cover it. This quantity is supposed to be sufficient for any distance within a hundred yards. A shot which comes very close to the nail is considered as that of an indifferent marksman; the bending of the nail is, of course, somewhat better; but nothing less than hitting it right on the head is satisfactory. Well, kind reader, one out of three shots generally hits the nail, and should the shooters amount to half a dozen, two nails are frequently needed before each can have a shot. Those who drive the nail have a further trial amongst themselves, and the two best shots out of these generally settle the affair, when all the sportsmen adjourn to some house, and spend an hour or two in friendly intercourse, appointing, before they part, a day for another trial. This is technically termed *driving the nail*.

Barking off Squirrels is delightful sport, and in my opinion requires a greater degree of accuracy than any other. I first witnessed this manner of procuring Squirrels whilst near the town of Frankfort. The performer was the celebrated Daniel Boone. We walked out together, and followed the rocky margins of the Kentucky River, until we reached a piece of flat land thickly covered with black walnuts, oaks, and hickories. As the general mast was a good one that year, Squirrels were seen gambolling on every tree around us. My companion, a stout, hale, and athletic man, dressed in a homespun hunting-shirt, bare-legged and moccasined, carried a long and heavy rifle, which, as he was loading it, he said had proved efficient in all his former undertakings, and which he hoped would not fail on this occasion, as he felt proud to show me his skill. The gun was wiped, the powder measured, the ball patched with six-hundred-thread linen, and the charge sent home with a hickory rod. We moved not a step from the place, for the Squirrels were so numerous that it was unnecessary to go after them. Boone pointed to one of these animals which had observed us, and was crouched on a branch about fifty paces distant, and bade me mark well the spot where the ball should hit. He raised his piece gradually, until the *bead* (that being the name given by the Kentuckians to the *sight*) of the barrel was brought to a line with the spot which he intended to hit. The whip-like report resounded through the woods and along the hills, in repeated echoes. Judge of my surprise when

I perceived that the ball had hit the piece of the bark immediately beneath the Squirrel, and shivered it into splinters, the concussion produced by which had killed the animal, and sent it whirling through the air, as if it had been blown up by the explosion of a powder magazine. Boone kept up his firing, and, before many hours had elapsed, we had procured as many Squirrels as we wished; for you must know, kind reader, that to load a rifle requires only a moment, and that if it is wiped once after each shot, it will do duty for hours. Since that first interview with our veteran Boone I have seen many other individuals perform the same feat.

The *snuffing of a candle* with a ball, I first had an opportunity of seeing near the banks of Green River, not far from a large Pigeon-roost to which I had previously made a visit. I heard many reports of guns during the early part of a dark night, and knowing them to be those of rifles, I went towards the spot to ascertain the cause. On reaching the place, I was welcomed by a dozen of tall stout men, who told me they were exercising, for the purpose of enabling them to shoot under night at the reflected light from the eyes of a Deer or Wolf, by torchlight, of which I shall give you an account somewhere else. A fire was blazing near, the smoke of which rose curling among the thick foliage of the trees. At a distance which rendered it scarcely distinguishable, stood a burning candle, as if intended for an offering to the goddess of night, but which in reality was only fifty yards from the spot on which we all stood. One man was within a few yards of it, to watch the effects of the shots, as well as to light the candle should it chance to go out, or to replace it should the shot cut it across. Each marksman shot in his turn. Some never hit either the snuff or the candle, and were congratulated with a loud laugh; while others actually snuffed the candle without putting it out, and were recompensed for their dexterity by numerous

hurrahs. One of them, who was particularly expert, was
very fortunate, and snuffed the candle three times out of
seven, whilst all the other shots either put out the candle
or cut it immediately under the light.

Of the feats performed by the Kentuckians with the
rifle, I could say more than might be expedient on the
present occasion. In every thinly peopled portion of the
State, it is rare to meet one without a gun of that description, as well as a tomahawk. By way of recreation, they
often cut off a piece of the bark of a tree, make a target of
it, using a little powder wetted with water or saliva, for the
bull's-eye, and shoot into the mark all the balls they have
about them, picking them out of the wood again.

After what I have said, you may easily imagine with
what ease a Kentuckian procures game, or despatches an
enemy, more especially when I tell you that every one in
the State is accustomed to handle the rifle from the time
when he is first able to shoulder it until near the close of
his career. That murderous weapon is the means of procuring them subsistence during all their wild and extensive
rambles, and is the source of their principal sports and
pleasures.

THE TRAVELLER AND THE POLE-CAT

ON a journey from Louisville to Henderson in Kentucky,
performed during very severe winter weather, in company
with a foreigner, the initials of whose name are D. T., my
companion, spying a beautiful animal, marked with black
and pale yellow, and having a long and bushy tail, exclaimed, " Mr. Audubon, is not that a beautiful Squirrel? "
" Yes," I answered, " and of a kind that will suffer you to
approach it and lay hold of it, if you are well gloved."
Mr. D. T., dismounting, took up a dry stick, and advanced
towards the pretty animal, with his large cloak floating in

the breeze. I think I see him approach, and laying the stick gently across the body of the animal, try to secure it; and I can yet laugh almost as heartily as I did then, when I plainly saw the discomfiture of the traveller. The Pole-cat (for a true Pole-cat it was, the *Mephitis americana* of zoölogists) raised its fine bushy tail, and showered such a discharge of the fluid given him by nature as a defence that my friend, dismayed and infuriated, began to belabor the poor animal. The swiftness and good management of the Pole-cat, however, saved its bones, and as it made its retreat towards its hole, it kept up at every step a continued ejectment, which fully convinced the gentleman that the pursuit of such Squirrels as these was at the best an unprofitable employment.

This was not all, however. I could not suffer his approach, nor could my horse; it was with difficulty he mounted his own; and we were forced to continue our journey far asunder, and he much to leeward. Nor did the matter end here. We could not proceed much farther that night; as, in the first place, it was nearly dark when we saw the Pole-cat, and as, in the second place, a heavy snow-storm began, and almost impeded our progress. We were forced to make for the first cabin we saw. Having asked and obtained permission to rest for the night, we dismounted and found ourselves amongst a crowd of men and women who had met for the purpose of *corn-shucking*.

To a European who has not visited the western parts of the United States, an explanation of this corn-shucking may not be unacceptable. Corn (or you may prefer calling it maize) is gathered in the husk, that is, by breaking each large ear from the stem. These ears are first thrown into heaps in the field, and afterwards carried in carts to the barn, or, as in this instance, and in such portions of Kentucky, to a shed made of the blades or long leaves that hang in graceful curves from the stalk, and which, when plucked and dried, are used instead of hay as food for horses and cattle. The husk consists of several thick leaves rather longer than the corn-ear itself, and which secure it from the weather. It is quite a labor to detach these leaves from the ear when thousands of bushels of the corn are gathered and heaped together. For this purpose, however, and in the western country more especially, several neighboring families join alternately at each other's plantations, and assist in clearing away the husks, thus preparing the maize for the market or for domestic use.

The good people whom we met with at this hospitable house were on the point of going to the barn (the farmer here being in rather good condition) to work until towards the middle of the night. When we had stood the few stares to which strangers must accustom themselves, no matter where, even in a drawing-room, we approached the fire. What a shock for the whole party! The scent of the Polecat, that had been almost stifled on my companion's vestments by the cold of the evening air, now recovered its primitive strength. The cloak was put out of the house, but its owner could not well be used in the same way. The company, however, took to their heels, and there only remained a single black servant, who waited on us till supper was served.

I felt vexed with myself, as I saw the good traveller displeased. But he had so much good-breeding as to treat this important affair with great forbearance, and merely said he was sorry for his want of knowledge in zoölogy. The good gentleman, however, was not only deficient in zoölogical lore, but, fresh as he was from Europe, felt more than uneasy in this out-of-the-way house, and would have proceeded towards my own home that night, had I not at length succeeded in persuading him that he was in perfect security.

We were shown to bed. As I was almost a stranger to him, and he to me, he thought it a very awkward thing to be obliged to lie in the same bed with me, but afterwards spoke of it as a happy circumstance, and requested that I should suffer him to be placed next the logs, thinking, no doubt, that there he should run no risk.

We started by break of day, taking with us the frozen cloak, and after passing a pleasant night in my own house, we parted. Some years after, I met my Kentucky companion in a far distant land, when he assured me that whenever the sun shone on his cloak or it was brought near a fire, the scent of the Pole-cat became so perceptible that he at last gave it to a poor monk in Italy.

The animal commonly known in America by the name of the Pole-cat is about a foot and a half in length, with a large bushy tail, nearly as long as the body. The color is generally brownish-black, with a large white patch on the back of the head; but there are many varieties of coloring, in some of which the broad white bands of the back are very conspicuous. The Pole-cat burrows, or forms a subterranean habitation among the roots of trees, or in rocky places. It feeds on birds, young Hares, Rats, Mice, and other animals, and commits great depredations on poultry. The most remarkable peculiarity of this animal is the power, alluded to above, of squirting for its defence a most nauseously scented fluid contained in a receptacle situated under the tail, which it can do to a distance of several yards. It does not, however, for this purpose sprinkle its tail with the fluid, as some allege, unless when extremely harassed by its enemies. The Pole-cat is frequently domesticated. The removal of the glands prevents the secretion of the nauseous fluid, and when thus improved, the animal becomes a great favorite, and performs the offices of the common cat with great dexterity.

DEER HUNTING

THE different modes of Deer hunting are probably too well understood, and too successfully practised in the United States; for, notwithstanding the almost incredible abundance of these beautiful animals in our forests and prairies, such havoc is carried on amongst them that, in a few centuries, they will probably be as scarce in America as the Great Bustard now is in Britain.

We have three modes of hunting Deer, each varying in some slight degree in the different States and districts. The first is termed *still hunting*, and is by far the most destructive. The second is called *fire-light hunting*, and is next in its exterminating effects. The third, which may be looked upon as a mere amusement, is named *driving*. Although many Deer are destroyed by this latter method, it is not by any means so pernicious as the others. These methods I shall describe separately.

Still hunting is followed as a kind of trade by most of our frontier-men. To be practised with success it requires great activity, an expert management of the rifle, and a thorough knowledge of the forest, together with an intimate acquaintance with the habits of the Deer, not only at different seasons of the year, but also at every hour of the day, as the hunters must be aware of the situations which the game prefers, and in which it is most likely to be found at any particular time. I might here present you with a full account of the habits of our Deer, were it not my intention to lay before you, at some future period, in the form of a distinct work, the observations which I have made on the various quadrupeds of our extensive territories.

Illustrations of any kind require to be presented in the best possible light. We shall therefore suppose that we are now about to follow the *true hunter*, as the " still hunter " is also called, through the interior of the tangled woods, across morasses, ravines, and such places, where the game may prove more or less plentiful, even should none be found there in the first instance. We shall allow our hunter all the agility, patience, and care which his occupation requires, and will march in his rear, as if we were spies, watching all his motions.

His dress, you observe, consists of a leather hunting-shirt, and a pair of trousers of the same material. His feet are well moccasined; he wears a belt round his waist; his heavy rifle is resting on his brawny shoulder; on one side hangs his ball pouch, surmounted by the horn of an ancient Buffalo, once the terror of the herd, but now containing a pound of the best gunpowder; his butcher knife is scabbarded in the same strap; and behind is a tomahawk, the handle of which has been thrust through his girdle. He walks with so rapid a step that probably few men, beside ourselves, that is, myself and my kind reader, could follow him, unless for a short distance, in their anxiety to witness his ruthless deeds. He stops, looks to the flint of his gun, its priming, and the leather cover of the lock, then glances his eye towards the sky, to judge of the course most likely to lead him to the game.

The heavens are clear, the red glare of the morning sun gleams through the lower branches of the lofty trees, the dew hangs in pearly drops at the top of every leaf. Already has the emerald hue of the foliage been converted into the more glowing tints of our autumnal months. A slight frost appears on the fence-rails of his little corn-field. As he proceeds he looks to the dead foliage under his feet, in search of the well-known traces of a buck's hoof. Now he bends towards the ground, on which something has attracted his attention. See! he alters his course, increases his speed, and will soon reach the opposite hill. Now he moves with caution, stops at almost every tree, and peeps forward, as if already within shooting distance of the game. He advances again, but how very slowly! He has reached the declivity, upon which the sun shines in all its growing splendor; but mark him! he takes the gun from his shoulder, has already thrown aside the leathern cover of the lock, and is wiping the edge of the flint with his tongue. Now he stands like a monumental figure, perhaps measuring the distance that lies between him and the game which he has in view. His rifle is slowly raised, the report follows, and he runs. Let us run also. Shall I speak to him, and ask him the result of this first essay? Assuredly, reader, for I know him well.

" Pray, friend, what have you killed? " for to say, " What have you shot at? " might imply the possibility of having missed, and so might hurt his feelings. " Nothing but a buck." "And where is it? " " Oh, it has taken a jump or so, but I settled it, and will soon be with it. My ball struck, and must have gone through his heart." We arrive at the spot where the animal had laid itself down among the grass in a thicket of grape-vines, sumach, and spruce bushes, where it intended to repose during the middle of the day. The place is covered with blood, the hoofs of the Deer have left deep prints in the ground, as it bounced in the agonies produced by its wound; but the blood that has gushed from its side discloses the course which it has taken. We soon reach the spot. There lies the buck, its tongue out, its eye dim, its breath exhausted; it is dead. The hunter draws his knife, cuts the buck's throat almost asunder, and prepares to skin it. For this purpose he hangs it upon the branch of a tree. When the skin is removed, he cuts off the hams, and abandoning the rest of the carcass to the Wolves and Vultures, reloads his gun, flings the venison, enclosed by the skin, upon his back, secures it with a strap, and walks off in search of more game, well knowing that, in the immediate neighborhood, another at least is to be found.

Had the weather been warmer, the hunter would have

sought for the buck along the *shadowy* side of the hills.
Had it been the spring season, he would have led us
through some thick cane-brake, to the margin of some
remote lake, where you would have seen the Deer immersed to his head in the water, to save his body from the
tormenting attacks of mosquitoes. Had winter overspread
the earth with a covering of snow, he would have searched
the low, damp woods, where the mosses and lichens, on
which at that period the Deer feeds, abound; the trees
being generally crusted with them for several feet from the
ground. At one time he might have marked the places
where the Deer clears the velvet from his horns by rubbing
them against the low stems of bushes, and where he frequently scrapes the earth with his fore-hoofs; at another
he would have betaken himself to places where persimmons and crab-apples abound, as beneath these trees the
Deer frequently stops to munch their fruits. During early
spring our hunter would imitate the bleating of the doe,
and thus frequently obtain both her and the fawn, or, like
some tribes of Indians, he would prepare a Deer's head,
placed on a stick, and creeping with it amongst the tall
grass of the prairies, would decoy Deer in reach of his rifle.
But, kind reader, you have seen enough of the *still hunter.*
Let it suffice for me to add that by the mode pursued by
him thousands of Deer are annually killed, many individuals shooting these animals merely for the skin, not caring
for even the most valuable portions of the flesh, unless
hunger, or a near market, induce them to carry off the
hams.

The mode of destroying deer by *fire-light,* or, as it is
named in some parts of the country, *forest-light,* never fails
to produce a very singular feeling in him who witnesses it
for the first time. There is something in it which at times
appears awfully grand. At other times a certain degree
of fear creeps over the mind, and even affects the physical
powers of him who follows the hunter through the thick

undergrowth of our woods, having to leap his horse over hundreds of huge fallen trunks, at one time impeded by a straggling grape-vine crossing his path, at another squeezed between two stubborn saplings, whilst their twigs come smack in his face, as his companion has forced his way through them. Again, he now and then runs the risk of breaking his neck, by being suddenly pitched headlong on the ground, as his horse sinks into a hole covered over with moss. But I must proceed in a more regular manner, and leave you, kind reader, to judge whether such a mode of hunting would suit your taste or not.

The hunter has returned to his camp or his house, has rested and eaten of his game. He waits impatiently for the return of night. He has procured a quantity of pine knots filled with resinous matter, and has an old frying-pan, that, for aught I know to the contrary, may have been used by his great-grandmother, in which the pine-knots are to be placed when lighted. The horses stand saddled at the door. The hunter comes forth, his rifle slung on his shoulder, and springs upon one of them, while his son, or a servant, mounts the other with the frying-pan and the pine-knots. Thus accoutred, they proceed towards the interior of the forest. When they have arrived at the spot where the hunt is to begin, they strike fire with a flint and steel, and kindle the resinous wood. The person who carries the fire moves in the direction judged to be the best. The blaze illuminates the near objects, but the distant parts seem involved in deepest obscurity. The hunter who bears the gun keeps immediately in front, and after a while discovers before him two feeble lights, which are produced by the reflection of the pine-fire from the eyes of an animal of the Deer or Wolf kind. The animal stands quite still. To one unacquainted with this strange mode of hunting, the glare from its eyes might bring to his imagination some lost hobgoblin that had strayed from its usual haunts. The hunter, however, nowise intimidated, approaches the object, sometimes so near as to discern its form, when, raising the rifle to his shoulder, he fires and kills it on the spot. He then dismounts, secures the skin and such portions of the flesh as he may want, in the manner already described, and continues his search through the greater part of the night, sometimes until the dawn of day, shooting from five to ten Deer, should these animals be plentiful. This kind of hunting proves fatal, not to the Deer alone, but also sometimes to Wolves, and now and then to a horse or cow, which may have straggled far into the woods.

Now, kind reader, prepare to mount a generous, full-blood Virginian hunter. See that your gun is in complete order, for hark to the sound of the bugle and horn, and the mingled clamor of a pack of harriers! Your friends are waiting for you, under the shade of the wood, and we must together go *driving* the light-footed Deer. The distance over which one has to travel is seldom felt when pleasure is anticipated as the result; so galloping we go pell-mell through the woods, to some well-known place where many a fine buck has drooped its antlers under the ball of the hunter's rifle. The servants, who are called the drivers, have already begun their search. Their voices are heard exciting the hounds, and unless we put spurs to our steeds, we may be too late at our stand, and thus lose the first opportunity of shooting the fleeting game as it passes by. Hark again! The dogs are in chase, the horn sounds louder and more clearly. Hurry, hurry on, or we shall be sadly behind!

Here we are at last! Dismount, fasten your horse to this tree, place yourself by the side of that large yellow poplar, and mind you do not shoot me! The Deer is fast approaching; I will to my own stand, and he who shoots him dead wins the prize.

The Deer is heard coming. It has inadvertently cracked a dead stick with its hoof, and the dogs are now so near that it will pass in a moment. There it comes! How beautifully it bounds over the ground! What a splendid head of horns! How easy its attitudes, depending, as it seems to do, on its own swiftness for safety! All is in vain, however; a gun is fired, the animal plunges and doubles with incomparable speed. There he goes! He passes another stand, from which a second shot, better directed than the first, brings him to the ground. The dogs, the servants, the sportsmen are now rushing forward to the spot. The hunter who has shot it is congratulated on his skill or good luck, and the chase begins again in some other part of the woods.

A few lines of explanation may be required to convey a clear idea of this mode of hunting. Deer are fond of following and retracing paths which they have formerly pursued, and continue to do so even after they have been shot at more than once. These tracks are discovered by persons on horseback in the woods, or a Deer is observed crossing a road, a field, or a small stream. When this has been noticed twice, the deer may be shot from the places called *stands* by the sportsman, who is stationed there, and waits for it, a line of stands being generally formed so as to cross the path which the game will follow. The person who ascertains the usual pass of the game, or discovers the parts where the animal feeds or lies down during the day, gives intimation to his friends, who then prepare for the chase. The servants start the Deer with the hounds, and by good management generally succeed in making it run the course that will soonest bring it to its death. But, should the Deer be cautious, and take another course, the hunters, mounted on swift horses, gallop through the woods to intercept it, guided by the sound of the horns and the cry of the dogs, and frequently succeed in shooting it. This sport is extremely agreeable, and proves successful on almost every occasion.

Hoping that this account will be sufficient to induce you,

kind reader, to go *driving* in our western and southern
woods, I now conclude my chapter on Deer Hunting by
informing you that the species referred to above is the
Virginia Deer, *Cervus virginianus*; and that, until I be able
to present you with a full account of its habits and history,
you may consult for information respecting it the excellent
"Fauna Americana" of my esteemed friend Dr. Harlan, of
Philadelphia.

THE ECCENTRIC NATURALIST

" WHAT an odd-looking fellow!" said I to myself, as,
while walking by the river, I observed a man landing from
a boat, with what I thought a bundle of dried clover on his
back; " how the boatmen stare at him! sure he must be
an original!" He ascended with a rapid step, and approaching me asked if I could point out the house in
which Mr. Audubon resided. "Why, I am the man," said
I, " and will gladly lead you to my dwelling."

The traveller rubbed his hands together with delight,
and drawing a letter from his pocket handed it to me
without any remark. I broke the seal and read as follows: " My dear Audubon, I send you an odd fish, which
you may prove to be undescribed, and hope you will do
so in your next letter. Believe, me always your friend
B." With all the simplicity of a woodsman I asked the
bearer where the odd fish was, when M. de T. (for, kind
reader, the individual in my presence was none else than
that renowned naturalist) smiled, rubbed his hands, and
with the greatest good-humor said, "I am that odd fish
I presume, Mr. Audubon." I felt confounded and blushed,
but contrived to stammer an apology.

We soon reached the house, when I presented my
learned guest to my family, and was ordering a servant to
go to the boat for M. de T.'s luggage, when he told me he

had none but what he brought on his back. He then loosened the pack of weeds which had first drawn my attention. The ladies were a little surprised, but I checked their critical glances for the moment. The naturalist pulled off his shoes, and while engaged in drawing his stockings, not up, but down, in order to cover the holes about the heels, told us in the gayest mood imaginable that he had walked a great distance, and had only taken a passage on board the *ark*, to be put on this shore, and that he was sorry his apparel had suffered so much from his late journey. Clean clothes were offered, but he would not accept them, and it was with evident reluctance that he performed the lavations usual on such occasions before he sat down to dinner.

At table, however, his agreeable conversation made us all forget his singular appearance; and, indeed, it was only as we strolled together in the garden that his attire struck me as exceedingly remarkable. A long loose coat of yellow nankeen, much the worse for the many rubs it had got in its time, and stained all over with the juice of plants, hung loosely about him like a sac. A waistcoat of the same, with enormous pockets, and buttoned up to his chin, reached below over a pair of tight pantaloons, the lower parts of which were buttoned down to the ankles. His beard was as long as I have known my own to be during some of my peregrinations, and his lank black hair hung loosely over his shoulders. His forehead was so broad and prominent that any tyro in phrenology would instantly have pronounced it the residence of a mind of strong powers. His words impressed an assurance of rigid truth, and as he directed the conversation to the study of the natural sciences, I listened to him with as much delight as Telemachus could have listened to Mentor. He had come to visit me, he said, expressly for the purpose of seeing my drawings, having been told that my representations of birds were accompanied with those of shrubs and plants, and he was desirous of knowing whether I might chance to have in my collection any with which he was unacquainted. I observed some degree of impatience in his request to be allowed at once to see what I had. We returned to the house, when I opened my portfolios and laid them before him.

He chanced to turn over the drawing of a plant quite new to him. After inspecting it closely, he shook his head, and told me no such plant existed in nature; for, kind reader, M. de T., although a highly scientific man, was suspicious to a fault, and believed such plants only to exist as he had himself seen, or such as, having been discovered of old, had, according to Father Malebranche's expression, acquired a "venerable beard." I told my guest that the plant was common in the immediate neighborhood, and that I should show it him on the morrow. "And why to-morrow, Mr. Audubon? Let us go now." We did so, and on reaching the bank of the river I pointed to the plant. M. de T., I thought, had gone mad. He plucked the plants one after another, danced, hugged me in his arms, and exultingly told me that he had got not merely a new species, but a new genus. When we returned home, the naturalist opened the bundle which he had brought on his back, and took out a journal rendered water-proof by means of a leather case, together with a small parcel of linen, examined the new plant, and wrote its description. The examination of my drawings then went on. You would be pleased, kind reader, to hear his criticisms, which were of the greatest advantage to me, for, being well acquainted with books as well as with nature, he was well fitted to give me advice.

It was summer, and the heat was so great that the windows were all open. The light of the candles attracted many insects, among which was observed a large species of Scarabæus. I caught one, and, aware of his inclination to believe only what he should himself see, I showed him the insect, and assured him it was so strong that it would crawl on the table with the candlestick on its back. " I should like to see the experiment made, Mr. Audubon," he replied. It was accordingly made, and the insect moved about, dragging its burden so as to make the candlestick change its position as if by magic, until coming upon the edge of the table, it dropped on the floor, took to wing, and made its escape.

When it waxed late, I showed him to the apartment intended for him during his stay, and endeavored to render him comfortable, leaving him writing materials in abundance. I was indeed heartily glad to have a naturalist under my roof. We had all retired to rest. Every person I imagined was in deep slumber save myself, when of a sudden I heard a great uproar in the naturalist's room. I got up, reached the place in a few moments, and opened the door, when to my astonishment, I saw my guest running about the room naked, holding the handle of my favorite violin, the body of which he had battered to pieces against the walls in attempting to kill the bats which had entered by the open window, probably attracted by the insects flying around his candle. I stood amazed, but he continued jumping and running round and round, until he was fairly exhausted, when he begged me to procure one of the animals for him, as he felt convinced they belonged to " a new species." Although I was convinced of the contrary, I took up the bow of my demolished Cremona, and administering a smart tap to each of the bats as it came up, soon got specimens enough. The war ended, I again bade him good-night, but could not help observing the state of the room. It was strewed with plants, which it would seem he had arranged into groups, but which were now scattered about in confusion. " Never mind, Mr. Audubon," quoth the eccentric naturalist, " never mind, I'll soon arrange them again. I have the bats, and that's enough."

Some days passed, during which we followed our several occupations. M. de T. searched the woods for plants, and I for birds. He also followed the margins of the Ohio, and picked up many shells, which he greatly extolled. With us, I told him, they were gathered into heaps to be converted into lime. "Lime! Mr. Audubon; why, they are worth a guinea apiece in any part of Europe." One day, as I was returning from a hunt in a cane-brake, he observed that I was wet and spattered with mud, and desired me to show him the interior of one of these places, which he said he had never visited.

The cane, kind reader, formerly grew spontaneously over the greater portions of the State of Kentucky and other western districts of our Union, as well as in many farther south. Now, however, cultivation, the introduction of cattle and horses, and other circumstances connected with the progress of civilization, have greatly altered the face of the country, and reduced the cane within comparatively small limits. It attains a height of from twelve to thirty feet, and a diameter of from one to two inches, and grows in great patches resembling osier-holts, in which occur plants of all sizes. The plants frequently grow so close together, and in course of time become so tangled, as to present an almost impenetrable thicket. A portion of ground thus covered with canes is called a *cane-brake.*

If you picture to yourself one of these cane-brakes growing beneath the gigantic trees that form our western forests, interspersed with vines of many species, and numberless plants of every description, you may conceive how difficult it is for one to make his way through it, especially after a heavy shower of rain or a fall of sleet, when the traveller, in forcing his way through, shakes down upon himself such quantities of water as soon reduce him to a state of the utmost discomfort. The hunters often cut little paths through the thickets with their knives, but the usual mode of passing through them is by pushing one's self backward, and wedging a way between the stems. To follow a Bear or a Cougar pursued by dogs through these brakes is a task the accomplishment of which may be imagined, but of the difficulties and dangers accompanying which I cannot easily give an adequate representation.

The canes generally grow on the richest soil, and are particularly plentiful along the margins of the great western rivers. Many of our new settlers are fond of forming farms in their immediate vicinity, as the plant is much relished by all kinds of cattle and horses, which feed upon it at all seasons, and again because these brakes are plentifully stocked with game of various kinds. It sometimes happens that the farmer clears a portion of the brake. This is done by cutting the stems — which are fistular and knotted, like those of other grasses — with a large knife or cutlass. They are afterwards placed in heaps, and when partially dried set fire to. The moisture contained between the joints is converted into steam, which causes the cane to burst with a smart report, and when a whole mass is crackling, the sounds resemble discharges of musketry. Indeed, I have been told that travellers floating down the rivers, and unacquainted with these circumstances, have been induced to pull their oars with redoubled vigor, apprehending the attack of a host of savages, ready to scalp every one of the party.

A day being fixed, we left home after an early breakfast, crossed the Ohio, and entered the woods. I had determined that my companion should view a cane-brake in all its perfection, and after leading him several miles in a direct course, came upon as fine a sample as existed in that part of the country. We entered, and for some time proceeded without much difficulty, as I led the way, and cut down the canes which were most likely to incommode him. The difficulties gradually increased, so that we were presently obliged to turn our backs to the foe, and push

ourselves on the best way we could. My companion
stopped here and there to pick up a plant and examine it.
After a while we chanced to come upon the top of a fallen
tree, which so obstructed our passage that we were on the
eve of going round, instead of thrusting ourselves through
amongst the branches, when, from its bed in the centre of
the tangled mass, forth rushed a Bear, with such force, and
snuffing the air in so frightful a manner, that M. de T.
became suddenly terror-struck, and, in his haste to escape,
made a desperate attempt to run, but fell amongst the
canes in such a way that he looked as if pinioned. Perceiving him jammed in between the stalks, and thoroughly
frightened, I could not refrain from laughing at the ridi-
culous exhibition which he made. My gayety, however,
was not very pleasing to the *savant*, who called out for
aid, which was at once administered. Gladly would he
have retraced his steps, but I was desirous that he should
be able to describe a cane-brake, and enticed him to follow
me by telling him that our worst difficulties were nearly
over. We proceeded, for by this time the Bear was out
of hearing.

The way became more and more tangled. I saw with
delight that a heavy cloud, portentous of a thunder gust,
was approaching. In the mean time, I kept my companion
in such constant difficulties that he now panted, perspired,
and seemed almost overcome by fatigue. The thunder
began to rumble, and soon after a dash of heavy rain
drenched us in a few minutes. The withered particles of
leaves and bark attached to the canes stuck to our clothes.
We received many scratches from briers, and now and
then a switch from a nettle. M. de T. seriously inquired
if we should ever get alive out of the horrible situation in
which we were. I spoke of courage and patience, and told
him I hoped we should soon get to the margin of the
brake, which, however, I knew to be two miles distant. I
made him rest, and gave him a mouthful of brandy from

my flask; after which, we proceeded on our slow and painful march. He threw away all his plants, emptied his pockets of the fungi, lichens, and mosses which he had thrust into them, and finding himself much lightened, went on for thirty or forty yards with a better grace. But, kind reader, enough — I led the naturalist first one way, then another, until I had nearly lost myself in the brake, although I was well acquainted with it, kept him tumbling and crawling on his hands and knees until long after mid-day, when we at length reached the edge of the river. I blew my horn, and soon showed my companion a boat coming to our rescue. We were ferried over, and on reaching the house, found more agreeable occupation in replenishing our empty coffers.

M. de T. remained with us for three weeks, and collected multitudes of plants, shells, bats, and fishes, but never again expressed a desire of visiting a cane-brake. We were perfectly reconciled to his oddities, and, finding him a most agreeable and intelligent companion, hoped that his sojourn might be of long duration. But, one evening when tea was prepared, and we expected him to join the family, he was nowhere to be found. His grasses and other valuables were all removed from his room. The night was spent in searching for him in the neighborhood. No eccentric naturalist could be discovered. Whether he had perished in a swamp, or had been devoured by a Bear or a Gar-fish, or had taken to his heels, were matters of conjecture; nor was it until some weeks after that a letter from him, thanking us for our attention, assured me of his safety.

SCIPIO AND THE BEAR

THE Black Bear (*Ursus americanus*), however clumsy in appearance, is active, vigilant, and persevering; possesses great strength, courage, and address; and undergoes with little injury the greatest fatigues and hardships in avoiding the pursuit of the hunter. Like the Deer, it changes its haunts with the seasons, and for the same reason, namely, the desire of obtaining suitable food, or of retiring to the more inaccessible parts, where it can pass the time in security, unobserved by man, the most dangerous of its enemies. During the spring months, it searches for food in the low rich alluvial lands that border the rivers, or by the margins of such inland lakes as, on account of their small size, are called by us ponds. There it procures abundance of succulent roots, and of the tender juicy stems of plants, upon which it chiefly feeds at that season. During the summer heat, it enters the gloomy swamps, passes much of its time in wallowing in the mud, like a hog, and contents itself with crayfish, roots, and nettles, now and then, when hard pressed by hunger, seizing on a young pig, or perhaps a sow, or even a calf. As soon as the different kinds of berries which grow on the mountains begin to ripen, the Bears betake themselves to the high grounds, followed by their cubs. In such retired parts of the country where there are no hilly grounds, it pays visits to the maize fields, which it ravages for a while. After this, the various species of nuts, acorns, grapes, and other forest fruits, that form what in the western country is called *mast*, attract its attention. The Bear is then seen rambling singly through the woods to gather this harvest, not forgetting meanwhile to rob every *Bee-tree* it meets with, Bears being, as you well know, expert at this operation. You also know that they are good climbers, and

may have been told, or at least may now be told, that the
Black Bear now and then *houses* itself in the hollow trunks
of the larger trees for weeks together, when it is said to
suck its paws. You are probably not aware of a habit in
which it indulges, and which, being curious, must be interesting to you.

At one season, the Black Bear may be seen examining
the lower part of the trunk of a tree for several minutes
with much attention, at the same time looking around, and
snuffing the air, to assure itself that no enemy is near. It
then raises itself on its hind-legs, approaches the trunk,
embraces it with its fore-legs, and scratches the bark with
its teeth and claws for several minutes in continuance. Its
jaws clash against each other, until a mass of foam runs
down on both sides of the mouth. After this it continues its rambles.

In various portions of our country, many of our woodsmen and hunters who have seen the Bear performing the
singular operation just described, imagine that it does so
for the purpose of leaving behind it an indication of its
size and power. They measure the height at which the
scratches are made, and in this manner can, in fact, form
an estimate of the magnitude of the individual. My own
opinion, however, is different. It seems to me that the
Bear scratches the trees, not for the purpose of shewing
its size or its strength, but merely for that of sharpening
its teeth and claws, to enable it better to encounter a rival
of its own species during the amatory season. The Wild
Boar of Europe clashes its tusks and scrapes the earth with
its feet, and the Deer rubs its antlers against the lower
part of the stems of young trees or bushes, for the same
purpose.

Being one night sleeping in the house of a friend, I
was wakened by a negro servant bearing a light, who gave
me a note, which he said his master had just received.
I ran my eye over the paper, and found it to be a com-

munication from a neighbor, requesting my friend and myself to join him as soon as possible, and assist in killing some Bears at that moment engaged in destroying his corn. I was not long in dressing, you may be assured, and, on entering the parlor, found my friend equipped and only waiting for some bullets, which a negro was employed in casting. The overseer's horn was heard calling up the negroes from their different cabins. Some were already engaged in saddling our horses, whilst others were gathering all the cur-dogs of the plantation. All was bustle. Before half an hour had elapsed, four stout negro men, armed with axes and knives, and mounted on strong nags of their own (for you must know, kind reader, that many of our slaves rear horses, cattle, pigs, and poultry, which are exclusively their own property), were following us at a round gallop through the woods, as we made directly for the neighbor's plantation, a little more than five miles off.

The night was none of the most favorable, a drizzling rain rendering the atmosphere thick and rather sultry; but as we were well acquainted with the course, we soon reached the house, where the owner was waiting our arrival. There were now three of us armed with guns, half a dozen servants, and a good pack of dogs of all kinds. We jogged on towards the detached field in which the Bears were at work. The owner told us that for some days several of these animals had visited his corn, and that a negro who was sent every afternoon to see at what part of the enclosure they entered, had assured him there were at least five in the field that night. A plan of attack was formed: the bars at the usual gap of the fence were to be put down without noise; the men and dogs were to divide, and afterwards proceed so as to surround the Bears, when, at the sounding of our horns, every one was to charge towards the centre of the field, and shout as loudly as possible, which it was judged would so intimidate the animals as to induce them to seek refuge upon the dead trees with which the field was still partially covered.

The plan succeeded. The horns sounded, the horses galloped forward, the men shouted, the dogs barked and howled. The shrieks of the negroes were enough to frighten a legion of Bears, and those in the field took to flight, so that by the time we reached the centre they were heard hurrying towards the tops of the trees. Fires were immediately lighted by the negroes. The drizzling rain had ceased, the sky cleared, and the glare of the crackling fires proved of great assistance to us. The Bears had been so terrified that we now saw several of them crouched at the junction of the larger boughs with the trunks. Two were immediately shot down. They were cubs of no great size, and being already half dead, we left them to the dogs, which quickly despatched them.

We were anxious to procure as much sport as possible, and having observed one of the Bears, which from its size we conjectured to be the mother, ordered the negroes to cut down the tree on which it was perched, when it was intended the dogs should have a tug with it, while we should support them, and assist in preventing the Bear from escaping by wounding it in one of the hind-legs. The surrounding woods now echoed to the blows of the axemen. The tree was large and tough, having been girded more than two years, and the operation of felling it seemed extremely tedious. However, it began to vibrate at each stroke; a few inches alone now supported it; and in a short time it came crashing to the ground, in so awful a manner that Bruin must doubtless have felt the shock as severe as we should feel a shake of the globe produced by the sudden collision of a comet.

The dogs rushed to the charge, and harassed the Bear on all sides. We had remounted, and now surrounded the poor animal. As its life depended upon its courage and strength, it exercised both in the most energetic manner. Now and then it seized a dog, and killed him by a single stroke. At another time, a well administered blow of one of its fore-legs sent an assailant off yelping so piteously that he might be looked upon as *hors de combat.* A cur had daringly ventured to seize the Bear by the snout, and was seen hanging to it, covered with blood, whilst a dozen or more scrambled over its back. Now and then the infuriated animal was seen to cast a revengeful glance at some of the party, and we had already determined to despatch it, when, to our astonishment, it suddenly shook off all the dogs, and, before we could fire, charged upon one of the negroes, who was mounted on a pied horse. The Bear seized the steed with teeth and claws, and clung to its breast. The terrified horse snorted and plunged. The rider, an athletic young man, and a capital horseman, kept his seat, although only saddled on a sheep's-skin tightly girthed, and requested his master not to fire at the Bear. Notwithstanding his coolness and courage, our anxiety for his safety was raised to the highest pitch, especially when in a moment we saw rider and horse come to the ground together; but we were instantly relieved on witnessing the masterly manner in which Scipio despatched his adversary, by laying open his skull with a single well-directed blow of his axe, when a deep growl announced the death of the Bear, and the valorous negro sprung to his feet unhurt.

Day dawned, and we renewed our search. Two of the remaining Bears were soon discovered, lodged in a tree about a hundred yards from the spot where the last one had been overpowered. On approaching them in a circle, we found that they manifested no desire to come down, and we resolved to try *smoking.* We surrounded the tree with a pile of brushwood and large branches. The flames ascended and caught hold of the dry bark. At length the tree assumed the appearance of a pillar of flame. The Bears mounted to the top branches. When they had reached the uppermost, they were seen to totter, and soon after, the branch cracking and snapping across, they came to the ground, bringing with them a mass of broken twigs. They were cubs, and the dogs soon worried them to death.

The party returned to the house in triumph. Scipio's horse, being severely wounded, was let loose in the field, to repair his strength by eating the corn. A cart was afterwards sent for the game. But before we had left the field, the horses, dogs, and Bears, together with the fires, had destroyed more corn within a few hours than the poor Bear and her cubs had during the whole of their visits.

A KENTUCKY BARBECUE

BEARGRASS CREEK, which is one of the many beautiful streams of the highly cultivated and happy State of Kentucky, meanders through a deeply shaded growth of majestic beechwoods, in which are interspersed various species of walnut, oak, elm, ash, and other trees, extending on either side of its course. The spot on which I witnessed the celebration of an anniversary of the glorious proclamation of our independence is situated on its banks near the city of Louisville. The woods spread their dense tufts towards the shores of the fair Ohio on the west, and over the gently rising grounds to the south and east. Every open spot forming a plantation was smiling in the luxuriance of a summer harvest. The farmer seemed to stand in admiration of the spectacle; the trees of his orchards bowed their branches, as if anxious to restore to their mother earth the fruit with which they were laden; the flocks leisurely ruminated as they lay on their grassy

JOHN WOODHOUSE AUDUBON, 1853.

beds; and the genial warmth of the season seemed inclined to favor their repose.

The free, single-hearted Kentuckian, bold, erect, and
proud of his Virginian descent, had, as usual, made arrangements for celebrating the day of his country's independence.
The whole neighborhood joined with one consent. No
personal invitation was required where every one was welcomed by his neighbor, and from the governor to the
guider of the plough, all met with light hearts and merry
faces.

It was indeed a beautiful day; the bright sun rode in
the clear blue heavens; the gentle breezes wafted around
the odors of the gorgeous flowers; the little birds sang
their sweetest songs in the woods, and the fluttering insects
danced in the sunbeams. Columbia's sons and daughters
seemed to have grown younger that morning. For a whole
week or more many servants and some masters had been
busily engaged in clearing an area. The undergrowth had
been carefully cut down, the low boughs lopped off, and
the grass alone, verdant and gay, remained to carpet the syl-
van pavilion. Now the wagons were seen slowly moving
along under their load of provisions which had been prepared for the common benefit. Each denizen had freely
given his ox, his ham, his venison, his Turkeys and other
fowls. Here were to be seen flagons of every beverage used
in the country; "la belle rivière" had opened her finny
stores, the melons of all sorts, peaches, plums, and pears,
would have sufficed to stock a market. In a word, Kentucky, the land of abundance, had supplied a feast for her
children. A purling stream gave its waters freely, while
the grateful breezes cooled the air. Columns of smoke
from the newly kindled fires rose above the trees; fifty
cooks or more moved to and fro as they plied their trade;
waiters of all qualities were disposing the dishes, the glasses
and the punch-bowls, amid vases filled with rich wines.
"Old Monongahela" filled many a barrel for the crowd.

And now the roasting viands perfume the air, and all appearances conspire to predict the speedy commencement of a banquet such as may suit the vigorous appetite of American woodsmen. Every steward is at his post ready to receive the joyous groups that at this moment begin to emerge from the dark recesses of the woods.

Each comely fair one, clad in pure white, is seen advancing under the protection of her sturdy lover, the neighing of their prancing steeds proclaiming how proud they are of their burden. The youthful riders leap from their seats, and the horses are speedily secured by twisting their bridles round a branch. As the youth of Kentucky lightly and gayly advanced towards the barbecue, they resembled a procession of nymphs and disguised divinities. Fathers and mothers smiled upon them as they followed the brilliant cortége. In a short time the ground was alive with merriment. A great wooden cannon bound with iron hoops was now crammed with home-made powder; fire was conveyed to it by means of a train, and as the explosion burst forth, thousands of hearty huzzas mingled with its echoes. From the most learned a good oration fell in proud and gladdening words on every ear, and although it probably did not equal the eloquence of a Clay, an Everett, a Webster, or a Preston, it served to remind every Kentuckian present of the glorious name, the patriotism, the courage, and the virtue of our immortal Washington. Fifes and drums sounded the march which had ever led him to glory; and as they changed to our celebrated " Yankee-Doodle," the air again rang with acclamations.

Now the stewards invited the assembled throngs to the feast. The fair led the van, and were first placed around the tables, which groaned under the profusion of the best productions of the country that had been heaped upon them. On each lovely nymph attended her gay beau, who in her chance or sidelong glances ever watched an opportunity of reading his happiness. How the viands diminished under the action of so many agents of destruction, I need not say, nor is it necessary that you should listen to the long recital. Many a national toast was offered and accepted, many speeches were delivered, and many essayed in amicable reply. The ladies then retired to booths that had been erected at a little distance, to which they were conducted by their partners, who returned to the table, and having thus cleared for action, recommenced a series of hearty rounds. However, as Kentuckians are neither slow nor long at their meals, all were in a few minutes replenished, and after a few more draughts from the bowl, they rejoined the ladies and prepared for the dance.

Double lines of a hundred fair ones extended along the ground in the most shady part of the woods, while here and there smaller groups awaited the merry trills of reels and cotillons. A burst of music from violins, clarionets, and bugles gave the welcome notice, and presently the whole assemblage seemed to be gracefully moving through the air. The "hunting-shirts" now joined in the dance, their fringed skirts keeping time with the gowns of the ladies, and the married people of either sex stepped in and mixed with their children. Every countenance beamed with joy, every heart leaped with gladness; no pride, no pomp, no affectation were there; their spirits brightened as they continued their exhilarating exercise, and care and sorrow were flung to the winds. During each interval of rest refreshments of all sorts were handed round, and while the fair one cooled her lips with the grateful juice of the melon, the hunter of Kentucky quenched his thirst with ample draughts of well-tempered punch.

I know, reader, that had you been with me on that day you would have richly enjoyed the sight of this national *fête champêtre*. You would have listened with pleasure to the ingenuous tale of the lover, the wise talk of the elder on the affairs of the State, the accounts of improvement in stock and utensils, and the hopes of continued prosperity to the country at large, and to Kentucky in particular. You would have been pleased to see those who did not join in the dance shooting at distant marks with their heavy rifles, or watched how they showed off the superior speed of their high bred "Old Virginia" horses, while others recounted their hunting exploits, and at intervals made the woods ring with their bursts of laughter. With me the time sped like an arrow in its flight, and although more than twenty years have elapsed since I joined a Kentucky barbecue, my spirit is refreshed every Fourth of July by the recollection of that day's merriment.

But now the sun has declined, and the shades of evening creep over the scene. Large fires are lighted in the woods, casting the long shadows of the live columns far along the trodden ground, and flaring on the happy groups loath to separate. In the still, clear sky, begin to sparkle the distant lamps of heaven. One might have thought that Nature herself smiled on the joy of her children. Supper now appeared on the tables, and after all had again refreshed themselves, preparations were made for departure. The lover hurried for the steed of his fair one, the hunter seized the arm of his friend, families gathered into loving groups, and all returned in peace to their happy homes.

And now, reader, allow me also to take my leave, and wish you good-night, trusting that when I again appear with another volume,[1] you will be ready to welcome me with a cordial greeting.

A RACCOON HUNT IN KENTUCKY

THE Raccoon, which is a cunning and crafty animal, is found in all our woods, so that its name is familiar to every child in the Union. The propensity which it evinces to capture all kinds of birds accessible to it in its

---

[1] The last Episode in vol. ii. of the "Ornithological Biographies."

nightly prowlings, for the purpose of feasting on their flesh, induces me to endeavor to afford you some idea of the pleasure which our western hunters feel in procuring it. With your leave, then, reader, I will take you to a "Coon Hunt."

A few hours ago the sun went down far beyond the "far west." The woodland choristers have disappeared, the matron has cradled her babe, and betaken herself to the spinning-wheel; the woodsman, his sons, and "the stranger," are chatting before a blazing fire, making wise reflections on past events, and anticipating those that are to come. Autumn, sallow and sad, prepares to bow her head to the keen blast of approaching winter; the corn, though still on its stalk, has lost its blades; the wood-pile is as large as the woodsman's cabin; the nights have become chill, and each new morn has effected a gradual change in the dews, which now crust the withered herb-age with a coat of glittering white. The sky is still cloudless; a thousand twinkling stars reflect their light from the tranquil waters; all is silent and calm in the forest, save the nightly prowlers that roam in its recesses. In the cheerful cabin all is happiness; its inmates gener-ously strive to contribute to the comfort of the stranger who has chanced to visit them; and, as Raccoons are abun-dant in the neighborhood, they propose a hunt. The offer is gladly accepted. The industrious woman leaves her wheel, for she has listened to her husband's talk; now she approaches the fire, takes up the board shovel, stirs the embers, produces a basket filled with sweet pota-toes, arranges its contents side by side in front of the hearth, and covers them with hot ashes and glowing coals. All this she does because she "guesses" that hungry stomachs will be calling for food when the sport is over. Ah! reader, what "homely joys" there are in such scenes, and how you would enjoy them! The rich may produce a better, or a more sumptuous meal, but his feelings can never be like those of the poor woodsman. Poor, I ought not to call him, for nature and industry bountifully supply all his wants; the woods and rivers produce his chief dainties, and his toils are his pleasures.

Now mark him! the bold Kentuckian is on his feet; his sons and the stranger prepare for the march. Horns and rifles are in requisition. The good man opens the wooden-hinged door, and sends forth a blast loud enough to scare a Wolf. The Raccoons scamper away from the corn-fields, break through the fences, and hie to the woods. The hunter has taken an axe from the wood-pile, and returning, assures us that the night is fine, and that we shall have rare sport. He blows through his rifle to ascertain that it is clear, examines his flint, and thrusts a feather into the touch-hole. To a leathern bag swung at his side is attached a powder-horn; his sheath-knife is there also; below hangs a narrow strip of homespun linen. He takes from his bag a bullet, pulls with his teeth the wooden stopper from his powder-horn, lays the ball on one hand, and with the other pours the powder upon it until it is just overtopped. Raising the horn to his mouth, he again closes it with the stopper, and restores it to its place. He introduces the powder into the tube; springs the box of his gun, greases the "patch" over with some melted tallow, or damps it; then places it on the honey-combed muzzle of his piece. The bullet is placed on the patch over the bore, and pressed with the handle of the knife, which now trims the edge of the linen. The elastic hickory rod, held with both hands, smoothly pushes the ball to its bed; once, twice, thrice has it rebounded. The rifle leaps as it were into the hunter's arms, the feather is drawn from the touch-hole, the powder fills the pan, which is closed. "Now I'm ready," cries the woodsman. His companions say the same. Hardly more than a minute has elapsed. I wish, reader, you had seen this fine fellow — but hark! the dogs are barking.

All is now bustle within and without; a servant lights a torch, and off we march to the woods. "Don't mind the boys, my dear sir," says the woodsman, "follow me close, for the ground is covered with logs, and the grape-vines hang everywhere across. Toby, hold up the light, man, or we'll never see the gullies. Trail your gun, sir, as General Clark used to say — not so, but this way — that's it; now then, no danger, you see; no fear of snakes, poor things! They are stiff enough, I'll be bound. The dogs have treed one. Toby, you old fool, why don't you turn to the right? — not so much; there — go ahead, and give us light. What's that? Who's there? Ah, you young rascals! you've played us a trick, have you? It's all well enough, but now just keep behind, or I'll — " And, in fact, the boys, with eyes good enough to see in the dark, although not quite so well as an Owl's, had cut directly across the dogs, which had surprised a Raccoon on the ground, and bayed it until the lads knocked it on the head. "Seek him, boys!" cried the hunter. The dogs, putting their noses to the ground, pushed off at a good rate. "Master, they're making for the creek," says old Toby. On towards it therefore we push. What woods, to be sure! No gentleman's park this, I assure you, reader. We are now in a low flat; the soil thinly covers the hard clay; nothing but beech-trees hereabouts, unless now and then a maple. Hang the limbs! say I — hang the supple-jacks too — here I am, fast by the neck; cut it with your knife. My knee has had a tremendous rub against a log; now my foot is jammed between two roots; and here I stick. "Toby, come back; don't you know the stranger is not up to the woods? Halloo, Toby, Toby!" There I stood perfectly shackled, the hunter laughing heartily, and the lads glad of an opportunity of slipping off. Toby arrived, and held the torch near the ground, on which the hunter, cutting one of the roots with his hatchet, set me free. "Are you hurt, sir?" — "No, not in the least." Off we start again. The boys had got up with the dogs, which were baying a Raccoon in a small puddle. We soon joined them with the light. "Now, stranger, watch and see!" The Raccoon was all but swimming, and yet had hold of the bottom of the pool with his feet. The glare of the lighted torch was doubtless distressing to him; his coat was ruffled, and his rounded tail seemed thrice its ordinary size; his eyes shone like emeralds; with foaming jaws he watched the dogs, ready to seize each by the snout if it came within reach. They kept him busy for several minutes; the water became thick with mud; his coat now hung dripping, and his draggled tail lay floating on the surface. His guttural growlings, in place of intimidating his assailants excited them the more; and they very unceremoniously closed upon him, curs as they were, and without the breeding of gentle dogs. One seized him by the rump, and tugged, but was soon forced to let go; another stuck to his side, but soon taking a better directed bite of his muzzle than another dog had just done of his tail, Coon made him yelp; and pitiful were the cries of luckless Tyke. The Raccoon would not let go, but in the mean time the other dogs seized him fast, and worried him to death, yet to the last he held by his antagonist's snout. Knocked on the head by an axe, he lay gasping his last breath, and the heaving of his chest was painful to see. The hunters stood gazing at him in the pool, while all around was by the flare of the torch rendered trebly dark and dismal. It was a good scene for a skilful painter.

We had now two Coons, whose furs were worth two quarters of a dollar, and whose bodies, which I must not forget, as Toby informed us, were worth two more. "What now?" I asked. "What now?" quoth the father; "why, go after more, to be sure." So we did, the dogs ahead, and I far behind. In a short time the curs treed another, and when we came up, we found them seated on their haunches, looking upwards, and barking. The hunters now employed their axes, and sent the chips about at such a rate that one of them coming in contact with my cheek, marked it so that a week after several of my friends asked me where, in the name of wonder, I had got that black eye. At length the tree began to crack, and slowly leaning to one side, the heavy mass swung rustling through the air, and fell to the earth with a crash. It was not one Coon that was surprised here, but three — ay, three of them, one of which, more crafty than the rest, leaped fairly from the main top while the tree was staggering. The other two stuck to the hollow of a branch, from which they were soon driven by one of the dogs. Tyke and Lion, having nosed the cunning old one, scampered after him, not mouthing like the well-trained hounds of our southern Fox-hunters, but yelling like furies. The hunter's sons attacked those on the tree, while the woodsman and I, preceded by Toby, made after the other; and busy enough we all were. Our animal was of extraordinary size, and after some parley, a rifle-ball was sent through his brain. He reeled once only; next moment he lay dead. The rest were despatched by the axe and the club, for a shot in those days was too valuable to be spent when it could be saved. It could procure a Deer, and therefore was worth more than a Coon's skin.

Now, look at the moon! how full and clear has she risen on the Raccoon hunters! Now is the time for sport! Onward we go, one following the long shadow of his precursor. The twigs are no impediment, and we move at a brisker pace, as we return to the hills. What a hue and cry! here are the dogs. Overhead and all around, on the forks of each tree, the hunter's keen eye searches for something round, which is likely to prove a coiled-up Raccoon. There's one! Between me and the moon I spied the cunning thing crouched in silence. After tak-

ing aim, I raise my barrel ever so little, the trigger is
pressed; down falls the Raccoon to the ground. Another
and another are on the same tree. Off goes a bullet,
then a second; and we secure the prey. "Let us go
home, stranger," says the woodsman; and contented with
our sport, towards his cabin we trudge. On arriving
there, we find a cheerful fire. Toby stays without, prepares the game, stretches the skins on a frame of cane,
and washes the bodies. The table is already set; the
cake and the potatoes are all well done; four bowls of
buttermilk are ranged in order, and now the hunters
fall to.

The Raccoon is a cunning animal, and makes a pleasant
pet. Monkey-like, it is quite dexterous in the use of its
fore-feet, and it will amble after its master, in the manner of a Bear, and even follow him into the street. It is
fond of eggs, but prefers them raw, and it matters not
whether it be morning, noon, or night when it finds a
dozen in the pheasant's nest, or one placed in your pocket
to please him. He knows the habits of mussels better
than most conchologists. Being an expert climber he
ascends to the hole of the Woodpecker, and devours the
young birds. He knows, too, how to watch the soft-
shelled Turtle's crawl, and, better still, how to dig up her
eggs. Now, by the edge of the pond, grimalkin-like,
he lies seemingly asleep, until the Summer-Duck comes
within reach. No negro knows better when the corn is
juicy and pleasant to eat; and although Squirrels and
Woodpeckers know this too, the Raccoon is found in the
corn-field longer in the season than any of them, the havoc
he commits there amounting to a tithe. His fur is good
in winter, and many think his fleʃh good also; but for my
part, I prefer a live Raccoon to a dead one; and should
find more pleasure in hunting one than in eating him.

PITTING OF WOLVES

THERE seems to be a universal feeling of hostility among men against the Wolf, whose strength, agility, and cunning, which latter is scarcely inferior to that of his relative, Master Reynard, tend to render him an object of hatred, especially to the husbandman, on whose flocks he is ever apt to commit depredations. In America, where this animal was formerly abundant, and in many parts of which it still occurs in considerable numbers, it is not more mercifully dealt with than in other parts of the world. Traps and snares of all sorts are set for catching it, while dogs and horses are trained for hunting the Fox. The Wolf, however, unless in some way injured, being more powerful and perhaps better winded than the Fox, is rarely pursued with hounds or any other dogs in open chase; but as his depredations are at times extensive and highly injurious to the farmer, the greatest exertions have been used to exterminate his race. Few instances have occurred among us of any attack made by Wolves on man, and only one has come under my own notice.

Two young negroes who resided near the banks of the Ohio, in the lower part of the state of Kentucky, about twenty-three years ago, had sweethearts living on a plantation ten miles distant. After the labors of the day were over, they frequently visited the fair ladies of their choice, the nearest way to whose dwelling lay directly across a great cane-brake. As to the lover every moment is precious, they usually took this route to save time. Winter had commenced, cold, dark, and forbidding, and after sunset scarcely a glimpse of light or glow of warmth, one might imagine, could be found in that dreary swamp, excepting in the eyes and bosoms of the ardent youths, or the hungry Wolves that prowled about. The snow covered the earth, and rendered them more easy to be scented from a distance by the famished beasts. Prudent in a certain degree, the young lovers carried their axes on their shoulders, and walked as briskly as the narrow path would allow. Some transient glimpses of light now and then met their eyes, but so faint were they that they believed them to be caused by their faces coming in contact with the slender reeds covered with snow. Suddenly, however, a long and frightful howl burst upon them, and they instantly knew that it proceeded from a troop of hungry, perhaps desperate Wolves. They stopped, and putting themselves in an attitude of defence, awaited the result. All around was dark, save a few feet of snow, and the silence of night was dismal. Nothing could be done to better their situation, and after standing a few minutes in expectation of an attack, they judged it best to resume their march; but no sooner had they replaced their axes on their shoulders and begun to move, than the foremost found himself assailed by several foes. His legs were held fast as if pressed by a powerful screw, and the torture inflicted by the fangs of the ravenous animal was for a moment excruciating. Several Wolves in the meantime sprung upon the breast of the other negro, and dragged him to the ground. Both struggled manfully against their foes; but in a short time one of them ceased to move, and the other, reduced in strength, and perhaps despairing of maintaining his ground, still more of aiding his unfortunate companion, sprung to the branch of a tree, and speedily gained a place of safety near the top. The next morning the mangled remains of his comrade lay scattered around on the snow, which was stained with blood. Three dead Wolves lay around, but the rest of the pack had disappeared, and Scipio, sliding to the ground, took up the axes, and made the best of his way home, to relate the sad adventure.

About two years after this occurrence, as I was travelling between Henderson and Vincennes, I chanced to stop for the night at a farmer's house by the side of the road. After putting up my horse and refreshing myself, I entered into conversation with mine host, who asked if I should like to pay a visit to the Wolf-pits, which were about half a mile distant. Glad of the opportunity I accompanied him across the fields to the neighborhood of a deep wood, and soon saw the engines of destruction. He had three pits, within a few hundred yards of each other. They were about eight feet deep and broader at bottom, so as to render it impossible for the most active animal to escape from them. The aperture was covered with a revolving platform of twigs attached to a central axis. On either surface of the platform was fastened a large piece of putrid venison, with other matters by no means pleasing to my olfactory nerves, although no doubt attractive to the Wolves. My companion wished to visit them that evening, merely as he was in the habit of doing so daily, for the purpose of seeing that all was right. He said that Wolves were very abundant that autumn, and had killed nearly the whole of his sheep and one of his colts, but that he was now "paying them off in full;" and added that if I would tarry a few hours with him next morning, he would beyond a doubt show me some sport rarely seen in those parts. We retired to rest in due time, and were up with the dawn.

"I think," said my host, "that all's right, for I see the dogs are anxious to get away to the pits, and although they are nothing but curs, their noses are none the worse for that." As he took up his gun, an axe, and a large knife, the dogs began to howl and bark, and whisked around us, as if full of joy. When we reached the first pit, we found the bait all gone, and the platform much injured; but the animal that had been entrapped had scraped a subterranean passage for himself, and so escaped. On peeping into the next, he assured me that "three famous fellows were safe enough" in it. I also peeped in and saw the Wolves, two black, and the other brindled, all of goodly size, sure enough. They lay flat on the earth, their ears laid close over the head, their eyes indicating fear more than anger. "But how are we to get them out?" "How, sir?" said the farmer; "why, by going down, to be sure, and hamstringing them." Being a novice in these matters, I begged to be merely a looker-on. "With all my heart," quoth the farmer; "stand here and look at me through the brush." Whereupon he glided down, taking with him his axe and knife, and leaving his rifle to my care. I was not a little surprised to see the cowardice of the Wolves. He pulled out successively their hind legs, and with a side stroke of the knife cut the principal tendon above the joint, exhibiting as little fear as if he had been marking lambs.

"Lo!" exclaimed the farmer, when he had got out, "we have forgotten the rope; I'll go after it." Off he went accordingly, with as much alacrity as any youngster could show. In a short time he returned out of breath, and wiping his forehead with the back of his hand — "Now for it." I was desired to raise and hold the platform on its central balance, whilst he, with all the dexterity of an Indian, threw a noose over the neck of one of the Wolves. We hauled it up motionless with fright, as if dead, its disabled legs swinging to and fro, its jaws wide open, and the gurgle in its throat alone indicating that it was alive. Letting him drop on the ground, the farmer loosened the rope by means of a stick, and left him to the dogs, all of which set upon him with great fury and soon worried him to death. The second was dealt with in the same manner; but the third, which was probably the oldest, as it was the blackest, showed some spirit the moment it was left loose to the mercy of the curs. This Wolf, which we afterwards found to be a female, scuffled along on its fore-legs at a surprising rate, giving a snap every now and then to the nearest dog, which went off howling dismally, with a mouthful of skin torn from its side. And so well did the furious beast defend itself, that apprehensive of its escape, the farmer levelled his rifle at it, and shot it through the heart, on which the curs rushed upon it, and satiated their vengeance on the destroyer of their master's flock.

THE OPOSSUM

THIS singular animal is found more or less abundant in most parts of the Southern, Western, and Middle States of the Union. It is the *Didelphis virginiana* of Pennant, Harlan, and other authors who have given some accounts of its habits; but as none of them, so far as I know, have illustrated its propensity to dissimulate, and as I have had opportunities of observing its manners, I trust that a few particulars of its biography will prove amusing.

The Opossum is fond of secluding itself during the day, although it by no means confines its predatory rangings to the night. Like many other quadrupeds which feed principally on flesh, it is also both frugivorous and herbivorous, and, when very hard pressed by hunger, it seizes various kinds of insects and reptiles. Its gait, while travelling, and at a time when it supposes itself unobserved, is altogether ambling; in other words, it, like a young foal, moves the two legs of one side forward at once. The Newfoundland dog manifests a similar propensity. Having a constitution as hardy as that of the most northern animals, it stands the coldest weather, and does not hibernate, although its covering of fur and hair may be said to be comparatively scanty even during winter. The defect, however, seems to be compensated by a skin of considerable thickness, and a general subcutaneous layer of fat. Its movements are usually rather

slow, and as it walks or ambles along, its curious prehensile tail is carried just above the ground, its rounded ears
are directed forward, and at almost every step its pointed
nose is applied to the objects beneath it, in order to discover what sort of creatures may have crossed its path.
Methinks I see one at this moment slowly and cautiously
trudging over the melting snows by the side of an unfrequented pond, nosing as it goes for the fare its ravenous
appetite prefers. Now it has come upon the fresh track
of a Grouse or Hare, and it raises its snout and snuffs the
keen air. At length it has decided on its course, and it
speeds onward at the rate of a man's ordinary walk. It
stops and seems at a loss in what direction to go, for the
object of its pursuit has either taken a considerable leap
or has cut backwards before the Opossum entered its
track. It raises itself up, stands for a while on its hind
feet, looks around, snuffs the air again, and then proceeds;
but now, at the foot of a noble tree, it comes to a full
stand. It walks round the base of the huge trunk, over
the snow-covered roots, and among them finds an aperture
which it at once enters. Several minutes elapse, when
it re-appears, dragging along a Squirrel already deprived
of life, with which in its mouth it begins to ascend the
tree. Slowly it climbs. The first fork does not seem to
suit it, for perhaps it thinks it might there be too openly
exposed to the view of some wily foe; and so it proceeds,
until it gains a cluster of branches intertwined with grapevines, and there composing itself, it twists its tail round
one of the twigs, and with its sharp teeth demolishes the
unlucky Squirrel, which it holds all the while with its
fore-paws.

The pleasant days of spring have arrived, and the trees
vigorously shoot forth their buds; but the Opossum is
almost bare, and seems nearly exhausted by hunger. It
visits the margins of creeks, and is pleased to see the
young frogs, which afford it a tolerable repast. Gradually

the poke-berry and the nettle shoot up, and on their tender and juicy stems it gladly feeds. The matin calls of the Wild Turkey Cock delight the ear of the cunning creature, for it well knows that it will soon hear the female and trace her to her nest, when it will suck the eggs with delight. Travelling through the woods, perhaps on the ground, perhaps aloft, from tree to tree, it hears a cock crow, and its heart swells as it remembers the savory food on which it regaled itself last summer in the neighboring farm-yard. With great care, however, it advances, and at last conceals itself in the very hen-house.

Honest farmer! why did you kill so many Crows last winter? ay and Ravens too? Well, you have had your own way of it; but now hie to the village and procure a store of ammunition, clean your rusty gun, set your traps, and teach your lazy curs to watch the Opossum. There it comes. The sun is scarcely down, but the appetite of the prowler is keen; hear the screams of one of your best chickens that has been seized by him! The cunning beast is off with it, and nothing can now be done, unless you stand there to watch the Fox or the Owl, now exulting in the thought that you have killed their enemy and your own friend, the poor Crow. That precious hen under which you last week placed a dozen eggs or so is now deprived of them. The Opossum, notwithstanding her angry outcries and rufflings of feathers, has removed them one by one, and now look at the poor bird as she moves across your yard; if not mad, she is at least stupid, for she scratches here and there, calling to her chickens all the while. All this comes from your shooting Crows. Had you been more merciful or more prudent, the Opossum might have been kept within the woods, where it would have been satisfied with a Squirrel, a young Hare, the eggs of a Turkey, or the grapes that so profusely adorn the boughs of our forest trees. But I talk to you in vain.

There cannot be a better exemplification of maternal tenderness than the female Opossum. Just peep into that curious sack in which the young are concealed, each attached to a teat. The kind mother not only nourishes them with care, but preserves them from their enemies; she moves with them as the shark does with its progeny, and now, aloft on the tulip-tree, she hides among the thick foliage. By the end of two months they begin to shift for themselves; each has been taught its particular lesson, and must now practise it.

But suppose the farmer has surprised an Opossum in the act of killing one of his best fowls. His angry feelings urge him to kick the poor beast, which, conscious of its inability to resist, rolls off like a ball. The more the farmer rages, the more reluctant is the animal to manifest resentment; at last there it lies, not dead, but exhausted, its jaws open, its tongue extended, its eye dimmed; and there it would lie until the bottle-fly should come to deposit its eggs, did not its tormentor at length walk off. "Surely," says he to himself, "the beast must be dead." But no, reader, it is only "'possuming," and no sooner has its enemy withdrawn than it gradually gets on its legs, and once more makes for the woods.

Once, while descending the Mississippi, in a sluggish flat-bottomed boat, expressly for the purpose of studying those objects of nature more nearly connected with my favorite pursuits, I chanced to meet with two well-grown Opossums, and brought them alive to the "ark." The poor things were placed on the roof or deck, and were immediately assailed by the crew, when, following their natural instinct, they lay as if quite dead. An experiment was suggested, and both were thrown overboard. On striking the water, and for a few moments after, neither evinced the least disposition to move; but finding their situation desperate, they began to swim towards our uncouth rudder, which was formed of a long slender tree, extending from the middle of the boat thirty feet beyond its stern. They both got upon it, were taken up, and afterwards let loose in their native woods.

In the year 1829, I was in a portion of lower Louisiana, where the Opossum abounds at all seasons, and having been asked by the President and the Secretary of the Zoö-logical Society of London, to forward live animals of this species to them, I offered a price a little above the common, and soon found myself plentifully supplied, twenty-five having been brought to me. I found them excessively voracious, and not less cowardly. They were put into a large box, with a great quantity of food, and conveyed to a steamer bound for New Orleans. Two days afterwards, I went to that city, to see about sending them off to Europe; but, to my surprise, I found that the old males had destroyed the younger ones, and eaten off their heads, and that only sixteen remained alive. A separate box was purchased for each, and some time after they reached my friends, the Rathbones of Liverpool, who, with their usual attention, sent them off to London, where, on my return, I saw a good number of them in the Zoölogical Gardens.

This animal is fond of grapes, of which a species now bears its name. Persimmons are greedily eaten by it, and in severe weather I have observed it eating lichens. Fowls of every kind, and quadrupeds less powerful than itself, are also its habitual prey.

The flesh of the Opossum resembles that of a young pig, and would perhaps be as highly prized, were it not for the prejudice generally entertained against it. Some "very particular" persons, to my knowledge, have pronounced it excellent eating. After cleaning its body, suspend it for a whole week in the frosty air, for it is not eaten in summer; then place it on a heap of hot wood embers; sprinkle it when cooked with gunpowder; and now tell me, good reader, does it not equal the famed Canvas-back Duck? Should you visit any of our markets, you may see it there in company with the best game.

A MAPLE–SUGAR CAMP

WHILE advancing the best way I could through the magnificent woods that cover the undulating grounds in the vicinity of the Green River in Kentucky, I was overtaken by night. With slow and cautious steps I proceeded, feeling some doubt as to my course, when the moon came forth, as if purposely to afford me her friendly light. The air I thought was uncommonly keen, and the gentle breeze that now and then shook the tops of the tall trees more than once made me think of halting for the night, and forming a camp. At times I thought of the campaigns of my old friend, Daniel Boone, his strange adventures in these very woods, and the extraordinary walk which he performed to save his fellow creatures at Fort Massacre from the scalping knives of the irritated Indians.[1] Now and then a Raccoon or Opossum, causing the fallen leaves to rustle, made me pause for a moment; and thus I was forcing my way, thinking on many things dismal as well as pleasing, when the glimmer of a distant fire suddenly aroused me from my reveries, and inspired me with fresh animation. As I approached it, I observed forms of different kinds moving to and fro before it, like spectres; and ere long, bursts of laughter, shouts, and songs apprised me of some merry-making. I thought at first I had probably stumbled upon a camp meeting; but I soon perceived that the mirth proceeded from a band of sugar-makers. Every man, woman, and child stared as I passed them, but all were friendly, and, without more ceremony than was needful, I walked up to the fire, at which I found two or three old women, with their hus-

---

[1] "On the 16th [June, 1778], before sunrise, I departed in the most secret manner, and arrived at Boonesborough on the 20th, after a journey of 160 miles, during which I had but one meal." (Letter of Daniel Boone, who was then forty-three.)

bands, attending to the kettles. Their plain dresses of Kentucky homespun were far more pleasing to my sight than the ribboned turbans of city dames, or the powdered wigs and embroidered waistcoats of antique beaux. I was heartily welcomed, and supplied with a goodly pone of bread, a plate of molasses, and some sweet potatoes.

Fatigued with my long ramble, I lay down under the lee of the smoke, and soon fell into a sound sleep. When day returned, the frost lay thick around; but the party arose cheerful and invigorated, and after performing their orisons, resumed their labor. The scenery was most pleasing; the ground all round looked as if it had been cleared of underwood; the maples, straight and tall, seemed as if planted in rows; between them meandered several rills, which gently murmured as they hastened toward the larger stream; and as the sun dissolved the frozen dews the few feathered songsters joined the chorus of the woodsmen's daughters. Whenever a burst of laughter suddenly echoed through the woods, an Owl or Wild Turkey would respond to it, with a signal welcome to the young men of the party. With large ladles the sugar-makers stirred the thickening juice of the maple; pails of sap were collected from the trees and brought in by the young people, while here and there some sturdy fellow was seen first hacking a cut in a tree, and afterwards boring with an auger a hole, into which he introduced a piece of hollow cane, by which the sap was to be drained off. About half a dozen men had felled a noble yellow poplar, and sawed its great trunk into many pieces, which, after being split, they were scooping into troughs to be placed under the cane-cocks, to receive the maple juice.

Now, good reader, should you ever chance to travel through the maple grounds that lie near the banks of that lovely stream the Green River of Kentucky, either in January or in March, or through those on the broader

Monongahela in April; nay, should you find yourself by
the limpid streamlets that roll down the declivities of the
Pocano Mountains to join the Lehigh, and there meet
with a sugar camp, take my advice and tarry for a while.
If you be on foot or on horseback, and are thirsty, you
can nowhere find a more wholesome or more agreeable
beverage than the juice of the maple.   A man when in
the Floridas may drink molasses diffused in water; in
Labrador he may drink what he can get; and at New
York or Philadelphia he may drink what he chooses; but
in the woods a draught from the sugar maple is delicious
and most refreshing.   How often, when travelling, have
I quenched my thirst with the limpid juice of the receiv-
ing-troughs, from which I parted with regret; nay, even
my horse, I have thought, seemed to desire to linger as
long as he could.

But let me endeavor to describe to you the manner in
which the sugar is obtained.   The trees that yield it
(*Acer saccharinum*) are found more or less abundantly in
all parts of the United States from Louisiana to Maine,
growing on elevated rich grounds.   An incision is made
into the trunk at a height of from two to six feet; a pipe
of cane or of any other kind is thrust into the aperture,
a trough is placed beneath and receives the juice, which
trickles by drops, and is as limpid as the purest spring
water.   When all the trees of a certain space have been
tapped, and the troughs filled, the people collect the
juice, and pour it into large vessels.   A camp has already
been pitched in the midst of a grove; several iron boilers
have been fixed on stone or brick supports, and the business proceeds with vigor.   At times several neighboring
families join, and enjoy the labor, as if it were a pastime,
remaining out day and night for several weeks; for the
troughs and kettles must be attended to from the moment
when they are first put in requisition until the sugar is
produced.   The men and boys perform the most laborious

part of the business, but the women and girls are not less busy.

It takes ten gallons of sap to produce a pound of fine-grained sugar; but an inferior kind in lumps, called *cake sugar*, is obtained in greater quantity. When the season is far advanced, the juice will no longer grain by boiling, and only produces a syrup. I have seen maple sugar so good, that some months after it was manufactured it resembled candy; and well do I remember the time when it was an article of commerce throughout Kentucky, where, twenty-five or thirty years ago, it sold at from $6\frac{1}{2}$ to $12\frac{1}{2}$ cents per pound, according to its quality, and was daily purchased in the markets or stores.

Trees that have been thus bored rarely last many years; for the cuts and perforations made in their trunks injure their health, so that after some years of *weeping* they become sickly, exhibit monstrosities about their lower parts, gradually decay, and at length die. I have no doubt, however, that, with proper care, the same quantity of sap might be obtained with less injury to the trees; and it is now fully time that the farmers and land-owners should begin to look to the preservation of their sugar-maples.

THE WHITE PERCH AND ITS FAVORITE BAIT

No sooner have the overflowing waters of early spring subsided within their banks, and the temperature become pleasant, than the trees of our woods are seen to unfold their buds and blossoms, and the White Perch which during the winter has lived in the ocean, rushes up our streams, to seek the well-known haunts in which it last year deposited its spawn. With unabating vigor it ascends the turbulent current of the Mississippi, of which, however, the

waters are too muddy to suit its habits; and glad no doubt
it is to enter one of the numberless tributaries whose
limpid waters are poured into the mighty river. Of these
subsidiary waters the Ohio is one in whose pure stream
the White Perch seems to delight; and towards its head-
springs the fish advance in numerous shoals, following the
banks with easy progress. Over many a pebbly or gravelly bar does it seek its food. Here the crawling Mussel
it crunches and devours; there, with the speed of an
arrow, it darts upon the minnow; again, at the edge of a
shelving rock, or by the side of a stone, it secures a cray-
fish. No impure food will " the Growler " touch; therefore, reader, never make use of such to allure it, otherwise
not only will your time be lost, but you will not enjoy the
gratification of tasting this delicious fish. Should you
have no experience in fishing for Perch I would recommend
to you to watch the men you see on that shore, for they
are excellent anglers.

Smooth are the waters, clear is the sky, and gently does
the stream move — perhaps its velocity does not exceed a
mile in the hour. Silence reigns around you. See, each
fisher has a basket or calabash, containing many a live
cray; and each line, as thick as a crowquill, measures
scarce a furlong. At one end two Perch-hooks are so fastened that they cannot interfere with each other. A few
inches beyond the reaching point of the farthest hook, the
sinker, perhaps a quarter of a pound in weight, having a
hole bored through its length, is passed upon the line, and
there secured by a stout knot at its lower extremity. The
other end of the line is fastened ashore. The tackle, you
observe, is carefully coiled on the sand at the fisher's feet.
Now on each hook he fixes a cray-fish, piercing the shell
beneath the tail, and forcing the keen weapon to reach the
very head of the suffering creature, while all its legs are left
at liberty to move. Now each man, holding his line a yard
or so from the hooks, whirls it several times overhead, and

sends it off to its full length directly across the stream. No sooner has it reached the gravelly bed than, gently urged by the current, it rolls over and over, until the line and the water follow the same direction. Before this, however, I see that several of the men have had a bite, and that by a short jerk they have hooked the fish. Hand over hand they haul in their lines. Poor Perch, it is useless labor for thee to flounce and splash in that manner, for no pity will be shown thee, and thou shalt be dashed on the sand, and left there to quiver in the agonies of death. The lines are within a few yards of being in. I see the fish gasping on its side. Ah! there are two on this line, both good; on most of the others there is one; but I see some of the lines have been robbed by some cunning inhabitant of the water. What beautiful fishes these Perches are! So silvery beneath, so deeply colored above! What a fine eye, too! But, friend, I cannot endure their gaspings. Pray put them on this short line, and place them in the water beside you, until you prepare to go home. In a few hours each fisher has obtained as many as he wishes. He rolls up his line, fastens five or six Perches on each side of his saddle, mounts his horse, and merrily wends his way.

In this manner the White Perch is caught along the sandy banks of the Ohio, from its mouth to its source. In many parts above Louisville some fishers prefer using the trot-line, which, however, ought to be placed upon, or very little above, the bottom of the stream. When this kind of line is employed, its hooks are more frequently baited with mussels than with cray-fish, the latter being, perhaps, not so easily procured there as farther down the stream. Great numbers of Perches are also caught in seines, especially during a transient rise of the water. Few persons fish for them with the pole, as they generally prefer following the edges of the sand-bars, next to deep water. Like all others of its tribe, the White Perch is fond of depositing its spawn on gravelly or sandy beds, but rarely at a depth of less than four or five feet. These beds are round, and have an elevated margin formed of the sand removed from their centre, which is scooped out for two or three inches. The fish, although it generally remains for some days over its treasure, is by no means so careful of it as the little " Sunny," but starts off at the least appearance of danger. I have more than once taken considerable pleasure in floating over their beds, when the water was sufficiently clear to admit of my seeing both the fish and its place of deposit; but I observed that if the sun was shining, the very sight of the boat's shadow drove the Perches away. I am of opinion that most of them return to the sea about the beginning of November; but of this I am not certain.

The usual length of this fish, which on the Ohio is called the White Perch, and in the state of New York the Growler, is from fifteen to twenty inches. I have, however, seen some considerably larger. The weight varies from a pound and a half to four, and even six pounds. For the first six weeks of their arrival in fresh-water streams they are in season; the flesh is then white and firm, and affords excellent eating; but during the heats of summer they become poor, and are seldom very good. Now and then, in the latter days of September, I have eaten some that tasted as well as in spring. One of the most remarkable habits of this fish is that from which it has received the name of Growler. When poised in the water, close to the bottom of the boat, it emits a rough croaking noise, somewhat resembling a groan. Whenever this sound is heard under a boat, if the least disturbance is made by knocking on the gunwale or bottom, it at once ceases; but is renewed when everything is quiet. It is seldom heard, however, unless in fine, calm weather.

The White Perch bites at the hook with considerable care, and very frequently takes off the bait without being caught. Indeed, it requires a good deal of dexterity to hook it, for if this is not done the first time it touches the bait, you rarely succeed afterward; and I have seen young hands at the game, who, in the course of a morning, seldom caught more than one or two, although they lost perhaps twenty crays. But now that I have afforded you some information respecting the habits of the White Perch, allow me to say a few words on the subject of its favorite bait.

The cray is certainly not a fish, although usually so styled; but as every one is acquainted with its form and nature, I shall not inflict on you any disquisition regarding it. It is a handsome crustaceous animal certainly, and its whole tribe I consider as dainties of the first order. To me " *Ecrevisses*," whether of salt or fresh water, stripped of their coats and blended into a soup or a " Gombo," have always been most welcome. Boiled or roasted, too, they are excellent in my estimation, and mayhap in yours. The cray-fish, of which I here more particularly speak — for I shall not deprive them of their caudal appendage, lest, like a basha without his tail, they might seem of less consequence — are found most abundantly swimming, crawling at the bottom or on shore, or working at their muddy burrows, in all the southern parts of the Union. If I mistake not, we have two species at least, one more an inhabitant of rocky streamlets than the other, and that one by far the best, though the other is good too. Both species swim by means of rapid strokes of the tail, which propel them backwards to a considerable distance at each repetition. All that I regret concerning these animals is that they are absolutely little aquatic vultures — or, if you please, crustacea with vulturine habits — for they feed on everything impure that comes in their way, when they cannot obtain fresh aliment. However this may be, the crays somehow fall in with this sort of food, and any person may catch as many as he may wish, by fastening a piece of flesh to a line, allowing it to remain under water for a while, and drawing it up with care, when, with the aid of a hand-net, he may bring it ashore with *a few!* But although this is a good method of procuring cray-fish, it answers only for those that live in running waters. The form of these is delicate, their color a light olive, and their motions in the water are very lively. The others are larger, of a dark, greenish brown, less active in the water than on land, although they are most truly amphibious. The first conceal themselves beneath shelving rocks, stones, or waterplants; the others form a deep burrow in the damp earth, depositing the materials drawn up as a man would do in digging a well. The manner in which they dispose of the mud you may see by glancing at the plate of the White Ibis, in my third volume of illustrations, where also you will find a tolerable portrait of one of these creatures.

According to the nature of the ground, the burrows of this cray-fish are more or less deep. Indeed, this also depends partly on the increasing dryness of the soil, when influenced by the heat of summer, as well as on the texture of the substratum. Thus, in some places, where the cray can reach the water after working a few inches, it rests contented during the day, but crawls out for food at night. Should it, however, be left dry, it renews its labors; and thus while one burrow may be only five or six inches deep, another may be two or three feet, and a third even more. They are easily procured when thus lodged in shallow holes; but when the burrow is deep, a thread is used, with a small piece of flesh fastened to it. The cray eagerly seizes the bait, and is gently drawn up, and thrown to a distance, when he becomes an easy prey. You have read of the method used by the White Ibis in procuring crays,[1] and I leave you to judge whether the bird or the

---

[1] This bird [the White Ibis], to procure the Cray-fish, walks with remarkable care to the mounds of mud which the latter throws up while forming its hole, and breaks up the upper part of the fabric, dropping the fragments into the deep cavity that has been made by the animal. Then

man is the best fisher. This species is most abundant round the borders of the stagnant lakes, bayous, or ponds of the Southern Districts; and I have seen them caught even in the streets of the suburbs of New Orleans, after a heavy shower. They become a great pest by perforating embankments of all sorts, and many are the maledictions that are uttered against them, both by millers and planters, nay, even by the overseers of the levees along the banks of the Mississippi. But they are curious creatures, formed no doubt for useful purposes, and as such they are worthy of your notice.

THE AMERICAN SUN PERCH

FEW of our smaller fresh-water fishes excel, either in beauty or in delicacy and flavor, the species which I have chosen as the subject of this article, and few afford more pleasure to young fishers. Although it occurs in all our streams, whether rapid or gentle, small or large, in the mill-dam overshadowed by tall forest trees, or in the open lake margined with reeds, you must never expect to find it in impure waters. Let the place be deep or shallow, broad or narrow, the water must be clear enough to allow the sun's rays to fall unimpaired on the rich coat of mail that covers the body of the Sunfish. Look at him as he poises himself under the lee of the protecting rock beneath our feet! See how steadily he maintains his position, and yet how many rapid motions of his fins are necessary to preserve it! Now another is by his side glowing with equal beauty, and poising itself by equally easy and grace-

the Ibis retires a single step, and patiently waits the result. The Cray-fish, incommoded by the load of earth, instantly sets to work anew, and at last reaches the entrance of its burrow; but the moment it comes in sight the Ibis seizes it with his bill. (The White Ibis, *Ibis Alba*, Plate CCXXII., Ornith. Biog., vol. iii., p. 176).

ful movements. The sun is shining, and under the lee of every stone, and sunk log, some of the little creatures are rising to the surface to enjoy the bright blaze, which enhances all their beauty. The golden hues of some parts of the body, blend with the green of the emerald, while the coral tints of the lower parts and the red of its sparkling eye, render our little favorite a perfect gem of the waters.

The rushing stream boils and gurgles as it forces its way over the obstacles presented by its bed, the craggy points, large stones and logs that are strewn along the bottom. Every one of these proves a place of rest, safety, and observation to the little things, whose eyes are ever anxiously watching their favorite prey as it passes. There an unfortunate moth, swept along by the current, labors in vain to extricate itself from the treacherous element; its body, indeed, at intervals, rises a little above the surface, but its broad wings, now wet and heavy, bear it down again to the water. The Sunfish has marked it, and as it passes his retreat, he darts towards it, with twenty of his fellows, all eager to seize the prize. The swiftest swallows it in a moment, and all immediately return to their lurking-places, where they fancy themselves secure. But, alas! the Sunfish is no more without enemies than the moth, or any other living creature. So has nature determined, evidently, to promote prudence and industry, without which none can reap the full advantage of life.

On the top of yon miller's dam stands boldly erect the ardent fisher. Up to the knees and regardless of the danger of his situation, he prepares his apparatus of destruction. A keen hook attached to his grass line is now hid within the body of a worm or grasshopper. With a knowing eye he marks one after another every surge of the water below. Observing the top of a rock scarcely covered, he sends his hook towards it with gentleness and certainty; the bait now floats and anon sinks; his reel slowly lengthens the line, which is suddenly tightened, and he feels that a fish is secured. Now whirls the reel again; thrice has the fish tried its utmost strength and speed, but soon, panting and exhausted, it is seen floating for a moment on the surface. Nothing now is required but to bring it to hand, which done, the angler baits anew, and sends forth the treacherous morsel. For an hour or more he continues the agreeable occupation, drawing from the stream a fish at every short interval. To the willow twig fastened to his waist a hundred "Sunnies" are already attached. Suddenly the sky is overcast, and the crafty fisher, although aware that with a different hook and bait he might soon procure a fine eel or two, carefully wades to the shore, and homeward leisurely plods his way.

In this manner are the Sunfishes caught by the regular or "scientific" anglers, and a beautiful sight it is to see the ease and grace with which they allure the objects of their desire, whether in the open turbulence of the waters, or under the low boughs of the overhanging trees, where, in some deep hole, a swarm of the little creatures may be playing in fancied security. Rarely does his tackle become entangled, whilst, with incomparable dexterity, he draws one after another from the waters.

Thousands of individuals, however, there are, who, less curious in their mode of fishing, often procure as many "Sunnies" without allowing them to play for a moment. Look at these boys! One stands on the shore, while the others are on fallen trees that project over the stream. Their rods, as you perceive, are merely shoots of the hazel or hickory, their lines are simply twine, and their hooks none of the finest. One has a calabash filled with worms and grubs of many sorts, kept alive in damp earth, and another is supplied with a bottle containing half a gross of live "hoppers;" the third has no bait at all, but borrows from his nearest neighbor. Well, there they are, "three merry boys," whirling their rods in the air to

unroll their lines, on one of which, you observe, a cork is
fastened, while on another is a bit of light wood, and on
the third a grain or two of large shot, to draw it at once
to a certain depth.   Now their hooks are baited and all
are ready.   Each casts his line as he thinks best, after
he has probed the depth of the stream with his rod, to
enable him to place his buoy at the proper point.   Bob,
bob, goes the cork; down it moves; the bit of wood dis-
appears, the leaded line tightens; in a moment up swing
the "Sunnies," which, getting unhooked, are projected
far among the grass, where they struggle in vain, until
death ends their efforts.   The hooks are now baited anew,
and dropped into the water.   The fish is abundant, the
weather propitious and delightful, for it is now October;
and so greedy have the "Sunnies" become of grasshoppers
and grubs that dozens at once dash at the same bait.   The
lads, believe me, have now rare sport, and in an hour
scarcely a fish remains in the hole.   The happy children
have caught, perhaps, some hundreds of delicious "pan-
fish," to feed their parents and delight their little sisters.
Surely their pleasure is fully as great as that experienced
by the scientific angler.

I have known instances when the waters of a dam having been let out, for some reason better known to the
miller than to myself, all the Sunfish have betaken themselves to one or two deep holes, as if to avoid being carried away from their favorite abode.   There I have seen
them in such multitudes that one could catch as many as
he pleased with a pin-hook, fastened to any sort of line,
and baited with any sort of worm or insect, or even with
a piece of newly caught fish.   Yet, and I am not able to
account for it, all of a sudden, without apparent cause,
they would cease to take, and no allurement whatever
could entice them or the other fishes in the pool to seize
the hook.

During high freshets, this species of Perch seldom bites

at anything; but you may procure them with a cast-net
or a seine, provided you are well acquainted with the
localities.   On the contrary, when the waters are clear
and low, every secluded hole, every eddy under the lee
of a rock, every place sheltered by a raft of timber, will
afford you amusement.   In some parts of the Southern
States, the negroes procure these fishes late in the autumn
in shallow ponds or bayous, by wading through the water
with caution, and placing at every few steps a wicker
apparatus, not unlike a small barrel, open at both ends.
The moment the fishes find themselves confined within
the lower part of this, which is pressed to the bottom
of the stream, their skippings announce their capture, and
the fisher secures his booty.

This species, the *Labrus auritus* of Linnæus, the *Pomo-
tis vulgaris* of Cuvier, seldom exceeds five or six inches
in length, but is rather deep in proportion.   The usual
size is from four to five inches, with a depth of from two
to two and a half.   They are not bony, and at all seasons
afford delicate eating.   Having observed a considerable
change in their color in different parts of the United
States, and in different streams, ponds, or lakes, I was
led to think that this curious effect might be produced
by the difference of color in the water.   Thus the Sunfish caught in the deep waters of Green River, in Kentucky, exhibit a depth of olive-brown quite different from
the general tint of those caught in the colorless waters
of the Ohio or Schuylkill; those of the reddish-colored
waters of the bayous of the Louisiana swamps look as if
covered with a coppery tarnish; and, lastly, those met
with in streams that glide beneath cedars or other firs,
have a pale and sallow complexion.

The Sun Perch, wherever found, seems to give a
decided preference to sandy, gravelly, or rocky beds of
streams, avoiding those of which the bottom is muddy.
At the period of depositing their eggs this preference

is still more apparent. The little creature is then seen
swimming rapidly over shallows, the bed of which is
mostly formed of fine gravel, when after a time it is observed to poise itself and gradually sink to the bottom,
where with its fin it pushes aside the sand to the extent
of eight or ten inches, thus forming a circular cavity.   In
a few days a little ridge is thus raised around, and in the
cleared area the roe is deposited. By wading carefully
over the extent of the place, a person may count forty,
fifty, or more of these beds, some within a few feet of
each other, and some several yards apart.   Instead of
abandoning its spawn, as others of the family are wont
to do, this little fish keeps guard over it with all the care
of a sitting bird.   You observe it poised over the bed,
watching the objects around.   Should the rotten leaf of
a tree, a piece of wood, or any other substance, happen to
be rolled over the border of the bed, the Sunfish carefully
removes it, holding the obnoxious matter in its mouth,
and dropping it over the margin.   Having many times
witnessed this act of prudence and cleanliness in the
little sunny, and observed that at this period it will not
seize on any kind of bait, I took it into my head one fair
afternoon to make a few experiments for the purpose of
judging how far its instinct or reason might induce it to
act when disturbed or harassed.

Provided with a fine fishing-line, and such insects as I
knew were relished by this fish, I reached a sand-bar
covered by about one foot of water, where I had previously
seen many deposits. Approaching the nearest to the
shore with great care, I baited my hook with a living
ground-worm, the greater part of which was left at liberty
to writhe as it pleased, and, throwing the line up the
stream, managed it so that at last it passed over the
border of the nest, when I allowed it to remain on the
bottom.   The fish, I perceived, had marked me, and as
the worm intruded on its premises, it swam to the farther

side, there poised itself for a few moments, then approached the worm, and carried it in its mouth over the side next to me, with a care and gentleness so very remarkable as to afford me much surprise. I repeated the experiment six or seven times, and always with the same result. Then changing the bait, I employed a young grasshopper, which I floated into the egg-bed. The insect was removed, as the worm had been, and two attempts to hook the fish proved unsuccessful. I now threw my line with the hook bare, and managed as before. The Sunny appeared quite alarmed. It swam to one side, then to another, in rapid succession, and seemed to entertain a fear that the removal of the suspicious object might prove extremely dangerous to it. Yet it gradually approached the hook, took it delicately up, and the next instant dropped it over the edge of the bed.

Reader, if you are one who, like me, have studied Nature with a desire to improve your mental faculties, and contemplate the wonderful phenomena that present themselves to the view at every step we take in her wide domain, you would have been struck, had you witnessed the actions of this little fish, as I was, with admiration of the Being who gave such instincts to so humble an object. I gazed in amazement at the little creature, and wondered that Nature had endowed it with such feelings and powers. The irrepressible desire of acquiring knowledge prompted me to continue the experiment; but with whatever dexterity I could in those days hook a fish, all my efforts proved abortive, not with this individual only, but with many others which I subjected to the same trials.

Satisfied that at this period the Sunfish was more than a match for me, I rolled up my line, and with the rod gave a rap on the water as nearly over the fish as I could. The Sunny darted off to a distance of several yards, poised itself steadily, and as soon as my rod was raised

from the water, returned to its station. The effect of
the blow on the water was now apparent, for I perceived
that the fish was busily employed in smoothing the bed;
but here ended my experiments on the Sunfish.

MY STYLE OF DRAWING BIRDS[1]

WHEN, as a little lad, I first began my attempts at
representing birds on paper, I was far from possessing
much knowledge of their nature, and, like hundreds of
others, when I had laid the effort aside, I was under the
impression that it was a finished picture of a bird because
it possessed some sort of a head and tail, and two sticks
in lieu of legs; I never troubled myself with the thought
that abutments were requisite to prevent it from falling
either backward or forward, and oh! what bills and claws
I did draw, to say nothing of a perfectly straight line for
a back, and a tail stuck in anyhow, like an unshipped
rudder.

Many persons besides my father saw my miserable
attempts, and so many praised them to the skies that
perhaps no one was ever nearer being completely wrecked
than I by these mistaken, though affectionate words. My
father, however, spoke very differently to me; he constantly impressed upon me that nothing in the world possessing life and animation was easy to imitate, and that
as I grew older he hoped I would become more and more
alive to this. He was so kind to me, and so deeply interested in my improvement that to have listened carelessly

[1] Audubon's drawings have been criticised for their *flatness*. Of this,
Cuvier says: "It is difficult to give a true picture of a bird with the same
effect of perspective as a landscape, and the lack of this is no defect in a
work on Natural History. Naturalists prefer the real color of objects to
those accidental tints which are the result of the varied reflections of light
necessary to complete picturesque representations, but foreign and even injurious to scientific truth."

to his serious words would have been highly ungrateful. I listened less to others, more to him, and his words became my law.

The first collection of drawings I made were from European specimens, procured by my father or myself, and I still have them in my possession.[1] They were all represented *strictly ornithologically*, which means neither more nor less than in stiff, unmeaning profiles, such as are found in most works published to the present day. My next set was begun in America, and there, without my honored mentor, I betook myself to the drawing of specimens hung by a string tied to one foot, having a desire to show every portion, as the wings lay loosely spread, as well as the tail. In this manner I made some pretty fair signs for poulterers.

One day, while watching the habits of a pair of Pewees at Mill Grove, I looked so intently at their graceful attitudes that a thought struck my mind like a flash of light, that nothing, after all, could ever answer my enthusiastic desires to represent nature, except to copy her in her own way, alive and moving! Then I began again. On I went, forming, literally, hundreds of outlines of my favorites, the Pewees; how good or bad I cannot tell, but I fancied I had mounted a step on the high pinnacle before me. I continued for months together, simply outlining birds as I observed them, either alighted or on the wing, but could finish none of my sketches. I procured many individuals of different species, and laying them on the table or on the ground, tried to place them in such attitudes as I had sketched. But, alas! they were *dead*, to all intents and purposes, and neither wing, leg, nor tail could I place according to my wishes. A second thought came to my assistance; by means of threads I raised or lowered a head, wing, or tail, and by fastening the threads

---

[1] This was in 1838; they have since been destroyed by fire, or, at least, the greater number.

securely, I had something like life before me; yet much was wanting. When I saw the living birds, I felt the blood rush to my temples, and almost in despair spent about a month without drawing, but in deep thought, and daily in the company of the feathered inhabitants of dear Mill Grove.

I had drawn from the "manikin" whilst under David, and had obtained tolerable figures of our species through this means, so I cogitated how far a manikin of a bird would answer. I labored with wood, cork, and wires, and formed a grotesque figure, which I cannot describe in any other words than by saying that when set up it was a tolerable-looking Dodo. A friend roused my ire by laughing at it immoderately, and assuring me that if I wished to represent a tame gander it might do. I gave it a kick, broke it to atoms, walked off, and thought again.

Young as I was, my impatience to obtain my desire filled my brains with many plans. I not infrequently dreamed that I had made a new discovery; and long before day, one morning, I leaped out of bed fully persuaded that I had obtained my object. I ordered a horse to be saddled, mounted, and went off at a gallop towards the little village of Norristown, distant about five miles. When I arrived there not a door was open, for it was not yet daylight. Therefore I went to the river, took a bath, and, returning to the town, entered the first opened shop, inquired for wire of different sizes, bought some, leaped on my steed, and was soon again at Mill Grove. The wife of my tenant, I really believe, thought that I was mad, as, on offering me breakfast, I told her I only wanted my gun. I was off to the creek, and shot the first Kingfisher I met. I picked the bird up, carried it home by the bill, sent for the miller, and bade him bring me a piece of board of soft wood. When he returned he found me filing sharp points to some pieces of wire, and I proceeded to show him what I meant to do. I pierced the

OLD MILL AND MILLER'S COTTAGE AT MILL GROVE ON THE PERKIOMEN CREEK.

FROM A PHOTOGRAPH FROM W. H. WETHERILL, ESQ.

body of the fishing bird, and fixed it on the board; another wire passed above his upper mandible held the head in a pretty fair attitude, smaller ones fixed the feet according to my notions, and even common pins came to my assistance. The last wire proved a delightful elevator to the bird's tail, and at last — there stood before me the *real* Kingfisher.

Think not that my lack of breakfast was at all in my way. No, indeed! I outlined the bird, aided by compasses and my eyes, colored it, finished it, without a thought of hunger. My honest miller stood by the while, and was delighted to see me pleased. This was what I shall call my first drawing actually from nature, for even the eye of the Kingfisher was as if full of life whenever I pressed the lids aside with my finger.

In those happy days of my youth I was extremely fond of reading what I still call the delightful fables of La Fontaine. I had frequently perused the one entitled "*L'hirondelle et les petits oiseaux*," and thought much of the meaning imparted in the first line, which, if I now recollect rightly, goes on to say that "*Quiconque a beaucoup vu, peut avoir beaucoup retenu.*" To me this meant that to study Nature was to ramble through her domains late and early, and if I observed all as I should, that the memory of what I saw would at least be of service to me.

"Early to bed, and early to rise," was another adage which I thought, and still think, of much value; 't is a pity that instead of being merely an adage it has not become a general law; I have followed it ever since I was a child, and am ever grateful for the hint it conveyed.

As I wandered, mostly bent on the study of birds, and with a wish to represent all those found in our woods, to the best of my powers, I gradually became acquainted with their forms and habits, and the use of my wires was improved by constant practice. Whenever I produced a better representation of any species the preceding one was destroyed, and after a time I laid down what I was pleased to call a constitution of my manner of drawing birds, formed upon natural principles, which I will try to put briefly before you.

The gradual knowledge of the forms and habits of the birds of our country impressed me with the idea that each part of a family must possess a certain degree of affinity, distinguishable at sight in any one of them. The Pewees, which I knew by experience were positively Flycatchers, led me to the discovery that every bird truly of that genus, when standing, was usually in a passive attitude; that they sat uprightly, now and then glancing their eyes upwards or sideways, to watch the approach of their insect prey; that if in pursuit of this prey their movements through the air were, in each and all of that tribe, the same, etc., etc.

Gallinaceous birds I saw were possessed of movements and positions peculiar to them. Amongst the water-birds also I found characteristic manners. I observed that the Herons walked with elegance and stateliness, that, in fact, every family had some mark by which it could be known; and, after having collected many ideas and much material of this kind, I fairly began, in greater earnest than ever, the very collection of Birds of America, which is now being published.

The better I understood my subjects, the better I became able to represent them in what I hoped were natural positions. The bird once fixed with wires on squares, I studied as a lay figure before me, its nature, previously known to me as far as habits went, and its general form having been frequently observed. Now I could examine more thoroughly the bill, nostrils, eyes, legs, and claws, as well as the structure of the wings and tail; the very tongue was of importance to me, and I thought the more I understood all these particulars, the better representations I made of the originals.

AUDUBON.

FROM A PENCIL SKETCH AFTER DEATH, BY JOHN WOODHOUSE AUDUBON.
January 28, 1851.

My drawings at first were made altogether in water-colors, but they wanted softness and a great deal of finish. For a long time I was much dispirited at this, particularly when vainly endeavoring to imitate birds of soft and downy plumage, such as that of most Owls, Pigeons, Hawks, and Herons. How this could be remedied required a new train of thought, or some so-called accident, and the latter came to my aid.

One day, after having finished a miniature portrait of the one dearest to me in all the world, a portion of the face was injured by a drop of water, which dried where it fell; and although I labored a great deal to repair the damage, the blur still remained. Recollecting that, when a pupil of David, I had drawn heads and figures in different colored chalks, I resorted to a piece of that material of the tint required for the part, applied the pigment, rubbed the place with a cork stump, and at once produced the desired effect.

My drawings of Owls and other birds of similar plumage were much improved by such applications; indeed, after a few years of patience, some of my attempts began almost to please me, and I have continued the same style ever since, and that now is for more than thirty years.

Whilst travelling in Europe as well as America, many persons have evinced the desire to draw birds in my manner, and I have always felt much pleasure in showing it to any one by whom I hoped ornithological delineations or portraitures would be improved.

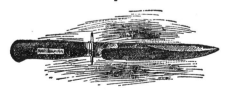

BOWIE KNIFE.

Presented by Henry Carleton.

INDEX

Canso. *See* Canseau.
Canterbury, i. 304.
Cape Breton Island, i. 353, 354.
—— Florida Songster, i. 88.
Caprimulgus, ii. 163.
Cariacus macrotis, i. 4£4.
Caribou, i. 378, 389, 403, 407–409, 432, 433;
ii. 394, 399, 400, 412, 418.
—— flies, i. 411 : ii. 404.
Carleton, Lieut. James Henry, ii. 172, 173.
Carlisle, Eng., i. 141–144.
——, Penn., ii. 117.
Carolinas, ii. 445.
Carré, Charles, i. 52; ii. 249, 251, 253.
Carrier, Gen. Jean B., i. 10.
Carrière, Michel, ii. 136, 137.
Carroll Co., Mo., i. 462.
Cash Creek, i. 31; ii. 274.
Cat-bird, i. 219, 245, 470; ii. 7, 253.
Catchfly, i. 399.
Catfish, i. 282; ii. 213.
Cathartes aura, i. 458. *See also* Buzzard,
Turkey.
Catlin, George, i. 497, 498; ii. 10, 15, 24,
27, 49, 96, 108, 180.
"Cavalier," ii. 305.
Cavendish Square, i. 69.
Cedar birds, i. 475.
—— Island, i. 505, 508; ii. 166, 167.
Centrocircus urophasianus, ii. 126.
Ceritronyx bairdii, ii. 117.
Cerré, M., i. 493, 494, 498.
Cervus macrotis, i. 484.
—— virginianus, ii. 473.
Chaffinch, i. 226.
Chamois, ii. 56, 153.
Champ de Mars, i. 326.
Chapel En-La-Frith, i. 136.
Charadrius, i. 423.
—— semipalmatus, i. 386, 398, 412.
Charbonneau River, ii. 93, 98, 101.
Charbonnière River, ii. 175.
Chardon, Mr., i. 524, 526, 528, 529; ii. 11–
16, 22, 24, 38, 40–44, 47, 50, 71.
Charing Cross, i. 303.
Chariton River, i. 462 ; ii. 174.
"Charity, Mr.," i. 510, 511.
Charles I., i. 235, 236.
Charleston, S. C., i. 66–72; ii. 97, 347.
Charrette, F. A. de, i. 273.
Charwell River, i. 292.
Chastelleux, Marquis de, i. 270.
Chat, Yellow-breasted, i. 470, 504; ii. 7.
Chenopòduum album, ii. 14.
Chester, Eng., i. 249.

Chevalier, M., i. 410, 413.
Cheyenne River, i. 529; ii. 133, 136.
Chicha River, i. 527.
Chickadee, i. 400.
Chickasaw, ii. 260.
Children, John George, i. 252, 254, 257, 258,
264, 276, 277, 294, 301, 342.
Chillicothe, ii. 218.
Chippeway Indian, ii. 126, 127.
Chittenden, Capt. Hiram M., i. 479, 492.
Choctaw Indians, ii. 260.
Chorley, Henry, i. 269.
——, John, i. 248, 249, 264, 269, 273, 276.
Chouans, i. 10.
Chouteau, Auguste, ii. 33.
——, Pierre, i. 452, 454, 463, 468, 499; ii.
33, 35.
——, Madam Pierre, i. 468; ii. 173.
Chouteau's River, i. 503.
Chucknill's Widow, i. 132.
Cincinnati, i. 36, 37, 48–50, 454; ii. 175,
250, 454.
Clancarty, Lord, i. 171, 183.
Clapham, i. 254.
Clarence, Duchess of, i. 259.
Claridge, Mr., ii. 436.
Clark, David, i. 46.
——, Jonathan, i. 31.
——, Lady Mary, i. 187.
——, William, i. 31.
Clay, Henry, i. 126, 157, 272.
Clayton, John, i. 263.
Clementi, Muzio, i. 115.
Clifton, Lord, i. 257.
Clinton, De Witt, i. 120, 167, 192.
Clyde River, i. 266.
Cocks of the plain, ii. 126.
Cod, i. 357; ii. 419, 422–425.
Colaptes aurato-mexicanus, ii. 41.
—— ayresii, ii. 53.
—— cafer, ii. 53. *See also* Woodpecker,
Red-shafted.
—— hybridus, ii. 41.
Cold Water River, ii. 260, 261.
Colinus virginianus, i. 457.
Collins, John, ii. 53, 57, 68, 70, 72, 76, 82,
86, 102, 124.
Colmesnil, Louis, i. 19.
"Columbia" (ship), i. 60, 342 ; ii. 56.
—— College, i. 77.
—— Fur Co., i. 499.
—— River, i. 302.
Colymbus glacialis, i. 389, 392.
—— septentrionalis, i. 390. *See also* Diver,
Red-throated.

534 *INDEX*

Combe, Andrew, i. 191, 207.
——, George, i. 157, 160, 164, 166, 168, 188, 191, 204, 225.
Condolleot, M., i. 309, 316.
Connecticut, ii. 262.
Constant, M., i. 327.
Contopus richardsonii, i. 405, 406.
—— virens, i. 406.
Coolidge, Capt., i. 350; ii. 432.
—— Joseph, i. 67, 68; companion in Labrador, 345–420; 428, 436, 439.
Cooper, J. F., ii. 207.
—— Co., Mo., i. 459.
Coot, i. 472, 532; ii. 7, 337.
——, White-winged, i. 418.
Cormorant, i. 157, 370, 384–386, 393–395, 459; ii. 337, 353, 360, 361, 404, 433.
——, Double-crested, i. 398, 400.
——, Florida, i. 459.
Corn-shucking, ii. 463.
Cornwall, Eng., i. 142.
Corpus Christi, i. 288.
Couëron, i. 11.
Coues, Dr. Elliott, i. 29, 64, 402.
Cougar, i. 74; ii. 260–269, 374, 441, 478.
Council Bluffs, i. 475, 477, 478, 482.
Covent Garden Theatre, i. 253, 291, 315.
Cowbirds, i. 477, 481.
Craighlockhart, i. 164.
Crane, Sand-hill, i. 475; ii. 9, 95, 171, 174.
—— Whooping, i. 87.
Cree Indians, ii. 109, 123, 132.
Creeper, Black-and-White, i. 471.
——, Chestnut-sided, i. 471.
——, Yellow-back, i. 471.
Crisp, Major, i. 516.
Croghan, Major, i. 30.
—— family, ii. 200, 207.
Cross, Mr., i. 279–281.
Crossbills, i. 396, 400, 416, 433.
——, White-winged, i. 385, 412, 415, 431, 434.
Crow, i. 379, 385, 434, 471, 475, 476; ii. 36, 212, 323, 353, 503.
—— Blackbird, i. 477, 480, 481.
——, Carrion, i. 181, 183, 190, 352; ii. 249, 252.
——, Fish, ii. 170, 365.
—— Fort, ii. 50, 65, 178.
—— Indians, ii. 10, 33, 48, 54, 178, 180.
"Crow-feather" (boat), i. 499.
Cruden, Alexander, i. 212.
Cruikshank, George, ii. 236.
Cuba, i. 88; ii. 306, 309.
Cuckoo, i. 180, 245.

Cuckoo, Black-billed, ii. 8.
Culbertson, Alexander, 1843, i. 528; ii. 29, 177; 182, 188.
——, Mrs. Alexander, ii. 81, 85, 88, 89, 111, 112, 121, 154, 157, 163.
Cumberland, i. 454.
—— Isle, ii. 277.
—— River, ii. 277.
Cummings, Capt. Samuel, i. 48, 49; ii. 175.
Curlew, i. 96, 176, 419, 423, 427, 428; ii. 63, 310, 350, 426.
——, Esquimaux, i. 420, 422. *See also* Numenius borealis.
——, Labrador, i. 425.
——, Long-billed, i. 489.
——, Rose-colored, ii. 364.
Curlew-berry, i. 423.
Currie, W. W., i. 269, 270.
Cushat, i. 338.
Cutting, Mr., i. 520, 521, 524; ii. 37, 168.
Cuvier, Baron, i. 235, 294, 306–308, 312, 315–326, 331, 333, 334, 338, 339, 519, 522.
——, Baroness, i. 39, 319, 325.
——, Mlle., i. 309, 316–319, 324.
Cymochorea leucorrhoa, i. 396.

Da Costa, i. 19, 21–24, 26, 27, 39.
Dakota River, i. 501.
Dalmahoy Castle, i. 186, 192, 195.
Damelaphus hemionus, i. 484.
Darlington, i. 238.
Dauphine St., New Orleans, i. 49.
David, Jacques Louis, i. 24, 36, 39, 313, 324; ii. 524, 527.
Davy, Messrs., i. 246.
Day, Capt. Robert, ii. 346, 371.
Dearman, Mr., i. 129.
Decatur, i. 485.
Deer, i. 182, 375, 378, 389, 407, 461, 473, 481, 482, 490, 493–496, 501, 502, 504, 507, 512, 516, 517, 527; ii. 8, 20, 23, 26, 35–42, 49–57, 65, 74, 75, 80, 92, 117, 126, 139, 154, 155, 158, 165–168, 174, 175, 205, 206, 222, 245, 261, 262, 266, 269, 270, 273, 300, 319, 324, 347, 350, 382, 383, 390, 396, 399, 400, 439, 441, 452, 457, 461, 468–472, 481, 482.
——, Black-tailed, i. 516; ii. 57, 72, 74, 147, 165, 484.
——, Long White-tailed, ii. 65, 74, 75, 127, 176.
——, Mule, i. 484; ii. 167.
——, Virginia, i. 485; ii. 473.
Deer-hunting, ii. 466, 473.

THE FACSIMILES OF THE DIPLOMAS WHICH FOLLOW ARE TAKEN FROM A FEW OF THE VERY MANY WHICH AUDUBON RECEIVED FROM THE SCIENTIFIC SOCIETIES OF EUROPE AND AMERICA. UNFORTUNATELY, AMONG THE MANY WHICH THE REPEATED FIRES HAVE DESTROYED WAS THAT OF THE ROYAL SOCIETY OF ENGLAND. THE LETTER ANNOUNCING TO AUDUBON HIS ELECTION TO THAT CELEBRATED SOCIETY, THE HIGHEST HONOR HE RECEIVED, IS THEREFORE SUBSTITUTED, WITH THE SIGNATURE OF SIR (FORMERLY CAPTAIN) EDWARD SABINE, THE ARCTIC EXPLORER.

THE DIPLOMAS GIVEN ARE:

La Société Linnéenne de Paris. 6 Novembre, 1823.

Lyceum of Natural History, New York. January 13, 1824.

Société d'Histoire Naturelle de Paris. 5 Decembre, 1828.

American Academy of Arts and Sciences, Massachusetts. November 10, 1830.

Royal Society of Edinburgh. March 5, 1831.

Royal Jennerian Society, London. July 15, 1836.

Literary and Historical Society of Quebec. November 19, 1836.

Western Academy of Natural Sciences, St. Louis, Mo. April 17, 1843.

Natural History Society of Montreal. March 29, 1847.

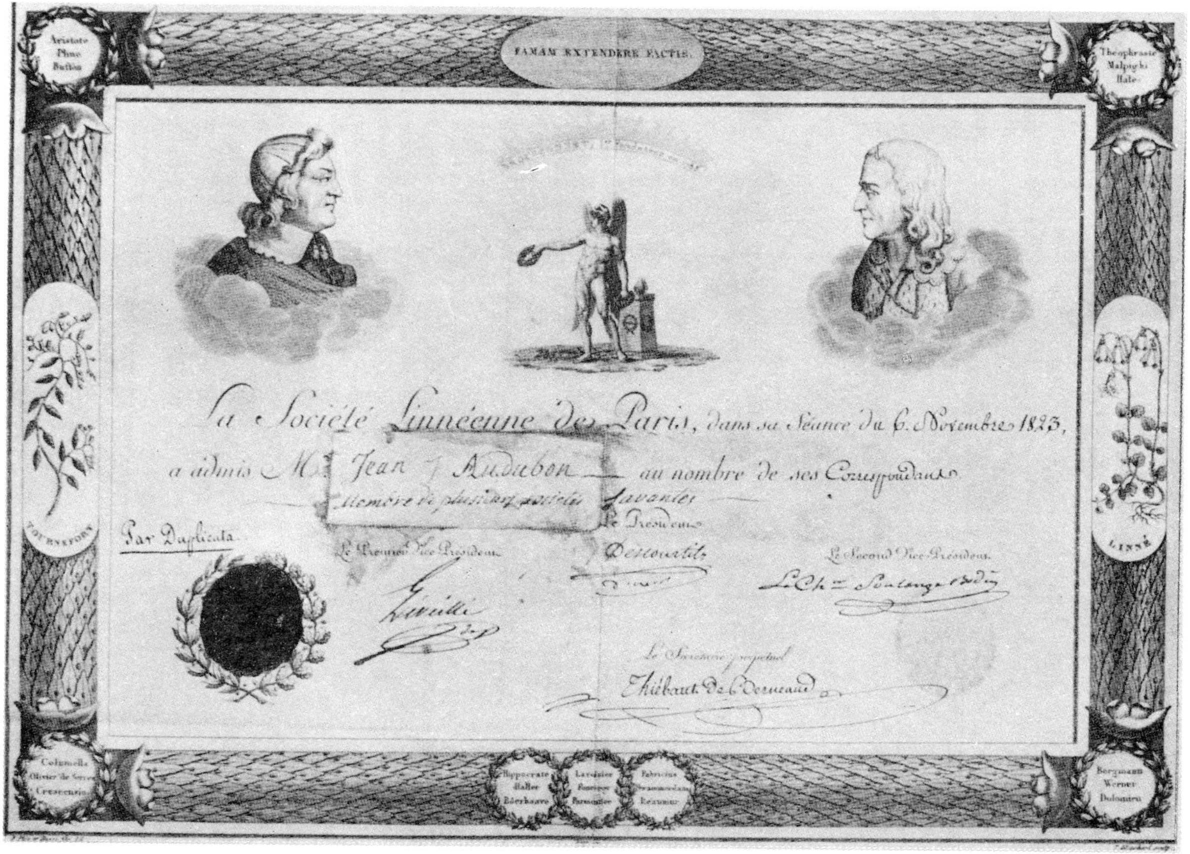
FAMAM EXTENDERE FACTIS
Aristote
Pline
Buffon
Théophraste
Malpighi
Hale
TOURNEFORT
LINNÉ
Columella
Olivier de Serres
Crescenzio
Hippocrate
Haller
Boerhaave
Lavoisier
Parmentier
Fabricius
Réaumur
Bergmann
Werner
Dolomieu
La Société Linnéenne de Paris, dans sa Séance du 6. Novembre 1823,
a admis M. Jean J Audubon au nombre de ses Correspondans
Membre de plusieurs sociétés savantes
Par Duplicata
Le Président
Le Premier Vice Président
Le Second Vice Président
Le Secrétaire perpétuel

The Lyceum of Natural History,

OF

NEW-YORK.

Desirous of Promoting the interests of the INSTITUTION, by associating to themselves men distinguished for their Scientific Attainments, have elected *John James Audubon* a Corresponding MEMBER of said Lyceum, hereby granting unto him all the Rights and Privileges appertaining to the same.

In Witness Whereof, the Seal of the said SOCIETY is affixed to this Diploma, and the same signed by the proper Officers.   Dated New-York, this 13 day of January 1824.

Jn. De la Field, President.

Arthr. Anders. 1st. Vice President.

J. E. De Kay 2d. Vice President.

Jer. Van Rensselaer, M.D. Corresponding Secretary.

I. D. Lee, M.D. Recording Secretary.

SOCIÉTÉ D'HISTOIRE NATURELLE

DE PARIS.

La Société dans sa séance du cinq Décembre 1828 — a admis

au nombre de ses membres Correspondans Mr. Audubon

To all Persons to whom these Presents shall come,

GREETING.

The American Academy of Arts and Sciences, established by a Law of the Commonwealth of Massachusetts, at a Meeting held the tenth. Day of November One Thousand Eight Hundred and thirty for the purpose of promoting the design of their institution, elected

J. J. AUDUBON F.R.S.

a Fellow of their Society, and have granted unto him all the rights and privileges of a Member.

And In Testimony thereof, have affixed their Seal to this certificate, and caused the same to be duly attested.

Nath'l Bowditch   President

Josiah Quincy Vice-Presid.'

Secretaries

Attest
F. C. Gray.

Nathan Hale

Physica Edinburgena

Societas Regia

AD.MDCCLXXI INSTITUTA ET REGIA AUCTORITATE AD.MDCCLXXXIII CONFIRMATA

Omnibus ad quas hac pervenerint

SALUTEM.

Ingenuum virum Joannem Jacobum Audubon, quippe cujus gravissime commendata fuerit in moribus integritas, et in scientia literisque peritia, anno MDCCCXXXI, Maii decimo, in Societatem nostram adscripsimus In cujus testimonium has literas, manibus nos tatisque sigillo munitas, libentissime demamus.

Datum Edinburgi mense ... die ... AD.MDCCCX

Literary and Historical Society of Quebec

INCORPORATED BY ROYAL CHARTER, 1831.

"For the prosecution of researches into the early History of Canada; for the recovering, procuring, and publishing documents and useful information on the Natural, Civil and Literary History of British North America; and for the advancement of the Arts and Sciences in Canada."

DIPLOMA OF FELLOWSHIP.

_____ has been elected _____ member of the Literary and Historical Society of Quebec, and as such entitled to all the privileges of Fellowship as a member of the Corporation under the Royal Charter.

In testimony whereof the undersigned have hereunto affixed the Seal of the Corporation at Quebec, this _____ day of _____ one thousand eight hundred and Thirty Six. _____

Recording Secretary.

Council Secretary.

Corresponding Secretary.

President.

Vice President.

Vice President.

THE

WESTERN ACADEMY

OF

NATURAL SCIENCES,

AT

SAINT LOUIS, MO.

Have Elected

J. J. Audubon

an Honorary Member of their Association, this Seventeenth

Day of April 1843.

William McLaughlin Cor. Secretary.

_____ Rec. Secretary.

Geo. Engelmann M.D. President.

B. B. Brown M.D. Vice President.

Sir

I have the honor of acquainting you that you were on Thursday last elected a fellow of the *Royal Society*, in consequence of which the Statute requires your attendance for admission on or before the fourth Meeting from the day of your election, or within such further time as shall be granted by the Society or Council, upon cause shewed, to either of them: otherwise your election will be void.

You will therefore be pleased to attend at eight of the clock in the evening on one of the following days, viz:-

Thursday March 25th
Thursday April 1st
Thursday April 22nd
Thursday April 29th

I am

Sir

Your humble Servant

Edward Sabine

From the Apartments
of the Royal Society,
Somerset Place, Strand.
March 19th 1830

Secretary.

John J. Audubon Esqr.

A CATALOG OF SELECTED
DOVER BOOKS
IN ALL FIELDS OF INTEREST

A CATALOG OF SELECTED DOVER BOOKS IN ALL FIELDS OF INTEREST

CONCERNING THE SPIRITUAL IN ART, Wassily Kandinsky. Pioneering work by father of abstract art. Thoughts on color theory, nature of art. Analysis of earlier masters. 12 illustrations. 80pp. of text. 5⅜ × 8½. 23411-8 Pa. $2.50

LEONARDO ON THE HUMAN BODY, Leonardo da Vinci. More than 1200 of Leonardo's anatomical drawings on 215 plates. Leonardo's text, which accompanies the drawings, has been translated into English. 506pp. 8⅜ × 11¾. 24483-0 Pa. $10.95

GOBLIN MARKET, Christina Rossetti. Best-known work by poet comparable to Emily Dickinson, Alfred Tennyson. With 46 delightfully grotesque illustrations by Laurence Housman. 64pp. 4 × 6¾. 24516-0 Pa. $2.50

THE HEART OF THOREAU'S JOURNALS, edited by Odell Shepard. Selections from *Journal*, ranging over full gamut of interests. 228pp. 5⅜ × 8½. 20741-2 Pa. $4.50

MR. LINCOLN'S CAMERA MAN: MATHEW B. BRADY, Roy Meredith. Over 300 Brady photos reproduced directly from original negatives, photos. Lively commentary. 368pp. 8⅜ × 11¼. 23021-X Pa. $14.95

PHOTOGRAPHIC VIEWS OF SHERMAN'S CAMPAIGN, George N. Barnard. Reprint of landmark 1866 volume with 61 plates: battlefield of New Hope Church, the Etawah Bridge, the capture of Atlanta, etc. 80pp. 9 × 12. 23445-2 Pa. $6.00

A SHORT HISTORY OF ANATOMY AND PHYSIOLOGY FROM THE GREEKS TO HARVEY, Dr. Charles Singer. Thoroughly engrossing non-technical survey. 270 illustrations. 211pp. 5⅜ × 8½. 20389-1 Pa. $4.95

REDOUTE ROSES IRON-ON TRANSFER PATTERNS, Barbara Christopher. Redouté was botanical painter to the Empress Josephine; transfer his famous roses onto fabric with these 24 transfer patterns. 80pp. 8¼ × 10⅞. 24292-7 Pa. $3.50

THE FIVE BOOKS OF ARCHITECTURE, Sebastiano Serlio. Architectural milestone, first (1611) English translation of Renaissance classic. Unabridged reproduction of original edition includes over 300 woodcut illustrations. 416pp. 9⅜ × 12¼. 24349-4 Pa. $14.95

CARLSON'S GUIDE TO LANDSCAPE PAINTING, John F. Carlson. Authoritative, comprehensive guide covers, every aspect of landscape painting. 34 reproductions of paintings by author; 58 explanatory diagrams. 144pp. 8⅜ × 11. 22927-0 Pa. $5.95

101 PUZZLES IN THOUGHT AND LOGIC, C.R. Wylie, Jr. Solve murders, robberies, see which fishermen are liars—purely by reasoning! 107pp. 5⅜ × 8½. 20367-0 Pa. $2.00

TEST YOUR LOGIC, George J. Summers. 50 more truly new puzzles with new turns of thought, new subtleties of inference. 100pp. 5⅜ × 8½. 22877-0 Pa. $2.25

SURREAL STICKERS AND UNREAL STAMPS, William Rowe. 224 haunting, hilarious stamps on gummed, perforated stock, with images of elephants, geisha girls, George Washington, etc. 16pp. one side. 8¼ × 11.   24371-0 Pa. $3.50

GOURMET KITCHEN LABELS, Ed Sibbett, Jr. 112 full-color labels (4 copies each of 28 designs). Fruit, bread, other culinary motifs. Gummed and perforated. 16pp. 8¼ × 11.   24087-8 Pa. $2.95

PATTERNS AND INSTRUCTIONS FOR CARVING AUTHENTIC BIRDS, H.D. Green. Detailed instructions, 27 diagrams, 85 photographs for carving 15 species of birds so life-like, they'll seem ready to fly! 8¼ × 11.   24222-6 Pa. $2.75

FLATLAND, E.A. Abbott. Science-fiction classic explores life of 2-D being in 3-D world. 16 illustrations. 103pp. 5⅜ × 8.   20001-9 Pa. $2.00

DRIED FLOWERS, Sarah Whitlock and Martha Rankin. Concise, clear, practical guide to dehydration, glycerinizing, pressing plant material, and more. Covers use of silica gel. 12 drawings. 32pp. 5⅜ × 8½.   21802-3 Pa. $1.00

EASY-TO-MAKE CANDLES, Gary V. Guy. Learn how easy it is to make all kinds of decorative candles. Step-by-step instructions. 82 illustrations. 48pp. 8¼ × 11.
23881-4 Pa. $2.50

SUPER STICKERS FOR KIDS, Carolyn Bracken. 128 gummed and perforated full-color stickers: GIRL WANTED, KEEP OUT, BORED OF EDUCATION, X-RATED, COMBAT ZONE, many others. 16pp. 8¼ × 11.   24092-4 Pa. $2.50

CUT AND COLOR PAPER MASKS, Michael Grater. Clowns, animals, funny faces...simply color them in, cut them out, and put them together, and you have 9 paper masks to play with and enjoy. 32pp. 8¼ × 11.   23171-2 Pa. $2.25

A CHRISTMAS CAROL: THE ORIGINAL MANUSCRIPT, Charles Dickens. Clear facsimile of Dickens manuscript, on facing pages with final printed text. 8 illustrations by John Leech, 4 in color on covers. 144pp. 8⅜ × 11¼.
20980-6 Pa. $5.95

CARVING SHOREBIRDS, Harry V. Shourds & Anthony Hillman. 16 full-size patterns (all double-page spreads) for 19 North American shorebirds with step-by-step instructions. 72pp. 9¼ × 12¼.   24287-0 Pa. $4.95

THE GENTLE ART OF MATHEMATICS, Dan Pedoe. Mathematical games, probability, the question of infinity, topology, how the laws of algebra work, problems of irrational numbers, and more. 42 figures. 143pp. 5⅜ × 8½. (EBE)
22949-1 Pa. $3.50

READY-TO-USE DOLLHOUSE WALLPAPER, Katzenbach & Warren, Inc. Stripe, 2 floral stripes, 2 allover florals, polka dot; all in full color. 4 sheets (350 sq. in.) of each, enough for average room. 48pp. 8¼ × 11.   23495-9 Pa. $2.95

MINIATURE IRON-ON TRANSFER PATTERNS FOR DOLLHOUSES, DOLLS, AND SMALL PROJECTS, Rita Weiss and Frank Fontana. Over 100 miniature patterns: rugs, bedspreads, quilts, chair seats, etc. In standard dollhouse size. 48pp. 8¼ × 11.   23741-9 Pa. $1.95

THE DINOSAUR COLORING BOOK, Anthony Rao. 45 renderings of dinosaurs, fossil birds, turtles, other creatures of Mesozoic Era. Scientifically accurate. Captions. 48pp. 8¼ × 11.   24022-3 Pa. $2.50

TOLL HOUSE TRIED AND TRUE RECIPES, Ruth Graves Wakefield. Popovers, veal and ham loaf, baked beans, much more from the famous Mass. restaurant. Nearly 700 recipes. 376pp. 5⅜ × 8½. 23560-2 Pa. $4.95

FAVORITE CHRISTMAS CAROLS, selected and arranged by Charles J.F. Cofone. Title, music, first verse and refrain of 34 traditional carols in handsome calligraphy; also subsequent verses and other information in type. 79pp. 8⅜ × 11. 20445-6 Pa. $3.50

CAMERA WORK: A PICTORIAL GUIDE, Alfred Stieglitz. All 559 illustrations from most important periodical in history of art photography. Reduced in size but still clear, in strict chronological order, with complete captions. 176pp. 8⅜ × 11¼. 23591-2 Pa. $6.95

FAVORITE SONGS OF THE NINETIES, edited by Robert Fremont. 88 favorites: "Ta-Ra-Ra-Boom-De-Aye," "The Band Played On," "Bird in a Gilded Cage," etc. 401pp. 9 × 12. 21536-9 Pa. $12.95

STRING FIGURES AND HOW TO MAKE THEM, Caroline F. Jayne. Fullest, clearest instructions on string figures from around world: Eskimo, Navajo, Lapp, Europe, more. Cat's cradle, moving spear, lightning, stars. 950 illustrations. 407pp. 5⅜ × 8½. 20152-X Pa. $5.95

LIFE IN ANCIENT EGYPT, Adolf Erman. Detailed older account, with much not in more recent books: domestic life, religion, magic, medicine, commerce, and whatever else needed for complete picture. Many illustrations. 597pp. 5⅜ × 8½. 22632-8 Pa. $7.95

ANCIENT EGYPT: ITS CULTURE AND HISTORY, J.E. Manchip White. From pre-dynastics through Ptolemies: scoiety, history, political structure, religion, daily life, literature, cultural heritage. 48 plates. 217pp. 5⅜ × 8½. (EBE) 22548-8 Pa. $4.95

KEPT IN THE DARK, Anthony Trollope. Unusual short novel about Victorian morality and abnormal psychology by the great English author. Probably the first American publication. Frontispiece by Sir John Millais. 92pp. 6½ × 9¼. 23609-9 Pa. $2.95

MAN AND WIFE, Wilkie Collins. Nineteenth-century master launches an attack on out-moded Scottish marital laws and Victorian cult of athleticism. Artfully plotted. 35 illustrations. 239pp. 6⅛ × 9¼. 24451-2 Pa. $5.95

RELATIVITY AND COMMON SENSE, Herman Bondi. Radically reoriented presentation of Einstein's Special Theory and one of most valuable popular accounts available. 60 illustrations. 177pp. 5⅜ × 8. (EUK) 24021-5 Pa. $3.95

THE EGYPTIAN BOOK OF THE DEAD, E.A. Wallis Budge. Complete reproduction of Ani's papyrus, finest ever found. Full hieroglyphic text, interlinear transliteration, word-for-word translation, smooth translation. 533pp. 6½ × 9¼. (USO) 21866-X Pa. $8.95

COUNTRY AND SUBURBAN HOMES OF THE PRAIRIE SCHOOL PERIOD, H.V. von Holst. Over 400 photographs floor plans, elevations, detailed drawings (exteriors and interiors) for over 100 structures. Text. Important primary source. 128pp. 8⅜ × 11¼. 24373-7 Pa. $5.95

SOURCE BOOK OF MEDICAL HISTORY, edited by Logan Clendening, M.D. Original accounts ranging from Ancient Egypt and Greece to discovery of X-rays: Galen, Pasteur, Lavoisier, Harvey, Parkinson, others. 685pp. 5⅜ × 8½.
20621-1 Pa. $10.95

THE ROSE AND THE KEY, J.S. Lefanu. Superb mystery novel from Irish master. Dark doings among an ancient and aristocratic English family. Well-drawn characters; capital suspense. Introduction by N. Donaldson. 448pp. 5⅜ × 8½.
24377-X Pa. $6.95

SOUTH WIND, Norman Douglas. Witty, elegant novel of ideas set on languorous Meditterranean island of Nepenthe. Elegant prose, glittering epigrams, mordant satire. 1917 masterpiece. 416pp. 5⅜ × 8½. (Available in U.S. only)
24361-3 Pa. $5.95

RUSSELL'S CIVIL WAR PHOTOGRAPHS, Capt. A.J. Russell. 116 rare Civil War Photos: Bull Run, Virginia campaigns, bridges, railroads, Richmond, Lincoln's funeral car. Many never seen before. Captions. 128pp. 9⅜ × 12¼.
24283-8 Pa. $6.95

PHOTOGRAPHS BY MAN RAY: 105 Works, 1920-1934. Nudes, still lifes, landscapes, women's faces, celebrity portraits (Dali, Matisse, Picasso, others), rayographs. Reprinted from rare gravure edition. 128pp. 9⅜ × 12¼. (Available in U.S. only)
23842-3 Pa. $7.95

STAR NAMES: THEIR LORE AND MEANING, Richard H. Allen. Star names, the zodiac, constellations: folklore and literature associated with heavens. The basic book of its field, fascinating reading. 563pp. 5⅜ × 8½.
21079-0 Pa. $7.95

BURNHAM'S CELESTIAL HANDBOOK, Robert Burnham, Jr. Thorough guide to the stars beyond our solar system. Exhaustive treatment. Alphabetical by constellation: Andromeda to Cetus in Vol. 1; Chamaeleon to Orion in Vol. 2; and Pavo to Vulpecula in Vol. 3. Hundreds of illustrations. Index in Vol. 3. 2000pp. 6⅛ × 9¼.
23567-X, 23568-8, 23673-0 Pa. Three-vol. set $36.85

THE ART NOUVEAU STYLE BOOK OF ALPHONSE MUCHA, Alphonse Mucha. All 72 plates from *Documents Decoratifs* in original color. Stunning, essential work of Art Nouveau. 80pp. 9⅜ × 12¼.
24044-4 Pa. $7.95

DESIGNS BY ERTE; FASHION DRAWINGS AND ILLUSTRATIONS FROM "HARPER'S BAZAR," Erte. 310 fabulous line drawings and 14 *Harper's Bazar* covers, 8 in full color. Erte's exotic temptresses with tassels, fur muffs, long trains, coifs, more. 129pp. 9⅜ × 12¼.
23397-9 Pa. $6.95

HISTORY OF STRENGTH OF MATERIALS, Stephen P. Timoshenko. Excellent historical survey of the strength of materials with many references to the theories of elasticity and structure. 245 figures. 452pp. 5⅜ × 8½.   61187-6 Pa. $8.95

Prices subject to change without notice.
Available at your book dealer or write for free catalog to Dept. GI, Dover Publications, Inc., 31 East 2nd St. Mineola, N.Y. 11501. Dover publishes more than 175 books each year on science, elementary and advanced mathematics, biology, music, art, literary history, social sciences and other areas.